IMPOVERISHED

'Joanna Mack sets out her timely response to the "deeply flawed and inhumane" policies that led to rising poverty and destitution in the UK and the change that has to come including how to pay for it. It is comprehensive, detailed, and timely.'
Alison Garnham, Child Poverty Action Group

'Based on her unparalleled expertise, Mack exposes the political choices behind mass poverty and provides an urgent blueprint for renewal. This is a powerful, rigorous, and deeply humane book.'
Richard Wilkinson, The Equality Trust

'This powerful analysis from a seasoned observer demonstrates how and why poverty in Britain has worsened, and urgently needs fixing.'
Donald Hirsch, Loughborough University

'Forensic, comprehensive, informative. Few people are better placed than Joanna Mack to explain the rise in UK poverty and to set out realistic policy solutions.'
Jane Millar, University of Bath

'A no-nonsense account of the problem and – crucially – the solutions to poverty in the UK: a sorely needed book.'
Tania Burchardt, Centre for Analysis of Social Exclusion, London School of Economics and Political Science

'Joanna Mack is a pioneering poverty scholar and *Impoverished* provides an insightful analysis of how to repair Britain's worn and torn social fabric.'
**Stephen Sinclair,
Glasgow Caledonian University**

IMPOVERISHED

How to Fix Britain's Poverty Problem

Joanna Mack

First published in Great Britain in 2026 by

Policy Press, an imprint of
Bristol University Press
University of Bristol
1-9 Old Park Hill
Bristol
BS2 8BB
UK
t: +44 (0)117 374 6645
e: bup-info@bristol.ac.uk

Details of international sales and distribution partners are available at
policy.bristoluniversitypress.co.uk

© Bristol University Press 2026

DOI: 10.51952/9781447376071

British Library Cataloguing in Publication Data
A catalogue record for this book is available from the British Library

ISBN 978-1-4473-7606-4 paperback
ISBN 978-1-4473-7607-1 ePub
ISBN 978-1-4473-7608-8 ePdf

The right of Joanna Mack to be identified as author of this work has been asserted by her in
accordance with the Copyright, Designs and Patents Act 1988.

All rights reserved: no part of this publication may be reproduced, stored in a retrieval system, or
transmitted in any form or by any means, electronic, mechanical, photocopying, recording, or
otherwise without the prior permission of Bristol University Press.

Every reasonable effort has been made to obtain permission to reproduce copyrighted material.
If, however, anyone knows of an oversight, please contact the publisher.

The statements and opinions contained within this publication are solely those of the author and
not of the University of Bristol or Bristol University Press. The University of Bristol and Bristol
University Press disclaim responsibility for any injury to persons or property resulting from any
material published in this publication.

Bristol University Press and Policy Press work to counter discrimination on grounds of gender,
race, disability, age and sexuality.

Cover design: Ahlawat Gunjan
Front cover image: iStock/whitemay; Shutterstock/alberto clemares exposito

To those who, from 1983 onwards, shared their struggle in the hope of a better life for those who followed ...

Mavis: 'It's not a standard of living. It's existence.'
Ernie: 'Well, it's hard. It's the most difficult task to get by.'[1]

Contents

List of figures and tables viii
About the author x
Acknowledgements xi

Introduction: The promise of change 1

1 The breadth and depth of impoverishment 11
2 The collapse of the safety net 36
3 Blaming the vulnerable 62
4 Why isn't work a route out of poverty? 88
5 The dismantling of services tackling disadvantage 117
6 How the UK's housing system drives poverty 139
7 How destitution is designed into the UK's immigration system 163
8 The interlocking challenges of climate change and poverty 189
9 Lowering the basic costs of living 215
10 Renewing public services 235
11 Income security for all 259
12 Making change happen 284

Notes 293
Bibliography 340
Index 361

List of figures and tables

Figures

1.1	Relative poverty, before and after housing costs, 1963 to 2023/24	15
1.2	Absolute poverty, before and after housing costs, 1963 to 2023/24	17
1.3	How different groups have fared since 1992	18
1.4	The extent relative income poverty underestimates people's needs	21
1.5	The rise in material deprivation under the last Conservative government	24
1.6	The ways children are increasingly missing out because of family finances	25
1.7	The rise in food insecurity	28
1.8	The rise in deep financial problems	32
1.9	The rise in destitution	33
2.1	The RPI value of various benefits in 2022 prices	40
3.1	Actual and projected annual spending on working-age benefits	81
4.1	The shift to in-work poverty, adults	90
4.2	The shift to in-work poverty, children	91
4.3	The rising risk of poverty for adults and children in households in work, 2001 to 2024	92
4.4	The risk of poverty in different types of households in work, adults	93
4.5	A decade of stagnating earnings	99

4.6	The impact of the high inflation years on household costs	103
5.1	Local authority spending power in England, 2010/11 to 2023/24	119
5.2	Percentage change in spending since 2010 by deprivation level	120
5.3	Drop in spending on preventative children's services, 2009/10 to 2022/23	128
5.4	Drop in real spending on services for children and young people	131
5.5	Local and central government support for bus services, England, 2009 to 2023	134
6.1	The rising problem of homelessness	145
6.2	The rise in the use of temporary accommodation for the homeless	147
6.3	Sub-standard housing by tenure, England, 2022/23	151
6.4	Numbers of children living in sub-standard homes by tenure, England, 2022/23	152
6.5	Affordable homes completed by type, England	162
7.1	Net long-term migration 2012 to 2024	172

Tables

4.1	Average effective tax rates on different increases in hours of work for low-earning households	108
8.1	Poverty rates, number of people in poverty, and percentage of dwellings below energy standards, by tenure, 2022/23	212

About the author

Joanna Mack has been involved in poverty research for over 40 years, starting with the pioneering *Breadline Britain* survey in 1983, which established the measurement of poverty based on socially determined needs, now widely used internationally. A former award-winning TV producer and director, she has written extensively on poverty in the UK, including co-authoring, in 2015, *Breadline Britain: The rise of mass poverty*. She was co-editor of the *Journal of Poverty and Social Justice* until 2025 and is now a consulting editor. She is Visiting Fellow at The Open University.

Acknowledgements

This book owes its existence to Ginny Mills of Bristol University Press, who approached me asking if, given the continuing slump in living standards, I would be interested in writing a book on poverty in the UK today, updating my past work. Given the extent of the escalating crisis, it seemed an urgent undertaking and I would like to thank Ginny for making this happen and for the support she, and the team at BUP, have given throughout.

The contents of the book draw extensively on the academic work of others, without which analysis of the extent of the problem and possible solutions would not be possible. Across the UK, universities continue, despite the financial problems they face, to undertake extraordinarily important research to help us understand the world better. I am particularly grateful to the Townsend Centre for International Poverty Research at the University of Bristol and the School of Social Sciences at Cardiff University, with whom I have had the pleasure to work over the years, and, among many others, the Centre for the Analysis of Social Exclusion at the London School of Economics, the School for Business and Society at the University of York, the Centre for Research in Social Policy at the University of Loughborough, the Migration Observatory at the University of Oxford, and the Institute for Social Policy, Housing, and Equalities at Heriot-Watt University in Edinburgh.

I have also drawn extensively on the work of the many independent research bodies and think tanks that carry out so much important policy work in the UK, including the

Institute for Fiscal Studies, the Joseph Rowntree Foundation, the Resolution Foundation, the New Economics Foundation, Centre for Local Economic Strategies, the Fabians, Common Wealth, Institute for Public Policy Research, and the Institute for Government, among many others. I would also like to thank the many other bodies that do extensive work trying to understand the causes of poverty and advocating for change, including, but again not exclusively, Shelter, Crisis, the Food Foundation, Citizens Advice, Child Poverty Action Group, Disability Alliance, StepChange, the Poverty Alliance, the Refugee Council, the Trade Union Congress (TUC), and those who have shared their experiences. In reporting current events, I have drawn on various media outlets which I regard to be reliable and, where possible, open access, primarily, *The Guardian* newspaper, the BBC, and ITV, though some, such as the *Financial Times*, have only limited access. I have aimed to reference all sources throughout the book.

There are many individuals who have played a critical role in my thinking. I would like to give particular thanks to David Gordon, Stewart Lansley, and Shailen Nandy, with whom I have worked over many years, and to Marco Pomati, with whom I co-edited the *Journal of Poverty and Social Justice*. I have learnt a great deal from them all.

And finally, but by no means least, I would like to give a special thanks to my family who have supported me in these endeavours over very many years. My sisters Gaynor, Sally, and Emma have provided a continuing source of encouragement as has my sister-in-law and her husband, Jacqueline and Alan Bowman. But above all I would like to thank my sons, Jonathan and David, and husband Harold Frayman. They have shared their knowledge with me and challenged me. Above all, they have provided their continuing support and understanding.

All responsibility for content is, of course, mine.

Joanna Mack, November 2025

Introduction:
The promise of change

When the Labour Party swept to power in the General Election of 4 July 2024, the country was facing a social crisis. Poverty was deepening with people falling further below the poverty line than before. Growing numbers were facing destitution, unable to feed and clothe themselves properly, unable to keep warm and clean. Millions were turning to food banks with one in twenty households regularly running out of food.[1] Quite simply, people's fundamental human needs were not being met.

Poverty was also becoming more widespread with more and more people living below what the public regard as a minimum acceptable living standard, excluded from the options and opportunities most take for granted. Families with children had been the worst hit, far more likely to go without food and other essentials than other households. In an average class of thirty pupils, nine were living in poverty. For many, poverty was penetrating deep into their lives, affecting not just their material well-being and security but their friendships and opportunities.

After years of austerity, the UK's welfare system was in a fragile state, with a safety net that was failing to protect households from poverty and unable to cope with the additional pressures of the rolling crises of the 2020s. By the time of the 2024 election, income growth had been the weakest across any parliament since comparable records began in 1961 and living standards were declining for the majority of households.[2] Households' financial resilience was low with many households left with little to fall back on.

The Labour Party promised 'change'. But quite what and how was left vague. Tackling poverty was not mentioned as a priority or one of the 'first six steps'.[3] The emphasis of the campaign was on kick-starting economic growth as the way to enable change to be implemented. This, above all, was to be the driving 'mission' of Keir Starmer's Labour government. Nothing was to get in its way and nothing else was a higher priority.[4]

To lift living standards, renewed growth and overturning the stagnation of the last 15 years is important. Without it, wages will continue to flatline. But if the last 40 years has taught anything it is that growth, in itself, will not guarantee that those at the bottom end will reap the benefits. What matters is the kind of growth and how it is distributed.

Labour's manifesto did talk about 'family security' and, within that context, promised to 'develop an ambitious strategy to reduce child poverty'.[5] Beyond introducing 'free breakfast clubs in every primary school' no details were given. There was no commitment to increase working-age or child benefits, just a general commitment to review the workings of Universal Credit. In terms of concrete policies, there was nothing to match the scale or urgency of the challenge faced, just a general promise that a Labour government would do better at tackling child poverty, announcing after the election a taskforce to work out what this strategy might actually be.[6]

The omens were not looking good. One of the first tests for the new government came when the Scottish National Party (SNP) tabled a motion to abolish the two-child limit brought in by the Conservative government in 2017 and which restricted help through means-tested family benefits to two children. Poverty campaigners and experts had consistently argued that this was a priority[7] and had hoped that, despite its absence from the manifesto and campaign promises, the government would act decisively and immediately to scrap it.[8] An estimated 350,000 to 500,000 children would be lifted out of poverty by doing so, making it one of the simplest and quickest ways to make an impact.[9]

Introduction

This hope was shattered when the new government failed to submit any amendments to the SNP motion, whipped its new MPs to vote against it, and suspended the seven Labour MPs who did.[10] The government argued that its cost – estimated at around £1.7 billion,[11] rising to around £3.4 billion by the 2030s[12] – was not in their spending plans and was therefore unfunded, suggesting, vaguely, it might be done at a later date when 'fiscal limits allow'. In the meantime, it was hardly an encouraging start for a government that claimed that it would have an ambitious strategy to tackle child poverty and, whatever happened at a later date, it meant that in the meantime the families affected, and their children, suffered.

Then, days later, the government announced cuts to the winter fuel allowance for pensioners on the basis there was an additional 'black hole' in public finances inherited from the Conservative government that needed to be filled.[13] The allowance had been received by all pensioners, around 11 million people, and was worth £300 a year for a single pensioner and £200 for each member of a couple. But from now it was to be only available to those on pension credit, thereby limiting the allowance to around 1.3 million pensioners and turning what had been a universal benefit into a means-tested one.

The Chancellor, Rachel Reeves, argued that this would save around £1.5 billion. While Labour had inherited an exceptionally bad financial hand, with rising levels of public debt and ever-rising payments on these debts, the choice of targets for savings seemed quite contrary to what people expected from a Labour government. There was outrage with charities arguing that it would leave many elderly people cold in the coming winter, in particular those just outside the pension credit limit.[14]

But this was only the beginning of the disappointment for those who wished to see strong anti-poverty policies. Talk of the promise of change and renewal was increasingly replaced by talk of 'fiscal rules', and tough action on spending to improve the state of the government's finances. While concern that unfunded spending might spook the markets was understandable, the government had tied its hands in their election campaign by committing to rules to reduce the level of government debt, largely inherited from the previous government, while ruling out the main options for tax increases. This left no room for much-needed increases in day-to-day spending to repair Britain's social fabric.[15]

In the autumn of 2024, in her first budget, the Chancellor re-emphasised the government's commitment to 'fiscal responsibility'. Though the Chancellor did increase leeway for capital spending for investment by revising these 'rules',[16] tough controls were placed on day-to-day spending, with a requirement that the current account budget be either in balance or in surplus by the end of the parliament.

In particular, a welfare spending cap, first introduced by the coalition government in 2014,[17] remained in place. This cap, which excludes pensions and benefits dependent on external economic events such as Jobseeker's Allowance, covers about half of welfare spending and thereby limits the extent to which policy changes can increase social security spending. The government argued that this was necessary to 'ensure that welfare spending is sustainable in the medium term'[18] but the rule in effect limits increasing spending on social security to improve the quality of people's lives. Moreover, given the rising pressures on most benefits, the possibility of cuts loomed.

Disability groups were particularly concerned that the government would continue with savings on disability benefits that had been earmarked by the previous Conservative government. This would increase entrenched levels of deprivation among an already at-risk group.[19] Indeed, when these Conservative government proposals were challenged in the High Court by disability activists in December 2024,[20] the new Labour government defended them.

Then in March 2025, the government unveiled more than £6 billion of welfare savings that would see far tougher tests

Introduction

imposed on disability benefits, with some payments frozen from 2026.[21] When the new welfare reform bill was published, the government defended the move by saying the aim was to increase incentives to work. But it included savings of £5 billion from making it harder to qualify for Personal Independence Payments (PIP), a non-means-tested benefit not actually linked to work and that is aimed at helping people with the additional costs of their disability.

The language the government used sounded much like that used to justify the benefit cuts of the austerity years of previous governments. The Work and Pensions Secretary, Liz Kendall, talked of people 'taking the mickey' by claiming benefits when they should be working,[22] while the prime minister's spokesperson argued that there was an 'unsustainable rise in welfare spending' which was 'holding our economy back'.[23] The government's arguments were all about the 'spiralling' costs of disability benefits and the 'surge' in the numbers of claimants – not why this might be the case or how to help people's health improve.[24]

In reality, welfare spending as a proportion of GDP has remained remarkably stable, fluctuating around 10 to 12 per cent over the last thirty years and standing at just over 11 per cent in 2024/25.[25] Whatever the motivations, the impact of the proposed changes to disability benefits was clear; many would fall into poverty.[26]

Other changes also threatened to increase poverty levels, notably among migrants, a group already at higher risk of poverty. Since taking office, the new Labour government had taken an increasingly hard-line view on immigration, with the prime minister echoing the language of the far right when talking about recent rises in immigration as a 'squalid chapter' in UK history and the 'risk' of 'becoming an island of strangers'.[27] While Starmer subsequently said that he regretted using these phrases,[28] the policies being put forward remained. In May 2025, the Home Office announced tough new rules including extending the standard wait required to move from temporary visas to the right to remain – and ultimately to citizenship – from the current five to ten years.[29] Research has repeatedly found that acquiring the permanent right to remain improves economic outcome and lifts social integration,[30] while remaining on temporary visas denies access to many social security benefits, increases vulnerability, and pushes people into destitution.[31]

This was not what had been hoped for by those wanting a strong anti-poverty strategy. Nor, it seemed, was it what the electorate wanted. The Labour government's poll ratings plummeted, slipping to around just 23 per cent by May 2025. This represented a sharper fall in popularity than that experienced by any government since 1983.[32] Come the local elections in England that May, the Labour Party suffered huge losses,[33] notably in what were once strong Labour areas such Durham and Lancashire. 'People on the doorsteps are using the word "betrayal"', commented one Labour MP to the BBC. It was a conclusion echoed by others: 'It turns out that cutting disability and winter fuel payments comes at a cost – these are not Labour things to do.'[34]

Faced with such pressures, the government shifted its position on the winter fuel allowance, though not on disability benefit or the two-child limit, both substantially larger causes of rising poverty. Under the threadbare pretext that government finances had improved,[35] the government announced that all pensioners with incomes under £35,000, estimated at around three-quarters of pensioners, would now receive a payment, with those under 80 receiving £200 and those over 80, £300.[36] This would be achieved by paying all pensioners the allowance through the benefits system and then clawing it back for those on higher incomes through the tax system, a system already in use for child benefit and known to be problematic.[37]

At the end of all this, the resultant savings will be minimal[38] while, by moving away from a universal system, new anomalies and cliff edges – that are always present with means-testing – had been introduced. Better-off pensioners, for example, often have relatively low incomes but large pension pots of assets on which they can draw, and which do not count for the winter fuel payment limit.

While the sums of money involved are small in the scheme of government spending, it seemed like a lesson in how to botch change.[39] Rather than being produced as part of a coherent argument as to why the winter fuel allowance was not necessary for most pensioners (and then was), or as part of a discussion on the level of the state pension, or as part of a strategy to support low-income households with their heating bills, it was announced, out of the blue, on the basis that there was suddenly an unexpected shortfall in public finances. It thus seemed to be singling out pensioners for no reason other than that savings were said to be needed.

As the end of their first year in power approached, the government seemed to lack any overriding ambition to tackle poverty. Indeed, the government reasserted its determination to push on with its planned reforms to benefits for disabled people. In June 2025, it published its Universal Credit and Personal Independence Bill which, by its own estimates, would mean that by 2029–30, 800,000 people would not receive the daily living component of PIP who would otherwise have done so; and around 150,000 people on carer's allowance would see their allowance withdrawn.[40] Liz Kendall justified the changes by making an extraordinary claim: namely, that withdrawing an allowance designed to support disabled people with their higher living costs, 'marks the moment we take the road of compassion, opportunity and dignity' and that it would give 'people peace of mind'.[41] Independent research organisations estimate that some quarter of a million families would be pushed into poverty and nearly 700,000 families already in poverty would fall further below the poverty line.[42] By the time the bill was coming to a vote in the House of Commons, well over a hundred Labour MPs were threatening to vote against it, forcing the government to backtrack. Plans for a tightening of PIP were taken out, to be reviewed at a later date, though the bill still contained changes to the health element of Universal Credit (UC), paid to protect those with disabilities who face difficulties in undertaking paid work. These changes would mean that from 2026/27 new claimants of the health element of UC would receive £2,400 a year, around half that of existing claimants, whose current rate of £5,000 a year would be frozen until 2029/30.[43] The bill passed, though over 40 Labour MPs still voted against it.

The government's assessment of the impact of the bill as passed claimed that, overall, it would now lift 50,000 people out of poverty.[44] But this was completely misleading as it included planned changes by the previous Conservative government that had never happened. In reality, the new bill would result in 100,000 more people being pushed into poverty.[45]

In the autumn of 2025, the government started out on its next u-turn, this time on the two-child benefit limit, initially exploring various options for partial reform.[46] By the time of the November budget, the reversal of its position of 18 months earlier was complete, with Rachel Reeves announcing its end.[47] While welcomed by campaigners, the overall impression left, however, was of a government being dragged to take the most basic steps to tackle poverty. Shortly after, their delayed child poverty strategy was launched.[48] It was broad ranging, and a positive shift in approach from recent years. But in terms of policy, it was largely a consolidation of previously announced measures. It lacked the level of ambition needed for the challenge faced.

This is not to say that nothing else was being achieved that might make a difference. The government had taken a number of actions that had the potential to improve the quality of people's lives in the long term, notably new employment legislation to increase job security. It had made commitments to new investment in housing and to increase energy security in the light of climate change. In its spending review in June 2025, the government announced significant capital investment in a range of schemes to stimulate jobs and growth and a string of infrastructure projects.[49] In addition, overall day-to-day spending was to be increased for some areas with, in particular, more money for the National Health Service. But with sharp controls on spending elsewhere, notably in welfare and local authorities, the risk was that the potential long-term benefits from these investments would be undermined.

Meanwhile, the British economy was continuing to stagnate, with projections of a likely fall in people's living standards over this parliament.[50] Indeed, even with around 500,000 children being taken out of poverty by the reversal of the two-child benefit limit and other policies, the extent of child poverty would be expected by the end of this parliament to remain at around 30 per cent of children.[51] The scale and depth of the problems require more than the current policies on offer – they require deeper changes.

What is needed is a comprehensive and ambitious anti-poverty strategy that is both forward-looking and sustainable – that tackles the current high levels of poverty, is affordable in the long-term, and builds a system resilient to future challenges, including the rapidly growing climate crisis.

Fixing the UK's poverty problem would not be easy; a wide range of short-term and long-term actions would need to be taken that would begin to transform the kind of society we live in so that resources are more fairly shared. In a still-wealthy country like the UK, it is perfectly possible. But first it requires an ambition do so, and then a determination to find the money to make it happen. And it requires the argument to be made.

In this book, I try to set out the kinds of reforms and changes that would be necessary to fix the poverty problem. To do this, we first need to understand what's gone wrong. Why have such high levels of hardship and deprivation come about? What are the long- and short-term causes? The last decades of the 20th century saw sharply widening economic inequalities that in themselves saw relative poverty rise. But since 2010 the problem has become acute.

I will argue that the causes of Britain's impoverishment are wide ranging and not only stem from changes to the benefits system made during the austerity years but also include the move to a low-paid economy, the decline of social housing, the underfunding and privatisation of public services, and a rise in the price of basic goods. To fix the problem, we need to tackle these multiple causes.

The first step on this road is to understand the depth and extent of the problem.

1

The breadth and depth of impoverishment

Households in the UK are struggling just to make ends meet, juggling their bills, cutting back on the quantity and quality of food they buy, skipping meals, turning down the heating, and struggling with their rent or mortgages.[1] Increasing numbers feel that they are merely surviving rather than living.

It has become commonplace, in every town and city in every area of the country, even the more affluent ones, to see ever more food banks, donation boxes requesting basic household and personal hygiene items such as toilet paper or shampoo, and schools and GP surgeries setting up emergency supplies.

Changing Realities,[2] a project run by the Child Poverty Action Group in collaboration with the University of York, has been documenting the impact of the current crisis on the lives of people on low incomes:[3]

> It's the constant maths, the 'if I skip this bill this month and jiggle that grocery shop then I should be able to just afford it but not if something unexpected happens 'tween now and then, and I'll have to rearrange some appointments cos I'll not be able to afford travel for those til the month after now.' Just cos my kids need shoes. (Victoria B, April 2023)

> I have had to reduce the food shop budget by so much that my children are now noticing there is less and less in the house, and myself and my husband have had to start fibbing to them regarding why we are not eating by telling them we eat when they are in bed or we had a late lunch. I'm not sure what's worse, the guilt of lying or the hunger that is strangling my family. (Lexie H, March 2023)

> Not being able to afford the cost of heating and electricity to cook healthy meals has also had a big effect on my mental health, feeling that I am not able to care for my daughter in a way that I should be able to. There are also the appointments that I miss to try to get help as I simply don't have the money to pay for travel. ... I would not say at the moment that I have any sort of meaningful life, largely being at home struggling to keep warm and eating very basic foods. (Erik W, February 2023)

> We have cut out holidays, cinema trips, meals out etc. I feel like life is being slowly squeezed out of us families surviving on low incomes. (Sadie Q, April 2023)

The impact of these hardships and deprivations is devastating on their lives and opportunities, and increasingly severe on their health. For both men and women there has been a rise in the number of years spent with a disability or ill-health,[4] even before the impact of COVID-19. Over the previous decade, the average height of five-year-olds had declined,[5] while the obesity and diabetes rates for young people had soared.[6] Premature births and low birthweights were increasing for babies born in the most deprived areas[7] and for the first time in over a century, the predicted healthy lifespan of today's children was lower than the previous generation.

The breadth and depth of impoverishment

To understand why there is such a high level of impoverishment, we need to understand the long- and short-term trends in the numbers in poverty.

Measuring poverty

What poverty is has long been debated. Is it about the bare minimum for existence: not having a roof over your head, not having enough money to be able to eat healthily and properly, not being able to turn on the heating to keep warm? Or should it also incorporate ideas about people not being able to participate in the society in which they live? The first approach sets a basic survival standard and sees how many people today fall below that standard. The second provides a relative measure of what people require to participate in society and depends on the contemporary standards of the society in which they live. It moves with the times.

Historically, as living standards have improved, the standard set by relative measures rose but those at the bottom end struggled to keep up, leading to rising relative poverty and falling absolute poverty. In recent years, however, with living standards stagnating, this has not been the case. For those at the bottom end, while their relative position has changed less, their struggles to provide for the basic necessities of life have increased.

There are two main ways in which to look at people's standard of living. The first is income based, essentially using income as a proxy for people's living standards. People above the level of income set as the poverty line are seen as having enough money to be able to afford an adequate standard of living, those below are seen as being in poverty. The second approach is to look directly at what people have and don't have; at their level of deprivation. This approach sets a minimum standard covering all aspects of life – food, housing, social activities, access to services and the like – and finds out who has to go without these goods and activities and by how much.

The purpose of any measure is to find out which groups fall into poverty, how far they fall, and what they miss out on. The different measures provide somewhat different insights, so it is necessary to look at different sets of indicators to get a fuller picture. In this way a framework of the problem can be established and why it has come about explored.

The official poverty measures

The main measure of poverty in the UK – and the one you see in the headlines – is based on household incomes and looks at how many people fall below a set level of household income.[8] To allow comparison of living standards for different types of households, disposable household income is adjusted for household composition and size using equivalence scales.[9]

In the UK, there are two main measures.[10] The first (and most widely used one) takes a relative approach and is taken as the proportion of the population with incomes falling below 60 per cent of median household income in that year, that is the midpoint of the income range with equal numbers of households or individuals on incomes above and below that point. This is a measure widely used internationally and allows comparisons between countries and of trends over time.

The second is an absolute income measure using a fixed household income poverty line. This does not mean that it provides what is necessary for essential needs, just that the level is fixed and does not move each year. This means you can compare how people on low incomes are faring compared to those on low incomes in previous years, rather than, as with the relative measure, other households at the same point in time. Generally, you would expect that as living standards rise over time, absolute poverty will fall. As a result, the baseline is usually reset every decade or so. The current absolute poverty line is set at 60 per cent of median household income in 2010/11, with household incomes adjusted each year for inflation.

The breadth and depth of impoverishment

Figure 1.1: Relative poverty, before and after housing costs, 1963 to 2023/24

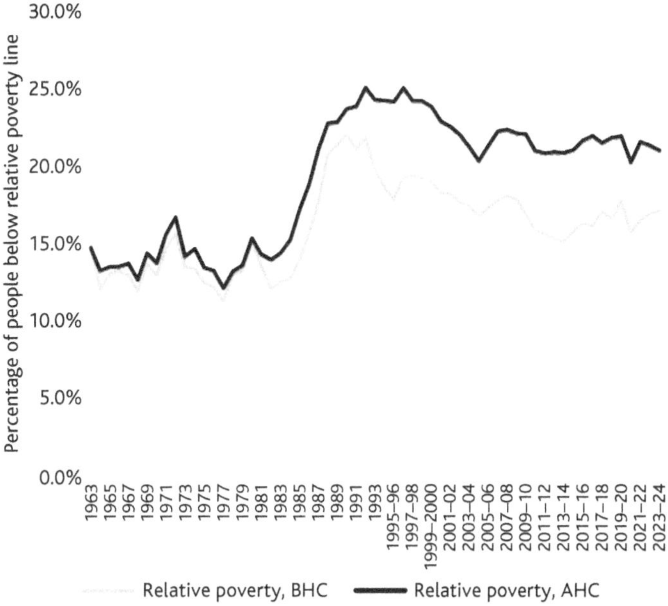

Note: Data up to 2002/03 refers to GB, from then to UK.
Source: Institute for Fiscal Studies[11]

In addition, household incomes can be taken *before* or *after* housing costs. The government measure of poverty uses *before* housing costs – since the 1980s, it has produced a lower percentage of people in poverty – but poverty after housing costs tells us more about what households have available to spend on a day-to-day basis.

Figure 1.1 shows the trends in relative income poverty, both before and after housing costs over the last 60 years and Figure 1.2 shows the trends for absolute income poverty. These long-term trends are crucial to understanding the roots of today's poverty levels.

Looking at relative income poverty (Figure 1.1), the levels for both before and after housing costs were fairly stable during the 1960s and 1970s and then shot up during the 1980s as a direct result of the Thatcher government's policies which were designed to encourage inequality – and did so.[12] In addition, poverty rates before and after housing costs were relatively similar during the 1960s and 1970s but began to pull apart during the 1980s with poverty after housing costs rising faster than poverty before housing costs – a trend that has widened sharply ever since. This was a direct result of government policies – across all parties – that oversaw a rise in the costs of housing at the bottom end.

Within these overall trends, relative poverty levels did drop during the first two terms of the last Labour government between 1997 and 2005. Government policies – in this case, primarily the introduction of the minimum wage and various tax credit schemes aimed at reducing poverty – made a difference. But importantly, this improvement was not maintained and 20 years later we are at much the same levels of relative poverty as in the mid-2000s.

The trends in absolute poverty are shocking (Figure 1.2). Up until the mid-2000s, absolute poverty had steadily declined; household incomes, including at the bottom end, had improved throughout this period so against a fixed line, poverty declined. But this came to an end: since the mid-2000s, household incomes at the bottom end have hardly improved and overall absolute poverty levels remain much as they were 20 years ago. This is primarily because growth in the UK over this period has been extraordinarily sluggish: it hardly grew in the years before the pandemic, then fell during the pandemic only rebounding slightly after.[13]

Moreover, since the 1990s, the fortunes of different groups have differed with pensioner poverty dropping sharply, particularly in the years up to 2010, while working-age households have fared far worse (see Figure 1.3). The decline in pensioner poverty is a major social policy success, the result of pensioner benefits increasing in the period up to 2010 both relative to prices and

Figure 1.2: Absolute poverty, before and after housing costs, 1963 to 2023/24

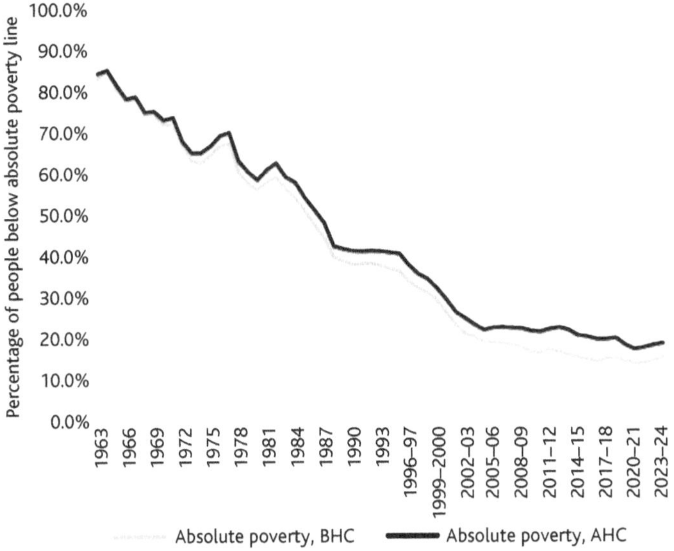

[Figure: line chart showing percentage of people below absolute poverty line, declining from ~85% in 1963 to ~20% in 2023/24, with BHC and AHC lines]

Absolute poverty, BHC — Absolute poverty, AHC

Note: Data up to 2002/03 refers to GB, from then to UK.
Source: Institute for Fiscal Studies[14]

to the relative income poverty line,[15] and then being largely protected. Essentially all governments of whatever political affiliation throughout this period have signed up to improving pensions and the result has been a drop in relative income pensioner poverty from around 30 per cent (after housing costs) in the late 1990s to around 16 per cent today.

By contrast, the rate of child poverty has remained consistently higher. Though the rate of child poverty has declined since the early 1990s, it is only by a little, from just over 33 per cent to around 30 per cent. The trend during this period can be broken down into three key periods and it useful to examine this as it demonstrates the impact of changes in the benefits system – and its limitations.

Between 1997 and 2005, the first two terms of the last Labour government, there was a significant improvement in

Figure 1.3: How different groups have fared since 1992

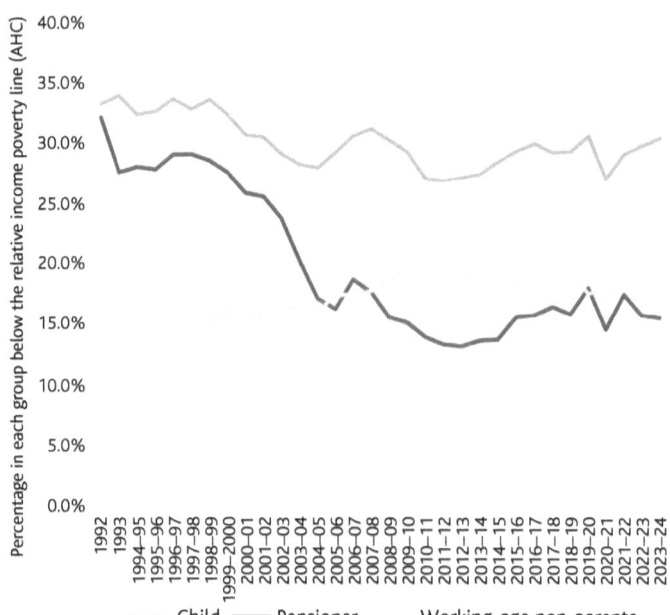

Note: Data up to 2002/03 refers to GB, from then to UK.
Source: Institute for Fiscal Studies[16]

child poverty. The percentage of children in relative income poverty (after housing costs) fell from around 34 per cent to 28 per cent. The government had set falling child poverty as a key priority, with the aim of cutting child poverty by a half by 2010, introducing a number of changes to the benefits system. The most important of these were an increase in child benefit for the first child (a universal benefit paid to all families), increases to the child allowance for workless families and the introduction of a new system of Child Tax Credit for low-paid working families.[17] Entitlements to state benefits for families with children rose, with those for families most at risk of poverty rising notably faster than both prices and median incomes.[18]

However, these improvements had started to peter out by the mid-2000s, and between 2005 and 2010, there was little overall improvement with the child poverty rate ending up at around 27 per cent (after housing costs). This was largely because the growth in benefits and tax credits for families with children became less generous and was no longer keeping up with the growth in median incomes.[19] But, in addition, the benefit and tax credit measures were fighting against a stagnation in wages at the bottom end which meant that, even with Child Tax Credits, work was no longer providing a route out of poverty.

Overall, by the end of the Labour government in 2010, some 700,000 children had been lifted out of relative poverty after housing costs (and 1 million before housing costs), a significant achievement even if below the ambitions set.

And then came austerity and its harsh benefit policies, particularly for families with children. By 2012, as austerity began to bite, poverty rates for children started to increase and, despite a dip during COVID, ended up a decade later notably higher. Indeed, child poverty, at 30 per cent, is back up at the levels of the early 2000s. Some 4.3 million children in the UK are living in relative income poverty, with all the limitations of opportunities and detrimental impact this brings.

The problems with the relative income measure

These relative income trends do not, however, get at the scale of the current problem and, as such, do not reflect the experiences of low-income households.

The problem here lies in the nature of these income-based measures. Income, in the end, is just a proxy for living standards and while household income is a key determinant of living standards, it doesn't necessarily tell us what households can and cannot afford in any one week. This depends on other factors, such as the security and reliability of their income, the level of debt, the degree of support from others, unexpected demands when things break down, or new demands such as sudden illness, redundancy, or when children move schools.

In addition, the relative measure can be quite misleading, implying an improvement when the actual income of those in poverty has fallen or stayed the same. When median incomes fall, as happened during the recession after the 2008 crash and the lockdowns during COVID, it can result in a decline in relative poverty rates. This is not because of any improvement in the lives of those on low incomes but because the median income had fallen. Similarly, during the cost-of-living crisis, the decline in the purchasing power of income meant that those on low incomes saw their standard of living decline but this is not reflected in relative income poverty measures as their incomes relative to the median were unchanged.

Most importantly, the line set is entirely arbitrary. While setting the relative poverty income line at 60 per cent of median income has the advantages of being widely used and allows international comparisons to be made, it is not based on an assessment of what people need. Since 2008, the Joseph Rowntree Foundation (JRF), an independent trust whose principal aim is working towards ending poverty in the UK, has been drawing up the level of income needed to reach a minimum standard of living for different types of households, the Minimum Income Standard (MIS). To set the standards a negotiated consensus is reached between groups of socially mixed members of the public as to what items and activities different types of households need. It sets out to identify wants and necessities, not luxuries, and covers not just the basics of food, clothes, and shelter, but a wider range of items needed to participate in society. These items are then costed by the research team and an overall budget reached. The items in the lists are updated every four years to make sure they reflect contemporary standards, and the items recosted each year to account for inflation.[20]

The budget needed to reach this minimum standard is consistently higher than the 60 per cent of median income

The breadth and depth of impoverishment

Figure 1.4: The extent relative income poverty underestimates people's needs

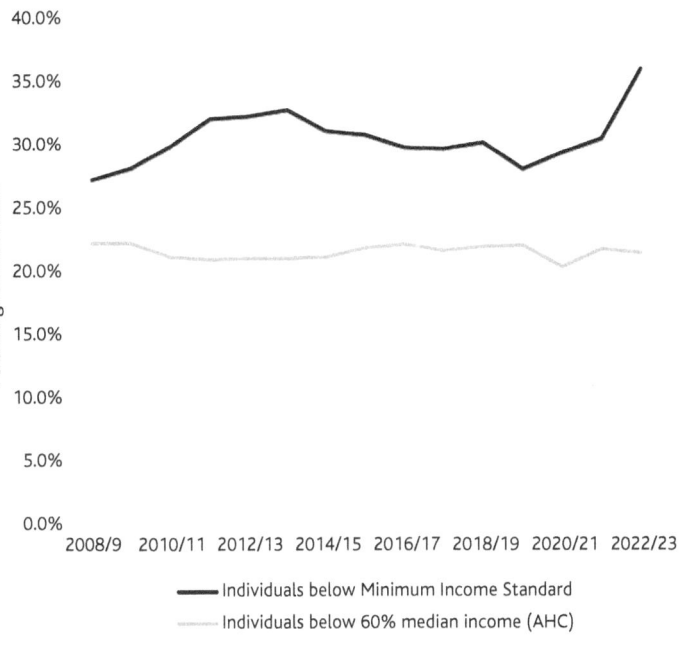

Source: Joseph Rowntree Foundation[21]

benchmark; that is, the relative poverty level is underestimating the numbers of people living in poverty (see Figure 1.4). In 2022/23, nearly 36 per cent of individuals were living below the MIS compared to just over 21 per cent below the relative income poverty line.[22]

Moreover, as can be seen in Figure 1.4, the gap between the percentage of individuals living below the MIS and the percentage living below 60 per cent of median income (after housing costs) has grown over the last decade or so. This is partly because new needs have arisen with items such as computers and internet access moving from nice to have, to being essential. It is also partly because certain essential costs have increased, in particular, for childcare, transport, and energy. And most recently, it is partly a result of the high inflation of 2021–23 resulting in baked-in higher prices for many essentials. The increase in the gap between those below the MIS and those below the relative income poverty line is true for all household groups, with children, again, faring the worst.

This finding is crucial to understanding why the relative income poverty measure doesn't seem to explain the increasing levels of hardship in society. But this measure, too, has some problems. At the end of the day, what we are really interested in, when looking at poverty, is identifying what it is that people go without which they need – in other words, the levels of deprivation. While the MIS provides a basis for setting a required income level at which to measure poverty, it doesn't overcome some of the other problems with using income to measure poverty. These relate to the security and reliability of incomes, other demands on income such as debt, and other sources of support. Deprivation levels are affected by resources *over time*, while income measures are based on a snapshot at one time.[23] Moreover, levels of deprivation depend on a wider view of resources than just income, depending on collectively provided services, such as education and health, which would otherwise be paid for.

To get a better picture, we need to look directly at what people have and don't have.

Going without

Material deprivation is a direct measure of poverty based on people's lack of items and activities deemed to be necessary for a minimum standard of living. Unlike the MIS approach, it does not try to identify a comprehensive list of the items and activities people need so that a budget can be created but identifies a

The breadth and depth of impoverishment

representative set of items and activities across a range of aspects of people's lives and, for each item, identifies who goes without that item and why. The lack of these can be taken as a strong indicator of a standard of living below a socially acceptable level.

As well as asking about income, the Department of Work and Pensions (DWP)'s annual Family Resources Survey collects data on material deprivation for families with children living in the UK. The survey asks respondents whether they have or do not have a range of items and activities indicative of a minimum acceptable living standard, covering food, housing, clothing, social and leisure activities, household goods, transport, and communications. If the respondent does not have an item, they are asked whether it was because they couldn't afford it or didn't want it. Only those who cannot afford an item are counted as materially deprived and results are weighted to provide an overall deprivation score. The survey also asks a similar set of questions for pensioners, though for pensioners all those who do not have an item are included as materially deprived because of concerns that pensioners are reluctant to admit they cannot afford something.

In 2010/11, there was a limited updating of child deprivation measures,[24] and these then remained unchanged up until 2023, enabling material deprivation during this period to be tracked. This provides an absolute measure, in the sense that the standard is fixed and has not moved over time. In the first part of this period up until 2019, there was some improvement in deprivation levels across all groups. For children it dropped from around 20 per cent to 18 per cent and pensioners around 10 per cent to 6 per cent. This is largely what you would expect, and hope for, in an absolute measure. You would expect more people to be able to afford a basket of goods set at the start of the period.

But during the last period of Conservative government, this changed dramatically. The COVID pandemic, the cost-of-living crisis, and the sheer chaos of government during this period resulted in household incomes and outgoings becoming more and more unpredictable, a particular problem for low-income

Figure 1.5: The rise in material deprivation under the last Conservative government

[Bar chart showing percentage in material deprivation for 2019/20 and 2022/23:
- All: 15%, 19%
- Children: 18%, 21%
- In-work: 14%, 17%
- Pensioners: 6%, 8%]

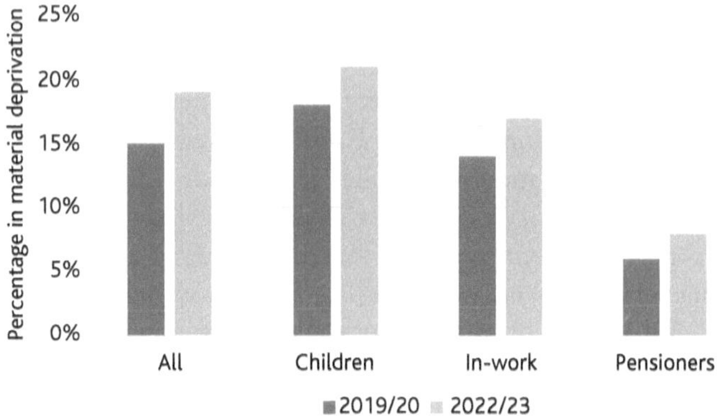

Source: Institute for Fiscal Studies[25]

families who have few, if any, reserves to fall back on. Moreover, the exceptionally high inflation between 2022 and 2023 was largely driven by energy and food prices soaring[26] – goods which make up a particularly high proportion of low-income households' expenditure. The result was that these households ended up cutting back on these basic items or on other necessities to be able to afford these items.

Figure 1.5 shows the results: between 2019/20 and 2022/23, material deprivation across all groups rose. The rise was sharpest for children and adults in work, ending up with 21 per cent of children and 17 per cent of adults in work suffering material deprivation, that is over 3 million children and 8.5 million adults. Moreover, at 21 per cent the child material deprivation rate was higher than it was back in 2010/11.

Figure 1.6 looks at each of the items that make up the overall material deprivation index for children and how the rates for each item have changed from the start of the last Conservative government to 2022/23. Apart from an outdoor space for children to play (which is unaffected by day-to-day expenditure),

The breadth and depth of impoverishment

Figure 1.6: The ways children are increasingly missing out because of family finances

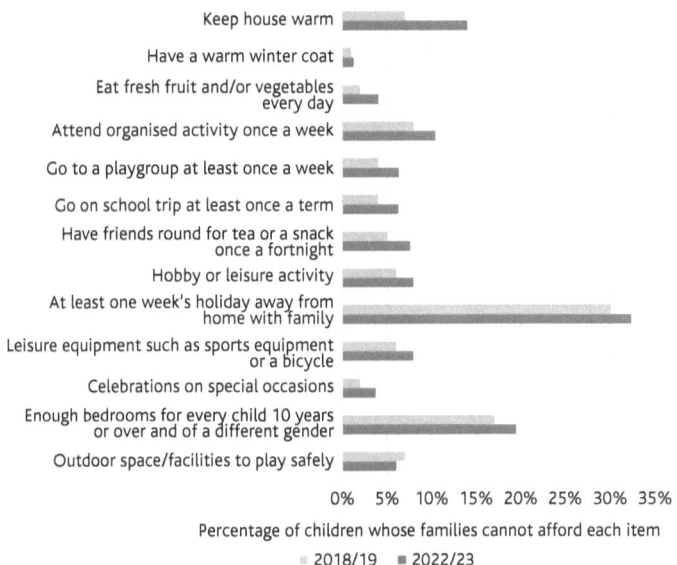

Source: DWP Households Below Average Income (HBAI) series, Table 4.7db[27]

for every other item, the percentage whose families cannot afford that item has risen. The rise is particularly sharp for children whose families cannot afford fresh fruit and vegetables each day and for those who cannot keep the house warm, where rates for both have doubled.

Families on higher incomes have been less affected by the turmoil of recent years. Despite the cost-of-living crisis, children in families whose incomes are in the top 20 per cent are very unlikely to be unable to afford any of these items. The rise is highly concentrated in those at the bottom of the income range. For example, the numbers of children in households in the top 20 per cent of incomes who cannot afford fresh fruit and/or vegetables is too low to calculate; for children in the bottom 20 per cent of household incomes it is 7 per cent. Similarly, 1 per cent of children in the top quintile live in a house that can't be kept warm because of lack of money compared to 13 per cent of those in the bottom quintile; for a lack of a week's holiday the percentages are 5 per cent and 56 per cent, respectively; and so on.

Indeed, these figures are an underestimate of the real extent to which children are missing out at the bottom end. The way the figures are calculated excludes those whose families say they do not have an item because they don't want it and the percentage of families who say they don't have an item because they don't want it is consistently higher in the bottom of the income range. People adjust their expectations. Looking again at having fresh fruit and/or vegetables daily, 5 per cent of families in the bottom 20 per cent say that they don't have this because they don't want it; for families in the top 20 per cent, it is 2 per cent. If this group is included, in 2022/23, 12 per cent of children in the bottom 20 per cent lacked a daily portion of fresh fruit and/or vegetables.

It is worth looking more deeply into food poverty, for this is one of the most shocking features of the last decade.

Food insecurity

The sharp rise in the number of food banks has become symbolic of the impact of the austerity years. The first food bank in the UK was opened by the Trussell Trust back in 2000 and by 2010 there were still only 35. The numbers then exploded. By 2013, there were 650 and by 2019 this had doubled to 1,300. By 2023/24, the number of food banks run by the Trussell Trust had risen to 1,700 and by then there were food banks run by other operators, at least another 1,172.[28] The UK had become a food bank nation. The Trussell Trust alone distributed 3.12 million emergency food parcels, nearly double the number supplied five years earlier in 2018/19.[29]

In 2021, the DWP started – for the first time ever – collecting data on food bank use. That year (2021/22), 2.1 million people lived in households that had used a food bank in the last year. A year later (2022/23), this had risen to 2.3 million. That's 3 per cent of the population. In 2022/23, 800,000 children lived in households that had turned to food banks in the last year, nearly 6 per cent of children.[30]

People only turn to food banks when they have run out of all other choices. Because of the shame and stigma attached to doing so, many people will look first to informal networks of family and friends for help[31] – or simply cut back on the quantity and quality of food they eat. The concept of 'food insecurity' tries to capture this wider problem, incorporating ideas such as whether people have sufficient food for an active and healthy lifestyle, whether they have certainty about their ability to access food, and whether they can access it in socially acceptable ways.[32]

Before the rapid rise in food banks, research into food insecurity in the UK was relatively rare and there had been little attempt to measure it. However, faced with the sharp rise in the numbers using food banks and the indications that this was the tip of deeper problems, this has all changed. Since 2019/20, the DWP' Family Resources survey has asked households about their experiences over the previous 30 days on a range of aspects of food quality and quantity. These tapped into different levels of food insecurity from whether respondents were ever worried food would run out before they could buy more and whether they could afford a balanced diet, through to questions about whether they skipped meals, whether they ever went hungry, whether they were losing weight because of lack of food, and down to whether they had not eaten at all for a day or days. From the answers, households that were food insecure and those on the margins of food insecurity were identified. Those who were food insecure covered both those who had low food security (that is, a reduced quality and variety of diet), and those who had very low food security (that is, those whose food intake had been reduced because of lack of money or other resources for food), while those on the margins of food insecurity covered those who had problems at times, or anxiety about, accessing adequate food.[33]

Figure 1.7 shows the rise in food insecurity between 2019/20 and 2023/24. The percentages living in households in the UK that are food insecure and those on the margins of food insecurity rose for all individuals and for children living in such households, with the rise in those living in households that are food insecure being particularly striking. In 2023/24, 11 per cent (7.5 million individuals), were living in food insecure households including nearly 4 million who had not at times had enough money to buy enough food. Families with children, again, fare the worst with 18 per cent of children (2.6 million) living with food insecurity.

Figure 1.7: The rise in food insecurity

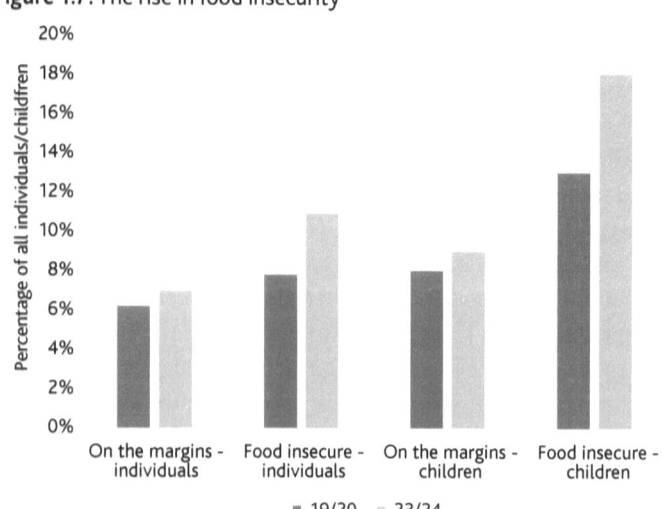

Source: DWP HBAI series, Food Insecurity Tables, 4.1ts and 4.4ts[34]

The breadth and depth of impoverishment

These figures could be an underestimate; The Food Foundation, an independent think tank set up in 2014 to campaign for everyone to have a healthy and sustainable diet, finds, using a slightly different method concentrating on a shortage of food, a somewhat higher percentage of households (at around 14 per cent in 2024 compared to the DWP's 11 per cent) to be food insecure.[35]

Equally important, of course, is the quality of food and the ability to access a healthy diet. The Food Foundation finds that healthier foods are more than twice as expensive per calorie than less healthy foods and less available, a gap that has been increasing in recent years.[36] The result is that to afford the government's recommended health diet, set out in the Eatwell Guide,[37] the most deprived fifth of UK households would need to spend 45 per cent of their disposable income (after housing costs) rising to 70 per cent for households with children.[38] This is clearly unrealistic. If a healthy diet is out of reach, families will turn to an unhealthy one with the result that children from the most deprived income groups eat a less healthy diet with all the long-term consequences this brings.

Financial insecurity

The rise in food insecurity is mirrored by a sharp rise in the numbers of households having financial problems. Indeed, the two are relatively interchangeable in that low-income households have long juggled their finances between paying their bills and having enough for their day-to-day needs, sometimes cutting back on food and heating to pay the bills and sometimes missing a payment just to have enough to eat. But the impact of the COVID pandemic and cost-of-living crises between 2021 and 2023 made these problems acute and, though inflation has fallen back, continue to do so.

In 2024, the Financial Conduct Authority's 'Financial Lives' survey[39] found that around one in four were not coping or were finding it difficult to cope or had very limited savings to fall back on. While renters were most affected, many mortgage holders were still struggling with their higher mortgage repayments, and while those out of work were by far the most likely to have deep problems, many in work were also struggling:[40]

> The rising cost of living is killing me. As a single parent with four children, I do everything I can to make sure they're fed and kept warm. I go without food so that they at least have something. I dread finding out how much more in debt I'm getting with gas and electric, because I just cannot afford to pay the extortionate amount it costs. (Female, 35–44, renting, long-term sick or disabled)

> I have to go without food most days and reduce my electricity usage. I only put the heating on once a week. I have had to reduce social outings to about once every other month and find it extremely hard to get by financially in months that have birthdays. (Female, 35–44, mortgage, employed)

> For me, the rising cost of living is making me feel more stressed out. … It affects everything from personal relationships to mental health. … I feel depressed most of the time, and I can't see any hope that it will be better in the near future. I can't figure out what we have done wrong to be in this situation. (Male, 45–54, renting, self-employed)

> Food has doubled, the mortgage is up 400 per cent, gas and electricity is up 200 per cent. It now costs more to live than the income we get. (Male, 55–64, mortgage, employed)

> Friends have helped me, but this impacts my emotional health as I feel a failure and feel embarrassed but am not in a place to say no. … I also worry about losing

> my dog if I can't afford to look after her. But I'd starve first, as she's so important to me. (Female, 55–64, own outright, self-employed)

> We simply can't afford enough food shopping or gas and electric bills. I'm nearly always hungry now. (Female, 25–34, renting, long-term sick or disabled)

> It's truly awful. Most days I'm stuck deciding if I'm going to starve or be cold. We worry about what bill is coming around the corner. ... We survive because of the kindness of others – charity and family. (Female, 25–34, renting, unemployed)

> The rise in living cost means that I have had to move back in with my mum after a relationship breakdown. I cannot afford to rent anywhere even though I am working full time. I am now sofa surfing and I still find myself struggling to afford food at the end of the month. (Female, 25–34, living rent-free, employed)

Most particularly these surveys have found that more and more households were getting into deep financial problems. Figure 1.8 shows the two indicators used to measure over-indebtedness and how the percentages of adults affected rose between 2017 (the last survey before the rolling crises and the first survey in this series) and 2024.

Debt and indebtedness create a long-term problem, often difficult to escape from. It is yet another indicator of the seriousness and depth of levels of poverty.

The rise of destitution

In 2015 the Joseph Rowntree Foundation, concerned about the growing evidence of severe hardship, set out to measure

Figure 1.8: The rise in deep financial problems

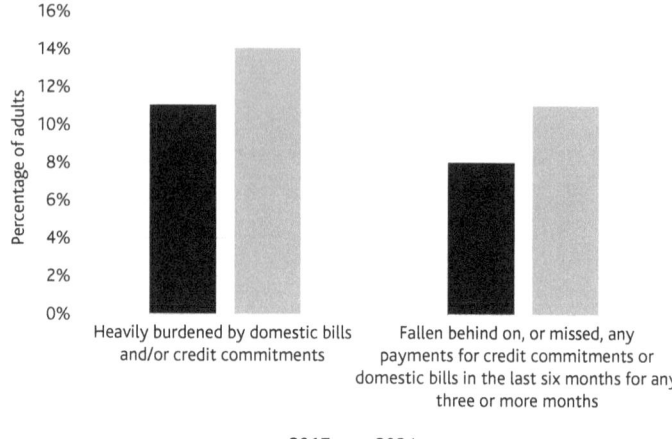

Source: Financial Conduct Authority 'Financial Lives' surveys, January 2017 and 2024[41]

destitution. They developed a measure that encompassed those who did not have basic, minimum material necessities or whose income level was so low that they were unable to provide these minimum material necessities for themselves and depended on family and friends or charities and voluntary organisations.

The result was a definition of destitution that encompassed people, including children, who had lacked two or more of the following six essentials over the past month, namely had fewer than two meals a day for two or more days, had been unable to heat their homes for five or more days, had been unable to light their homes for five or more days, did not have clothing and footwear appropriate for the weather and did not have basic toiletries such as soap, shampoo, toothpaste, and a toothbrush, and who lacked shelter or had slept rough for one or more nights.

This represents an extreme form of absolute poverty, previously thought to have been confined to British history rather than being of relevance today, a feature of the 19th century and its Poor Laws rather than a wealthy 21st-century economy with a developed welfare system. Indeed, if people were increasingly living in such conditions, they had been largely hidden. The measures of poverty used had not been picking this up, partly because of the questions asked (which were designed to measure poverty rather than destitution) and partly because of the limitations of the large-scale household surveys used to measure poverty – many of the people who face destitution simply don't live in the kind of households surveyed.[42]

To capture these hidden people, the researchers carried out a 'destitution survey' of users of a representative sample of crisis centres across the UK and combined these results with a wide variety of existing data gathered by government and charities to produce national estimates.[43]

The findings are alarming. As can be seen in Figure 1.9, back in 2017, over three-quarters of a million households covering over 1.5 million people were destitute – a shockingly high number for a wealthy country like the UK.[44] But of even more concern, there has a been a sharp rise since 2017. Over the five years between

Figure 1.9: The rise in destitution

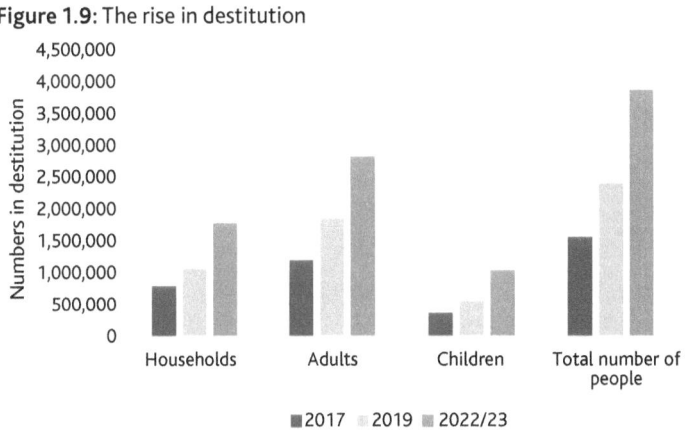

Source: Joseph Rowntree Foundation, Destitution in the UK reports 2018, 2020, and 2023

2017 and 2022/23, the number of households facing destitution more than doubled, with the rate of increase accelerating.[45] In 2022/23, there were 1.8 million households in destitution, affecting 3.8 million people, including around 1 million children.

Such problems are typically the end result of long periods of poverty and hardship. Once destitute, it is generally not temporary but extends onwards over a considerable period of time, often months or years, and often reoccurring.

The impact on people's lives is immense. There is a constant shortage of food and though many turned to food banks, this itself raised problems:[46]

> You get donated maybe tinned food and stuff. I have used that to top us up, but I think it's just because we eat more of the same types of food quite regularly too, like maybe dried foods and stuff, to make it last obviously. … I don't think you always get the same nutritional benefits for yourself or your children. (Woman, aged 25–45)

> Food banks only give you three days of supply and the area that I'm in, they're only open on Mondays and Tuesdays, so by Friday I'm out of food. (Man, aged 25–45)

Most struggled with basic toiletries, often reliant on family or friends or simply going without:

> The toilet rolls and stuff were so hard to get, they were so expensive, so obviously they are something you do need, and wipes and that for the children … we were getting the toiletries that our children needed and … we were getting less toiletries and hygiene things for ourselves. (Woman, aged 25–45)

> I can get them [toiletries], but I have noticed they've gone up in price quite a bit. But kind of lucky there,

> because at Christmas time, when the family ask what I want for Christmas and all that, I just say to them, 'Get us some deodorant and shampoos and things like that.' (Man, aged over 45)

> I sometimes have to borrow off my mum for [toiletries]. That's more my eldest daughter, her disability, she's incontinent at night-time, so she has to wear night-time pads. They're not covered on the NHS or I have to purchase them myself – they're £8 for 12 pads. (Woman, aged 25–45)

Then the soaring domestic energy costs in 2022 hit hard. Though the government provided support for domestic energy bills, it was insufficient for those already struggling:

> Quite a few times [we've run out of money for gas and electric]. … We invested in fleecy blankets to keep warm [over winter]. … It was quite literally between, as I said, between heating and eating. … I would prioritise my daughter to eat, and I would go without, and I would probably boost the heating for about an hour or two and then turn it off. (Man, aged over 45)

> I just try and stay out of the house, most of the time. I just try and stay out of the house. (Man, aged 25–45)

And problems just piled on top of each other:

> It's limited benefits. I had to stay in a hotel and go without food. I had to pay for a hotel, and I didn't have nowhere to stay. (Man, aged 25–45)

This is where the breakdown in the welfare safety net is most apparent.

2

The collapse of the safety net

In July 2019, before the impact of the COVID pandemic and before the cost-of-living crisis, the House of Commons select committee on Work and Pensions examined the impact of the reforms to Britain's welfare system since 2010. Its conclusions were stark: 'The welfare safety net is not fit for purpose for people living on the breadline.'[1]

This was hardly a surprise. The committee's previous report in 2016 found that: 'Reductions to benefit entitlements have left people on the lowest incomes more vulnerable to short-term financial crises.'[2] By 2019, the changes announced under the 2010–15 coalition government had continued to take effect and, from 2015, the new Conservative government had frozen most working-age benefits. This had, the 2019 report found, 'exacerbated' the problem, 'pushing households into poverty and creating additional stresses on household finance'.[3] The outcome, it concluded, was that 'People who cannot boost their incomes sufficiently through work – and who may find that work itself incurs additional costs (such as childcare) – face enormous, on-going challenges in simply meeting their basic day-to-day needs'.[4]

The previous year, the United Nations special rapporteur on extreme poverty and human rights, Professor Philip Alston, had described the ways in which the UK's social safety net was being 'systematically dismantled',[5] arguing that 'key elements of the post-war Beveridge social contract are being overturned'.[6] The reforms since 2010 should be seen as 'radical social re-engineering', replacing compassion with:

> a punitive, mean-spirited, and often callous approach apparently designed to instil discipline where it is least useful, to impose a rigid order on the lives of those least capable of coping with today's world, and elevating the goal of enforcing blind compliance, over a genuine concern to improve the well-being of those at the lowest levels of British society.[7]

What's gone wrong?

The erosion of the value of working-age benefits

One of the most significant – and less discussed – changes made to social security benefits has been the way in which they are increased in value each year to reflect changing prices, a process known as uprating. Since 1987, non-means-tested benefits had been uprated in April each year in line with the Retail Price Index (RPI), an all-item index based on a comprehensive list of household expenditure, as measured the previous September, while means-tested benefits and tax credits had been uprated in line with an index called 'Rossi' (basically the RPI without housing costs). From 2011, the coalition government changed the system to uprate most working-age benefits in line with the Consumer Price Index (CPI), an index based on national accounts rather than household spending, while child benefit was frozen for three years. The RPI/Rossi to CPI shift was significant because historically the CPI had grown more slowly than either the RPI or Rossi. Indeed, the CPI, unlike the

RPI, was never meant as a cost-of-living measure – but as a tool to measure price changes across different countries – and excludes some significant costs for low-income households (for example, TV licences).[8] The move from RPI/Rossi to CPI took out over £1 billion from working-age benefits in its first year and was projected to remove around £6 billion by 2014/15.[9]

The then-Chancellor, George Osborne, justified this by arguing that 'there was no money left' and that a key reason why this was the case was because of increases in welfare spending by the previous government. This in turn, he argued, had resulted in welfare support becoming excessively generous.[10] In fact, while the overall welfare cash transfers (to pensioner and working-age households) had risen somewhat as a percentage of GDP, this was a direct result of the 2008 economic crash, which had brought rising unemployment and lowered national income.[11] Moreover, despite the consequent increase in unemployment benefit, spending on working-age benefits (excluding transfers to children) was smaller as a percentage of GDP than when Labour took power.[12]

This was to be just the start. In 2012, Osborne shifted up a gear in his 'austerity' agenda and decided to limit increases for these benefits to 1 per cent for three years from 2013/14, taking out a further £3.7 billion from these benefits.

Even worse was to come. In 2015, when the 1 per cent limit was due to come to an end and benefits were due to rise again with inflation, the newly elected Conservative government announced a five-year freeze on most working-age benefits (this time also including benefits paid to people too unwell to work as well as extending the freeze on child benefit).[13] This kept benefits at their 2015/16 level until 2019/20. By the end of this four-year freeze, a further £4.4 billion had been taken out of working-age benefits compared to what would have happened if these benefits had been uprated in line with CPI.[14]

It had affected more than 27 million people and swept 400,000 into poverty.[15] For many, the impact was devastating:

> Before [the freeze], there would have been the occasionally miraculous situation where I could manage to save a few pounds. As the freeze has continued, those opportunities have become even fewer and further apart, and it is now a regular occurrence for me to run out of money days before my next payment.
>
> Since the benefit freeze, I have been choosing between eating, heating, paying bills to dealing with another essential need/emergency. It's not right that the cost of living continues to increase, while benefits have remained static. It is cruel and unrealistic to expect people to break free of poverty, while doing nothing to make this an achievable outcome. (Ashley, 42, a single, Employment Support Allowance claimant with no children interviewed by the JRF)[16]

The benefit freeze came to an end in 2020, after which most major working-age benefits returned to being uprated in line with the CPI. But the effects are permanent. Benefits are increased from a lower level and, without a one-off increase to benefit levels, the impact continues onwards indefinitely. Moreover, the return to uprating benefits was to the CPI, not the RPI, the change originally implemented by Osborne back in 2011.

The differential impact of austerity

In the meantime, and during the whole of this period, the basic state pension was protected. From 2012, the uprating of the state pension switched from being in line with RPI to whichever was the highest of CPI price inflation, the rate of earnings growth, or 2.5 per cent, known as the triple lock. The coalition and Conservative governments' austerity measures were, it turns out, quite selective.

The overall impact of these changes can be seen in Figure 2.1. This charts the real RPI value since 2010 of working-age benefits

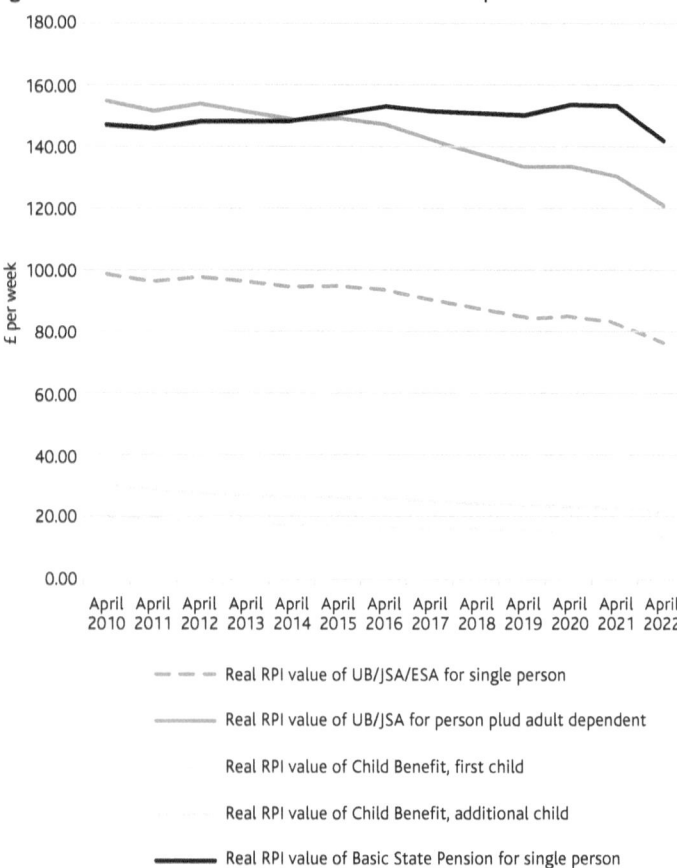

Figure 2.1: The RPI value of various benefits in 2022 prices

- – – Real RPI value of UB/JSA/ESA for single person
- ——— Real RPI value of UB/JSA for person plud adult dependent
- Real RPI value of Child Benefit, first child
- Real RPI value of Child Benefit, additional child
- ——— Real RPI value of Basic State Pension for single person

Source: DWP benefit rate statistics, 2022, Tables 6, 19, 20, 21, 39, and 40[17]

for those out of work, child benefit, and the basic state pension, at April 2022 prices; that is, it shows how far the value of benefits has fallen compared to the value they would have had if these benefits had been uprated in line with the RPI and had not been frozen.

As can be seen, the base level of benefits aimed at those out of work – unemployment benefit and its replacement Jobseeker's Allowance and the Work Support Allowance for those who are disabled but judged capable of work – have declined sharply; by 2022 the value for a single person was over £20 a week less than it would have been if uprated using the RPI and over £30 for someone on these benefits with an adult dependent.[18] Similarly, the value of child benefit has declined sharply and for a family of two children was over £12 a week less.

The basic state pension fared better and up until 2021 saw a modest increase in its value relative to RPI. For all the claimed generosity of the triple lock (and it has been more generous), it has not actually made a significant difference to the value of the state pension compared to what it would have been if it had continued to be uprated at the RPI rate. Its value dropped in 2022 as a result of a temporary suspension of the earnings element of the triple lock which meant that in April 2022 it was uprated, like all other benefits, in line with the CPI inflation rate the previous September. Because inflation in the meantime had soared, this led to a real-terms fall in the value of all benefits by the time of this uprating.

Though overall, pensioners have fared well compared to those of working age, low-income pensioners have not seen such a boost as increases in the state pension were partly offset by the consequent decrease in various mean-tested benefits for low-income pensioners.[19] As a result, low-income pensioners have in recent years increasingly faced financial difficulties.[20]

The overall picture for working-age benefits is far worse. These were never generous and are now far too low.[21] Basic unemployment support is now worth just 14 per cent of average earnings[22] and recipients are ever more reliant on other means-tested benefits. It has left many unable to withstand any, even minor, unexpected additional expenses, let alone achieve a decent standard of living.

While this attack on benefit levels by stealth has gone somewhat under the radar, other policies directly aimed at reducing the working-age benefit budget were far more controversial.

The targeting of larger families

The coalition, and then Conservative, governments of 2010 to 2019, made a fundamentally significant change to the way the benefits system operates; namely, a number of policies were introduced that removed the link, which had up until then been the norm, between a household's actual costs and the benefits to which they were entitled.[23] There were two policies that particularly hit larger families.

In 2013, the then-Secretary of State for Work and Pensions Iain Duncan Smith introduced, with some exemptions, a cap on the total amount of benefits a household could receive, initially set at £26,000 each year for a multi-person household, with a lower level for single-person household. The purported aim was to create a strong work incentive and, according to Duncan Smith, was 'returning fairness' to the system by ensuring that 'no-one can claim more than the average household earns in work'.[24] It was a concept of fairness that, as was so often the case, pitted the 'hardworking' taxpayer against the benefit claimant, stuck supposedly in 'welfare dependency', when no such sharp divisions exist. Households often go through periods in and out of the labour market as their circumstances change.

In 2016, the level of the cap was significantly reduced to £20,000 outside London and £23,000 in London,[25] and it wasn't until 2023 that the level was increased, ending up at £22,020 outside London and £25,323 in London. By this time some 114,000 households were being capped, with a particular harsh impact on larger families (who were more likely to hit the cap), resulting in an estimated 280,000 children being affected.

The second policy, announced in 2015, was to limit the child element of means-tested benefits, such as Child Tax Credit and UC, to two children from April 2017. After much campaigning, the government was forced to make concessions for, for example, children born after rape and multiple births but, otherwise, it went forward much as planned. By the time of the election in 2024, this had affected some 2 million children, with a loss for families of £3,500 a year for each additional child.[26]

The government's argument in this case was that the policy would encourage 'parents to reflect carefully on their readiness to support an additional child' and 'face the same financial choices around the number of children they can afford as those supporting themselves through work' as well as, as ever, being 'fair to those who pay for it'.[27] From the start, this was fundamentally flawed, since what people can afford today does not tell us what they will be able to afford in the future. Moreover, there was absolutely no evidence that the policy would influence conception rates.

Both these policies were targeted at changing adult behaviour as opposed to reflecting the needs of children. If people's behaviour did not change, the impact on children's lives would be devastating. This would be particularly the case for children in larger families, which made certain minorities, who generally had larger families, particularly vulnerable, including Pakistani, Bangladeshi, and Black African/Caribbean families.

Predictably, the policies caused extreme hardship to the affected families, not just the children but also the adults. A comprehensive three-year research project for the Nuffield Foundation – led by the University of York and the London School of Economics – found that there was 'no evidence that either policy meets its behavioural aims and, in some cases, has had the opposite effect'.[28]

Neither policy resulted in increased moves into paid work or increased hours of employment, a key aim of both policies. There were two main reasons. Some parents, though they had worked in the past and planned to do so in the future, prioritised caring for their children themselves, especially when they were young or had health problems, over increased income. Many others, who did want to work, faced a range of barriers which made it difficult, if not impossible; with lack of affordable childcare, health conditions, and a lack of flexibility for working hours being the main ones. Indeed, some families affected by the two-child limit were pushed further away from the prospect of employment as they could no longer afford the costs of even finding work (transport, suitable clothes, and training, for example).

This lack of connection between the stated policy aims and the reality of people's lives was equally evident in the attempts to influence parents' decision making as to how many children to have. The impact on fertility rates of families that might have been affected by the limit was statistically insignificant. Most couples weren't even aware of the policy before they conceived. For those who were aware and had, nevertheless, decided to have more children, they either thought that they could manage but their circumstances changed, or they prioritised family and future relationships above the financial impact. For others, becoming pregnant had not been a choice.

Essentially, these policies have one critical flaw: they assume people's lives are on a smooth and stable trajectory. But stuff happens and circumstances change; people lose their jobs or can no longer carry on because of ill health, they get divorced or separated, they face bereavement, they take on caring responsibilities for family members. Commitments taken on when things were going well can no longer be met.

The only impact was to push more children, not just the third child but all the children in a family, into poverty. This is likely to have long-term financial costs, with worse health outcomes and lower long-term educational outcomes for the children concerned,[29] making the policy not only morally objectionable and a failure on its own terms, but also questionable as to whether there were any financial savings in the long term. 'The worst social security policy ever' is the assessment of Professor Jonathan Bradshaw, one of the country's leading experts on child poverty.[30]

It made the disappointment for poverty campaigners even sharper when the incoming Labour government in 2024 failed to remove this policy on taking power, only moving to do so some 18 months later following intense criticism of the lack of action.

The second area in which the government introduced policies which removed the link between a household's actual costs and the benefits to which they were entitled was housing.

The targeting of low-income private renters

Much of the benefit system is essentially picking up problems stemming from other policy failures. Nowhere is this more apparent than housing. A long-term failure of the UK housing market has resulted in ever-rising rents for low-income households. However, rather than addressing the housing problem, it has been left to the benefits system, through housing benefit (a benefit available to low-income households who rent their homes), to try to pick up some of the resultant financial pressure for low-income households. And this, in turn, has resulted in a toxic combination of increasing amounts going out in housing benefit but, as housing benefit failed to cover all of the extra cost of the rising rents, an increasingly large share of the income of low-income households going on rent. As part of their austerity drive, the coalition government set about reducing this area of welfare spending.

For private rental tenants, this was done by repeatedly capping and then freezing Local Housing Allowance (LHA), the maximum amount you can claim in housing benefit if you are renting from a private landlord. Back in 2010 the LHA for a household was set at the 50th percentile of private sector rents in the local area for a property with the number of bedrooms deemed appropriate for the size of that household. The coalition government, soon after taking power, decided to drop this level to the 30th percentile and, in addition, set a cap (dependent on rental size) on the total amount of housing benefit any household could claim. This meant that from 2011 private sector renters on housing benefit could only afford to rent properties in the bottom third of the rental market (the worst properties) and in some high-rent areas (such as London) where the 30th percentile housing hit the cap, only properties below that level. Those in properties above the cap either had to move (often not an option) or pay the difference.

In 2012 this was followed up by limiting, with a few exceptions, the rate of rise of LHA values to 1 per cent, whatever the rise in rents of properties in the 30th percentile had been.[31] Then in 2016, the Conservative government imposed a four-year freeze on the LHA rate. This meant that by 2019/20, the average gap between the LHA rate and even the 30th percentile had grown significantly, with the result that in one in five areas of Britain, only 10 per cent or less of private rental properties in the area were affordable within the housing benefit allowed by these rates.[32]

If the effect of housing benefit had been, as some had argued and some international evidence had suggested,[33] to prop up rental prices by, in effect, being a subsidy to landlords, then one might have expected rents just above the cap to fall as affected renters moved to cheaper rentals. But, with a few exceptions for small subgroups of rental properties, this did not happen. Rents did not fall. Most of those affected did not have the choice of moving, their housing was already at the most basic level and there simply weren't cheaper rental properties they could move to that met even this basic level. The impact of the cap therefore fell almost entirely on the tenants whose housing benefit covered an increasingly small part of their rent.[34]

During COVID-19, the government lifted the LHA freeze, restoring much of the gap between LHA and the 30th percentile and then froze it again for another four years. After this latest freeze, in April 2024, the then-Chancellor Jeremy Hunt relinked the 30th percentile level, to again subsequently freeze it. The end result of all this is that around seven in ten private renters in the lowest 40 per cent of incomes spent above 30 per cent of their income on rent.[35]

As the homelessness charity Crisis has documented, the continuing low levels of the LHA have imposed impossible choices on low-income tenants in the private sector:[36]

> I had to move due to my landlord selling the house I was in. … I work part time and the support [from LHA rates] I get is leaving me so short each month. I'm a single parent with two teens trying to work but they make it so hard. (Female, a single parent)

> My daughter's landlord wants possession as he's selling. She can't find anything for the LHA of £350 a month. She is long-term sick, and this is exacerbating her severe anxiety. (Mother of a disabled daughter)

> My rent has gone up … but my housing benefit has not changed. I've worked since I was 16 until I was made redundant four years ago at 58, and I've not been able to get another job. I am lucky to have two brothers that help towards my rent otherwise I would find myself homeless. (Male, unemployed)

Families faced with such a shortfall have struggled to both pay their rent and have enough left over to pay their bills and feed the family. The result has been rising levels of indebtedness and hardship and increasing homelessness and destitution.[37] And while there have been some direct savings for the government on housing benefit (and the housing component of UC) as a result, because none of the underlying causes of high rents were being tackled, the government was still spending around £22 billion a year on housing benefit,[38] a rise in housing benefit spending per working-age person of around 40 per cent since the mid-1990s.[39] Moreover, any savings have been offset, at least to some extent, by higher costs to councils who have been left to pick up the pieces.[40]

It all makes this repeated capping and freezing of LHA another strong contender for the 'worst social security policy' prize.[41]

Despite all this evidence of hardship and counter-productive impacts, in the autumn budget in 2024, the Chancellor Rachel Reeves decided to continue with the LHA freeze at least until 2026, possibly beyond. The JRF calculates that the average private renter in receipt of housing benefits was £684 per year worse off from April 2025 than they would have been in 2011 before all the changes, the equivalent of having to find more than a month's worth of extra rent every year.[42]

Not surprisingly, homelessness charities were 'extremely disappointed' and found it 'deeply concerning'.[43] The JRF further calculates that as a result of the 2025 freeze private renters will be £243 worse off on average that year with a working-age couple with children being £340 worse off.[44] If this policy continued to the end of this parliament, these figures will increase to £703 and £882 a year, respectively, pulling increasing numbers of private renters into deep poverty.[45]

The infamous 'bedroom tax'

For social housing tenants, the coalition government took aim at what they saw as underoccupancy by reducing housing benefit payments to tenants of working age considered to be living in properties too large for the size of household, the

Social Housing Size Criteria, or what became known as the 'bedroom tax'. From 2012, for those deemed to have one spare room, 14 per cent of their benefit was to be deducted and for two or more, 25 per cent. Limiting the size of the property covered by housing benefit had been the case for private tenants for a number of years (whose maximum LHA depended on household size) but social and private tenants have very different characteristics. Social tenants are much more likely to be older, widowed, divorced, or separated, economically inactive, and to have lived in the property for a long time.[46] The impact on these tenants was therefore harsher and the 'bedroom tax' became highly controversial. Indeed, its consequences were attributed to pushing some tenants over the edge,[47] leading it to be described by some as 'a policy that kills'.[48]

It hit tenants with disabilities particularly hard, many of whom used a spare room to store their equipment and the like: of the half a million tenants affected, around three in five were in households with at least one registered disabled tenant.[49] And it has had a disproportionate impact on those who were bereaved who were given little time to adjust to their loss before the penalty was imposed.[50]

If the idea, as was claimed by the government at the time, was to force tenants perceived to be underoccupying their home to move to a smaller home, it was stunningly unsuccessful. In the early years of the policy fewer than a quarter registered to move; their work, their children's schooling, caring responsibilities, and social relationships tied them to the area. In many places, there were simply no smaller homes available, hardly surprising given the acute shortage of social housing. Those who did manage to be allocated a smaller place simply reduced the number of smaller homes available to new applicants, the very type of social housing most in demand. And in areas where demand for larger homes is small, it meant more properties being left empty for longer before being re-let.[51] In the end, nine in ten of those affected took the financial hit.[52] As a result of the policy, around a third of affected tenants fell into rent arrears and for those already in arrears their debts mounted.[53]

After extensive challenges from disabled claimants based on discrimination grounds – which eventually ended up in the Supreme Court – the government was, in 2017, forced to exclude some disabled tenants from its reach where there was a 'transparent medical need for an additional bedroom'.[54] But the changes were limited and fuzzy at the edges; much of the cruelty of the policy continued for households containing a person with a disability as it did for households without.[55]

The bedroom tax, like the LHA freeze, despite its clear and obvious failures, looks set to continue onwards with no prospect of ending.[56] Regardless of past promises, the incoming Labour government did not reverse the policy, arguing that its 'dire' economic inheritance made it impossible to undo all the policies it had stood against while in opposition, leaving the minority parties to press the issue.[57] On the latest figures, nearly half a million social housing tenants on housing benefit or receiving the housing element of UC are paying the bedroom tax.[58] Around 1.8 million private tenants receive housing benefit and continue to be affected by the lower LHA rate. For both social and private tenants, these policies continue to cause financial hardship and distress.

At the same time as these changes, in 2013, the roll out of UC began, arguably the most fundamental shakeup in the benefits system for decades.

Universal Credit or discredit?

UC was the signature welfare policy of the coalition government and brought together six existing benefits (the 'legacy' benefits), to create one giant, means-tested system. When fully rolled out UC would cover means-tested support for those on out-of-work benefits (including for those who have a long-term sickness or disability), families on low incomes with children, Working Tax Credit (a benefit for those in work on low pay, to be discussed in Chapter 4) and help with rental costs, all previously provided through separate benefits. The aim was to simplify and rationalise the system, and to bring the benefits system into the digital world. Claimants would make one application, rather than many separate claims, and this would be made online, with some allowance for those without the internet to phone in.

But as with any simplifying process, it removed flexibility and, at least to some extent, an ability to design and adapt support depending on circumstances. For example, bundling all payments into one prevented different benefits going to different household members. This worked fine for most households, but for those in more problematic relationships, in particular for women in coercive relationships, it, as the Women's Budget Group argued, 'set the scene for abuse'.[59] (In Scotland, split payments were subsequently introduced.)

Notably, to accommodate the time it took to gather the earnings information needed from employers to work out the level of the tax credit element, it was decided to make payments monthly, in arrears. This meant that, whereas the majority of unemployment claims under the 'legacy' system were sorted in two weeks and virtually all by three weeks,[60] under UC there was, at a minimum, a five-week wait period between application and the receipt of benefit, and often far longer.[61] While claimants could receive an advance payment – and around 60 per cent did – these are treated like debt and deducted from their subsequent UC. It left claimants with too little money to live off.

Surveys of social housing tenants during the roll out of UC found that almost three-quarters of UC tenants were in arrears compared to a quarter of other tenants.[62] Similarly, the Trussell Trust saw a sharp rise over time in foodbank use in areas where UC had been rolled out.[63]

Even after the initial assessments, there remained problems with unpredictability in the level of payment, with claimants finding that their payments could vary significantly, particularly for those in insecure work or zero hours contracts. Those who worked irregular hours and whose income fluctuated often found that their benefits would be reduced just when their income was also reduced, making it very difficult to cope. Indeed, some claimants reported that they felt it was better for their finances not to take a temporary job as at least then they had certainty in their payments.[64] What claimants need for budgeting is stability in the amounts paid.

The new system also took a more aggressive approach to reclaiming past debt, making it much easier to deduct money from a household's benefit entitlement to pay for outstanding monies owed to third parties – such as debts and fines on energy and other utility bills, council tax and social rent arrears, benefit advances and tax credit overpayments – and at much higher levels.[65] Debt deductions have long been part of the benefits system, justified as helping claimants manage their finances and the arrangements made, including maximum repayment rates, were negotiated with the claimants to reflect their resources and other commitments. But under UC, deductions were seen increasingly differently, as part of a policy to 'to protect public funds'[66] and, by making the deductions more punitive, as a way of pushing people off benefits and into work.

In 2023, nearly half of households on UC had deductions from their benefit payments for debt,[67] with one in ten of these deductions taking more than a quarter of their benefit entitlement.[68] These deductions no longer even pretend to be consensual, with deductions often starting with no warning or fluctuating with little explanation.[69] It left claimants struggling ever more to make ends meet – making this more aggressive approach to debt a powerful driver of deepening poverty.

Faced with deductions, claimants are more likely to turn to unauthorised lenders and loan sharks. Around one in ten of the clients of StepChange, the debt charity, report using unregistered lenders as a result of such deductions – which, as one their clients describes, can have serious consequences: [70]

> A friend of mine realised that I was struggling and gave me a phone number for a loan shark. I rang him, and after speaking he offered to lend me £500 on the condition that I pay him back £1,200 – I am still paying him back at the moment. I've heard horror stories about the violence others have endured if they haven't paid him back on time. (UC claimant)

Claimants get ever more trapped in a vicious poverty/debt cycle which spirals out of control. Their physical and mental health deteriorates, their problems get worse, they fail to pay their bills, resulting yet further deductions, they take out further loans and debts – and so it goes on. As a recent longitudinal study of those on very low incomes conducted in the north of England concludes:

> Over time, deductions set in motion events that wore away at the resources, resilience and relationships of claimants with many deprived of warmth, light, food and habitable accommodation. This profoundly damaged the physical and mental health of claimants pushing them (further) away from the labour market, as they struggled with everyday survival.[71]

As with so many of the changes made to benefit policy in recent years, it has been counterproductive on its own terms. Claimants have ended up further away from the jobs market and the cost to the public purse has ended up higher.

In October 2024, in her first budget, the newly elected Labour Chancellor, Rachel Reeves, reduced the overall cap for UC deductions from 25 per cent of the standard allowance to 15 per cent from April 2025. The move will affect an estimated 1.2 million families who will see their deductions reduced by, on average, £420 per year.[72] It does not reduce their overall level of indebtedness, it simply allows claimants to repay debts over a longer period. So, while it will have a significant impact on the current living standards of those in the deepest debt and should reduce the numbers being pushed into the deepest poverty, over the long term claimants will still be paying back the same amount and will continue to struggle.

Moreover, it does not remove the underlying reasons why debt has been rising for those on UC; namely, the five-week wait for claimants to get their first payment resulting in advance payments that must be paid back to bridge that gap and the unpredictability of the level of benefit. Nor does it remove the other causes of rising levels of debt for those on benefits due to the inadequate levels of benefits and the rising cost of rent, energy and other utility bills.

UC was introduced with the claim that it made the system simpler, but simpler for whom? Certainly not for many of those dependent on it who report continued and deep problems with how it operates, as well as the delays and errors in payments. StepChange found that 65 per cent of their clients said that receiving UC had made it harder for them to budget and manage their financial situation, and only 9 per cent found it easier. They also reported that the ongoing processes involved in constantly needing to update the information provided in the online journal that they are required to keep can often seem demeaning and stigmatising. As participants in Covid Realities[73] – a major research project which looked into the experiences of parents and carers on low incomes during the pandemic – explain:[74]

> It wasn't my choice to move to Universal Credit. I had no choice. And in the time that they moved me from the legacy benefit, I'd racked up a bill that I had no idea about because they'd overpaid me and they took that whole amount out in one Universal Credit payment which was right at the beginning of the first lockdown where I'd lost my job and it took multiple phone calls and journal entries for me to finally get hold of someone and I was crying I had to you know,

it really, really rinsed me for the month. I physically could not afford my bills. (Female claimant)

I'd much prefer to be able to simply email one consistent person who knows me and my case. Sending a message on the journal feels like you're sending it into the ether. I don't know who it's going to and if they ever get it. ... The journal often seems like simply a way for the DWP to send demands rather than a way for us to ask questions or ask for help. As soon as you do you're signposted out of the communication. (Female claimant)

It all gives the appearance of a system designed by people who had little to no contact with, or interest in, claimants themselves – and this is precisely its origins. It was initially thought up as a concept by Iain Duncan Smith's policy outfit, the Centre for Social Justice, in their 2009 report *Dynamic Benefits*,[75] and taken forward by the coalition government when Duncan Smith became Secretary of State for Work and Pensions.

However, the system came into its own on 23 March 2020 with lockdown.

Coping with the COVID-19 pandemic

During lockdown, the government's main strategy for protecting jobs and family incomes was the Coronavirus Job Retention Scheme, also known as furlough, and the Self-Employment Income Support Scheme, discussed in Chapter 4. But, even with these job protection schemes, unemployment was rising at unprecedented rates. This resulted in an avalanche of claims for UC with around 1.5 million claims made between 13 March and 9 April 2020.[76] To cope, the DWP suspended some of its verification procedures and all of the work conditionality requirements. Most claimants were assessed on time and those who qualified were paid on time and in full. For this group of claimants, the new system worked and, by being online, it did prove easier to manage for the DWP. It is difficult to imagine the old system having coped.

One reason for the system's efficiency during COVID-19 was because some of the rules were temporarily put on hold. But another was the make-up of the claimants. They were much more likely to be younger and with less complex problems than existing claimants.

In addition, to ease the impact on the living standards of moving on to UC, the government provided a temporary, flat-rate increase in UC of £20 a week (this applied to all UC claimants and those on Working Tax Credit though not those still on other 'legacy' benefits). It was, as one of the participants in Covid Realities notes,[77] an admission that benefits are too low:

> I'd like people to think about why it was necessary to introduce a £20 uplift at the start of Covid. Surely this is an acknowledgement in itself that the support given to low-income households just isn't enough for them to live on. (Caroline, mother of one, Northern Ireland)[78]

This enhanced level of UC, along with its ease of access, provided a lifeline for many, helping to prevent more households being swept into poverty. Even with the uplift, however, many new claimants, who often had existing financial commitments, found it difficult to manage; over a third reported having difficulties in keeping up with bill payments.[79] And for those already on benefits affected by the benefits cap, it made no difference.

To help cover some of these gaps, the government also introduced the COVID Winter Grant Scheme (from December 2020 to April 2021) and the COVID Local Support Grant (from June 2021 to September 2021). These schemes provided local authorities with almost £400 million for additional assistance to particularly vulnerable households to help cover the costs of food, energy, water bills, and other essentials, in a move the government described as providing 'peace of mind'.[80] The local authorities were responsible for administering the monies and were given discretion as to who received additional payments and how the support was given, such as food vouchers, direct cash transfers, support for utility bills and the like, though they then had to account for the spend to the government.

Making emergency support mainstream

These schemes are best seen as part of a move that started under the coalition government to transfer responsibility for ad hoc support for vulnerable households from central to local government. In 2013, it scrapped the centrally administered Social Fund and replaced it with the centrally funded but locally administered Local Welfare Assistance Schemes, though these were less well funded than the Social Fund. The coalition government's argument for this transfer of responsibility was that local councils were best placed to know what was needed in their area, but it is more accurately seen as buck-passing on a grand scale.[81] Councils were facing draconian funding cuts,[82] and were struggling to meet their minimum legal requirements, putting immense, competing pressures on these discretionary funds, which were not ring-fenced.

Within a few years many councils had either closed the fund or cut their spending on it substantially.[83] Moreover, as the benefits cuts bit, what was seen as a fund for exceptional one-off payments resulting from problems at a personal level swiftly became a fund to pick up the failure of the benefits system to cover standard, routine, everyday costs. But it enabled government ministers to talk about 'local spending decisions' whenever a case of a family facing problems hit the media, derided by Ruth Lister in the House of Lords as a 'Pontius Pilate response'.[84] The COVID Winter Grant Scheme and the

COVID Local Support Grant followed this blueprint: funds far too small to cover the extensive remit placed on them but allowing central government to disclaim responsibility.

With the COVID lockdowns ended, the UC uplift was withdrawn in September 2021, despite extensive opposition involving some 100 organisations. The removal of the uplift inevitably led to more financial hardship for low-income families with around 6 million families losing £1,040 from their annual income. The JRF estimated it would sweep a further 500,000 people into poverty, including 200,000 children.[85]

The government's 'solution' instead was to continue the use of discretionary funds run at the local level to mitigate the increasingly insufficient, centrally run benefits system. In doing this, the government turned the COVID-era emergency schemes into the Household Support Fund (HSF) which, like the earlier schemes, was funded centrally and administered locally. The HSF was set up originally to run from October 2021 to March 2022 but by then inflation had started to rise, initially fuelled by a post-COVID effect and then Russia's invasion of Ukraine. The fund was extended, first to October 2022, then to March 2023, and then March 2024. It was turning into a permanent, rather than temporary, measure and by then had accounted for £2.5 billion of expenditure: £2.15 billion in England and £350 million in comparator schemes in the devolved administrations.[86]

Far from being an emergency fund for those with particular and unexpected problems, it had become a way of trying to cover up for the failures of the benefits system itself. It was certainly used as such by the last government. For example, when, in the House of Commons, the then-Prime Minister Rishi Sunak was questioned about the case of Izzy, a struggling parent in Halifax, he referred the questioner to the fund, thus, attempting to transfer all accountability for the problem from the government to local councils: 'What I would say to Izzy and others who are in particular need is that they should talk to their council, because the Chancellor has provided more than £1 billion of funding to the Household Support Fund.'[87]

After taking power, the Labour government extended these schemes, first to 2025 and then in the spring of 2025 for another year to 2026.[88] And the government continues to play the same trick of pointing to discretionary funds provided to local authorities when defending failures to provide adequate basic benefits. When defending the freeze on the LHA for private renters, for example, the government pointed to the extra money for councils to help low-income households with other costs, such as food and energy through the HSF, and support for household housing costs available through Discretionary Housing Payments.[89]

But these discretionary funds are just sticking plasters and nowhere near enough to cope with the acute problems many households face. And, as one local authority participant commented in a research project supported by Research England:

> let's be clear about the Household Support Fund. It is the smallest of sticking plasters. You know, it's welcome. People will welcome it. But at the end of the day the levels of poverty and utter distress that we're seeing and hearing about are heart-breaking and what the Household Support Fund does is just ... you know, have a couple of quid and be a bit happy. And you know, the government can be all 'we've handed out all these large sums of money.' Really?[90]

But precisely because of the acute failures of the benefits system, there ends up being a dependence on these crisis funds, however inadequate they are. And this dependency applies not just to the households receiving emergency funding but also to an array of voluntary groups and charities working with families in crisis; food banks, welfare rights and debt advisory services, Citizens

Advice, other not-for-profit organisations working with specific vulnerable groups such as the elderly or homeless, and the like.

Over the last decade or so, these organisations have become increasingly important in picking up the pieces of the failing benefits system. They provide food, furniture, beds and bedding, clothes, and many other necessities to those struggling. They provide debt advice and on–off support for larger, unexpected expenditures (such as a broken-down fridge or washing machine). In effect, they have been 'acting as a "last safety net" for those financially struggling'.[91]

Local authorities, whose own capacity has been much reduced by a decade or more of funding cuts, have relied on such organisations in implementing the distribution of these emergency funds, either handing out block grants for providing support to vulnerable households or paying these organisations to administer the funds, giving them the power to refer service users for vouchers or cash transfers. But these organisations are themselves under increasing financial pressures and increasingly dependent on monies paid out of these funds just to survive.[92]

But none of this is sustainable. Nor is it satisfactory as a solution to the benefits crisis. The voluntary organisations themselves often feel they are put in an impossible position, being expected to solve problems for which they simply do not have the funding. Some resort to rationing their services, and in doing so often reflect a wider anti-benefit narrative with concerns about dependency and 'weaning people off' support.[93] This, in turn, leads to uneven support and exclusion.

For the recipients, it is a move of last resort and one which many find demeaning.[94]

UC is simply too low. This applies for all recipients of working age (whatever their work status and household setup) but is particularly the case for those out of work. Around six in ten adults without children in households with one or more unemployed are in relative income poverty (after housing costs) rising to a shocking nine in ten for households with children.[95]

A decade and more of cuts to working-age benefits has taken a heavy toll. At the same time, the system has been restructured to make it harsher for those out of work.

3

Blaming the vulnerable

When the Work and Pensions Secretary, Liz Kendall, told ITV News in March 2025 that the number of people on benefits who pretend they can't work is 'not good enough', and 'we have to end that', that they are 'taking the mickey',[1] she was just the latest in a long line of ministers, of all political persuasions, who have blamed benefit claimants for their own situation. While Kendall phrased it around also wanting to help people into work, the impact on claimants of such rhetoric is much the same.

Back in 2010 the Conservative Party posters in the general election campaign declared 'Let's cut benefits for those who refuse to work'.[2] While, even back then, attacks on benefit claimants, particularly those out of work, was nothing new, what followed was exceptional in the ferocity of the rhetoric used and the consequent policies adopted. The 'scrounger' rhetoric used by the government and much of the press in these years has been well documented.[3] It set out to harden people's attitudes towards those on benefits with claims of welfare dependency. It laid the ground for the punitive measures that were subsequently implemented.

Over the past 30 years or so, one of the main aims of changes to the benefit system has been to try to move people who are unemployed or not working through sickness or disability into paid work. Work is widely agreed to be potentially beneficial for the people concerned; it can increase household incomes, give a sense of purpose, widen social networks, and improve mental health. What is far more controversial is how this shift is achieved.

Governments have relied on two main ways: first, increasing the financial incentives to move into work, primarily through the use of Working Tax Credit (see Chapter 4) and, second, by making it difficult to survive on out-of-work benefits. As seen in Chapter 2 (see Figure 2.2), the value of unemployment benefits was reduced sharply over the lifetimes of the coalition and Conservative governments.

Unemployment benefit in the UK is now exceptionally low, especially compared to most European and OECD countries who have far more generous support levels for those out of work, often related to previous earnings. For a single person without children on average earnings, their overall benefits (including housing benefit) on becoming unemployed will be 40 per cent of their previous earnings compared to the OECD average of 59 per cent.[4]

But not only have levels of income for those out of work been cut, their lives have also – as a matter of deliberate policy – been made more difficult.

The explosion of the use of 'conditionality' regimes

The unemployed have always been required to 'sign on' for availability to work before claiming unemployment benefit but since the mid-1990s and the introduction of the Jobseeker's Allowance (JSA), this has been pursued through imposing tougher requirements to look for (and take up) a job; what's called 'conditionality', backed up by the withdrawal of benefit, through sanctions, if these conditions were not met. In addition, new groups of those out of work have fallen under these regimes as their use has become more widespread.

The most significant expansion in this use of conditionality took place under the Labour government of 2005–10. In 2007, incapacity benefit was replaced by the Employment Support Allowance (ESA) which, for the first time, extended the reach of welfare conditionality to many working-age, disabled adults. Then, in 2008, the rules for lone parents claiming out-of-work benefits were changed. Up until then, lone parents did not have to search for a job to receive these benefits until their youngest child turned 16; under the new rules the age was incrementally reduced so that by 2012, lone parents of five-year-olds had to look for work.

What happened under the coalition government of 2010–15 and then the Conservative government of 2015–19 was that a much tougher set of conditions were applied and much harsher sanctions were imposed on those who did not meet these conditions. This included full-time job search regimes with claimants required to meet certain conditions which were set in regular meetings with a 'work coach'; these could include the number of jobs they needed to apply for each week, the number of hours spent on job searching, the number of interviews attended, and the like. If these conditions were breached, the claimant could be subject to sanctions which for some benefits were up to 100 per cent of their standard benefit allowance and, if they had already been sanctioned twice before, could last up to three years.[5]

Moreover, with the rollout of UC even more claimants were subject to these requirements with the extension of conditionality to in-work recipients and to the partners of benefit recipients. This was a vast extension of conditionality and changed Working Tax Credits from being a support system for households with someone in work but on low wages to a punitive judgement system as to whether the person in work was working hard enough. In effect, it extended the stigma of being on benefits to those in work.[6]

In addition, from 2017, new conditions for parents of preschool children on UC were introduced. Parents of children aged three or four had to be available for, and actively look for, work, parents of two-year-olds had to take 'active steps' to prepare for work, and parents of one-year-olds had to undertake work-focused interviews – or be sanctioned. This included the main carer in couples with children as well as lone parents, while for lone parents various exemptions, which had been allowed under the predecessor JSA to restrict their hours of work under certain circumstances, became more limited. As of November 2024 (the latest available data) over 2 million people on UC were on conditionality regimes.[7] And this is placing more and more and more claimants under the threat of sanctions.

The detrimental impact of sanctions

Sanctioning was largely suspended during the COVID pandemic but has been rising sharply since its gradual reintroduction in April 2021. Between November 2022 and the end of October 2023, over half a million people on UC had had a sanction decision made against them.[8] While these levels of sanctioning, and the severity of the sanctions, are below the peak of the coalition years – when at its maximum over a million a year were sanctioned[9] – these are not trivial numbers. And sanctioning has an enormous impact on those sanctioned and their families.

While some level of hardship would be expected, the House of Commons Works and Pensions Committee review of benefit sanctions in 2018[10] found that the experience of sanctioned claimants went far beyond hardship. It forced claimants into borrowing money or moving into debt or arrears, any of which was often difficult to get out of after the sanctions had ended:[11]

> How do you catch up? … you are still getting yourself to work, but the ends are still not being met … when the sanction [ends], you've still got that backlog. You have still got bills that are outstanding and you are still being chased. (Female, a single parent)

It drove people to food banks, or to cut back on food and other essentials:

> I had to rely on food banks and the kindness of family to get through Christmas. It made me feel like a failure and caused my children stress. (Female, 31–45)

> I fell into debt with bills and at times was unable to top up my prepayment electric meter so was without heating or lighting. (Male, 31–45)

And sanctions had a severe effect on some claimants' mental health:

> I was already depressed, this worsened it, seriously knocking my confidence. I self-harmed. (Male, 31–45)

> It sent my mental and physical health spiralling out of control. I have severe anxiety at the mention of the DWP or sight of a brown envelope. (Female, 45+)

This discriminatory nature of conditionality and sanctions is particularly disturbing. In 2020, a team at the University of Glasgow, in a study on mental health and employment for the Health Foundation, interviewed people on benefits with a range of mental health problems who were subject to work search conditionality.[12] The research found that the pressure and poverty arising from conditionality and sanctions was likely to exacerbate mental health problems:[13]

> The only role they've had is just destroying my life, not bettering it. They're just making is harder every time for you. It's driving people to depression and everything. (Male, 45–47, employed and on UC)

> So you end up falling back into a deeper little hole. And then it just subsides and that hole gets bigger and bigger, and you're stuck in it and you think which way am I going to turn? I took an overdose, because of the

stress. (Male, 35–39, disabled person not in paid work and on Employment and Support Allowance)

The result was that conditionality, far from increasing employment, as is its stated aim, was likely to move people with mental health problems further away from the labour market.

These counter-productive outcomes do not, however, apply just to people with pre-existing conditions but seem more general. A major Economic and Social Research Council (ESRC)-funded longitudinal study,[14] interviewing claimants on UC at three intervals between 2014 and 2018, found that for the majority the whole process of stringent conditionality did 'far more harm than good' and that the mandatory conditions imposed – constantly applying for any old job, long hours just documenting job search activity and the like – were often 'futile and counter-productive':[15]

> I was looking for jobs that I had no training in. … I've never worked in a kitchen. The first thing you do when you ring up is, 'Have you got any experience?' 'No' 'Well sorry'. … Basically, my job adviser was saying, 'Apply for it just so I can see you're applying for jobs.' (Male, on UC)

For those claiming UC and in work (one of the new groups for which UC meant that conditionality applies) the situation was often even more difficult because of shift work, unpredictable hours or caring responsibilities:

> I go down [to JobCentre Plus] and say, 'Look, I'm doing 16 hours with more hours promised.' [The work coach says] 'Well you'll have to look for another job'. … That's scurrilous. … I never get told what day I'm working. So, I can't go to another employer and say, 'Look … I can probably fit in another 20 hours work a week but I don't know when I can work for you'. (Male on UC)

But the system itself was pushing people into jobs with low pay, no security, and no predictable hours:

> They said to me when I first signed on, 'Would you do a zero-hours contract?' I said, 'Well what if I say no?' She said, 'We'll sanction you, you won't get any money.' (Male on UC)

The justification for stringent conditionality backed up by harsh sanctions for those out of work – and its extension to those in work – is that it will produce behavioural change that will result in people moving into work and progressing in work. But studies with UC claimants suggest this is not the case.[16] In the aforementioned ESRC longitudinal study, the recipients were keen to work but, with a few exceptions, the conditions imposed on claimants did not help them find suitable jobs and often created barriers by demanding ineffective actions to find jobs. When sanctions were imposed the financial hardship made finding work even more difficult, while the threat of sanctions ended up pushing people into unsuitable, short-term jobs.

The extent to which conditionality impacts work status can be tested by looking at the introduction of conditionality for lone parents of children aged 5 to 16 between 2008 and 2012.[17] This created a sharp increase in the proportion of lone parents potentially subject to conditionality and sufficient time has passed for its long-term impact to be assessed.

The work search regimes which single parents became subject to did have some success in getting lone parents into work; a year and a half after their introduction, the proportion of targeted lone parents in employment went up by just over 4 percentage points from 63 per cent in work to 67.4 per cent.[18] Most of this rise was among parents of primary-age children, rates of employment among parents of secondary school-age children already being high, but once this higher level was reached the proportion of lone parents in work plateaued; the proportion who remained out of work remained steady and the policy was having no further long-term impact in moving them into employment.

Moreover, this increase in employment was almost entirely into low-paid, part-time jobs. This meant that these lone parents were still dependent on benefits – moving on to in-work benefits – which, because of the way tax credits work made it difficult to increase their earnings (see Chapter 4). Furthermore, and critically, these jobs were of the kind that had very limited opportunities for career progression and were likely to be insecure. It was not a route out of poverty.[19]

For the lone parents themselves the impact varied. Those who went into work saw some benefits in terms of their finances and well-being but, because of the nature of the work and their dependency on Working Tax Credits, many remained in relative poverty. For those who remained on lone-parent benefits and were subject to the conditionality regime, the impact, particularly on their mental health, was almost entirely detrimental. And some moved on to incapacity and disability benefits, ending up further away from the prospect of work. Overall, and despite increasing employment levels, poverty rates among lone parents have gone up since 2013, when work conditionality for single parents was first implemented in full. In 2020, pre-pandemic, almost half of all children in lone-parent families lived in relative poverty.[20]

The punitive targeting of those with disabilities

Of all the policy changes to the benefits system in recent years, the most damaging have been those targeted at people with disabilities and long-term health problems. The charge sheet is long and grim: causing avoidable harm, resulting in death and suicide, pushing people with disabilities and their carers into destitution, and flawed and dishonest assessments.[21]

There have been two types of benefits aimed at working-age people with disabilities and long-term sickness which use different criteria for eligibility. Because of this, a person with disabilities and long-term sickness can be entitled to just one of these benefits or both.

The first is means tested and based on an assessment of a person's ability to work or not, generically known as incapacity benefits. The most recent version is the ESA introduced in 2008 under the last Labour government.[22] To qualify for ESA, most applicants have had to undergo a Work Capability Assessment (WCA) – the main exemption being those with a terminal illness. Following successful assessment, applicants are placed into one of two groups: those deemed capable of work are placed in the work-related activity group (WRAG) and those who are seen to have limited capacity for work and work-related activities in what is called the support group. Those in the WRAG are subject to work conditionality (as discussed previously), those in the support group (who receive a higher level of benefit) are not. ESA has now become the 'health element' of UC, though the rules for eligibility (though not the payment levels, see later in the chapter) remain much the same.

The second benefit is not means tested and depends solely on a person's ability to do certain tasks. It is intended to compensate individuals unable to do these tasks for the associated higher living costs and claimants can work without affecting their benefit. Scope estimates the additional costs (in 2024) of living with a disability as just over £1,000 a month.[23] These are inescapable costs associated with managing conditions and supporting accessibility, not somehow optional costs to be cut if some benefit savings are deemed necessary.

The precise additional costs vary but are likely to include transport, food, clothing, heating, and a wide variety of additional aids, as interviewees for Scope report:[24]

> I can't just choose cheaper food or cheaper brands. I have to eat what I've got to eat, because of my

[conditions] – I can't just eat whatever I want. If that goes up in price, there's nothing I can do about it. (Male, 20s, living in the north-west of England)

In winter, I have to have the heating on all the time. I can't just have it on at set times. The temperature needs to be at a constant temperature for me, otherwise my pain increases and I'm cold. Then I'm in agony. (Female, 40s, living in the north-east of England)

I'm still reliant quite heavily on taxis, because I find the bus routes and the buses are just really quite inaccessible. … That causes me a lot of anxiety, which then pushes me towards using taxis. (Male, 30s, living in the north-east of England)

Up until 2013, these needs were covered by the Disabled Living Allowance (DLA), but this was replaced under the coalition government by PIP. Ostensibly introduced to provide a more 'holistic' approach to support those with disabilities, it was also, and more significantly, aimed at reducing costs, estimated when it was introduced at around £1.4 billion.[25] This was to be achieved by limiting the numbers claiming so that around one in five of those who had received DLA would not be eligible for PIP, removing the automatic entitlement that had previously come from certain conditions, introducing more regular reassessments, and by making assessments themselves more complex with claimants required to go through more hoops to meet eligibility requirements.[26] The PIP assessment has two elements, one about daily life (with questions such as 'can you dress yourself?'), the second about mobility ('how far can you walk?', and the like), with both elements having different levels of severity (and payments) attached to them.

The assessment regimes to gain entitlement to these two benefits (ESA and PIP) are currently separate – they assess different things – but both rely on outside providers to carry out the health assessments. These providers are large, commercial, for-profit companies: Maximus currently run the WCAs, and Capita and Independent Assessment Services (IAS) split the PIP assessments. IAS is part of ATOS, the company which had, from 2008, handled the WCAs and about whom there had been so many complaints about poor performance that, in 2014, their contract was terminated early.[27]

These companies employ what are called 'healthcare professionals' (HCPs) to make the assessments, though many of these HCPs have no formal expertise. Despite some reforms since the introduction of the assessments, the process remains deeply flawed. Many of the decisions made are simply incorrect, as can be seen from the high proportion that are overturned when challenged. Claimants who disagree with the decision can have what's called a Mandatory Reconsideration (though this process, in itself, is problematic as many who disagree with the initial decision find it too stressful to proceed to the next stage). Of the decisions that go to Mandatory Reconsideration about a quarter of the PIP assessments are overturned and well over half of the WCAs. Claimants who still disagree can go to a tribunal and of those who take this route about 70 per cent for both PIP and WCA are successful.[28] It is not surprising therefore that confidence in the system is low with most disabled people concluding that the system does not make accurate decisions.[29]

Even more concerning is the devastating impact of the whole process on many applicants. DWP research itself finds that the process of completing the questionnaires is commonly seen as 'stressful', 'worrying', 'daunting', 'overwhelming', and 'emotional'.[30] It focuses on what you can't do and the worst experiences of your life rather than what you might be able to do with the right support. In evidence submitted to the DWP select committee inquiry into health assessments in 2022/23, claimants recall the stress of filling in the form:[31]

> For the twelve days we took considering and writing on the form, my mother refused to eat, drink, or sleep save the smallest amount. She began to self-harm from the stress and cry in the despair of admitting how she is limited, how she is constantly in pain, how she cannot complete simple tasks. (Disabled claimant)

> I felt embarrassed and ashamed for having these difficulties. I usually try to stay positive and focus on what I can do ... but I had to lay out every single problem and failure to function normally on paper ... so that some stranger can read all of my shameful secrets and judge me on them. (Female claimant)

They reported fundamental errors in their reports and the omission of important information:

> The report we received was a work of fiction and bore no resemblance to what actually took place. ... For example the assessor said my husband took off his jacket with my assistance. My husband did not wear a jacket that day. (Husband of claimant)

> Apparently I walk my dog daily, which was baffling because I can barely walk and I do not have a dog! (Female claimant)

> I was asked if I had tried to self-harm and I said yes I have tried to hang myself, but this was not in the report. (Male claimant)

Some assessors simply seemed to make up the information:

> The assessor claimed in the report to have completed an extensive examination of me during the assessment. She

listed a breakdown of her observations regarding the movement of all my limbs and joints. In reality though my assessment was only fifteen minutes long and the assessor didn't examine me at all. (Female claimant)

I opened the door and walked the 5 metres back to my sofa, using my walking stick and that was all I was seen to do. How can somebody then say that I can walk between 20 and 50 metres? (Female claimant)

And some were appallingly insensitive:

> The assessor also asked my mother if she were suicidal. As I recall, that went like this:
>
> Assessor: Are you suicidal?
> K: Yes
> Assessor: How often are you suicidal?
> K: Every day
> Assessor: Have you tried?
> K: Yes
> Assessor: And why didn't you succeed? Why did you fail?
> K: My family would miss me.
>
> Each of K's answers was slow and ashamed. She had not yet told me these things, but she had been trying to bring them up at therapy to work through these feelings safely. For her to be forced to admit this and for there to be no after care, but the continuation of an exam, shattered her. I genuinely believe that without my constant assurances after the event that K would have made another suicide attempt that week. (Name withheld)

The impact of these health assessments on those with mental health problems was, as for the impact of work conditionality discussed previously, particularly concerning. The evidence suggests that for many the process makes their mental health problems worse and, at its extreme, increases the risk of suicide.[32] With the proportion of those on incapacity and disability benefits due to mental health problems increasing in recent years, this has significant and worrying implications.

But this was not the end of the ramping-up of problems for those with disabilities and ill-health. UC was to make their situation significantly worse.

How UC has hit people with severe disabilities

In general, the rates of these different elements of UC were the same as the legacy benefit they replaced but because of the decisions made in creating the new combined system, the total amount received by claimants often changed. These decisions were based on two main aims, to 'make work pay', while at the same time cutting the overall cost to the Exchequer.

Under the legacy system, with its different benefits, as household incomes increased, these benefits were withdrawn independently of one another, resulting in, at times, benefits being withdrawn simultaneously. This could create very weak incentives to work with overall benefit payments being withdrawn at much the same rate as earnings increased, reaching at times 96p being taken in higher taxes and lower benefits for an additional £1 earned.[33] This was particularly true for those in low-paid work who rented – that is, those on tax credit and housing benefit.

To 'make work pay', UC introduced changes to various entitlements and the rate at which benefit was withdrawn. As a result, there were winners and losers, though, as there was a net loss to claimants of around £5 billion at 2024/25 prices,[34] there were fewer gainers than losers and the gainers, on average, gained less and the losers lost more.

The gainers were those for whom, as a result of combining the different benefits, the withdrawal of benefits was less sharp as earnings increased, in particular working renters (see Chapter 4).

The losers were those out of work because of poor health or a disability. For this group, the shift to UC has resulted in a loss of income – and for some by a huge amount. The Resolution Foundation, a think tank focusing on the living standards of those on low-to-middle incomes, calculates that 'families who would previously have been eligible for Employment Support Allowance (the means-tested benefit aimed at supporting those with disabilities based on their inability to work) would be, on average, £2,100 per year worse off on Universal Credit'.[35]

The reason for this is that under UC the Severe Disability Premium – an additional benefit paid to some of the most severely disabled recipients of ESA – was abolished on the basis of simplifying the system. To compensate, the basic rate of ESA for those out of work increased – but the increase was far less than the value of the Severe Disability Premium – and some lost heavily; for a single person previously eligible for the Severe Disability Premium this could be up to around £2,800 a year.[36]

This change has transformed the composition of the poorest in society towards the sick and disabled. Following the switch to UC, families in receipt of ill-health or disability benefits are more likely to be in the bottom tenth of the household income distribution than before, with over half of those falling into the bottom decile following the switch coming from families previously eligible for ESA.[37]

The result is that people with disabilities and long-term health problems are far more likely to be in relative poverty. Overall, around 30 per cent of people who live in a household with someone with a disability or long-term illness are in relative income poverty (AHC) around 10 percentage points higher than households with no-one with a disability.[38] With regional variations in the proportions of the population with a disability varying immensely – rising to nearly a quarter of the population in the north-east,[39] this has large implications for the distribution of poverty.[40] Further more, people with disabilities and long-term health problems are much more likely to fall into destitution. In the JRF destitution survey almost two-thirds of those who were destitute reported a disability, rising to nearly three-quarters for those born in the UK (as opposed to recent migrants).[41]

Scotland's different direction

From 2018, the Scottish government took over responsibility from Westminster for the parts of the social security system related to the additional costs of disability, carers, heating, and for children born after that date. With these new powers the Scottish government could also alter select elements of UC, including creating new payments to 'top up' existing provision. In 2017, in anticipation of these new powers, the Scottish government set up a number of Social Security Experience Panels to help work on the development of new policy.[42]

At the heart of these new policies were people with disabilities and health conditions; in 2024, of the total devolved social security budget of £5.2 billion, £4.2 billion was forecast to be spent on payments for disabled people and those with health conditions, including PIP and Carer's Allowance. Here was a chance to redesign the inadequate system of support for people with disabilities. In particular, the Scottish government sought to replace the non-means-tested PIPs with an improved benefit for covering the additional costs of living with a disability, the Adult Disability Payment (ADP).

In the end the Scottish government decided to adopt a gradualist approach to change and to ensure that changes made were 'achievable, affordable and realistic',[43] with changes relating to the process of claiming the benefit rather than the design, criteria and levels of the benefit. This included conducting a full assessment for entitlement to receive the benefits only when the evidence provided is not sufficient to make a decision, removing some of the barriers for applying to the benefit experienced under PIP, reducing the number of assessments, increasing the award length to, for most cases, between five and ten years though, where the condition is unlikely to change, for longer, and improving the appeal process making it easier for claimants to trigger a full reassessment of the claim.[44]

Though the ADP is relatively new, having only been launched across all of Scotland in August 2022,[45] the new system does seem to have made the process of applying 'easier, more accurate, less stressful and less oppositional'.[46] In doing so it has increased application rates, success rates, and more awards have been awarded at the higher enhanced rate. This has, as predicted and anticipated, resulted in the overall bill for ADP being higher than it was for PIP (by about 15 per cent).

Yet more problems for people with disabilities

In Westminster, meanwhile, the priority was getting under control what the government saw as a ballooning benefits budget.

The problem, from this point of view, was that none of the changes to benefits to date had succeeded in moving people with disabilities into work and thereby reducing the benefits bill. Prior to COVID-19, the employment gap (that is, the difference between the rate of employment for those reporting a disability and those who are not) remained large and enduring at around 30 percentage points.[47]

This is not surprising as the primary problem has nothing to do with levels of disability payment, and is certainly not that they are too high. It is to do with pathways into work, discrimination from employers, and lack of support at work.[48] These would include travelling to work, the lack of support available in work, the reluctance of employers to take on people with disabilities, and the lack of flexibility at work to adjust to different needs, including flexibility for hospital appointments or fluctuating conditions. There are some schemes, such as Access to Work grants,[49] but these are discretionary, limited, have few rights of appeal, and have done little to improve the employment levels of people with disabilities.

In addition, the proportion of those with disabilities with low levels of qualifications is high, over 50 per cent compared to around 36 per cent for the non-disabled population.[50] This matters not just because it is more difficult for those with low qualifications to find work but because the type of work available is less likely to be suitable. It is more likely to require hard physical work or place employees under constant observance and stress. It is less likely to be adaptable. The result is the gap between those with disabilities and those without disabilities is much higher for those with low educational qualifications, at around 43 per cent.

In general, people with disabilities are simply more vulnerable in the work setting. This was highlighted during the pandemic itself when disabled workers were more likely to be temporarily away from work than non-disabled workers (for example, furloughed) and more likely to contract long-COVID, increasing their chances of being off work and potentially having a long-term impact on their health.

By the time the pandemic ended, there had been a sharp rise in the proportion of the working-age population receiving at least one health-related benefit: in 2019 there were 3.2 million such claimants in Britain (7.9 per cent of the working population), by 2022 this had risen to 4.2 million (10.2 per cent).[51] Some of this will have been a direct result of the pandemic, either long-COVID or the result of delays in hospital appointments and surgery, and some of this is due to longer-term trends which the impact of the pandemic has magnified. Even before the pandemic the result of austerity had been deteriorating health for those living in deprivation.[52] For both men and women there has been a rise in the number of years spent with a disability or ill-health,[53] which could explain some of the rise, particularly when associated with the rising pension age.

But, most notably, there has been a rise in claims for mental health problems, such as anxiety and depression, with an increase between 2019/20 and 2023/24 of over 8,000 a month (from around from 3,900 claims to 12,100). This has been the case across all ages but particularly among the young.[54] Again, this trend started pre-pandemic and reflects a general trend for a higher reporting of mental health problems, indicating a worsening mental health problem across the population. However, the government seems to be writing off some of those with mental health problems as being, as the Health Secretary, Wes Streeting, put it, overdiagnosed.[55] This seemed to be shifting the blame rather than addressing the very real problems those with mental health conditions faced, of struggling to get the mental health support they need, of fighting for financial stability, of facing inadequate levels of benefit, and of failing to get the right support from workplaces to be able to work.[56] There are questions as to where the lines for diagnoses should lie and how best to support people with varying degrees of mental health problems, but for those caught in the crosshairs of predetermined cuts to benefits such dismissals were worrying.[57]

Similarly, successive governments have tried to argue that the rise is due to more people claiming rather than deteriorating health conditions. Indeed, most people who are defined under the Equalities Act as disabled do not claim for a wide variety of reasons, so it is possible that cost of living pressures have led to more claiming. However, the proportions of disabled people claiming has only risen slightly (from 41 per cent in 2018 to 46 per cent in 2023)[58] and nowhere near explains the rise. Moreover, the success rate of claims has hardly change, suggesting the rise is due to an underlying worsening of health.

Whatever the reasons, the rise has had significant implications for the benefits budget. Figure 3.1 shows the total spent on disability and incapacity benefits (including its replacement with employment support element of UC) for Britain (excluding

Figure 3.1: Actual and projected annual spending on working-age benefits

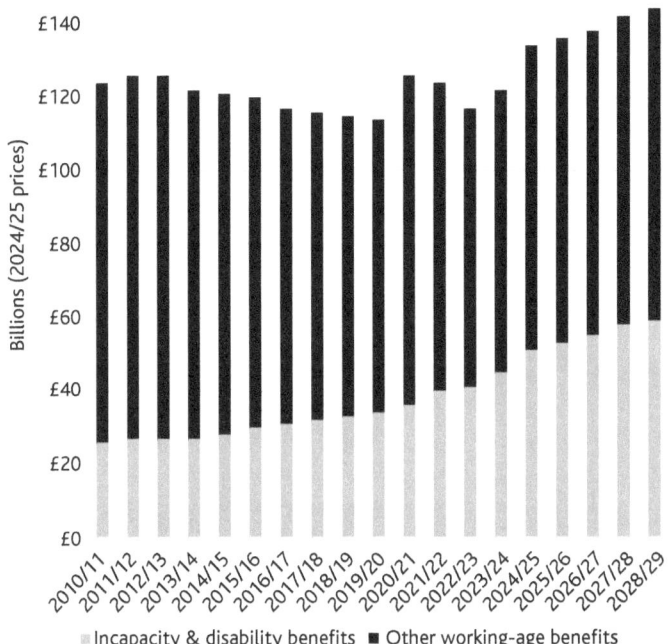

Note: Excludes disability benefit spending in Scotland which is devolved and child Disability Living Allowance which is not a working-age benefit.

Source: Institute for Fiscal Studies[59]

disability benefit spending in Scotland which is devolved) and that spent on other working-age benefits. As can be seen, while spending on working-age benefits other than disability benefits has fallen since 2010/11 and is now fairly static, spending on disability and incapacity benefits has risen and is projected to rise further. The total spent on disability and incapacity benefits rose from around £34 billion in 2019/20 to £45 billion in 2023/24, with a projected rise to £58 billion in 2028/29.

The current level is not in itself particularly high. Even following the recent increases, UK health-related benefits spending is similar to that in comparable countries. The Institute for Fiscal Studies notes that across the OECD, spending on working-age health-related benefits averaged 1.6 per cent of GDP in 2019 (the latest data) while at that point, UK spending on such benefits was considerably below that level, at 1.3 per cent of GDP.[60] Even with the recent increases it is at 1.7 per cent, much the same level as comparable countries.

The projections would push this up to 2.1 per cent of GDP by 2028. These are, of course, just projections, given the lack of understanding of why there has been a rise, to some extent they are more like a guess. If the numbers of new claimants for disability benefits returned to their pre-pandemic level the increase would be far lower.[61] Tackling this requires addressing the underlying causes for rising ill-health, and in particular mental health.

Instead, the government has decided to focus on the numbers receiving disability benefit, by raising the bar for qualification.

In 2023, then-Chancellor Jeremy Hunt announced plans to target those on incapacity benefit. While the plan was dressed up in the language of helping people into work, the purpose was simple, to reduce government spending by an estimated £3 billion.

Much to the disappointment of disability groups,[62] the incoming Labour government pushed on with the aim to target disability benefits for cuts and indeed set about an even greater shake-up of the system. The talk from government was, as then-Work and Pensions Secretary Liz Kendall put it, to get 'the welfare bill on a more sustainable footing'[63] or from Chancellor, Rachel Reeves, 'getting a grip' on the welfare budget. Prime Minister, Keir Starmer's phrasing of the same sentiment was that there is no 'bottomless pit'.[64]

At the same time, the government argued that their plans would help the many people with disabilities who are desperate to work and don't have adequate support to find the right job with Liz Kendall arguing that 'We start first, last and always with people, who've actually got hopes and dreams.'[65]

In March 2025, when the government finally announced the planned shake-up of disability benefits, it was keen to emphasise various schemes to be introduced which would be aimed at helping people into work and supporting them when in work.[66] Around £1 billion was set aside for investment in new work initiatives and a programme of changes including overhauling jobcentres and the role of work coaches.[67] There were plans to trial a system where GPs refer people to employment advisers rather than signing them off sick and to help people into jobs, and to stay in those jobs, through more rights to work from home. And there was to be a 'keep Britain working' review to investigate what employers can do to keep disabled people in work.

All this would take a while to see any results. And in the meantime, there were to be cuts – and these were to be drastic. Overall, they were aimed at saving around £5 billion a year by 2030, as deep a cut to the benefits system as that made by the Conservative Chancellor, George Osborne, when he reduced the benefit budget in 2015.[68] To achieve these cuts, the main target was reducing the eligibility requirement for PIP. Given the rhetoric about wanting to help people into work, this was a perverse target; PIP is aimed at helping people with the extra costs of living with a disability and, far from disincentivising work, provides people with a basis on which people can move into work.

It completely undermines Prime Minister Keir Starmer's claim that 'There is a clear moral case, which is: the current system doesn't help those who want to get into work. It traps people. I think it's 1,000 people a day going on to PIP.'[69] PIP, to repeat, does not prevent people from working, it is not withdrawn as people work (which might create a 'trap'); it helps with daily living costs. It enables people with disabilities a chance to live with dignity and it provides support to move into work. There is no moral case for cutting PIP.

'It disgusts me really,' says Jo, a 46-year-old with various disabilities who would no longer be able to work as she would have lost her PIP entitlement, interviewed by *The Guardian* newspaper,[70] 'When this first came out, the rhetoric was [framing PIP] as an out-of-work benefit. It's not. It keeps a lot of people *able* to work.'

Under these proposals, only the most severely disabled would in future have been eligible for PIP. The government's plan was to tighten the assessment for qualification for the 'daily living element' of PIP from November 2026. While for those who still qualified and who had the severest conditions, which would never improve, there was promise that in future they would not need to be reassessed, for others there was to be a higher bar for qualification. Under the proposed rules, someone who needed, for example, prompting to prepare food, help with showering or washing, dressing the lower body, and using the toilet, would not have qualified.[71] It would also exclude those needing help to engage and communicate with others and many people with mental health problems, leading mental health charities to argue that it would 'only serve to deepen the nation's mental health crisis'.[72]

This would have had a devastating impact. The Resolution Foundation estimated that between 800,000 and 1.2 million people would lose support, ranging between £4,200 and £6,300 per year by 2029–30.[73] It would have resulted in misery and would not help the people concerned into finding work, the supposed aim of the changes.

The bill also included savings to be made by cutting the level of the health-related element of UC, currently claimed by 1.6 million people. These cuts were focused on young people, who it proposed would no longer be eligible for any extra support until they reached the age of 22, and those who fall ill in the future, with payments for future claimants halved, from £97 per week in 2024–25 to £50 per week in 2026–27 and frozen at that level for four years. Current claimants would continue to receive £97 a week though this too would be frozen for four years. Those new claimants with the severest disabilities, with no prospects of improvement or being able to work, would be protected from these cuts with a new additional premium and would, in addition, no longer require reassessment in the future. However, on the government's own assessment,[74] only 200,000 people would be protected, just under 8 per cent of those claiming the benefit.

To mitigate, though not compensate for the cuts, UC recipients would receive an above-inflation increase. For those who are not eligible for the health element of UC (and therefore not seeing the benefit cut), this would be worth around £3 more per week in 2029–30.[75] This is a pittance, merely a sixth of the temporary £20 a week uplift to UC during the pandemic, and nothing compared to the loss for new claimants.

The government's overall aim is that the whole of the WCA system would be scrapped from 2028. The government hopes that by removing the exemptions from job-search requirements currently given to claimants with limited capability for work and by removing the additional payments, more people with disabilities will move into work, thus reducing the number of disabled people claiming UC. The argument is that the current system is 'trapping' ill and disabled people in poverty by preventing them from receiving support.

This is, again, disingenuous, there is absolutely no reason why those claiming the health element of WCA should not receive extra support; what the current system does mean is that they are excluded from conditionality and the threat of sanctions, not from support – and, as seen, conditionality tends to be both damaging and ineffective, in particular for those with existing mental health problems.[76]

It was difficult to see the government's approach as anything other than crude cuts designed to meet an arbitrary savings target, determined by self-imposed fiscal rules – rather than a genuine effort to help those with disabilities and sickness move into work. If that were the case, those elements helping disabled people into work and, in addition, moves to tighten requirements on employers to support disabled people in work would be put in place and seen to be working, before withdrawing benefits. The advice of disabled rights and anti-poverty groups, who had warned against any such moves as 'devastating' and as counter to moves to help people into work,[77] had clearly been ignored.

In the end, as seen in the Introduction, the government backtracked on its plans for PIP, promising instead a review to be led by Disability Minister Stephen Timms to be co-produced with disabled people, while pressing ahead with its plans for restricting the health element of UC. Though the government insists on framing it in terms of helping people, this is not how many people with disabilities see it. 'They might have bought votes with promises of co-producing the PIP review but how can we trust a government like this?', said Ellen Clifford from the campaign group Disabled People Against Cuts talking to *The Guardian* newspaper,[78] 'Let's not forget that the huge Universal Credit cut for new claimants remained in the bill unchanged. It makes a mockery of any claims to be protecting vulnerable people.'

In September 2025, following the Welfare bill fiasco, the prime minister replaced Liz Kendall as Work and Pensions Secretary with Pat McFadden, a shift in personnel rather than indicating a change in direction. McFadden had been a strong supporter of the planned cuts to PIP and regularly defended the tightening of the criteria for claiming such benefits on the basis that many could, and should, be in paid work and that there was a need to make savings.[79]

That the benefit system needs reform is undoubtedly the case. As seen in this chapter, the current system results in immense stress and hardship for many with disabilities. But change needs to be approached with the interests of those with disabilities at its heart rather than with a single-minded emphasis on forcing people into paid work.

There is, furthermore, something fundamentally discriminatory about an approach which simply sees people as a burden if they are not in paid work rather than human beings in their own right with their own hopes and aspirations and with the right to a decent life, whether able to work or not.[80] People with disabilities should be enabled to make decisions as to what is best for them.

Policies that push some of the most vulnerable in society into poverty and yet deeper poverty are – whatever their supposed intentions – deeply flawed and inhumane.

4

Why isn't work a route out of poverty?

Making work a route out of poverty has been a consistent mantra of all governments, Labour, Conservative, and coalition, for at least the last 30 years. In the run-up to her first budget, the new Labour Chancellor, Rachel Reeves, reiterated this desire, saying: 'We will build a Britain where people who can work, will work, turning the page on the recent rise in economic inactivity and decline and towards a future where people have good jobs and our benefits bill is under control.'[1]

For those of working age and able to work, being in work is generally beneficial in terms of health and well-being, while being out of work is far the more likely to lead to poverty. Yet for many, work has not been a route out of poverty. Indeed, the problem of poverty is increasingly a problem of in-work poverty and the lives of those in work and in poverty are becoming more, not less, stressful, as testimony to the House of Commons All-Party Parliamentary Group on Poverty, 2021–22 inquiry into in-work poverty made clear:[2]

> In-work poverty to me means working for nothing. I'm not working so we can get nice new things and visit new places. I'm working to keep me and my children alive. I'm not living life; I'm only just surviving. …

> I compare in-work poverty to a hamster's wheel. No matter how hard I work and how much I push myself, I get nowhere. I feel like I'm going round and round in circles and there's nowhere for me to get off, and no way to make it stop. (Hazel)

> Going to work often feels like it's about 'doing the right thing' or 'doing your part for society'. It's also about working your fingers to the bone to put an extra few quid in the gas meter so we can dry the school uniforms before tomorrow because we can only afford one jumper with a logo on it, and it got covered in paint today. Being in poverty means hiding all of this from the outside world because the shame can be unbearable, but as long as you're in work then you're not a burden to society, right? (Mel)

The rising importance of in-work poverty

Over the last 30 years, working-age poverty has been changing from being primarily due to being out of work to a situation where most of those in poverty are in work. Figure 4.1 shows the proportions of working-age adults in relative income poverty (AHC) by whether the household has no-one in work or whether it has one or more in work. Back in 1996/97, most (56 per cent) of those in poverty were out of work; by 2019, before the impact of COVID-19, this had fallen to a minority (39 per cent), with the remainder (61 per cent) in working households. Post-COVID, with a rise in long-term sickness, the proportion out of work rose a bit (to 43 per cent), though it has now fallen back again to its pre-COVID level (39 per cent).

The trend for children in relative poverty is even more stark. Figure 4.2 shows that until 2003/04, just over half of children in poverty were in households where no-one worked. This

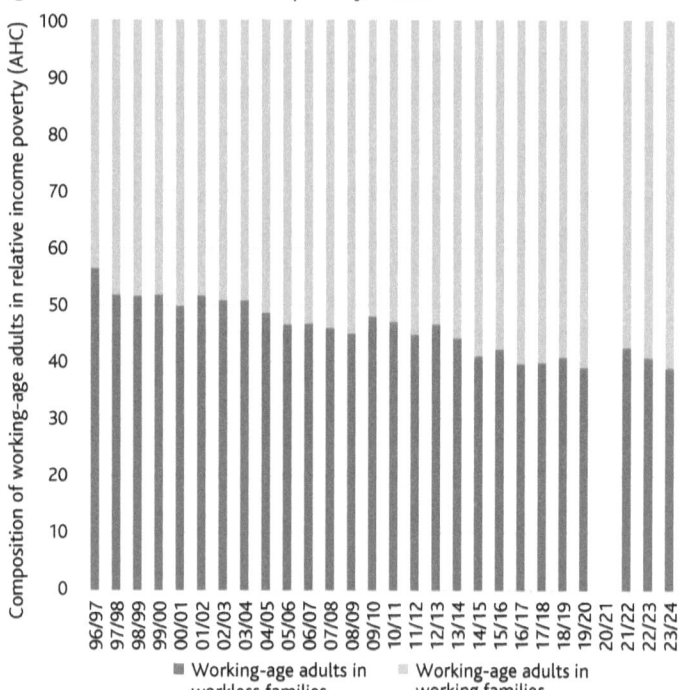

Figure 4.1: The shift to in-work poverty, adults

Note: Data is not available for 2020/21 because of COVID-19.

Source: HBAI 2023/24, working-age series, Table 5.5ts[3]

proportion then fell dramatically so that by 2019/20 (just before COVID-19) only a quarter of children in poverty were in such households.

Some of this increase in the proportion of those in poverty in work is due to trends which are positive, in particular the fall in unemployment. But it is also due to an increasing risk of poverty for those in work. This can be seen in Figure 4.3, which shows the percentage of working-age adults in working households (that is one or more household members in work)

Why isn't work a route out of poverty?

Figure 4.2: The shift to in-work poverty, children

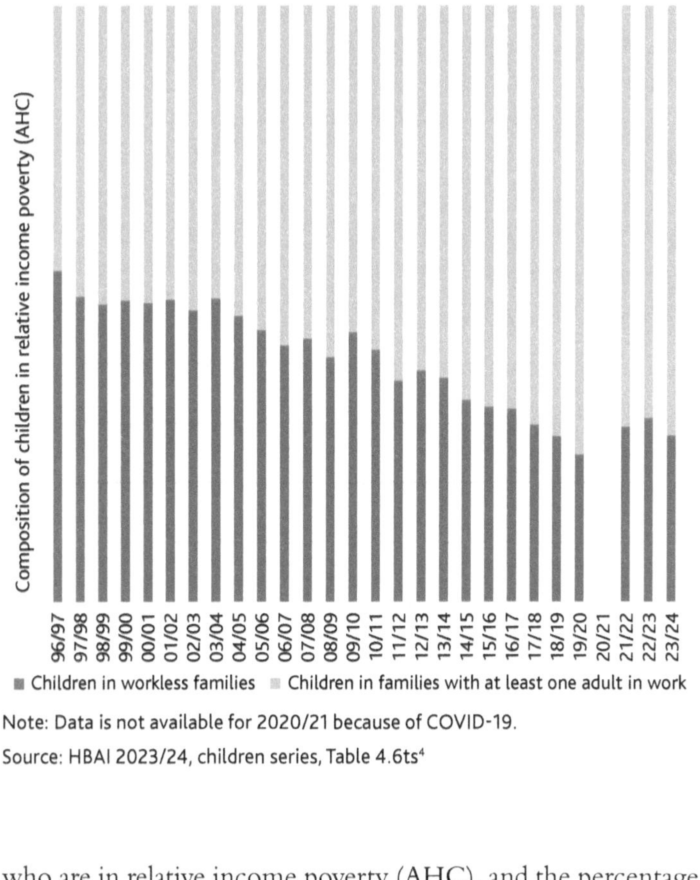

Y-axis: Composition of children in relative income poverty (AHC)

X-axis: 96/97 to 23/24

■ Children in workless families ▪ Children in families with at least one adult in work

Note: Data is not available for 2020/21 because of COVID-19.
Source: HBAI 2023/24, children series, Table 4.6ts[4]

who are in relative income poverty (AHC), and the percentage of children in such households.

Overall, the increase in the risk of poverty for adults in working families seems relatively small, rising from 11 per cent in the early 2000s to 15 per cent in 2019/20 (pre–COVID). But as most adults live in working households, the implications for poverty levels are large. Even without population increases during this period, well over 1 million extra adults would have been in poverty as a result of this increased rate; with the population increase that

Figure 4.3: The rising risk of poverty for adults and children in households in work, 2001 to 2024

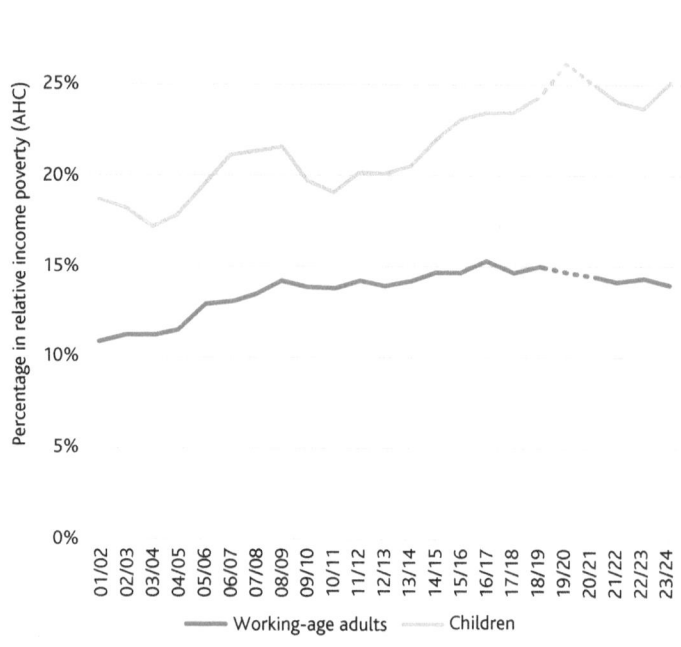

Note: Data is not available for 2020/21 because of COVID-19.

Source: HBAI 2023/24, working-age series, Table 5.11ts and children series, Table 4.14ts[5]

has taken place, it is almost 2 million, resulting in over 5 million adults in working families in relative poverty. The increase in the risk of poverty for children in working families has been sharper rising from 17 per cent in 2003/04 to 26 per cent in 2019/20 (pre-COVID) with a particularly sharp increase since 2010.

It is worth looking at the trend since 2010 in more detail. Figure 4.4 which shows the rate of relative income poverty

Why isn't work a route out of poverty?

Figure 4.4: The risk of poverty in different types of households in work, adults

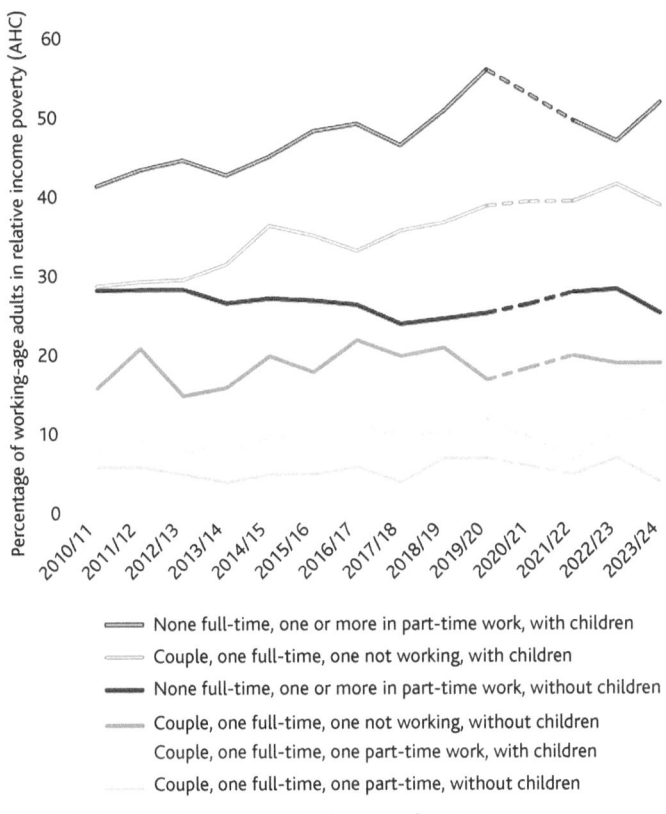

None full-time, one or more in part-time work, with children
Couple, one full-time, one not working, with children
None full-time, one or more in part-time work, without children
Couple, one full-time, one not working, without children
Couple, one full-time, one part-time work, with children
Couple, one full-time, one part-time, without children

Note: Data is not available for 2020/21 because of COVID-19.
Source: HBAI, 2023/24, working-age series, Table 5.11ts[6]

(AHC) for working-age adults living in households with different levels of work intensity, with and without children, from 2010/11 to 2023/24.

There are a number of striking features. Firstly, households with children are more likely to be in poverty, whatever the work status of the household, than those without children. Secondly, households with low levels of work are more likely to be in poverty than those with high levels of work, whether they have children or not. Work is much more likely to be a route out of poverty if it is full-time and households are much more likely to be in poverty if there is only one earner or part-time earners. If adults have other responsibilities that limit the amount of work undertaken, such as caring for others or for reasons of disability, the risk of poverty is higher. And thirdly, households with children where no-one works full-time are far more likely to be in poverty than other households, with the risk having risen rapidly. Over half of such households are now in poverty. Similar trends apply to single-parent families with those in part-time work being more likely to be in poverty than those in full-time work, while even single parents in full-time work have a high risk of poverty, simply because there is only one worker in the house.

On the face of it, these trends may seem surprising given the enormous emphasis that all recent governments have placed on solving poverty by getting people into work and making work a route out of poverty. Under the then Conservative governments of 2015 to 2024, there was one policy in particular that was aimed at making work pay: the minimum wage.

The impact of the minimum wage

In 2015 the then-Chancellor, George Osborne, rebranded the National Minimum Wage as a 'National Living Wage', introducing a higher rate for adults aged over 25 (later lowered to age 21) and subsequently promising substantial increases to its rate over time.[7] It was presented as offsetting the cuts to other working-age benefits being made.[8] 'The new National Living Wage', Osborne argued, 'is an essential part of building the higher wage, lower welfare, lower tax society that Britain needs.'[9]

Overall, the minimum wage policy, since its introduction in 1999, had had considerable success at raising the hourly wages of the lowest paid, not just for those on the minimum wage but also having some spillover effect on those just above, pushing up their hourly wages as well.[10] It is undoubtedly important for the around 3 million workers currently receiving it.

But Osborne's spin that that increase to the minimum wage would offset cuts to benefits was misleading. The minimum wage affects an *individual's* hourly pay, pushing up those who would otherwise have had low hourly wages. But Working Tax Credit and other means-tested working-age benefits are transfers of money to households whose *household* income is insufficient. Those on low hourly wages are not necessarily part of low-income households.[11] Indeed, minimum wage workers are often second earners and most commonly are in households whose household income is towards the middle of the income range.[12] So, contrary to Osborne's assertion, for most benefit recipients in work a higher minimum wage does not compensate for lower benefits.

Indeed, analysis by the Institute for Fiscal Studies on the impact of the National Living Wage finds that the biggest gains have gone to the middle of the working-age *household* income distribution, both in cash and percentage terms. These gains reach up through the top half of the household income distribution with those in the eighth decile gaining more than those in the second decile. There is very little impact on the poorest households, mostly because these households tend not to have anyone in work. If you look just at households where someone is in work, the gains are more evenly spread towards the bottom half of household incomes, but the impact is small.[13] This is primarily because only just under half of people experiencing in-work poverty have a low-paid member of their household.[14]

Even when a minimum wage worker is in a lower-income household, any increase in their income has a muted effect on the household's income. Such households will be on Working Tax Credit (or the UC Working Tax Credit element) and a rise in wages will see their benefit reduced as a result, not by as much as the increase but often by a significant proportion of the increase.

The minimum wage protects the lowest paid from exploitation and acts as a wage floor. In these important respects, it has been a successful policy. In her first budget in October 2024, the Chancellor, Rachel Reeves, increased the National Living Wage by 6.7 per cent, arguing that it was 'a significant move towards delivering a genuine living wage',[15] followed by a further increase, in line with the Low Pay Commission recommendations, in November 2025.[16]

But there are questions as to whether the main emphasis in moves to ensure wages sufficient to live off should simply be on pushing up the minimum wage. For if you want to use increases in wages to combat poverty, you need to look at wages across the income range.

The long-term rise in earnings inequality

Over the last 40 years the gap between the earnings of the top and bottom parts of the earnings distribution has widened substantially, and faster than other comparable countries. It has left the UK with one of the highest levels of wage and earnings inequality in the developed world.[17]

This has partly been driven by technological changes which have automated and replaced some middle-income jobs, pushed up the earnings at the top where more highly skilled, graduate labour has demanded a premium, and increased the number of low-paid insecure jobs. Overall, higher earnings levels are strongly associated with higher qualifications, with an increased level of earnings for each level of additional qualification. The median earnings for a 40-year-old graduate are twice as much as the median for someone qualified to GCSE level or below,[18] with across the age range high earnings overwhelmingly going to those with the highest qualifications. Moreover, while graduates can expect their earnings to increase over their working life, peaking during their forties and fifties, for those with low educational qualifications, there is remarkably little change in their earnings across this period.[19] The result is that low lifetime earnings are heavily concentrated among those with low qualifications.

But widening wage inequalities have also been driven by a huge shift of power between workers and firms. The sharp decline in unionisation and the loosening of contractual arrangements have weakened the bargaining power of traditional employees and strengthened that of employers and top executives. Research for the Institute for Fiscal Studies Deaton Review of Inequalities finds that among men declining unionism accounts for around a third of the rise in earnings inequality since 1985, though the impact is much less for women who have traditionally had lower levels of unionisation.[20]

The result of these trends is that the rewards of economic growth during this period went largely to those at the top end of the income scale. Between 1980 and 2008 just before the financial crash, real weekly earnings growth was fastest for the top 10 per cent (at around 2.6 per cent a year), relatively modest at the median (just below 2 per cent a year), and slow for those at the bottom (1 per cent a year),[21] and of those at the top end, by far the fastest was the top 1 per cent. The trickle down from growth was very much a trickle. The pay of the CEOs of the top FTSE 100 companies now stands at around 80 times that of that of those on the median wage, up from 20 times in the 1970s.[22]

In addition, there has been a sharp rise at the bottom end of the employment ladder in high levels of earnings insecurity and low levels of job security, brought about by a rise in on-call workers, temporary workers, zero-hours contracts, contracting out and similar, often exploitative, employment arrangements, and the more general rise of the so-called gig economy and of self-employment.

The number of zero-hours contract workers has skyrocketed from 143,000 in 2008 to around 1 million in 2019. Zero-hours workers earn on average around £5 less per hour than the average employee and work 10 hours fewer per week.[23] Similarly, the numbers of solo self-employed has also risen sharply and, again, most work fewer hours a week than employees and are more likely to have lower hourly wages.

In addition, part-time work – a major cause of household poverty – has been rising. The percentage of men on low hourly wages working part-time has increased sharply, rising from 5 per cent in 1994 to around 20 per cent, while, despite a decline, the percentage of women on low hourly wages in part-time work still stands at around 60 per cent.[24]

These trends have been made far worse by an overall stagnation in wages since 2010.

Rolling from crisis to crisis

Since the 2008 financial crash, the UK has stumbled from crisis to crisis, all of which have contributed to anaemic growth. As can be seen in Figure 4.5 (which shows trends in inflation-adjusted median hourly and weekly earnings indexed with January 2008 as 100) median weekly earnings had still not reached their 2008 level by 2021.

Just as the incipient shoots of recovery seemed under way after the financial crash, the new coalition government, on the pretext of tackling the deficit, brought in sharp cuts in public spending and ushered in the age of austerity. This had a devastating impact on the living standards of the poorest, but it also had a wider, detrimental impact on economic growth,[25] with some economists estimating that by 2018 growth had been stifled by as much as 16 per cent.[26] Both hourly and weekly median earnings plunged.

Then, in June 2016, came the vote to leave the European Union. The large majority of economists agree that this too had a negative impact on the UK economy and, as a consequence, on real wages. The National Institute of Economic and Social Research estimates that three years after the departure of the UK

Why isn't work a route out of poverty?

Figure 4.5: A decade of stagnating earnings

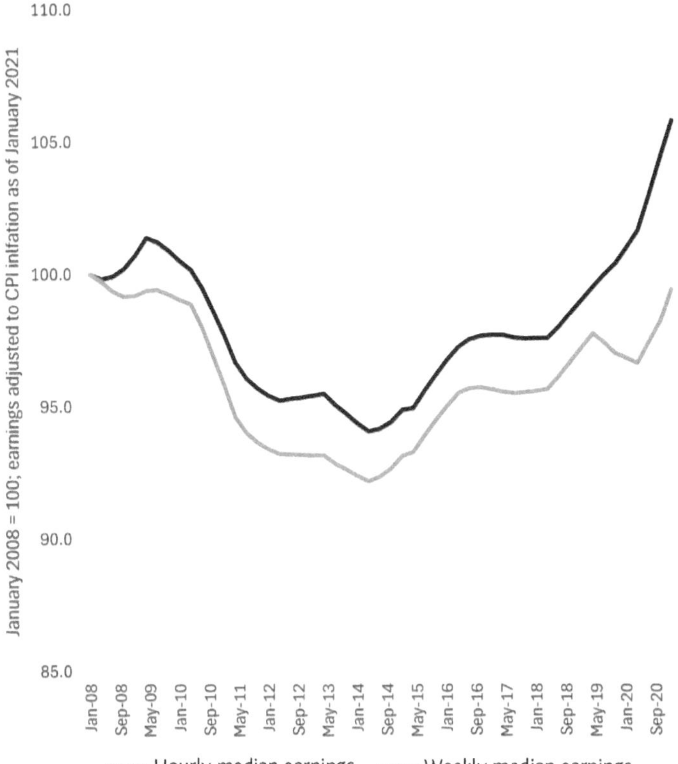

January 2008 = 100; earnings adjusted to CPI inflation as of January 2021

— Hourly median earnings   — Weekly median earnings

Source: The Resolution Foundation[27]

from the EU, UK real GDP was around 2 to 3 per cent lower due to Brexit than it would have been if the UK had remained in the EU,[28] a very similar estimate to that made by the Centre for Economic Policy Research.[29] That's a loss of about £850 per person.

And then, as wages began to return to their 2008 level, came COVID-19.

The COVID-19 pandemic and its aftermath

The enormous disruption of the global pandemic effectively closed down a significant part of the UK economy as the government struggled to control the spread of the coronavirus through a series of lockdowns. For those who did not work in essential occupations or who could not work remotely, unemployment loomed. The government needed to take action to prevent mass unemployment and, following consultations with employers and unions, came up with a novel (for the UK) response, the Coronavirus Job Retention Scheme (CJRS). Rather than wait for workers to be made redundant – and then provide assistance directly to those individuals through the benefit system – the government chose to subsidise employers to keep workers who could no longer carry out their work functions on temporary but paid leave (that is, 'furloughed'). The CJRS covered 80 per cent of the wages of furloughed workers on its introduction in March 2020, with employers encouraged to top up the remaining 20 per cent. This level dropped to 60 per cent by August 2021 before ending in September 2021.

The number of employees on furlough peaked at 8.9 million on 8 May 2020[30] and its costs were huge, around £70 billion. But it had an equally huge impact. Over the scheme's lifetime it supported nearly 12 million people. If these workers had been made unemployed and moved onto benefits, they would have faced dramatic falls to their income, on average halving. On furlough their incomes were, on average, kept to about 90 per cent of pre-furlough income.[31]

Overall, the scheme prevented mass unemployment, maintained the employer–employee relationship, and provided crucial support for many households throughout the crisis.[32] Even so, many took a financial hit; around half of furloughed employees did not receive any top-up from their employers. This was particularly true of low-paid workers and left around 2 million effectively paid less than the National Minimum Wage.[33]

The government also introduced a scheme to help the self-employed, the Self-Employed Income Support Scheme, though the outcomes of this scheme are less clear-cut, partly because of the diversity of the people involved and partly because of lack of timely information on them.[34] While for some it protected them from a drop of income they would otherwise have experienced, it didn't seem to have had an effect on their business's long-term survival, perhaps because some businesses simply never had a long-term future and were being kept above water by the scheme itself.[35]

Nevertheless, many still ended up unemployed. Some, like the newly employed or self-employed, were excluded from these schemes, while some employers chose not to participate in the scheme, choosing instead to make employees redundant.[36] Many of these workers will have ended up on UC, and often as a result in financial difficulties. And some, while they had lost their job, were simply not eligible for UC, either because they had a partner working or because they had savings over £16,000 (the limit for UC eligibility). This meant they dipped substantially into their savings or simply went without.

Overall, and because the government stepped in, the impact of COVID was relatively modest on household living standards compared to the immensity of the disruption. But, nevertheless, the impact was highly unequal. Those who were previously poorly paid, many from ethnic minorities and the young, were more likely to take a hit financially, more likely to go into debt, and more likely to have been pushed further away from the labour market.[37] Many of those in work and in a precarious financial situation prior to the pandemic, ended up in an even more precarious state.

But more problems were to come.

The long-term legacy of soaring inflation

In February 2022, soon after COVID-19 restrictions were eased, Russia invaded Ukraine. Inflation, which had already begun to rise post-COVID, soared, primarily because of sharp rises in energy and food prices, with food inflation peaking at nearly 20 per cent by the spring of 2023.[38] And, as discussed in earlier chapters, this had a particularly devastating impact on low-income households as these households spend a greater proportion of their household income on these essential items than higher-income households.[39]

The Office of National Statistics has been developing a Household Costs Index (HCI) which aims to better reflect a household's experience of changing prices and costs and to enable a comparison of how these affect different types of households.[40] While the CPI measures the percentage change in the prices of a basket of goods weighted by the proportion of total spending for each item, the HCI measures the changes weighted by the average household expenditure on each of these items. This means that whereas the CPI results in high-spending households having a greater weight than low-spending households, the HPI gives all households equal weights, commonly known as 'democratic' weighting.[41] The HCI therefore gives a better insight into the experience of low- and average-expenditure households of changing prices.

Figure 4.6 shows that during these high-inflation years the overall rise in inflation for households based on this new HCI was considerably higher than that based on the standard CPI. Moreover, inflation, as measured by the HCI, was higher for those in the bottom end of the income range than the top.[42]

Then, in September 2022, in the midst of this already high inflation came the now infamous budget of the then-new prime minister, Liz Truss, and her Chancellor, Kwasi Kwarteng. Side-stepping any independent oversight, the budget proposed unfunded tax cuts for high earners on the basis that it would promote growth. Economic analysts, and more particularly the financial markets, thought the idea these tax cuts would lead to growth was pie in the sky and that, instead, this would lead to an increasing budget deficit, higher interest rates, and further

Figure 4.6: The impact of the high inflation years on household costs

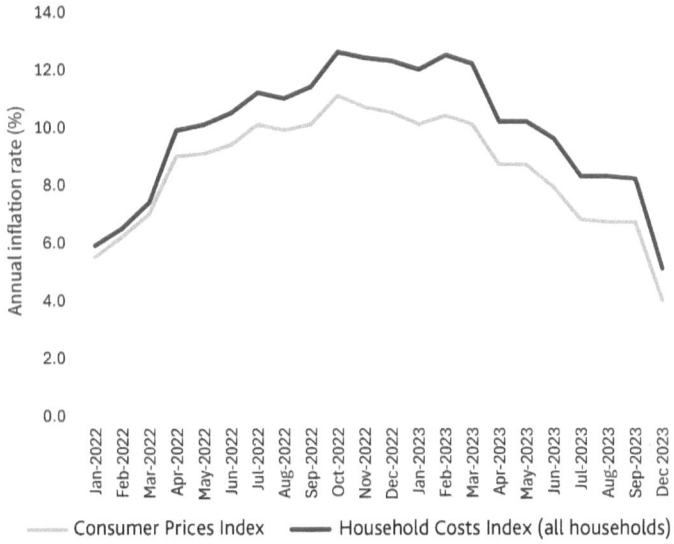

Source: ONS, Household Cost Indices[43]

inflation on top of already rising levels. The financial markets were spooked; sterling fell sharply against the dollar, the rate of interest on gilts, the way the government raises money to cover its debt, went up dramatically, and mortgage rates rose sharply.[44] Those who had to renew an existing mortgage were suddenly faced with long-term higher costs while private renters saw a further twist upwards to already rising rents.[45]

Liz Truss was forced to resign – her premiership famously being outlasted by a lettuce[46] – and the new prime minister, Rishi Sunak, and his Chancellor, Jeremy Hunt, reversed the budget's main policies. The panic subsided.

Eventually, by mid-2023, inflation started to go down and earnings started slowly to recover – but by nowhere near enough to make up for past losses. Indeed, real wages are not expected to recover to their pre-pandemic level until towards the end of the decade.[47] The impact of these years of high inflation are deeply baked into people's living standards, particularly at the bottom end of the income range.

To recover, earnings growth needs to be a lot stronger in the middle and bottom half of the income range to make a dent in the issue of in-work poverty.

A new direction

Reforms to work were a central plank of the Labour Party's offer at the 2024 general election. 'A New Deal for Working People' offered a long-term plan to reform the labour market so as to 'make work pay'.[48] Aiming to provide 'the biggest upgrade to rights at work for a generation', it promised a comprehensive set of policies to 'boost wages, make work more secure and support working people to thrive', with the aim of 'delivering a genuine living wage, banning exploitative zero hours contracts, and ending fire and rehire'.[49] The package aimed to enhance employment rights and ban exploitative practices, thereby raising workers' pay. It set to draw an end to the long era of ultra-flexible labour market policies which had benefited employers at the expense of employees.

Within the first months of office, Labour introduced its 'Employment Rights Bill', the first phase of this new plan.[50] The bill, which had been championed by then-Deputy Prime Minister, Angela Rayner, largely implemented the promise to end zero-hours contracts (with exceptions for those who chose such contracts), banned fire and rehire practices, and proposed employment rights from day one of employment, as opposed to the current two years, though this was subsequently increased to six months. It also made better provision for flexible working around other caring commitments 'where practical' – a provision that could help close the gender pay gap. It established a new enforcement agency, called the Fair Work Agency, to enforce these rights, though its exact remit was left fairly vague. And it repealed the previous government's Strikes Act which had required minimum service levels during strikes, aiming to reset industrial relations within the public sector.[51]

The government's assessment of its impact suggested it would cost businesses around £5 billion a year with the greatest financial benefits going to workers currently on insecure contracts, some of whom could benefit by up to £600 a year.[52]

The government sees this as the first step with other changes, including strengthening trade union rights, promised down the line though whether this takes place following Rayner's enforced departure from government in September 2025 is less certain.[53] If these intentions are followed through and not weakened under pressure from business, in particular small businesses who are most affected, then this new approach has the potential to be transformative in the longer term.[54]

Until this takes effect, the other key policy tool to make work a route of poverty is Working Tax Credits.

The impact of tax credits

When Working Tax Credit was introduced by the last Labour government in 1999, it was set up to encourage unemployed men, affected by technological change, back into work by providing a means-tested cash transfer for lower-income households in work. Unlike most other means-tested benefits (such as housing benefit or JSA) there was no savings limit for the recipient household, all that mattered was the level of household income.

The scheme was overhauled in 2002, splitting it into Working Tax Credit and Child Tax Credit, as part of the government's strategy for combatting child poverty. While Working Tax Credit was only payable if the household worked more than 16 hours a week, Child Tax Credit was payable whether the household worked or not, payable for each child up until the year they are 16. In doing this, the impact of the system shifted from one of encouraging people into jobs into one that redistributed resources into lower-income households with children.

During this period of Labour government, the value of tax credits diminished gradually as earnings increased; which is referred to as a long taper with a low taper rate. In addition, there was a relatively high earnings threshold (known as the work allowance) at which this reduction started. Up until 2010/11, the taper rate was 39 per cent and the threshold £6,420, meaning that for every extra pound earned above £6,420 a year, entitlement for tax credit was progressively reduced by 39p, first reducing the Working Tax Credit element and then the Child Tax Credit element.

Some of this financial support simply combatted widening earnings inequality which, without the benefit reforms, would have seen relative child poverty (before housing costs) rise from 26 per cent to over 32.1 per cent.[55] With the reforms it dropped to 18.4 per cent, though its impact was lessening towards the end of this period, even before the financial crash.

With the arrival of the coalition and then Conservative governments from 2010 onwards, the system became more aggressively focused on low-income households, lowering the threshold from which the reduction took place to £3,850 and withdrawing Child Tax Credit at lower income levels and increasing the basic taper rate for Working Tax Credit to 48 per cent.[56]

The then-Chancellor, George Osborne, argued that it directed the money where it was most needed and that it brought down costs, the argument always deployed for tightly means-tested benefits. However, tight means testing with its sharper cutoffs for the receipt of benefits *always* has a downside. For those who receive Working Tax Credit, higher taper rates make it harder to increase net income from employment as much of a recipient's increased wages is taken away in reduced benefit. Lower thresholds reduce the level of household income at which this disincentive starts. Once your earnings reach the income tax threshold, this disincentive effect becomes very high. A withdrawal rate of 48 per cent (the Osborne rate) combined with tax and national insurance contributions meant that the marginal tax rate (that is, the amount of money withdrawn for every pound extra earned) was around 73 per cent – much higher, indeed, than the top tax rate.

Moreover, the situation for those in rented accommodation receiving housing benefit was even worse as, at the same time, housing benefit was also withdrawn, at a slightly higher rate and from a slightly lower level. This meant that for working families in rented accommodation the marginal tax rate could be much higher; for lone parents, it was not uncommon to face a marginal tax rate of 96 per cent. The result was that for these households, better-paid work or longer hours were simply not a way out of poverty and shifting from part-time to full-time work had little financial incentive.

The introduction of UC brought Working Tax Credit, Child Tax Credit, and housing benefit into a single payment and reduced some of the worst of these overlapping withdrawal rates, though the taper rate for UC, at 63 pence in every pound earned, remained high.[57] It also, and importantly, introduced a savings threshold of £6,000 after which benefit entitlements reduced by £4.35 for every additional £250 of savings up £16,000, at which point entitlement was withdrawn. This effectively meant that if you were in a low- to middle-income household, where you might well end up entitled to the working tax element of UC, there was no or little point at all in saving.

In 2021, the Conservative government reduced this taper rate to 55 per cent, still higher than when Working Tax Credit was first introduced. The result of these continuing high taper rates is that increasing income from work remains a slow route out of poverty.

This can be seen in Table 4.1, which looks at households in work, with and without children, in the bottom third of the

Table 4.1: Average effective tax rates on different increases in hours of work for low-earning households

	0 to 20 hours per week	20 to 40 hours per week
Households with children		
2022–23 (legacy)	45.5%	58.6%
2022–23 (UC)	37.9%	58.3%
All households		
2022–23 (legacy)	41.5%	47.0%
2022–23 (UC)	36.1%	48.0%

Source: Institute for Fiscal Studies[87]

earnings distribution and their effective tax rates (that is the average rate at which benefit is withdrawn plus the average rate of tax on earnings) under the past and current system.

The first column shows the tax rate on entering work and the second the rate when moving from part-time to full-time work, the higher the difference in the effective tax rate, the weaker the incentive to work longer hours. As can be seen, the move to UC has improved the incentive to move into work but has made little difference to the incentive for households to move from part-time to full-time work and for households with children, in particular, the effective tax rate remains high.[58]

Out-of-work benefits are now so low (see Chapter 2) that there is a strong incentive anyway to find any work even if it is far below your past earnings potential. The incentive to move into work is strong, even if it's a low-paid, part-time job with no prospects. It's that or living in extreme poverty.

But the failure of the system to incentivise full-time work more generally has substantial long-term impacts. Part-time work is strongly associated with low wage rates and a lack of career progression. Households that are dependent on part-time workers have high rates of poverty. To move out of poverty, such households need the prospect of and opportunities for wage progression, moving into better jobs with better hours. Part of this is clearly due to the way the UK economy has developed into one which has a large share of low-paid, low-skilled workers. But it is also about the way the benefits system is structured to encourage, or force, people into work but does little or nothing to encourage career and wage progression. If the system could be redesigned to do that, work could become a more effective route out of poverty.

This does not, of course, mean that everyone would choose to work full-time, just that the financial gain from doing so would be greater and there would therefore be more of a financial incentive to do so. Parents, particularly those looking after very young children or a child with a disability or long-term ill health, may choose not to, or not be able to. These decisions will often go well beyond their financial impact and into questions of what is valued about life. But the cost of childcare will also be an important factor.

The childcare gap

One of the biggest social policy shifts in recent years has been the emphasis placed on getting parents, and mothers in particular, into work. Going out to work brings, it is argued, not just financial benefits for your children but makes you a better parent by providing a role model for your children. As former Prime Minister, Theresa May, put it: 'A child can grow up seeing a parent go out to work every day, and inwardly form the expectation that they will do the same. Imagine that child a few years later, taking the step from education into employment and starting her working life on the front foot. She is setting herself on the road to a fulfilling career and a happier life.'[59]

This shift can be seen clearly in the way benefit entitlements for lone parents have changed from exempting them from having to look for work until their youngest child reached 16 years of age to the current position where parents of children as young as a year old have to prepare for work.

To help support these changes, government investment in childcare rose considerably.[60] Back in the mid-2000s, the then-Labour government introduced limited free childcare hours for parents in work and the subsequent coalition and Conservative governments expanded this provision. By the end of 2020, in England and Wales parents of three- and four-year-olds where both parents worked were entitled to 30 hours' free childcare a week for 38 weeks. In Scotland the equivalent hours were spread over the year but provided whether or not parents worked.[61] While there was some provision for childcare support for children under two, it was limited to parents on benefits for just 15 hours.

This level of provision of free hours was clearly not enough and left parents working full-time picking up huge costs for childcare: the Women's Budget Group (WBG) estimated that a nursery place for a child under two cost between 45 per cent and 60 per cent of women's average salaries in England, and between a fifth and a quarter for three- and four-year-olds, even with the free hours entitlement for this age group taken into account.[62] For many women, it does not pay to work full-time, with the WBG estimating 1.7 million women were prevented from taking on more hours of paid work due to childcare issues.

The problem was not just the lack of entitlement to free or subsidised hours but the sharply rising costs of childcare. Since 2010, fees for childcare and nursery places per hour for pre-school-age children rose faster than either price inflation or wages. The Institute for Fiscal Studies calculated that for parents of a child under two costs grew by 60 per cent in cash terms between 2010 and 2021 – twice as fast as average earnings.[63]

These sharply rising costs are primarily a result of how pre-school provision has developed over the last 20 years. When free, albeit limited, childcare hours were first introduced, the then-Labour government did so by urging local authorities to promote the private-for-profit sector as the main resource for providing childcare.[64] As hours were limited, parents needed to pay these providers for additional hours. The coalition and then Conservative governments from 2010 to 2024 continued the expansion of free hours, gradually increasing the free hours covered and extending it to the under-threes, again subsidising the private sector to provide the childcare. However, the hourly rate received by providers from the government for the 'free hours' did not reflect the true cost of providing care and was generally cross-subsidised by higher charges to parents for additional hours of childcare.[65]

As a result of these choices, there was an expansion of private childcare providers which could cross-subsidise nurseries and raise loans on the financial markets. The result is that 84 per cent of provision is now delivered by for-profit providers as opposed to not-for-profit organisations such as local authorities or third sector organisations. Moreover, these private providers are increasingly consolidating with larger companies taking over smaller ones with private sole traders and partnerships going out of business. It's become big business, and it has all been driven by public subsidy. It is now seen as a 'hot market', offering high, short-term returns for investors,[66] with private equity companies and venture capital companies already buying into the sector.[67]

When the University College London Social Research Unit investigated how the sector had changed over the last 20 years, they found the for-profit companies they examined were dominated by highly leveraged financial models, characterised by high levels of indebtedness, very complex financial structures involving foreign investors and shareholders, and with considerable sums being extracted for debt repayments.[68] No wonder costs have risen so sharply – both for the government that subsidises the free hours and the parents who pay for the additional hours.

Moreover, the research finds staff costs are low, either by employing fewer or cheaper staff. Nearly a fifth of adult workers (aged 23 or over) employed in nurseries outside of schools are paid below the National Living Wage and levels of staff with qualifications in such nurseries are well below those in school-based ones.[69] This risks lowering the quality of the care provided. And, of course, these companies go where they can make the most money and this results in inadequate provision for children with disabilities[70] and in areas of deprivation.[71] By 2020, the Coram Childcare Survey found only just over half of local authorities in England had enough childcare for the children of parents who work full-time, less than a fifth for those who work atypical hours or whose children had special educational needs or disability, a slight decline in all these types of provision on the previous year.[72] While there is high quality provision, particularly in wealthier areas, this market-dominated system can leave poorer areas underserved.[73] And these are precisely the areas where provision needs to be highest to achieve the aim of getting parents into work.

In 2023, the then-Chancellor, Jeremy Hunt, announced, at a cost of around £4 billion a year, a major expansion of this system, by extending the existing 30 free hours a week during term-time for working parents of two-year-olds and over to those of children aged nine months and over. On winning the election, the incoming Labour government promised to ensure this commitment was met and while some of this was to be achieved through additional provision through new state nurseries (see Chapter 9), most of the expansion would be through subsidies to the private provider system.

But this is a model that is costly to both parents and the Exchequer and uneven in its distribution. Without addressing the inequalities of provision, places, and costs (see Chapter 9), it will not make work a route out of poverty.

Meanwhile for those who undertake unpaid care for a member of their household with a disability for a relative or friend outside their immediate household, the problems of combining full-time work with caring responsibilities can be even harder, and the poverty trap even more difficult to get out of.

The undervaluing of care

Informal unpaid carers provide services which would otherwise cost the state billions of pounds. The most recent census in 2021 estimated that there were around 5.7 million informal carers in the UK, though Carers UK, the UK's leading charity for unpaid carers, estimates it could be over 10 million. While many carers value and gain satisfaction from the support that they give,[74] it comes at a huge financial cost – informal caring remains enormously undervalued.

This stems, in part, from gendered assumptions about family life; historically, caring has been seen as part of a woman's role and it remains the case that the majority of unpaid carers of working age are women, often older.[75] The result has been that the Carer's Allowance, like its predecessors, has a limited monetary value and tight restriction on undertaking paid work without penalty. The benefit is not means tested (anyone can qualify whatever the household income) but it is not seen as a payment for work undertaken. The assumption remains that care is not really 'work'.

To claim the benefit, the carer must show that they are caring for a person in receipt of the standard or enhanced levels of the element of the PIP related to daily care or the care component of the Child Disability Payment. As such it is an unusual benefit as it depends entirely on the benefit status of another person – and many of those currently receiving the Carer's Allowance fear that the government's review of PIP will lead to tighter requirements and thereby result in their entitlement being lost.[76] The carer must then show that they provide care for this person for at least 35 hours a week. If successful, they can then get (at 2024 rates) £81.90 a week. This works out at about a fifth of the hourly rate of the National Living Wage. Perhaps it is not surprising that take-up of those eligible for the allowance, at around 65 per cent, is relatively low.[77]

The Carer's Allowance is not enough to live off, so many apply for means-tested benefits to cope, primarily UC. It then gets fiendishly complicated. UC counts the Carer's Allowance as income and therefore it affects your level of benefit and qualification for benefit.

The alternative way to top up your income is to work. But this option is not easy for most carers, primarily because of their caring responsibilities, but, in addition, for those who do work and who claim the Carer's Allowance, it can be a minefield.

Those receiving the Carer's Allowance can only continue to receive the allowance up to a strict, and low, earnings limit; in 2024/25, it was £151 per week. There is then a cliff-edge cutoff; if they earn any amount (even pence) over that limit, they lose all their benefit. And if that happens without you noticing – and that is very easy if you are asked to work an extra hour's overtime, or your rate of pay has gone up fractionally – and you have not notified the DWP, you are liable to be fined for not declaring that you are now over the limit.[78] And even if you do notify the DWP, it can take, because of staff shortages, months and months to process the information leaving the claimant having been overpaid and having to pay this debt off, often in a short period of time which the claimant is often unable to do.[79] And, as *The Guardian* has uncovered, because the DWP has been taking a more aggressive approach to reclaiming overpayments – what they see as 'fraud' – claimants can then find themselves prosecuted.[80]

The impact, as the House of Commons Work and Pensions Committee has found, can be devastating:[81]

> I have always worked and a few years ago I was put in a position that turned my life upside down. My mum had dementia and Alzheimer's. I accidentally did too

many hours, I was caring for my mum and my mentally ill son and holding down my job, I wasn't aware that I'd done wrong until I was called for an interview at the job centre. I was charged with fraud and taken to court, I was given community service of 180 hours unpaid work as if I didn't have enough to deal with. My son went into care because I couldn't cope, and I have now had to give up work and care for mum. I had to move in with her and give up my home, my job, my life. I am now having to pay the money back. My own health has suffered, and my finances are rock bottom. I feel my life has been in a downward spiral and I haven't been able to cope since. (Respondent with overpayment of £3,000)

While the Labour government has promised to end the scandal of debts building up as a result of overpayments,[82] and consequent prosecutions, more needs to be done. In her first budget, the Chancellor, Rachel Reeves increased the weekly earnings limit for Carer's Allowance by an additional £45 a week from April of 2025, making an additional 60,000 in-work carers eligible for the allowance. But, while the government has accepted recommendations to make the system more transparent,[83] barriers to work remain, notably the cliff-edge cutoff, and there is still little done to help carers balance their caring responsibilities and work.

Moreover, many carers of working age simply do not qualify for even the limited benefits of the Carer's Allowance. Many provide care for less than the qualifying time of 35 hours a week or for those who reach this time requirement do so for more than one person (caring for multiple people does not count). Research suggests that for those providing care for over 20 hours, undertaking full-time paid work becomes especially difficult.[84] Nearly four in ten caring for between 20 to 35 hours a week are not in work, and of those who are a third work part-time.[85]

The result of all this is that, overall, informal carers face a financial penalty. Research by the JRF estimates that the average pay penalty is around £5,000 a year, rising after six years of providing care to nearly £8,000 a year. It is not therefore surprising that informal carers are more likely to be in relative income poverty than non-carers and more likely to be in deep poverty.[86]

Clearly, for those who have to take on caring responsibilities, work is not a route out of poverty and compensation paid through the benefits system is vastly inadequate. In Scotland, where the Scottish government has since 2016 taken over responsibility for some benefits, a rethink of the Carer's Allowance has been underway but so far, apart from some additional lump-sum payments, little has changed.

In the meantime, the crisis in social care leaves many with little choice but to provide care themselves, on their own. Despite having the right to receive support, such as respite care, help undertaking specific tasks, or with juggling work and care, the crisis in social care makes this very difficult to access.

For a decade and more, cuts have left local services struggling to cope.

5

The dismantling of services tackling disadvantage

Councils are in crisis. Caught between rising demand for statutory services, such as adult social care, and long-term cuts to their budgets, less and less has been spent on almost everything else. The consequent closure of libraries, reduced facilities at leisure centres, more infrequent and more expensive bus services, less regular rubbish collections, poorly tended parks, an increase in potholes and broken streetlights, and much else, affects everyone, rich or poor, and in every part of the country, wealthy or deprived.[1] The fabric of people's everyday lives has been impoverished.

But this has also driven up poverty. The severest cuts to funding have been in the most deprived areas and it is in these areas especially that many services provide a crucial lifeline. Further, some of the services that have been cut back most severely are those that help prevent people falling into poverty in the first place. And then what happens is a vicious cycle creating yet more acute need. How has this all come about?

The differential impact of austerity (again)

The deep financial problems of local authorities started, as with the collapse of the benefit safety net, back in 2010 when the newly elected coalition government began its austerity drive. Councils took a disproportionate share of the overall cuts: by 2019, real-terms funding from central government to local authorities in England dropped (on a like-for-like basis) by 46 per cent overall.[2]

At the same time, the government initially froze council tax rises meaning that councils could not offset these sharp cuts at all. It then introduced a tight limit on how much a council could raise taxes without a local referendum, making it very difficult to offset the cuts. From the mid-2010s, local authorities with social care duties could, in addition, raise their council tax rates by small further percentages without a local referendum seeking approval[3] but this was simply to cover some of the increase in demand.

The result was that the overall money available for local authorities in England to spend on services (that is the total of government grants, council tax and business rates, and other small income streams such as parking fees) fell by over 20 per cent in real terms between 2010/11 and 2019/20 and per person by some 26 per cent.[4] In Wales, the situation was similar though less severe, with overall spending per person dropping during this period by some 10 per cent.[5] Scotland, because of the way funding allocation from central government worked, escaped most of the sharp cuts to local authority funding experienced in England, and Scottish government spending has been, as a result, relatively protected with overall spending falling by 4.5 per cent per person during this period.[6]

From 2019/20, the re-elected Conservative government, now under Boris Johnson, started to increase central government funding to local authorities in England as part of its promised 'levelling up' agenda. But then came COVID-19, which placed enormous pressure on local authorities, which had to take on a wide range of extra responsibilities from test and trace to additional support for vulnerable households. Though much of the immediate additional costs were covered by additional central government grants, these additional monies had ended by 2022, though the long-term problems caused by the pandemic had not. And by then, inflation was soaring away and the increase in central government funding was being eroded by the much higher than expected inflation. The result was that, despite increases to funding, in 2024/25 the money local authorities in England had to spend on services remained far below the level in 2010/11, as can be seen in Figure 5.1.

But the overall reduction in spending power, striking as it is, hides a very uneven impact. Because of the way the coalition

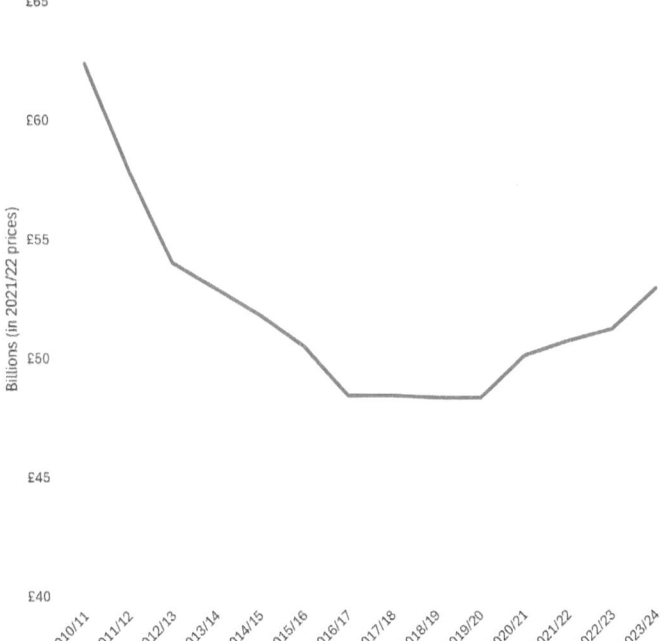

Figure 5.1: Local authority spending power in England, 2010/11 to 2023/24

Source: Institute for Government[7]

government chose to distribute the cuts, the impact was felt more heavily in more deprived areas that were more dependent on central government funding. In addition, when the freeze on council tax that had been imposed by central government was lifted, it was wealthier areas, where there was a larger and more well-off tax base, that benefited most. The overall result, as can be seen in Figure 5.2, is that local authorities serving the most deprived areas of England have taken a far bigger financial hit on services than authorities in wealthier areas.

The result was an exacerbation of already large and deep-seated regional inequalities. The rapid deindustrialisation of the 1980s – and the lack of any replacement industries – left many parts of the country with a long-term legacy of deprivation. The UK is now one of the most geographically unequal countries in the developed world,[8] with substantial gaps in income levels, educational outcomes, health, and poverty between

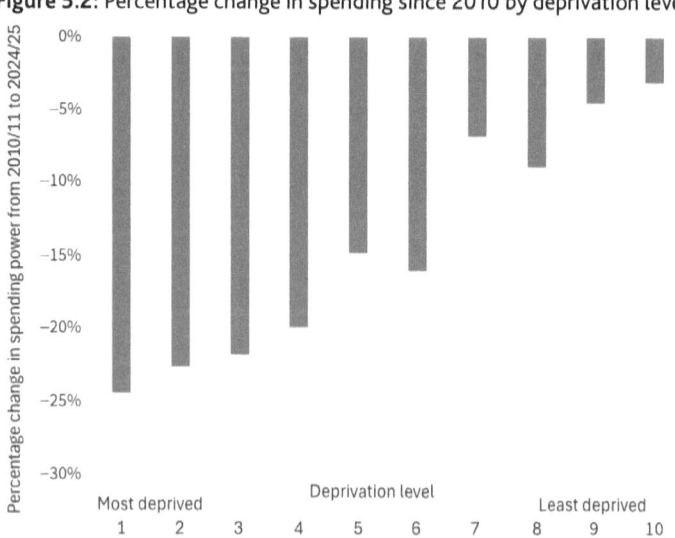

Figure 5.2: Percentage change in spending since 2010 by deprivation level

Source: Institute for Government[9]

different regions but also between areas within a region. Areas of exceptionally high deprivation can be found across the country but are particularly concentrated in deindustrialised towns such as Merthyr Tydfil or Ashfield, coastal towns such as Blackpool and Clacton, as well as in the large metropolitan areas, including London.[10]

When Boris Johnston stood on the steps of 10 Downing Street after his re-election in 2019, he promised to 'level up across Britain' and 'answer the plea of the forgotten people and the left-behind towns'.[11] But the rhetoric was never really matched by funds. Five years after 'levelling up' was launched, the Institute for Fiscal Studies' verdict was that progress towards levelling up had been 'glacial' and that 'on many metrics, the UK as a whole has gone into reverse'.[12]

In the meantime, the demand for services that councils have to provide by law was rising.

The crisis in social care

Across the UK, the proportion of the population who are elderly is growing, and growing faster than the population at large. This, in itself, increases demand for social care as those over 65 are more likely to need help. At the same time the average healthy life span has been relatively stable, increasing marginally for men and decreasing marginally for women,[13] which combined with a growing elderly population pushes up demand yet further, and particularly in more deprived areas where a person's healthy life span is on average 12 years below that of the least deprived local authorities.[14]

So just when local authority funding was experiencing cuts, and particularly for the most deprived authorities, demand for adult social care was increasing.

Publicly funded adult social care in England is means-tested and is only available for those with assets under £23,250. Low-asset households are, of course, most concentrated in local authorities with the highest levels of deprivation, pushing up demand yet further in these areas.

Anyone else who has the misfortune to face long-term care needs has to pay entirely for their own care. For those needing residential care this can be extraordinarily expensive and, as housing is included as an asset, it affects anyone owning their own home. The Department of Health and Social Care estimated that one in seven people will face costs of more than £100,000.[15] For many the consequence of paying these unforeseen and often huge costs can be devastating and can push them into a spiral of poverty, as respondents to research by Carers UK report:[16]

> Downsized property in very poor condition, it was all we could afford after paying Dad's care costs in the last year of his life. ... I had to sell my home too to fund this and Mum's costs. ... I have three ceilings with black mould, shower leaking through to hall and plaster on walls destroyed, can't afford repairs, I need new radiators cannot afford them so turned off. I have [broken] windows ... can't afford repairs. I have boiler not working properly for hot water or heat, can't afford repairs. I can't afford heat in winter so piles of blankets, Mum is immobile. My nearly 14-year-old car needs new brakes, can't afford them. ... Survive on cheap food. Oven is not working properly can't afford repairs so rely on microwave food i.e. jacket potatoes etc. ... Garden is not suitable for Mum can't afford to get it done. Mum has difficulty getting out of front ... can't afford alterations. (Carer of elderly, disabled parent)

It is widely accepted that this system is unfair – whether you get, say dementia, or not is largely unpredictable. Successive governments have promised to do something about this, but plans have repeatedly been postponed or abandoned, costing more than governments were prepared to pay.

In the meantime, the demand for publicly funded social care has increasingly outstripped the ability of councils to provide it.[17] While government funding levels for social care have increased since 2020, and the government did provide some extra crisis funding in 2022 and 2023, it has been nowhere near enough and has not even kept pace with rising costs in the sector, let alone rising demand. In 2022/23, less than half of those requesting adult social care support received any support at all.[18] This is not because the level of need of the people applying is lower but because publicly funded social care is being rationed with local authorities, in effect, raising the threshold of needs that a person requires to receive care.[19]

But even this is not the full picture of the extent to which people are being excluded from social care. Since 2010, the means-tested threshold of £23,250 has been frozen, meaning that it has not kept pace with inflation. If it had risen in line with inflation, the threshold in 2023 would have been over £30,000.[20] This means that fewer people are even eligible to apply, leaving more and more people struggling on a day-to-day basis and, as ever with means testing, disincentivising saving.

But those who are turned down still need help, often with the most basic aspects of life such as feeding, personal hygiene, dressing, or just getting around. Without help, their quality of life would deteriorate and, in all likelihood, the condition creating the need for help in the first place would get worse. Often the help will instead come from family and friends. This has led to a rise in the numbers of people providing unpaid care which, as seen in Chapter 4, is often a route to poverty and this, in turn, can result in carers struggling to provide the care needed:[21]

> Mum is always cold so heating bills are £500 a month. She likes heating on 24/7 even in July. (Carer of parent)

My wife's diet is complicated. She needs foods that are higher in iron, which is mainly red meat, the cost of that is horrendous. We do what we can and shop in the cheapest shops. We also need to make sure the meat has low carb amounts as she has diabetes. We also need to keep her B12 and potassium levels up as she has had issues in the past. So we struggle to tick all the boxes. (Carer of spouse)

At the same time as the demand for adult social care has been rising, so has the demand for child social care. Since 2010, the number of children in care has risen steadily and in 2023 stood at nearly 84,000, a rise of about 30 per cent.[22] The reasons for this are complex,[23] but it is at least partly due to a reduction in the sources available for early intervention to support families before a crisis arises.[24] At the same time, there has been a striking rise in the costs of placing a child in a residential home, as there already had been for adult social care.

The rise and rise of for-profit social care

Since 2010, there has been a significant increase in the outsourcing of child residential services with the result that children's homes have largely become a for-profit industry. This resulted in more than 80 per cent of homes being run by such companies in 2022/23, squeezing out public and non-profit provision.[25] This route of privatisation had already been pursued in the adult social care sector, so that by 2018 85 per cent of care homes in England were already being run by for-profit companies, with most of the remainder run by third sector organisations.[26]

The progressive privatisation of adult social care over the last 30 years has been based on the argument that it would provide choice and deliver a more efficient care service. While the initial idea was that there would be a mixed market with providers from

The dismantling of services tackling disadvantage

private for-profit companies, non-profit organisations, and local authorities themselves, this did not happen. Provision became dominated by private companies and, while some of these were small, often family, businesses, others were large, investor-led companies seeking to maximise profit.

These private companies became increasingly interested in richer, self-funded residents in affluent areas, from whom they made more money than those qualifying for free care and funded by local authorities. The result, in the words of the Care Quality Commission is that 'there is the risk that people who live in more deprived areas, and are more likely to receive local authority-funded care, may not be able to get the care they need.'[27] What then emerges is a two-tier system where those who cannot afford to pay wait longer; in the meantime their health deteriorates with the result that they may end up in hospital.

At the same time, the dominance of a few providers makes the whole system vulnerable to the sudden collapse of a provider, as happened in 2011 to Southern Cross Healthcare, then the largest providers of care homes to adults in the UK. Set up in the mid-1990s, the company swiftly expanded and started to attract the attention of investment bankers. By the time it was acquired by US private equity company Blackstone in 2004, it was pursuing aggressive expansion through complicated financial dealings including the sale and leaseback of its properties – and making huge profits. In 2006 Blackstone sold it shares in Southern Cross, reportedly making a profit of £1.1 billion on its original investment[28] and leaving behind a company overloaded with debt. Then came the financial crash, and this financial wheeler-dealing strategy hit the end of the road.[29] The company went bankrupt, leaving its 31,000 residents anxious about whether they were about to be evicted – and the government were forced to pick up the pieces.[30]

Subsequently, many of Southern Cross's homes were sold to Four Seasons, another larger provider of care homes and again a highly leveraged company. In 2019, Four Seasons collapsed, this time leaving some 14,000 older people in distress. This is a system that gives rights to private equity companies to extract profit at the expense of the right of older people to a secure home.[31]

The fragility of this model was next exposed during the COVID-19 pandemic. Residents of care homes, being elderly, were extremely vulnerable to catching the infection but to make matters worse the government decided to discharge COVID-infected patients from hospital to care homes so that the NHS was not overwhelmed. Over 42,000 care home residents died from COVID-19 between March 2020 and April 2021 while in the first two years of the pandemic nearly 1,300 care workers died.[32] For those affected this was obviously heartbreaking and for many a foreseeable and unforgivable tragedy.

For the care homes it caused financial problems as they were now operating on below-maximum occupancy rates and more reliant on (more expensive) agency workers. To ensure their financial viability the government pumped some £2.1 billion into the sector. Little of this trickled down to the workers who had to work longer hours, in difficult and dangerous conditions, facing daily trauma. But it did allow profit margins to soar.

Warwick Business School found that over a quarter of companies receiving government support increased the dividends paid to shareholders compared to the previous year, by an average of 11 per cent.[33] For some larger chains the profit extraction was huge. Runwood Homes, for which the Care Quality Commission rated a quarter of its homes as 'requires improvement' (the second lowest rating), saw its profits rise from £15 million in 2019 to £25.4 million in 2020.[34] Profiteering from the pandemic was rife.

This expansion has taken place despite the transparent problems that have emerged with the private ownership of adult care homes and increasing evidence that the quality of provision in for-profit homes is lower.[35] Treatment in some adult care private homes is shocking.

In March 2025, Daniel Hewitt, the investigations editor for ITV News, uncovered allegations of multiple failings at residential and supported-living homes run by Lifeways, the UK's largest provider of community care for adults with complex conditions.[36] In one home in Coventry a young man with learning disabilities, autism, and bipolar disorder, needing 24-hour, one-on-one care, was filmed eating out of a rubbish bin in the middle of the night. In another Lifeways home in North London, photos were obtained showing a man with Down's Syndrome whose foot had turned black after an infection was left undetected and untreated for weeks, resulting in the need for hospital treatment.

Analysis for ITV News by public service analysts Tussell, found Lifeways had received almost £1.5 billion in contracts with local councils and the NHS since 2016, with the company's revenue increasing in 2024 to £295 million. The four directors, including the Chief Executive Officer, had received total annual pay of £1.6 million between them, with the highest paid director receiving £923,000.

Yet, of the 19 Lifeways services inspected by the Care Quality Commission in 2024, 63 per cent were rated 'requires improvement', with numerous and increasing safeguarding alerts and concerns.

Still the privatisation of social care rolls on, increasingly taking in children's homes as well as increasing their hold on adult social care. And this shift to for-profit operators is pushing up the costs of child social care. The Competitions and Markets Authority have found 'the largest private providers of placements are making materially higher profits, and charging materially higher prices than we would expect if this market were functioning effectively',[37] while at the same time failing to provide the therapies and facilities the children need.[38] Others, including local council leaders, have accused the larger companies of 'profiteering on the backs of young people'.[39]

The result of this ever-increasing spending on children's homes and other statutory, often emergency, child social care services is that less and less is spent on preventative services. Figure 5.3 shows local authority spending on children's services between

Figure 5.3: Drop in spending on preventative children's services, 2009/10 to 2022/23

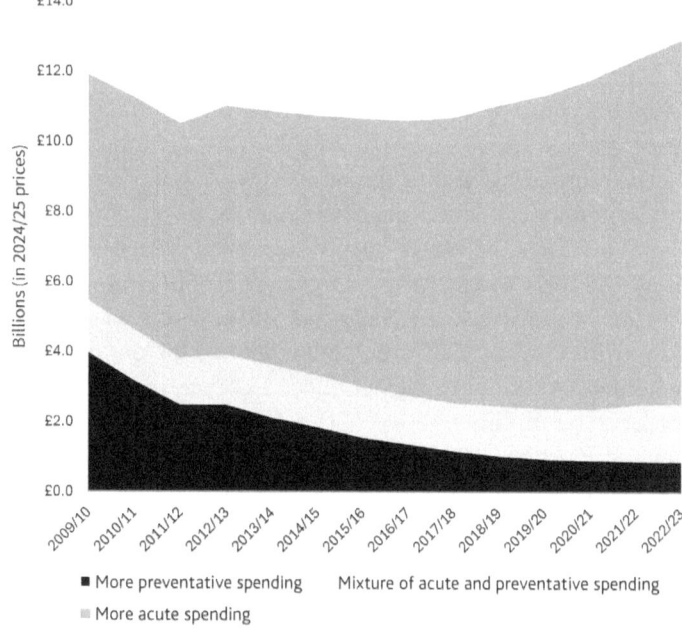

Source: Institute for Government[40]

2009/10 and 2022/23 (at 2024/25 prices) by the type of service provided. This shows that while spending on acute services rose from £6.5 billion to £10.4 billion, that on preventative services fell from £4 billion to under £1 billion.

This is completely counterproductive as cuts to preventative services create long-term (and usually more expensive) demands elsewhere, as investment in such services stops needs escalating. Research has found that for every £20 increase per child in non-safeguarding spending in a previous year, there was an average reduction of almost 2.5 children in need of help and protection the following year.[41] Cutting spending on preventative services thus creates a vicious spiral whereby the subsequent rising demand for acute services leads to yet further cuts to preventative services.

Moreover, it diminishes lives and prospects, increasing chances of poverty and deprivation in the future.

The hollowing out of support for young people and children

It is long and well established that children living in deprivation, on average, have lower educational outcomes[42] and poorer long-term health.[43] In general, the wealthier the parent, the better the future prospects for the child. We also know that these differences emerge at an early age. For example, the vocabulary performance of children at the ages of three and five increases as parental income increases, but the difference between the lowest-income families and those in the middle is far greater than that between the middle and the top.[44] There is a sharp penalty for being born poor.

By the age of five, children from the most advantaged groups are over a year ahead in vocabulary, compared to those from disadvantaged backgrounds. Similar patterns emerge for behavioural problems. This does not necessarily mean that the life chances of children living in deprivation are inevitably lower but it makes it more likely. Of course, much of the solution to this is tackling inequality. But strategic interventions for children and young people facing poverty can make a difference.

Back in 1997, the last Labour government launched Sure Start, an ambitious programme specifically aimed at improving educational, health, and development outcomes for children in disadvantaged areas by establishing early-age, integrated children's centres. Around 500 centres were set up, offering a range of services including healthcare, early learning and play, childcare, and support for children with special needs.

In 2003, this programme was expanded with the aim to eventually provide access to Sure Start in wealthier as well as more deprived neighbourhoods.[45] At the same time, though the focus on helping children from disadvantaged backgrounds remained, access to places was made universal – the new centres were open to all. By 2009, there were 3,632 Sure Start children's centres.[46]

But then came the coalition government and priorities shifted. The Sure Start budget was no longer ring-fenced by central government, and local authorities, faced with severe cuts to their funding and the sharp rise in spending on acute child services, were looking for large reductions in spending on non-statutory services. This pressure intensified under the subsequent Conservative governments. As can be seen in Figure 5.4, spending on children under five and on services for young people which was not related to children's social care and protection fell dramatically.

The Sure Start centres, which from the start had never really been embedded in the public education system, were vulnerable. Between 2009/10 and 2021/22, spending on Sure Start children's centres and other services for children under five fell by nearly three-quarters and by 2018 as many as 1,400 had been closed,[47] with those that remained, now referred to as just children's centres, reduced in capacity to such an extent that many were no longer offering childcare,[48] which had been found to be particularly important for improving cognitive skills and social behaviours.[49]

The idea of children's centres 'in pram-pushing distance' with open access services had been hollowed out to just a few centres for referred families in high need.[50] These remaining centres, faced with financial restraints themselves, were struggling, failing to provide the needed variety of programmes and dependent on staff lacking the training and experience to cope with families with complex needs.[51]

And all this builds up future problems and disadvantages. The Institute for Fiscal Studies has carried out two assessments on the long-term impacts of Sure Start centres, one on health and

Figure 5.4: Drop in real spending on services for children and young people

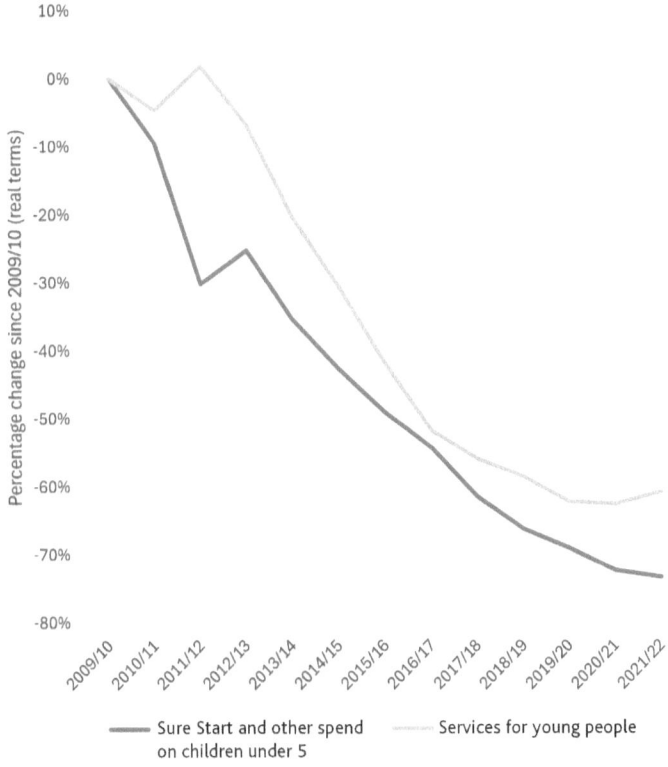

Source: Institute for Government[52]

the other on education. The study on health[53] found that for children born from the opening of such centres in 1999 to Sure Start's peak in 2009–10, living in an area within walking distance of such centres reduced the likelihood of hospitalisation among children of primary school age, with these benefits getting bigger as children got older. By the age of 11 the reduced probability of hospitalisation was strongly significant and equivalent to averting

5,500 hospitalisations of 11-year-olds each year.[54] Moreover, these reductions were greatest for children living in the most disadvantaged areas. Reducing these hospitalisations can have a lifetime's impact for the children involved.

The study into the impact of Sure Start on educational outcomes[55] similarly found positive outcomes. By age five, children had been given better foundations to succeed, in particular better communication and mathematical skills. The impact of this increased over the years, and by age 11, the academic performance of those in Sure Start areas was much improved, and these improvements could still be seen at age 16.[56]

In the push to focus on getting parents into work, the importance of early years provision in ensuring the best possible start for all children has been ignored. Early years provision has become dominated by private providers who are more likely to base their centres in richer areas where they can charge higher prices to parents. Children from more deprived areas are getting left behind.

A very similar picture emerges for youth services. These include the provision of youth clubs, youth work, activities for young people, and teenage pregnancy services and, as seen in Figure 5.4, spending on these services has dropped by some 60 per cent between 2009/10 and 2022/23. Research by UNISON, the public services union, estimates that since 2012 councils have shut at least 350 youth centres, 41,000 youth service places for young people have been cut, and at least 35,000 hours of outreach work by youth workers have been removed.[57] These services can help raise confidence and well-being, develop social skills, encourage skills development and training, counter loneliness and isolation, help develop an interest in creative and physical activities whether sport, music, the arts or the like, help tackle substance abuse, and much else.[58]

Research suggests that these closures have led to significant declines in educational performance at ages 15–16 (Key Stage 4 or GCSEs), comparable to the effects of closures of Sure Start centres, and an increase in youth offending rates with the impact being larger for teenagers from lower-income backgrounds.[59] The result is a stocking up of long-term future problems.

The decline of local bus services

Since 1985, outside of London, bus services in England, Scotland, and Wales have been privatised and deregulated, run by private companies for profit with no statutory required minimum service levels. The bus operators themselves, outside London, decide where most services run, the frequency of service and the level of fare. The provision of unprofitable routes or affordable fares has depended on subsidies from local government which cover direct payments to operators to run particular services and reimbursements for concessionary bus fares. In addition, central government directly subsidises bus companies through a fuel duty rebate. The result is that private bus companies still receive high levels of public money while having little public accountability for their service levels.

Figure 5.5 shows the financial support for bus services in England from these various sources between 2010 and 2023. As can be seen, since 2010 these subsidies have declined, with the exception of the pandemic years when, because of the loss of income resulting from large numbers of passengers being no longer allowed to travel, subsidies increased both from local government and central government including additional government emergency funding. Most notably, subsidies to companies to provide services dropped sharply, from nearly £1.6 billion in 2009 to around £0.83 billion in 2020, a fall of around 47 per cent. Cash-strapped local authorities could no longer afford such a high level of subsidy.

The result was that, outside of London, over 3,000 routes were reduced or completely withdrawn, resulting in the miles on local authority-supported bus services declining by over 50 per cent.[60] Not surprisingly, given these routes were subsidised

Figure 5.5: Local and central government support for bus services, England, 2009 to 2023

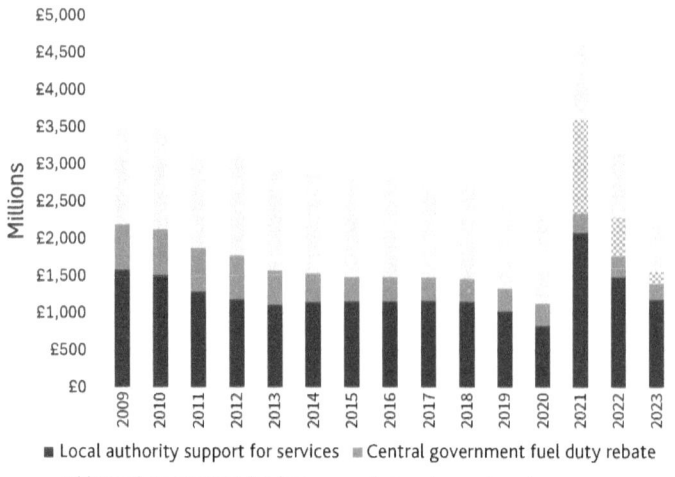

Note: Prices adjusted for inflation as of June 2024.
Source: Department for Transport, Table BUS05bii[61]

because they were uncommercial, this was not made up by new services provided by the bus companies themselves. It has left many rural areas and small towns as bus service deserts, but it has also affected the frequency and reliability of services in sub-urban estates in larger metropolitan areas. A 2020 review of services in South Yorkshire, for example, found that the number of bus miles operated across the network had fallen an average of 11.8 per cent between 2009/10 and 2016/17 with the services that remained facing significant reliability issues.[62] Even the government's own review of bus services in 2021, Bus Back Better, admitted that:

> Many communities have lost their daily bus services altogether. Others have services for only a few hours a

day, suitable perhaps for a short shopping trip but not for work or longer distance journeys. Others might have relatively good services in the daytime but no service at all in the evenings.[63]

This decline has a serious impact on the lives of those dependent on bus services. This includes those in rural areas,[64] older people, people with disabilities, and women (who take the bus more frequently than men). But it is particularly important for low-income households of whom some 40 per cent do not have access to a car.[65] The decline in services affects their quality life, their ability to take part in social, leisure, and cultural activities, to visit family and friends. It can impact on their access to healthcare, education, and food. And cutting services can cost people their job, as one respondent explains:

> This particular bus route cost me a job. ... I had to quit because of the bus. At the time, 2008–2009 we had the big market crash, jobs were few and far between to start with, for Stagecoach to pull a really important bus route was a kick in the teeth for a lot of people. ... It took a while to find another job, about two years.[66] (Lee, Hartlepool)

For many young people, the cost of transport is one of the biggest issues they face[67] and in some worst-affected areas it can result in young people dropping out of post-16 education. This all jeopardises people's ability to lift themselves out of poverty.

Research by the Institute for Transport Studies (ITS) at the University of Leeds finds that unemployed people have 'extremely high levels of dependence on buses for accessing employment, much more so than the general working population'.[68] In this study, based on Brighton, Nottingham, Kent towns, and West Yorkshire, nearly one in five participants had not applied for a job because of a lack of suitable or affordable bus service with over one in ten having turned down a job offer for that reason.[69] Phil, aged 36, who has had to turn down jobs because there was no guarantee he could make the shift on time or make it home, explains the problems that can then result as a consequence:

> I learned to restrict my job search to the close local mileage, but that leads you to getting into trouble with [the DWP], because you aren't fulfilling what they say you should be doing by looking only local. I got my money stopped ... because over a two-month span, my job search wasn't deemed adequate.[70] (Phil, 36)

Cost is also a factor. When the Thatcher government introduced the privatisation and deregulation of buses, the promise was lower fares from competition;[71] in reality between 1987 and 2021, average bus fares rose by 403 per cent compared to 163 per cent for motoring costs[72] and compared to CPI inflation at around 203 per cent.[73] As Dean, aged 35, in Newcastle, explains the resultant high costs can cause cascading problems:

> There are times when I won't pay for another thing because travel is the most important, because I have to get to the hospital. ... Sometimes it might be a bill, like the gas bills.[74] (Dean, 35, Newcastle)

To counter these rising fares, in January 2023, following the decline in bus service use post-pandemic and the rapid inflation of 2022, the then Conservative government did introduce subsidies for a £2 maximum single fare for certain (by no means all) services outside London up until the end of 2024, a cap which the new Labour government extended for a year, though lifting it to £3.[75]

It is now widely agreed that the privatisation and deregulation of bus services brought in by Margaret Thatcher's government has not worked.[76] It promised more routes and resulted in fewer, it promised lower fares, but resulted in higher fares. And it promised that the transfer to the private sector would also remove any potential future liability on the taxpayer to provide capital or make good losses[77] whereas, as the substantial subsidies during COVID-19 (see Figure 5.5) demonstrate, this was not the case. At the end of the day, the government picked up the pieces from the private sector to ensure that a vital public service continued.[78]

It is, however, a system that is beginning to change.

The promise of a better bus service

In 2017, franchising – the system that allows an authority to take public control of the bus network, including where and when buses operate, fare levels, and service and quality standards – was permitted in metro mayoral combined authorities in England. This system is the one operated in London through Transport for London, and since 2019 it has also been permitted in Scotland. This has led to some considerable improvements, notably in Greater Manchester where the Mayor, Andy Burnham, has used these new powers to bring in a London-style system of integrated local transport back under public control. The new 'Bee Network' has turned the corner on bus use, with passenger numbers rising by 5 per cent in its first year of operation.[79]

In 2021, as part of its 'levelling-up agenda', Boris Johnson's government promised a new national bus strategy, which would provide, according to Johnson, 'main road services in cities and towns to run so often that you don't need a timetable'.[80] A promised £3 billion was attached to it. But, as so often with the then-prime minister's promises, it was more hype than reality. Within a year, the funding had been cut by half to £1.4 billion over three years[81] – and it soon became clear that only around £1 billion over three years would be available for bus improvement plans, with this funding available to just 40 per cent of the Local Transport Authorities applying.[82]

Soon after the Labour government was elected in 2024, a new Buses Bill was published, extending franchising powers to all local authorities,[83] offering new guidance on how to do so and to reduce the costs of doing so.[84] Getting on for an extra £1 billion was allocated for 2025/26 for local councils to improve bus services.[85] And notably, it also allowed councils – for the first time since Thatcher prohibited it – to set up new publicly owned bus companies, enabling authorities to own, as well as run, services. The few municipal bus companies, notably in Nottingham and Lothian – that had survived the post-Thatcher years had proved successful, with high customer satisfaction, more routes and, indeed, they proved profitable for the councils.[86] This move away from privatisation could be transformative, if followed through and with sufficient funding provided.

But, despite these additional monies for bus services, overstretched local authorities do not have the cash to do this properly on their own. Spending now would not just improve people's lives but would have the potential to shift the poverty dial over the longer term. Research by KMPG with ITS Leeds finds that, allowing for other factors that influence deprivation, a 10 per cent improvement in local bus service connectivity in town and city neighbourhoods was associated with a 3.6 per cent reduction in deprivation.[87]

As with other services explored in this chapter, more investment now would create a virtuous circle whereby less spending on emergency support and services is necessary in future years. And there is one area where this is particularly true.

6

How the UK's housing system drives poverty

The high cost of housing in the UK has become an increasingly important driver of poverty. Private rents have been soaring in recent years, with average rents going up by more than a quarter in the three years between mid-2021 and 2024.[1]

Indeed, over the last 30 years or so, private rents have risen substantially faster than inflation.[2] At the same time, as social housing stock levels have fallen and house prices rocketed, more and more people have been forced into private renting. It has left increasing numbers of renters struggling to cope with their payments, even after housing benefit:[3]

> I am 68 years old and about to be evicted from my home … while I was waiting for my application for Discretionary Housing Payment to be processed, arrears accrued and my landlord started legal proceedings to evict me. … The council will provide me with bed and breakfast accommodation after I am evicted at a cost greater than my current rent – [it] makes no sense. (Private renter, 68)
>
> I had to resign from work last year due to stress … and my finances suffered and I am still struggling to pay

> rent/bills. Most of what I receive goes on rent. ... It just feels like you are being kicked when you're at your lowest. (Out-of-work private renter)

If the rising rents reflected improved housing, with more and larger rooms of better quality, it might be seen as a choice people have made. But this is not the case. People are simply paying more for similar properties.[4] Indeed, housing conditions at the bottom end of the private rented sector are at times appalling.

Overall, poorer households now spend a much higher proportion of their income on housing than richer ones. This is perhaps unsurprising given that housing is a basic necessity. But what is striking is that the gap has grown substantially. Back in 1980, households in the bottom quarter of household income spent around 10 per cent of their income on housing, the proportion then shot up so that by the mid-1990s poorer households were spending about a quarter of their income (before housing benefit) on housing and has remained around 22 to 25 per cent ever since. By the 2020s, even after housing benefit, poorer households are spending around 19 per cent of their income. In the same period, the proportion of income being spent on housing by richer households was around 5 per cent in the early 1980s and, having risen somewhat during the 1990s, was back to around 5 per cent by the 2020s.[5]

To understand how housing has become such a driver of poverty, we need to take a whistle-stop tour of how the housing market has changed.

The decline of social housing

This story starts, as is well documented,[6] with the sale of council housing under the Conservative government of Margaret Thatcher and the subsequent slow death of social housing. The Right to Buy tapped into people's aspirations to own their own home and offered council housing tenants highly discounted prices to buy their council house. Initially, this was set at a minimum of 33 per cent discount after three years' tenancy, rising for each year of tenancy to a maximum of 50 per cent; these discounts were subsequently increased.[7] Councils, who had to sell the houses if the tenants wanted to buy, were not allowed to keep most of the proceeds from the sales but had to pass them on to the Treasury (the proportion was 50 per cent when first introduced but dropped to 25 per cent by 1990). The proportion they were allowed to keep had to be used first to reduce any debt rather than building new homes. This meant that for new builds councils were largely dependent on government grants which were far less generous than what was needed to replace the existing stock.

Subsequent governments of all political persuasions have continued with what's been widely seen as a popular, vote-winning policy, though with differing degrees of enthusiasm. In particular, the incentives on offer varied. Under the last Labour government, the maximum discounts were reduced going down from £50,000 to £16,000 (outside London) in 2003. The coalition government, by contrast, set about 're-incentivising' purchasing, with the maximum discount raised to £75,000 in 2012 and then the rate going up to 70 per cent in 2014.[8] Overall, since its inception some 2 million houses have been sold in England under Right to Buy.[9] The one counter trend has been due to devolution, which in 1997 handed powers over housing to Scotland and Wales, eventually resulting in the ending of the scheme in Scotland in 2014 and Wales in 2018.

The resultant decline in social housing provision was also hastened by the coalition government's decision to introduce a new type of housing tenure, 'affordable housing'. In their spending review in 2010, investment in new homes for social rent was cut by two-thirds and this money was diverted into their new 'affordable rent programme'. These homes were to be built by housing associations but while social housing rents are tied to local earnings and are considerably below market rents, these tenancies were to be set at up to 80 per cent of market rent in the area, resulting in affordable rents being double that of social rents in some areas, notably parts of London. This has transformed the type of housing for social need being built; by 2022/23, only 15 per cent of new homes built for social need were for social rent rather than 'affordable rent'.[10]

Moreover, under this scheme the government covered a much smaller percentage of the cost of building these new homes than previously, dropping from around 50–75 per cent of the cost to around 25–30 per cent. To make up the difference, housing associations were told to convert their existing social housing into 'affordable housing' as they fell vacant, thereby raising extra revenue. By the end of 2021, nearly 121,000 social rent tenancies had been converted to 'affordable rent' tenancies.[11]

The result of these polices has been, not surprisingly, a very sharp decline in social housing stock. There are now 1.4 million fewer households in social housing in England than there were in 1980.[12] There has also been a steady rise in the cost of social renting.[13] Looking just at working-age households in the bottom 40 per cent of the household income range (those most likely to be in social housing and claiming benefits), the Institute for Fiscal Studies calculates that over the last 25 years, social rents have increased by 58 per cent in real terms.[14]

The initial idea behind the sale of council housing was to help create a 'property owning democracy'[15] and in the early days of Right to Buy it did indeed extend the reach of homeownership. But that did not last; it subsequently declined and is back now to just above the level it was in 1981. This is partly because the former council houses that were sold into homeownership were subsequently sold into the private rented sector; by 2017, in England, over 40 per cent of former council homes had ended up in the private rented sector. But it is also, and more importantly, because house prices rose dramatically, pricing increasing numbers of people out of homeownership. People between the ages of 16–44 are now less likely to own a home than they were in 1981,[16] as are those in the bottom 40 per cent of the household income distribution.[17]

The result of all this is that the private rented sector has boomed. This shift to private renting was particularly sharp in the decade after the economic crash, as homeownership became increasingly out of reach for many households and the buy-to-let sector became an easy route to wealth.[18] The number of households living in the private rented sector in the UK in the decade from 2007 to 2017 increased by 63 per cent from 2.8 million in 2007 to 4.5 million in 2017,[19] where it has remained, with a slight increase since. Much of this increase is among those in the mid- to higher-income range households and is the mirror image of the decline in the numbers able to buy with a mortgage. But there has also been an increase in private renting among lower-income households, in this case largely as a result of the decline in the availability of social housing.[20] Indeed, by 2013, the percentage of households in private rental housing began to overtake the percentage on social housing and by 2021 (the latest census data) 19.5 per cent of households were private renters and 17.5 per cent social renters.[21]

What's crucial here is that private rents are considerably higher than social rents, even though these have risen. Shelter estimates that in 2022/23 social rents were 64 per cent more affordable than private rents, with social tenants in England paying on average £828 less per month in rent than private tenants.[22]

And these trends, set in motion years back, have erupted into a crisis that has put enormous pressure on already-struggling local authorities.

The crisis of homelessness

In 2017, in light of a sustained rise in homelessness since 2011,[23] the Conservative government, then led by Theresa May, published its optimistically named 'Homelessness Reduction Act'. Its aims were worthy. It placed a renewed focus on the prevention of homelessness and gave new powers to local authorities to try to help those at risk of homelessness and at an earlier stage in the process, for example by providing support to access private rented accommodation.[24] It widened the range of people local authorities had a duty to protect to cover all groups, including importantly young people for whom homelessness had become an increasing problem, rather than just those deemed most vulnerable. Some small, additional funds to local authorities were made available, though, as the National Audit Office subsequently noted, not enough to cover the costs of the new requirements.[25]

More importantly, nothing was done about the key underlying drivers of the rise:[26] in particular, the surge in both private and social rents and the lack of availability of social housing pushing people into the more expensive and less secure private rented sector. Nor did it deal with landlords enforcing no-fault evictions, though the newly elected Labour government did move to ban such evictions within months of taking office.[27]

The act was, not surprisingly, completely unsuccessful in achieving its aim of reducing homelessness. Homelessness continued to rise and by 2024 was at its highest level since comparable data collection began in the early 2000s.[28] Figure 5.5 shows the trends for England for the two main official indicators: the numbers of households that are threatened with homelessness and are accepted by local authorities as needing help (that is, in official jargon, that were 'owed a prevention or relief duty') and of these the numbers actually classed as statutorily homeless, for whom the local authority must find alternative accommodation (that is, to whom the local authority owed a 'relief duty'). While there was a slight drop in the upward trend during COVID-19 (when the government temporarily introduced some protections for private renters), in the six years following the act, the number of households needing help with homelessness rose by some 20 per cent to around 325,000 in 2023/24, and the numbers of statutorily homeless rose by around 40 per cent to 179,000.

And these figures for those who are statutorily homeless underestimate the real extent of the problem for they exclude 'hidden homelessness', people who sofa-surf with family and friends and the like. The Homelessness Monitor, an independent analysis of homelessness conducted for the homelessness charity Crisis, has developed a measure of 'core homelessness'.[29] This aims to capture the most severe and immediate forms of homelessness and includes sleeping on the streets, spending night after night on friends and families' sofas, being stuck in unsuitable temporary accommodation like

Figure 6.1: The rising problem of homelessness

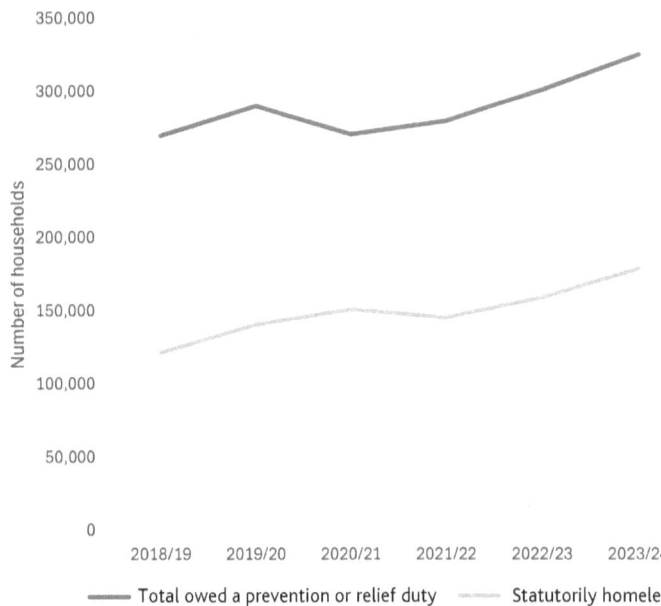

Source: Ministry of Housing, Communities and Local Government, statutory homelessness live tables, Table A1[30]

nightly, paid B&Bs, or some similar form of severe homelessness such as sleeping in a garage. On these estimates, the number of households in England who are homeless has now risen to nearly a quarter of a million.[31] Homelessness in Scotland and Wales, where the devolved administrations have stronger policies, is consistently lower than in England and has not seen such rises.[32]

The rising use of temporary accommodation

In England, the overall rise in homelessness has led to a striking increase in the use of temporary accommodation. While local authorities have a statutory duty to house the homeless in priority need, they do not have the capacity to do so and have increasingly turned to emergency accommodation, usually a single room in the private rented sector, B&B accommodation, or hostels. As can be seen in Figure 6.2, this rise in the use of temporary accommodation has been a long-term trend since 2010 but, after a slight pause during COVID-19, has been escalating since 2022, with a rise of around 30 per cent in the two years from the second quarter of 2022.

Conditions in temporary accommodation are often appalling, marked by damp and mould, a lack of space, sparse facilities for washing and cooking, and lack of cleanliness.[33] Some are unsafe with buildings in a dangerous state of disrepair, infestations ranging from mice and cockroaches to slugs and snails, leaks, and a lack of fire safety.[34] In the words of those living in temporary accommodation giving evidence to the All-Party Parliamentary Group for Households in Temporary Accommodation:[35]

> It's worse [than] a nightmare. The house is almost 50 staircases without lifts, cockroaches, mice. I fell [downstairs] severely when I was pregnant. Leaking,

Figure 6.2: The rise in the use of temporary accommodation for the homeless

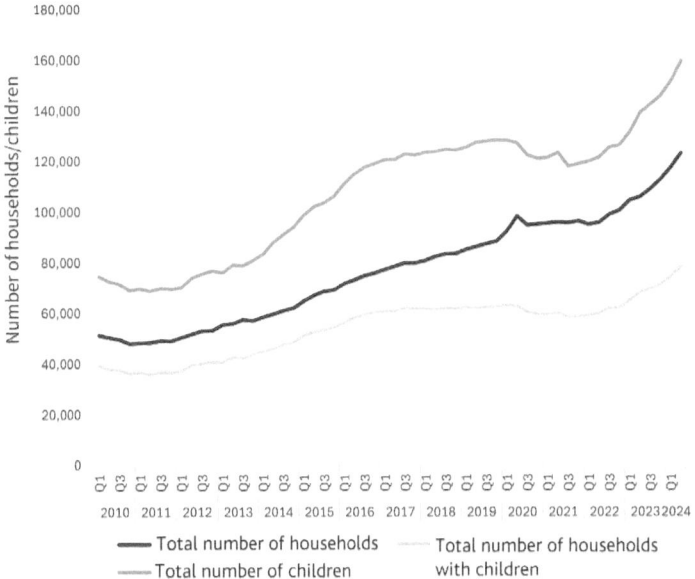

Source: Ministry of Housing, Communities and Local Government, statutory homelessness live tables, Table TA1[36]

> damp, roof touching our head, tiny rooms, we sleep on the ground. (Female, pregnant)

> Filthy. Heating not working properly – no hot water. Bin bags from previous residents in yard. No one responded to our calls for weeks. Totally ashamed to live like this. (Resident in temporary accommodation)

> Terrible conditions, cramped, no ventilation, alarms going off in the night. (Resident in overcrowded accommodation)

> Have had three fires since I've lived here. All related to dodgy wiring. Can't get repairs done through Council as 'out of borough'. (Resident in 'out of area' placement)

And, as advocates for residents reported, no consideration is given to those with disabilities:[37]

> My client has a severely disabled daughter who is blind & in a wheelchair and has multiple health conditions as well as severe scoliosis and seizures and restricted lung disease. ... Her severely disabled teen child has to be carried up and down the stairs which is a hazard and quite dangerous as mum is terrified of her falling. (Advocate for residents)

> Her fibromyalgia is also very bad and she desperately needs to be either [on the] ground floor or in a block with a lift as she is not often able to manage the stairs. When there was a fire outside the block, it was terrifying for her as she was barely able to escape down the narrow stairway. Similarly, when an ambulance came to her when she was having acute vomiting and body pains, the paramedics could not get her down the stairs and she had to be carried on the back of her eldest son. (Church pastor)

Often households are isolated, with increasing numbers placed outside their local area.[38] It all increases anxiety and mental health problems and for children can be extremely disruptive to their schooling, damaging life chances.

It is sometimes not even temporary. The Homelessness Monitor estimates that as of March 2022, almost 26,000 households had been living in temporary accommodation for between two to five years, with a further almost 19,000 households in temporary accommodation for more than five years.[39]

For local authorities the costs are huge. Local authorities pay for temporary accommodation and then can reclaim some of the costs from the DWP. But in 2011, as part of the 'austerity' drive, these rates were frozen and did not rise again until 2023. This led to a growing gap between the rising costs of temporary accommodation and the government subsidy: in 2022–23, for local authorities in England the gap was over £200 million, compared with around £40 million in 2012–13 (in 2022–23 prices).[40] Some small district councils in high-cost areas, such as Eastbourne or Hastings, have ended up spending up to half of their total net budget on temporary accommodation, putting them under severe financial strain.[41]

And it is an important contributor to the increasing proportion of local authority spending on housing services (excluding council housing) allocated to homelessness: this rose from 25 per cent in 2010/11 to 60 per cent in 2022/23.[42] This leaves an increasing shortfall elsewhere.

The failure to tackle poor housing conditions

Controlling and monitoring housing standards is a direct, and legal, responsibility of local authorities – but it is failing. And yet there is an enormous problem to be tackled.

Britain's housing standards are among the worst in Europe, with England having the highest proportion of inadequate housing of all countries.[43] At the bottom end, it is all too common to find properties wracked with mould, damp, rats, cockroaches, and other safety and hygiene hazards. Many poor households are still living in conditions typically seen in the slum estates of the 1930s, '40s, and '50s.

In England, Wales, and Northern Ireland there are three main official measures of sub-standard housing[44] (Scotland uses a somewhat different system). Housing is classed under the

Housing Health and Safety Rating System, with a category 1 hazard posing an immediate and severe threat to life and wellbeing. If a property fails to meet this level of safety, then councils are legally obliged to take action, but for private tenants only if they have complained.

The Decent Home Standard is slightly broader and to pass this level the property must not only meet the category 1 hazard level but also provide a reasonable degree of thermal comfort, be in a reasonable state of repair, and have reasonably modern facilities and services. Finally, homes classified as having 'damp' when the damp levels pose a risk to health.

In 2022–23, 3.5 million households (14 per cent) in England lived in a home that failed to meet the Decent Homes Standard, 2.1 million households (9 per cent) lived in a home which failed the category 1 hazard level, and 1 million households (4 per cent) lived in a home with damp.[45] In Wales, where the housing stock is older, in 2017–18, an estimated 238,000 houses failed the category 1 hazard level, some 18 per cent of the total housing stock.[46]

Private renters are more likely than any other tenure to live in a poor-quality home, a matter of increasing concern as not only are more households living in private rented accommodation, but they are doing so for longer and increasingly include a more diverse range of households, including families with children. As Figure 6.3 shows, nearly 13 per cent of private renters are living in a home that poses an immediate risk to life, nearly 9 per cent in a damp home, and over 21 per cent in a home that is not considered decent, all far higher than for social renters or for owner-occupiers. These figures for private renting are probably an underestimate as some tenants will be concerned that reporting problems might lead to eviction.

Moreover, the improvements that had been seen in housing conditions in the past, across all types of tenure, have stopped in recent years.[47]

Poor housing diminishes the lives of all residents and leads directly to ill-health, resulting in additional costs to the NHS of

Figure 6.3: Sub-standard housing by tenure, England, 2022/23

Source: English Housing Survey 2022/23, Tables AT3.1, AT3.2, and AT3.3[48]

some £1.1 billion a year.[49] But it can be a particular problem for elderly residents, whose own health and mobility is diminishing and whose vulnerability to infection from damp and cold are high, and for children, especially young children, where such conditions can cause both long-term and acute health problems.

Children living in damp homes are almost three times more likely to have breathing problems; one in five acute respiratory admissions into hospital for under twos would be prevented if housing was damp- and mould-free.[50] Of those admitted to hospital with breathing problems, many will go on to develop asthma and a lifetime of continuing ill-health. And it can lead directly to death. In December 2020, just before his second birthday, Awaab Ishak died in Rochdale from, the coroner concluded, 'a severe respiratory condition due to prolonged exposure to mould in his home environment',[51] the family's complaints about the condition of their council flat having been ignored.

Figure 6.4: Numbers of children living in sub-standard homes by tenure, England, 2022/23

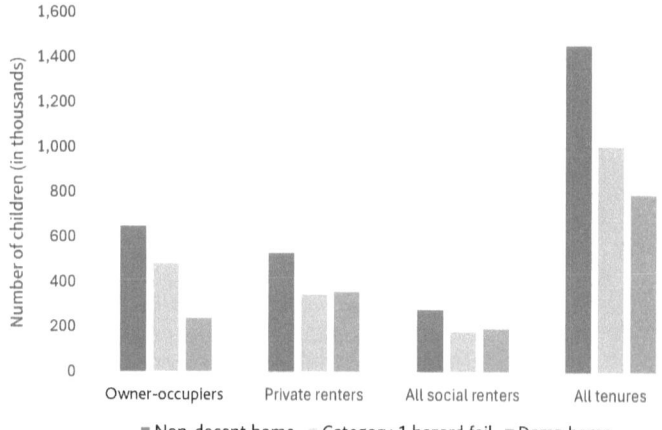

Source: English Housing Survey 2022/ 23, Table 1.7[52]

Figure 6.4 shows the number dependent children (in thousands) living in the three measures of substandard housing by tenure. There are around 1.5 million children living in homes that failed the Decent Homes Standard (13 per cent of children), around 1 million in a home that has a category 1 hazard present (9 per cent of children), and 790,000 living in a damp home (7 per cent). As with all households, children in privately rented housing are more likely to face these inadequate housing conditions than those living in all other types of tenure (see Figure 6.3) but because more households are owner-occupied, for the two of these three categories (non-decent homes and homes with a category 1 hazard) the largest number of children facing these problems are in owner-occupier homes.

The picture for damp is different. The largest number of children (over 355,000) living in a damp home live in a privately rented one, that's over one in ten children living in a privately rented home.

So why, when the dangers of poor housing have been known and accepted for years, has any improvement come to a halt?

A failure of regulation

Landlords have no requirement to meet minimum standards, including health and safety standards, before renting; councils only have an obligation to investigate if a complaint is made, but tenants fear eviction or rent increases if they complain as they are not protected. If the council investigates and finds the property is substandard and fails to meet the safety hazard level, they can issue an enforcement order, at which point the tenant is protected from eviction. The landlord only commits an offence if they then fail to comply with this order. It is a system that has been described by the chair of the Association of Chief Environmental Health Officers in England, Peter Wright, as having 'serious systemic failings'.[53]

But what has made matters even worse is that these inspections are increasingly not taking place. The National Residential Landlords Association has found that between 2021 and 2023, just a third of complaints raised by renters were responded to with an inspection.[54] The House of Commons Public Accounts Committee report on the 'regulation of private renting' found that local authorities were just firefighting and 'do not have the capacity to protect tenants and ensure landlords comply with regulations'.[55] Shelter report that four out of five local authorities said they did not have sufficient numbers of staff to ensure landlords were within the law.[56] When a local authority runs out of money, this is the impact.

To make matters worse, even for the complaints that were investigated, most did not result in action being taken: between 2021 and 2023, just 7 per cent led to an enforcement notice.[57] Taking action and ensuring it is followed takes more time and resources. The result is that rogue and criminal landlords can simply get away with it.

And to make matters even worse most of these landlords, because they are dealing with the poorest tenants, will be being subsided by housing benefit payments. Analysis from the Mayor of London's office finds that that across the country, landlords are collecting £9 billion a year in rent for 'non-decent', privately rented homes, with £1.6 billion of this coming from housing benefit.[58] To put it simply, public money is ending up in the pockets of private landlords who are letting out dangerous and dilapidated homes which are putting the health of their tenants at risk.

The problem of sub-standard social housing is somewhat different, in that it is more regulated. Many feel that one of the problems here is the lack of attention paid to tenants' concerns which, if tackled earlier, could avert future problems.[59] Essentially, as social housing has declined as a proportion of housing and become increasingly targeted at lower-income and more vulnerable households, it has also become marginalised, its tenants stigmatised, and their voices and concerns dismissed.[60] This was certainly the case at Grenfell Tower where tenants of the tower block that so devastatingly went up in flames in October 2017 had complained about fire safety for years and been ignored.[61]

The Grenfell fire resulted in the deaths of 72 people,[62] deaths that Sir Martin Moore-Bick, the chair of the public inquiry into the causes of the fire,[63] described on launching the final inquiry's report as 'all avoidable'.[64] The Royal Borough of Kensington and Chelsea and the Tenant Management Organisation that administered the tower on its behalf and ran the £10 million refurbishment programme that installed the highly flammable cladding material at the root of the fire, had shown a 'persistent indifference to fire safety, particularly the safety of vulnerable people'.[65] This included small, but ultimately critical, concerns that had been raised, such as faulty safety doors with automatic door-closing mechanisms that did not work.[66] Many argue the fire also exposed serious concerns about racial inequalities and class discrimination.[67] And it also exposed a 'serious and longstanding' failure of government regulation, its implementation and its oversight, that had allowed unscrupulous companies to exploit a weak regulatory regime and install unsafe cladding on the tower block.[68]

Following the Grenfell fire, over 4,500 tower blocks of over 11 metres have been identified as having unsafe cladding of which nearly 2,000 are in the social housing sector, and, as of 2024, of these unsafe social housing tower blocks more than half were still awaiting even a start to sorting out the problem.[69] And at the heart of this failure is resources. Research for the Local Government Association by the consultancy firm Savills estimates that the costs of fire safety remediation to meet the fire requirements bought in after Grenfell alone would be £7.7 billion to 2030.[70] This would require ether a sharp rise in council rents across the board or far more additional funding from central government than has not so far been forthcoming. At the end of the day, this is a choice as to who is valued and who is not.

The problem of lack of action due to lack of resources applies, however, not just to meeting fire safety standards but to substandard social housing more generally.

Back in the early 2000s, under the last Labour government, a comprehensive programme of investment, backed by an estimated £37 billion of government funding, was brought in to bring all social homes up to the newly defined Decent Homes Standard within ten years. This decade-long programme reduced the number of non-decent social homes by 1.1 million, so that by 2010 over 90 per cent of the target had been met.[71] But in the years since, funding for both council and housing association social housing has become tighter and more uncertain while costs have risen. While this primarily affects the number of new builds it has also impacted on repairs.

Councils who own council housing (and following a transfer of council housing stock to housing associations many do not), are required to keep their housing income and expenditure in a ring-fenced account, the Housing Revenue Account (HRA). In 2012, under the coalition government, a 'self-financing' settlement was introduced which required councils to fully cover their housing maintenance, management, and debt servicing costs from their rent and service charge income. It was based on various assumptions about rent levels, maintenance, and major repair costs, improvement costs to raise the standard of housing, and the level of Right-to-Buy sales.

In the subsequent years, the coalition and then Conservative governments did not keep to the terms of this settlement.[72] In particular, from 2016 the Conservative government imposed rent cuts on councils while at the same time promoting a rapid increase in Right-to-Buy sales with increased discounts and looser eligibility criteria. This has resulted in huge budget 'black holes' in councils' HRAs[73] and councils have struggled to keep up with repairs, let alone improve standards. They have also struggled to meet the new requirements that have been placed on social housing landlords to take action within specified timeframes, such as those brought in following the death of Awaab Ishak. Simply issuing new regulations without the financial backing to make it happen becomes performative politics.

The problem of substandard socially rented housing run by housing associations is somewhat different. Over the last 30 years housing associations have been transformed from small community-based organisations into mega organisations, many with tens of thousands of houses across the country.

This all started under the 1988 Housing Act, which prioritised housing associations over council housing and allowed housing associations to borrow from the private sector – and has continued ever since. While housing associations remain non-profit organisations, the introduction of private financing has transformed how they operate. These associations, while continuing to provide social housing for need, have diversified. Now seen as an investment opportunity, housing associations have moved away from their core mission of serving social housing needs to venturing into property sales and investments and some expanding their services into areas like social care and supported living. Yield Investing, a UK-based investment company specialising in property, sets out the advantages for investors as 'an opportunity to secure long-term, steady returns while addressing the growing demand for affordable housing in the UK'.[74]

The overall result has been that as government grants dropped, housing associations became more reliant on private financing and more driven by commercial rather than social purpose.[75] New builds were prioritised at the expense of renovation programmes.

Recognising these problems, the National Housing Federation (NHF), the voice of housing associations, commissioned an independent review of the issue of the poor quality of some social housing. The resultant report, The Better Social Housing Review, argued that housing associations need to return to their core purpose of providing quality housing for social need but that this could not be done alone and needed the government to commit to sustainably funding the regeneration of homes.[76]

Overall, The English Household Survey estimates that it would cost £7,511 on average to bring social housing properties up to the decent household standard.[77] Quite apart from the strong moral case for ensuring decent housing for all, this would be a good investment given that poor-quality housing, as seen, creates long-term problems.

The need for more for social housing

In its 2024 election manifesto, the Labour Party promised to build 1.5 million new homes over the course of the parliament and provide 'the biggest increase in social and affordable housebuilding in a generation'.[78] This is ambitious and a much-needed resetting of the UK housing policy.

Its success, or otherwise, is widely seen to depend on what sort of houses are built and the balance between homeownership and social housing. Building more housing for homeownership, while potentially helpful for those trying to get on the housing ladder, will not solve the housing crisis. This has been tried over the last decade or more and it has not worked as the supply of housing has not increased sufficiently, in particular, in areas of high demand. This is because most housebuilding for home ownership is carried out by 'speculative' private development; that is, the private developers obtain land, acquire planning permission, and construct homes prior to selling them.[79]

The problem is that this model works better for builders if they drip-feed homes onto the market houses at a rate that maintains market prices rather than to build sufficient houses to meet demand, as this keeps prices high and keeps their profits up while supplying more houses would drive prices down.[80] Indeed, the Competition and Markets Authority investigation into the housebuilding market in 2024 concluded that reliance on this speculative 'model has seen the gap widen considerably between what the market will deliver and what communities need'.[81]

It is widely agreed that the only way to provide what communities need is through more social housing with a widespread consensus that at least 90,000 social rent homes a year, for ten years, are needed in England.[82] This would largely clear social housing waiting lists and be sufficient to house all homeless families. Moreover, research commissioned by Shelter, in conjunction with the NHF, calculated that upfront costs in doing this would be balanced by wider economic benefits within only a few years.[83]

The Labour government's plans, set out soon after winning the election by Angela Rayner, Deputy Prime Minister and Secretary of State for Housing, Communities and Local Government, included the reintroduction of compulsory housebuilding targets for local authorities, with targets of 50 per cent affordable housing with a focus on social rent.[84] To achieve the scale of housebuilding it was looking for, the government would introduce legislation to speed up the planning processes and reform planning laws. While building on brownfield sites remained a priority, the government proposed making it easier to build in the Green Belt, as long as it was in the poor-quality parts of the Green Belt, what Labour describes as 'grey belt areas', though in practice it took a more dismissive attitude towards special environmental protections for rare species.[85] And it promised to build the next generation of new towns, with up to 12 under construction by the end of the parliament.[86]

Importantly, the government planned to reform the National Planning Policy Framework (NPPR), the guide that sets out the rules that local authorities must follow when granting permission to private developers for development and building projects in their area. Once a developer gets permission to build, the value of the land zooms up and developers, dominated by a small number of housebuilding companies, such as Barratt, Persimmon, and Taylor Wimpey,[87] are looking at big profits. The idea of the NPPR was that, in return for permission, the builders would be required to put something back into the community. Under the system, the developers negotiate with the local authority as to how much 'affordable housing' they will need to include for their planning application to get provisional approval along with other possible contributions.

The system has been repeatedly changed over recent years and currently, while the 'affordable' housing element can include social housing, it often does not have to and moreover can include shared ownership as part of the 'affordable' housing contribution. In addition, developers use what's called 'viability assessments' – by which it means that developers will have a profit margin of at least 20 per cent – to negotiate down their affordable housing commitments, leaving developers with no commitment at all for affordable housing on some sites.[88]

As a result, the system is almost completely ineffective at delivering social housing – the percentages agreed are usually small and the builders find loopholes to back out of commitments made, including the percentage of affordable homes. In 2023, only 3,454 social rent homes were delivered through this system.[89] A tightening of these rules to force builders to include a higher percentage of social housing, as opposed to affordable housing, would make a difference.

While the government has committed to an overall target for new builds, it needs to be more explicit and specific on requiring targets for social housing. Shelter have called for a requirement on plans for more than ten homes to set a minimum percentage of social housing. Research commissioned from Arup showed that a 20 per cent social rent requirement on large sites would result in 25,300 social rent homes.[90] While this change on its own is not enough to solve the crisis, it would account for far more homes than are produced under the current system.

However, even if the requirements placed on developers to include a higher percentage of social housing in its developments are tightened, there is a limit to what the private sector can be expected to contribute. Builders can be forced to include more social housing, and the planning system can be improved to speed up the rate at which houses are built, but neither is a panacea that will solve everything. This is because the total amount of affordable and social housing provided in this way depends on the rate at which developers can, or will, sell the proportion of the development that will go for private sale. Past governments have tried to stimulate private sales through subsides for first-time buyers, but these have tended to backfire. A 2022 House of Lords report on meeting housing demand concluded that 'Help to Buy' simply 'inflates house prices by more than their subsidy'.[91]

This means that to meet the number of social houses needed to solve the crisis, the government will have to fill the gap between what the market will support and what is needed. Research for the NHF by Savills finds that it would be near impossible for the government to reach its housebuilding targets without such additional support and that the quickest way of plugging the gap, and indeed the most sure-fire way, is with targeted, direct grant funding for councils and housing associations.⁹² And this support needs to be long term as large-scale projects take time to develop and build.

The main way of doing this would be through direct grants provided from central government under an updated and revised Affordable Homes Programme. Originally launched in 2010, the Affordable Homes Programme provides grant funding to local authorities and housing associations to help support the capital costs of developing affordable housing for rent or sale.⁹³ Under its different iterations during the coalition and Conservative government years, the emphasis has been on building 'affordable' rented housing as opposed to social rent housing, and on various subsidies for 'affordable' homeownership (such as shared ownership and 'affordable' homeownership schemes).

Overall, the programme has failed to deliver enough affordable housing with less than 50,000 a year being delivered for much of this period, though numbers have increased since the 2020s. But more importantly, as can be seen in Figure 6.5, the introduction of the scheme led to a sharp decline in the number of social rent homes being built, bottoming out at under 6,000 in the year 2016/17, while the numbers of 'affordable' housing for rent increased as did the numbers of affordable houses for sale. Of the total homes built in 2023/24, only around 15 per cent were social homes, while around 35 per cent were for sale and just under 50 per cent were 'affordable' rents. Overall, only around 85,000 social homes were built between 2013/14 and 2023/24. This is important as the average social rent is generally around 38 per cent of market rent for new lets, while 'affordable' rent is up to 54 per cent of market rent and in some areas much higher.⁹⁴

The government added £500 million to the current Affordable Homes Programme (which runs to 2026) in the autumn budget of 2024, bringing the total investment in housing supply to over £5 billion and which will support, on government estimates, the delivery of 33,000 new homes,⁹⁵ with a switch of emphasis to

Figure 6.5: Affordable homes completed by type, England

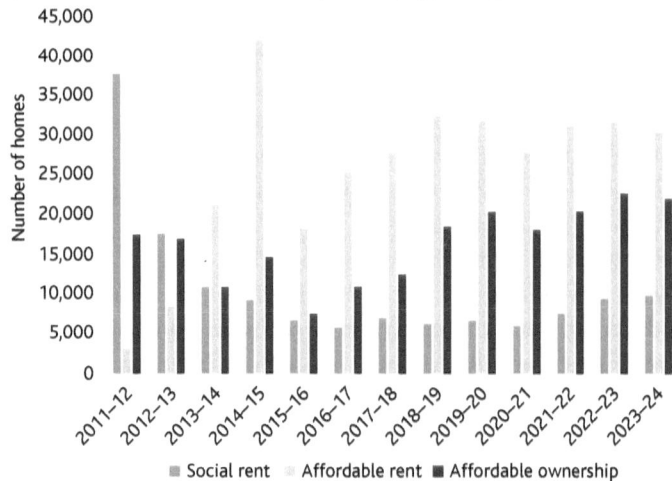

Source: Department for Levelling Up, Housing and Communities, live tables on affordable housing supply, live table 1000, December 2024[96]

supporting new homes for social rent. A further £350 million was added to the programme in February of 2025.

Moreover, in its June 2025 spending review, the government announced £39 billion for affordable and social housing over ten years from 2026–27 to 2035–36, providing a promised certainty for capital funding over the long term.[97] Out of this £39 billion programme, the government aims to build 300,000 social and affordable homes over the next decade with 60 per cent of these, 180,000, being for social rent.[98] These are significant steps in the right direction, and far more than has been done over the last decade.

In the meantime, the impact on local communities of the lack of affordable and decent housing and of the dismantling of services has had a profound impact – and one that has been particularly toxic.

7

How destitution is designed into the UK's immigration system

In late July and early August 2024, racist riots broke out in towns and cities throughout England. It all kicked off in Southport, a seaside town north of Liverpool, when hundreds of far-right extremists arrived and attacked a mosque.[1] The rioters had been stirred up into their hatred and rage by rumours surrounding a horrendous knife attack a few days earlier on the participants of a Taylor Swift-themed holiday dance class in the town, which had resulted in injuries to eight children and two adults and the tragic deaths of three young girls, Bebe King, Elsie Dot Stancombe, and Alice Dasilva Aguiar. The rumours, which had been widely spread on far-right-wing social media, claimed that the assailant was a Muslim, an undocumented asylum seeker who had arrived in the country by boat.[2]

The truth or otherwise of the rumours was, of course, no excuse for what happened. In fact, when the alleged assailant was arrested a few days later and named, so as to try to quell the rumours, it turned out he was born in Cardiff and at the time, lived in the Lancashire village of Banks.[3]

But by then the riot was underway. Joined by locals, the mob waved the flag of St George[4] and chanted Islamophobic abuse,[5] and slogans such as 'England till I die' and 'let's get them'.[6]

Hurling bricks and make-shift firebombs, they tried to break down the mosque's front door.[7]

Within a week, riots had spread across many of the poorer and more neglected areas of England and into Northern Ireland: in Hull, Liverpool, Stoke-on-Trent, Nottingham, Bristol, Manchester, Blackpool, Portsmouth, Aldershot, and Belfast among others. As the riots spread, the focus widened. In some, the hatred was targeted at anyone who was non-white. In Middlesbrough, North Yorkshire, rioters set up a 'race checkpoint' stopping cars to find out if the drivers were 'white and English' before letting them through.[8] In Sunderland, Tyne and Wear, two Filipino NHS nurses in a taxi on their way to work, as emergency cover for the casualties of the riots according to reports, were left terrified after their taxi was pelted with bricks.[9]

Others explicitly targeted asylum seekers. In Bournemouth, far-right protesters held on high a Union Jack emblazoned with 'Enough is enough – Stop the Boats',[10] a key plank of the premiership of the by-now-out-of-office Prime Minister Rishi Sunak. In Tamworth in Staffordshire, extremists smashed their way into the Holiday Inn hotel, believing it to be housing asylum seekers, and started fires within the property, cheering while lives were endangered inside.[11] In Rotherham, around 700 people gathered outside the Holiday Inn Express, a hotel housing asylum seekers, again trying to set fire to the hotel while the residents inside, including young children, looked out through the windows, powerless.[12]

There were plenty of others who lived in the towns and cities where the riots had taken place who came out in support of those being attacked and organised counter-protests. In Southport, volunteers from across the community came together to help clean up the town and rebuild the damaged wall of the attacked mosque.[13] In nearby Liverpool, when a local mosque was threatened, a strong counter protest gathered with placards such as 'Nans against Nazis'.[14] Eventually, the riots subsided.

The riots had been widely condemned by mainstream politicians but many had warned for years that the rhetoric surrounding government immigration policy, and its coverage in the press, were fomenting anti-immigration feelings which were, in turn, feeding the far-right agenda.[15] Baroness Sayeeda Warsi, once a co-chair of the Conservative Party, a former Conservative cabinet minister, and at the time of the riots still a member of the Conservative party, saw the riots as 'the culmination of two decades of stigmatising, demonising and othering refugees, Muslims and other minorities'.[16] In turn, people's concerns about their lives and communities – and the failure to tackle the deep inequalities in society and the stark disparities between different parts of the UK – were exploited and blamed on immigration. For the rioters, this had become a country into which migrants were flooding in, getting priority treatment at the expense of those already here, and once arrived, having an easy life.

The reality for migrants into the UK is quite the reverse. The immigration system, in its ostensible aim to limit immigration, or at least unskilled immigration, has incorporated into its design hardship and poverty. The policies have not in practice limited net migration; the UK economy is deeply dependent on migrant workers and many public services would collapse without such labour.

What the policies have achieved is to create misery and destitution.

The impact of the hostile environment

Back in 2012, when Theresa May was Home Secretary in the coalition government, she set out to reduce the number of immigrants in the UK with no right to remain by ensuring their lives were so difficult they would not be able to stay. Such migrants already had few rights and had no recourse to public funds, meaning they had very limited access to social security benefits and health services. But their lives were about to become even more restricted. Outlining her new policy in a *Telegraph* interview she explained: 'The aim is to create here in Britain a really hostile environment for illegal migration ... What we don't want is a situation where people think that they can come here and overstay because they're able to access everything they need.'[17]

A billboard campaign with a van covered in an advert stating that illegal migrants must 'go home or face arrest' was run in areas of London with high levels of immigrant populations, creating fear and anxiety among these communities even if here perfectly legally. A set of policies were introduced, mainly through the Immigration Acts of 2014 and 2016, to restrict migrants who were in the UK illegally – whether entering illegally, or entering legally and then overstaying their visas or breaking their visa conditions – from being able to work, study, rent a place to live, drive, have bank accounts, and obtain access to social protections like healthcare and benefits.[18] Local authorities, employers, landlords, banks, the police, the NHS, and many others were required to check immigration documentation and share data with the Home Office for enforcement purposes – or risk fines or criminal prosecution. It was in effect turning private citizens, civil servants, employers, and those responsible for public and social services into immigration enforcement agents.

Whether these measures encouraged those migrants classed as illegal in the UK to leave is completely unknown. As the Independent Chief Inspector of Borders and Immigration, David Bolt, told the House of Commons Home Affairs Committee in 2018: 'the Home Office does not have in place measurements to evaluate the effectiveness' of the hostile environment measures, or of the impact of the provisions brought in by the Immigration Acts of 2014 and 2016.[19]

It did, however, fuel exploitation.[20] Those unsure of their immigration status ended up turning to jobs in the least regulated sectors of the economy, where employers would turn a blind eye to their immigration status. Those on temporary visas tied to a specific job were particularly vulnerable to exploitation as any complaint could mean not just losing their job but thereby their immigration status.

What is also known is that these measures had a detrimental impact on immigrant communities living in the UK perfectly legally – and increased their risk of poverty and destitution. It did this by adding to the discrimination, already often experienced by immigrant communities, from a whole range of bodies – banks, landlords, employers – who wanted to avoid the risks and complications associated with dealing with immigrants, even if they were here legally. Research by the Residential Landlords Association and Crisis, for example, found that just under half of landlords would, as a result, only rent to those with documents familiar to them and were less likely to rent to someone without a British passport (which included the 17 per cent of British nationals without a passport).[21] It created mistrust, especially among migrant communities, and added to fears among non-immigrant communities who were in effect being told that immigrants were a big problem. A Warwick University study into the policy found that many people reported harassment for being 'illegal immigrants' when they had settled status or were British citizens.[22]

When the UN Special Rapporteur on Contemporary Forms of Racism, Racial Discrimination, Xenophobia and Related Intolerance, Professor Tendayi Achiume, visited the UK in 2018, she found the hostile environment policy was:

> destroying the lives and livelihoods of racial and ethnic minority communities more broadly, including many that have been instrumental to the prosperity of this nation for decades, and are rightful claimants of citizenship status.[23]

The policy had, the Special Rapporteur argued, permeated so many aspects of life that:

a hostile environment ostensibly created for and formally restricted to irregular immigrants, is in effect, a hostile environment for all racial and ethnic communities and individuals in the UK. This is because ethnicity continues to be deployed in the public and private sector as a proxy for legal immigration status.[24]

The most egregious consequence was the human rights violations and indignities suffered by members of the Afro-Caribbean British population who now found themselves caught by the new legislation. The Windrush scandal first came to widespread public attention in 2017 when *The Guardian* newspaper began reporting the experiences of long-standing residents of the UK who had been wrongly detained as undocumented migrants, often denied legal rights.[25]

Those from Commonwealth countries who had arrived in the UK prior to 1973, often with their parents who had come in response to the country's post-war labour shortage, were at that time citizens of the UK and Colonies and had an automatic 'right of abode' in the UK. No documentation was given at the time to state this and unless they had subsequently applied for a British passport (and up until 1985 they could still travel on their UK and Colonies passport), they now had to prove that their residency pre-dated 1973 by supplying the Home Office with at least one official document from every year they had lived here before that date. Failure to meet this near-impossible requirement meant they were classed as undocumented migrants, with the direct result that they could lose their jobs, housing, access to healthcare, bank accounts, benefit entitlements, driving licences, and much else. Many were placed in immigration detention centres, and some were deported to countries they hadn't seen since they were children.[26] The lives of those impacted and their families were destroyed.

It was, as even a review for the Home Office in 2020 concluded, the result of 'a profound institutional failure' to protect a group perfectly legally entitled to be in the UK, from the impact of the hostile environment.[27] The Conservative government, who by now had rebranded the hostile environment as the 'compliance environment', promised compensation, but little was delivered and the unit set up to deliver it was subsequently dismantled. While the Labour government subsequently promised to ensure that those affected receive full and swift compensation,[28] many of the hostile environment policies remain in place but under its new name of compliance.

Shifting the rhetoric from hostile to compliance and tackling the worst excesses of the policies does not alter the main thrust of the impact of these policies. Indeed, the Labour government has, if anything, ramped up the rhetoric against 'illegal' migrants and has been keen to boast of a crackdown.

In May 2025, the Home Office released video footage of alleged immigration offenders in handcuffs being forced onto a plane for deportation. It was, the Home Office announced, 'the first time' it had 'shared images of the inner working of the removals process'.[29] The aim, much like Theresa May's poster campaign, was, the Home Office explained, to send 'a clear signal' to illegal immigrants that they were not welcome. Then, in November 2025, the new Home Secretary, Shabana Mahmood, announced tougher new rules, adopting the language of the far right by talking of 'asylum shopping', and of illegal migration 'destabilising communities'.[30] The lessons as to what this sort of messaging sent to those in the UK perfectly legally had not been learnt; nor was it likely to succeed in driving down the numbers of asylum seekers for, as discussed below, the drivers of this lay elsewhere.[31]

In the meantime, Brexit had transformed legal immigration into the UK.

How Brexit has increased the poverty risks for migrants

When the UK voted to leave the EU back in 2016, one of the reasons proposed by those in favour was to 'take back control'.

Though never really defined or elaborated, a key aspect of the slogan's appeal reflected concern about the extent of migration to the UK from the EU.[32] In the year to March 2016, before the referendum, EU net migration had peaked at over 280,000, with EU citizens contributing a high share of the net migration into the UK.[33]

EU citizens coming to the UK were, pre-Brexit, treated very differently to non-EU migrants. As EU citizens, they had an unconditional right to reside in the UK for up to three months, and if they worked in the UK, they, and their dependents, had the right to the same welfare benefits as UK citizens; rights that were reciprocally granted to UK citizens in other EU countries. Up until 2014, job-seeking EU migrants also had similar rights though they became more restricted after that and were excluded from claiming JSA after six months and from claiming housing benefit and council tax reduction. Even so, this was far more generous than the rights for international workers on visas in the UK.

For non-EU migrants, entry was severely restricted. For those applying for a work visa there were various salary thresholds, quotas and skill levels, along with the need for sponsorship from an employer; for those seeking a family visa to join a partner in the UK, proof was needed of the relationship; and for a student visa, there were quota limits and strict time restrictions on the length of stay in the UK. All had to pay application fees, often high, and applicants could ultimately be refused entry. Since 2011, visas for low-skilled workers were largely restricted to those for seasonal workers, domestic workers, or those applying for work visas connected to a 'shortage occupation'. Moreover, all those entering, whether on work, family, or student visas, had very limited social rights; as a condition of their visa they had 'no recourse to public funds' (NRPF), meaning they were not entitled to most benefits, social housing or other housing help, and had a requirement to pay a healthcare surcharge for themselves and their dependents.

How destitution is designed into the UK's immigration system

Denying access to certain services and benefits to which long-term UK nationals are entitled has long been part of the country's immigration policies. From the 1980s onwards migrants granted temporary permission to live in the UK had NRPF as a condition of their visa and successive governments had taken further steps to limit eligibility to public funds for increasing categories of migrants.[34] Only migrants who had, with some exceptions, lived in the UK for five years or more could apply for 'indefinite leave to remain' status and thereby gain the entitlements of UK citizens. This process could be extremely lengthy, as well as fraught and costly, meaning that many migrants to the UK continued to have very limited social rights, despite having often settled in the UK, worked and paid their taxes for years. The Migration Observatory at the University of Oxford estimated that in 2020 around 1.376 million people in the UK had NRPF attached to their visa,[35] of whom four in ten had lived in the UK for over five years and one in ten for over a decade.[36]

Not surprisingly therefore, prior to the UK leaving the EU, non-EU migrants to the UK were more likely to be in poverty than EU migrants (and indeed non-migrants).[37] Much of this risk was dependent on the types of jobs being undertaken once in the UK; clearly those coming in with visas for higher-skilled jobs were much less likely to be in poverty. But for those coming in to cover shortages of workers in low-paid jobs – such as the social care sector – were much more likely to be in poverty than UK or EU nationals, simply because of their status as having very limited rights to benefits and having to pay the health surcharge.

When the UK formally left the EU on 1 January 2021, freedom of movement from the EU ended, though by then migration from the EU had already dropped substantially. Since then, all migrants have been treated 'equally', having the same limited social rights, including NRPF status and payments for healthcare. A new points-based system was introduced which was designed to exclude the vast majority of people earning between £20,480 and £25,600 a year, and anyone earning less than £20,480 from accessing work visas. The aim, according to the government, was, firstly, to bring down immigration altogether and secondly, to severely limit the number of low-paid migrants, forcing UK employers to be more productive, rather than relying on cheap labour, and to thereby lift wages.[38]

The first aim has, so far, completely failed. As can be seen in Figure 7.1, net long-term migration to the UK (that is, people coming to the UK for more than 12 months minus those leaving), rose rapidly, reaching record levels in 2022 and 2023 of over 850,000, more than double its pre-Brexit level in 2015

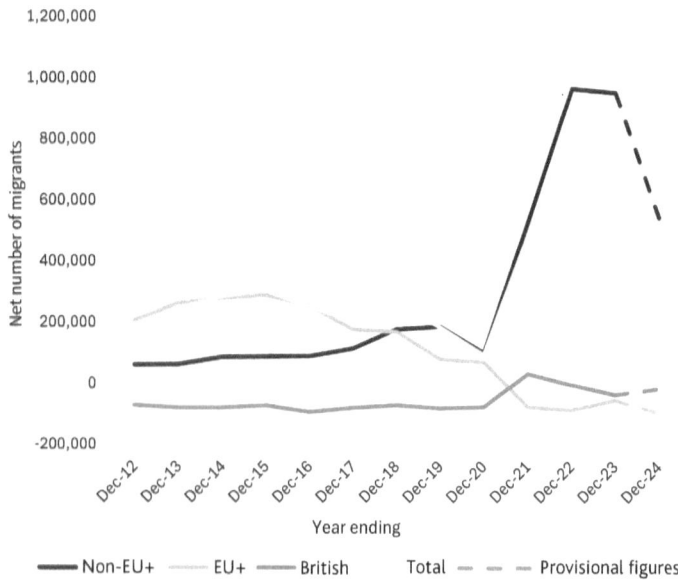

Figure 7.1: Net long-term migration 2012 to 2024

Note: EU+ covers EU countries plus Malta, Cyprus, and Croatia.
Source: ONS, long-term migration series, Figure 2[39]

of some 300,000.[40] It subsequently dropped in 2024, largely as a result of new restrictions introduced by the Conservative government in early 2024 including a ban on partners and children of care workers and most overseas students, and an increase in the salary threshold for general skilled workers to £38,700. Even so, it remains far higher than its pre-Brexit level. Moreover, as seen in Figure 7.1, the pattern has changed, with a sharp drop in net migration from the EU and associated areas as more people left for the EU than arrived from it and a sharp rise in the numbers arriving from non-EU countries.

As to the second aim, many felt that there was no reason to think that low-paid wages would rise as a result of limiting immigration. As Oxford University's Migration Observatory points out, 'past research has generally found that immigration has limited impacts on wages'.[41] Similarly, the New Economics Foundation (NEF) finds that 'there is no correlation between increases in immigration and decreases in real wages of less-skilled occupations'.[42]

Unless other actions were taken to raise wages, what seemed more likely was labour shortages in occupations where wages fell below the minimum salary levels set for migrants by the new system, and which had been heavily dependent on migrant labour from the EU, occupations such as hospitality, cleaning and domestic service, and the care sector. This, in turn, risked fuelling the exploitation of migrants here legally but on limited work visas or student visas;[43] as the Gangmasters and Labour Abuse Authority noted 'unscrupulous employers may look to fill this void by exploiting vulnerable workers'.[44] The Authority had, for example, found migrants on student visas being taken on by agencies supplying workers to the care sector, and then sleeping at work on mattresses on the floor in cramped, cold, and unsanitary conditions. In the process, they were being forced to work more than 20 hours a week, thereby breaching their visa conditions. And this made them into illegal migrants and therefore even more vulnerable.[45]

While the 2015 Modern Slavery Act has made it an offence to require people to perform forced labour, the government has at the same time created an environment around migration that encourages that very exploitation.[46] Most victims of human trafficking, for example, do not report the severe abuse they suffer, fearing, accurately, that they will not subsequently be supported and that, despite the act, they will not be granted leave to remain.[47] This effectively gives exploitative employers impunity to underpay and exploit their workers which, in turn, puts employers who want to be fair at a disadvantage and continues the cycle of low pay in these sectors.

As predicted, what happened was that shortages in key low-paid occupations – notably the health and social care sector – became so acute that new occupations were swiftly added by the Conservative government to the list of 'shortage occupations' allowed to pay below the minimum rate set by the points system.[48] Large numbers of low-paid migrant workers were as a result allowed visas into the country to keep essential services in these designated 'shortage occupations' running and were a key driver in the rise of immigration post 2022.

The Labour government, in its Immigration White Paper released in May 2025, set out its plans to control immigration numbers, including making migrants wait longer for British citizenship (discussed later) and closing the care route to immigration, pledging a domestic skills initiative to improve training of UK nationals to reduce demand for overseas workers. But as there is a continuing acute staffing crisis in social care,[49] and without action to increase pay, this seems like wishful thinking.

In the meantime, low-paid migrant workers, because of their lack of entitlements, face a high risk of poverty.

The impact of having 'no recourse to public funds'

For many, living with NRPF results in extreme hardship. Citizens Advice, in a 2021 study of a representative sample of migrants with NRPF,[50] found that without access to UC, tax credits, child benefit, or other benefits, most could not afford essential services: over 80 per cent were behind with at least one of their bills while 75 per cent had faced negative impacts such as not being able to heat or light their home, afford suitable clothing or shoes, or simply to eat.[51] As 'John', on a tier 2 visa for skilled workers sponsored by an approved employer, explained:

> It's been a lot of struggle, living to make ends meet with no entitlement to public funds. To pay rent, shelter and some other bills. I have been in debt to friends, that I lost some because I was unable to pay back; even my little salary is gone on debt and loans.[52] ('John', mixed White and Black African man)

Nearly one in five of those with NRPF status had at times been unable to feed themselves with migrants with children particularly badly affected. Families with NRPF status are not entitled to free school meals and, without this support, their children can go hungry for long periods of time. Aisha, in the UK on a family visa, explains the problems:

> I'm not going to lie to you, we would rather stay without food but I pay my rent, because I can't imagine where we would go. We can't afford private housing, we can't get support from the state for our housing, that really, really freaks me out. I would rather not eat for days and pay rent.[53] (Aisha, Black African, single mother)

To assess the financial impact of living with NRPF, researchers at the University of Southampton have calculated the net incomes (after taxes and benefits) of non-migrant and migrant workers in different types of households and in different types of work. They found that the net income of migrant households was consistently lower, pushing some migrant households in exactly the same type of job, household, and location as a non-migrant household into poverty where the non-migrant household was not pushed into poverty. For those where the non-migrant household was also in poverty, the depth of poverty of the migrant household was far deeper.[54]

By far the greatest difference was for households with children. Excluded from the social rights and benefits for children of UK citizens and, having to pay health surcharges for each household member, migrant households with children need to be earning well above average earnings to be out of poverty. For those on lower wages, where a non-migrant worker was likely to be in poverty, the migrant workers' situation was desperate: thus a worker in a shortage occupation earning just over £20,000 with a non-earning partner and a one-year-old would be in poverty whatever their citizenship status, but the migrant household would have a net income of just £222 a week compared to the non-migrant's £468 a week.[55]

Living with NRPF leaves households extremely vulnerable to any unforeseen change in their circumstances. Though those with NRPF status were eligible for furlough during the COVID-19 pandemic, if they were made unemployed, they still remained unable to claim most other forms of welfare such as UC. This left many dependent on friends, charities, religious groups, or other such voluntary organisations just to survive.[56] Similarly, such families were particularly badly affected by the soaring inflation of 2022/23 as the various emergency payments the government put in place could not be claimed by those with NRPF.

The JRF's 2023 report into destitution backs up these findings. While most of those who were destitute were born in the UK (72 per cent), migrants were disproportionately affected. They found:

> There has been an especially rapid increase in the size of the destitute migrant population since 2019. Migrants experiencing destitution are seriously and

increasingly lacking in access to both cash and in-kind forms of support.[57]

The report found that the overall rise in the numbers of migrants who were destitute was driven by a rise in the number of destitute migrants who were not from the European Economic Area and who were not asylum seekers. Their numbers rose as a proportion of the destitute population from 10 per cent in 2019 to 13 per cent in 2022.[58] And this group had fallen into destitution because, though generally here legally and often doing vital work, they did not receive benefits, were much less likely to be eligible for other forms of governmental support locally delivered and often did not have family in this country to turn to.

It is such findings that make the latest proposed changes to the immigration system making it harder to move from temporary visa status to indefinite leave to remain (and with that most of the rights that UK citizens have) so concerning. In the Immigration White Paper, the Labour government set out its intention to double the standard qualifying period from five to ten years, with some exceptions including family members of British citizens. In addition, it proposed a reduced qualifying period for those had 'earned settlement', a distinction to be based on 'points-based contributions to the UK economy and society'.[59] What that means is unclear. If, as seems likely, it refers to higher-paid migrants, it is particularly pernicious, as it is lower-paid migrants who would be kept in poverty by any extension to the qualifying period. It is this group who are hit particularly hard by having no recourse to public funds and for whom the costs of renewing their visa (in 2025 up to around £1,500 for a skilled worker for a three-year visa) and the annual paid-in-advance health surcharge (in 2025, £1,035 per year for most visas) can be devastating, leading many into debt.[60] For those migrants living and working in the UK perfectly legally these new rules are devastating; they feed a narrative that immigrants are not welcome and increase their vulnerability.

If the aim of the policy, as seems to be the case, is to reduce immigration, there is little evidence that longer waits for residence reduce migration levels.[61] What is clear is that increased qualifying periods would push more lower-paid migrants into poverty and hinder integration.

In the meantime, as well as the rise in legal migration, there has also been a sharp rise in illegal migration. This has largely driven by external, geo political factors, in the numbers of people fleeing persecution and other, often life-threatening situations, and trying to seek safety and protection in the UK – and a lack of legal routes to claim asylum. While those arriving illegally still form a small proportion of those migrating to the UK – those arriving by small boats account for only 3 to 4 per cent of overall immigration[62] – it has been rising and has increasingly led to a dangerous agenda, fuelled by the far right.

A race to the bottom

Under the UN Refugee Convention,[63] first established in 1951 in the aftermath of the Holocaust and the failures of countries before and during the Second World War to provide refuge for Jews trying to escape the Nazi regime,[64] seeking asylum from persecution is a human right to which everyone is entitled. Moreover, those seeking asylum do not need to go the nearest safe country, they are perfectly entitled to seek asylum in the UK. Indeed, the Convention requires all countries to share in the responsibility of providing asylum to refugees – not just neighbouring ones or those that are the first landing point.

Yet for the majority of those seeking asylum it has, with the exception of those from a few countries, become almost impossible to come to the UK in any way permitted by immigration rules. It is illegal to get into the UK without a visa and yet if you apply for a visa from within the country from which you seek asylum and are thought to be an asylum seeker you will be turned down. So, most asylum seekers end up taking dangerous, and not authorised, routes to get here, often in the hands of people smugglers. It is these rules that have pushed up the number of crossings made across the Channel in small boats, the backlog of asylum claims, and the dire situation of most asylum seekers, who are often left in limbo for years and in severe poverty.

The only exceptions are for those from Hong Kong, Ukraine and, to a lesser extent, Afghanistan. For these countries there are bespoke visa schemes which the then-Conservative government argued formed a new suite of 'safe and legal (humanitarian) routes' into the UK.[65] The schemes operate, however, on a different basis from the guiding humanitarian provisions based on the UN 1951 Refugee Convention, in that they explicitly discriminate on the grounds of nationality.[66]

The Hong Kong British National (Overseas) visa, established in 2021, is embedded in British colonial history and results from the Government's judgement that the 'One Country, Two Systems' solution agreed with China when Hong Kong was handed over, had broken down. The bespoke route that was set up for those from Hong Kong seeking, as a result, to move to the UK is more like ancestry and other visa routes than humanitarian ones for asylum: for each family member, you have to pay a visa fee, have to be able to support yourself for six months, have NRPF, and have to pay a health surcharge (up to for £3,120 for five years), none of which apply to those who successfully claim asylum.[67] However, like successful asylum seekers, those coming into the UK via the Hong Kong visa route can apply for indefinite leave to remain after five years and citizenship after a further year, though whether the government will try to retrospectively impose their proposed longer qualification period on this group is unclear. As of June 2024, around 150,000 people have arrived in the UK on this visa.[68]

The UK's Ukraine visa scheme followed the large-scale displacement brought about by Russia's invasion of Ukraine in February 2022 and was essentially a way of bypassing asylum application. There were two routes, the first for those with family members in the UK, and the second for those sponsored by someone in the UK. Successful applicants to either scheme had three years' leave to remain in the UK, the right to work, and a one-off interim payment of £200 administered by local authorities. Successful applicants were also allowed to claim benefits, though those providing accommodation under the scheme for family members could themselves experience a reduction in welfare benefit entitlement.[69] By June 2024, just over 209,000 people had arrived on these visas, most arriving in the first half of 2022.[70] After three years, applicants can apply for an extension, but the overall aim is to make the stay temporary rather than provide a route to settlement. In this respect, it is unlike those who successfully gain asylum and thereby are granted refugee status and gain the permanent right to remain.

The bespoke visa routes set up for Afghan nationals who, after the evacuation of Kabul by US and NATO forces in 2021 were at risk by staying in Afghanistan are more similar in terms of the eligibility and rights they bring to those granted refugee status. Successful applicants gain permission to work, access to education and healthcare, are eligible to apply for benefits classed as public funds, and can, after five years, apply for citizenship. However, the eligibility criteria for these schemes are very limited and, in practice, obtaining such visas is extremely difficult. The process lacks clarity and consistency and is convoluted, often requiring information and documentation which is near impossible to obtain under the Taliban. It can result in the need to travel to third countries such as Pakistan for biometrics and visas, which puts the lives of applicants in danger.[71] The numbers getting visas through this route has been low: around 29,000 between the start of the schemes in early 2021 to the second quarter of 2024, of whom more than half had come in the initial period during 2021.[72]

Ineligible for these schemes, or unable to access them, many Afghans instead try to travel to the UK to seek asylum. Indeed, since the start of 2022, this has become the main route for

Afghans seeking protection in the UK with the result that, by July 2024, around 24,400 Afghan nationals arriving in the UK through illegal routes claimed asylum in the UK, compared to roughly 12,600 Afghans who were resettled through the bespoke schemes.[73] Their journey is dangerous, with most crossing the Channel in small boats, but for those who do make the journey and apply for asylum, the chances of success once their application is heard is extremely high, around 95 per cent on initial decision.[74] Between the last quarter of 2022 and 2024 (the latest figures), Afghans have formed the largest proportion by nationality of people crossing the Channel in small boats,[75] and one would have thought that improving the Afghan resettlement schemes would be one easy way of reducing the numbers of small boat crossings and the additional pressures placed on an already broken asylum processing system.

But this has not been the approach and without legal routes, the number of asylum seekers arriving by unauthorised routes continued to increase. And this led to a huge backlog in cases. The Migration Observatory calculates that the share of asylum applications that received an initial decision within six months fell from 87 per cent in the second quarter of 2014 to 6 per cent in the third quarter of 2023.[76] By the end of June 2024, the asylum caseload consisted of 224,700 cases, quadruple the number in 2014.[77]

When then-Prime Minister, Rishi Sunak, declared that 'stopping the boats' was one of his top five priorities,[78] he did not have in mind ways of ensuring those seeking asylum could come to the country legally, and thus have no need for small boat crossings, but criminalising those who came to the country without documentation, enabling immediate deportation and ensuring their claims could not be heard. And this is what came to pass in the Illegal Immigration Act of 2023 (which is still in place). This gave the government additional powers to detain and remove anyone coming to the country without permission and to make any asylum claim inadmissible for anyone who arrived in the UK without authorisation on or after 7 May 2023.

The claim was that the act would remove the 'incentive to make dangerous small boat crossings',[79] but experts argued that this misunderstands what drives people fleeing persecution and would not stop people coming to the UK. Research, including the Home Office's own research, finds that most trying to cross do not know UK law and would be unlikely, even if they did, to be put off.[80] The most important factor influencing asylum numbers are global developments such as war, repression, or famine.

It also seemed unlikely that the new detention and deportation provisions would be workable. Under the act, deportation for those arriving illegally can only be to their home country if that country is deemed safe, which excludes the countries of origin of many migrants arriving illegally. Otherwise, it must be to a third 'safe' country. At the time of the act's passing, the then-Conservative government made the highly contentious claim that this country would be Rwanda. On taking power, the Labour government abandoned this Rwanda plan and looked at Albania instead to offshore failed asylum seekers.[81] Albania was, however, not interested, with Albania's Prime Minister, Edi Rama, accusing Britain of 'looking for places to dump immigrants'.[82] To date, nothing has come of these plans for third-country 'return hubs', nor does it seem likely to.[83]

The Labour government also shifted the talk from stopping the boats to cracking criminal gangs and to this end has created of a new Border Security Command with stronger powers.[84] At the same time, the new government restarted the process for making an asylum claim for those who had already arrived illegally, a process which had stalled under the Conservative government. The number of asylum-related returns increased, mainly to countries which had low asylum success rates rather than conflict countries. As a result, the backlog of claims started to reduce,[85] though at over 90,000 at the end of 2024, it was still high by historical standards.[86] The government has also come to an agreement with the French government for a 'one in one out' migrant deal where some of those arriving here illegally are returned to France in exchange for an equivalent number of asylum seekers who have not tried to enter the country illegally.[87] The pilot plan is to cover 2,600 people a year – about 6 per cent of the total number of crossings, and while not enough to make a substantial difference, it does open up the possibility of a legal way into the country for asylum seekers.

But overall, the Labour government's aim remains the same, trying to stop people seeking asylum in the UK through securitisation and enforcement. In February 2025, the government issued new Home Office guidance largely reinstating the previous government's policy of refusing citizenship to those who had entered via small boats. It was condemned by those who campaigned on behalf of refugees, who, along with many religious groups, wrote to the Home Office arguing that it risked turning asylum seekers into 'second class individuals' and risked 'playing into a toxic politics that pits "us vs them" and is then manipulated by the far right to bring hate and disorder to our streets'.[88] And indeed such criticisms proved to be prescient.

In September 2025 the largest 'nationalist' rally in recent memory, with some 100,000 or so marchers, took place in London under the banner of 'Unite the Kingdom'. Organised by the far-right activist Stephen Yaxley-Lennon, known as Tommy Robinson, the crowd expressed explicitly racist views, calling for migrants, illegal or otherwise, to be 'sent back'. But the government was not to be deflected, announcing yet more sweeping reforms.[89] While the proposals included new safe routes to the UK, the key to a more humanitarian system, these were limited and tightly capped. The main thrust was harsher treatment of those granted asylum, including the wait before being able to apply for the right to remain rising from five years to up to twenty years, with a requirement to reapply every two and a half years to retain their refugee status. This is both cruel and economically damaging.[90] It will mean that migrants are even more likely to live in poverty than they are currently.

How the UK's treatment of asylum seekers creates new depths of poverty

Contrary to the myths that fuelled the 2024 riots, which still persist, and the government's claim of generosity,[91] those awaiting a decision on their asylum claim are not living in luxury. On arriving in the UK, the large majority will not know anyone or have anywhere to go and will be housed by the Home Office in an accommodation centre, usually hostel-style accommodation of poor quality. This is meant to be temporary and after three or four weeks, asylum seekers are meant to be moved into dispersed accommodation – self-contained flats or houses, either single or shared.

Partly because of the backlog, partly because of the rise in numbers seeking asylum, and partly because of a shortage of housing, after 2020 this broke down and asylum seekers were instead being moved into 'contingency accommodation', which includes the use of hotels, one of the factors that proved so controversial for the rioters. The Migration Observatory estimates that while only 5 per cent of supported asylum seekers were housed in contingency accommodation or an accommodation centre in the first quarter of 2020, by the first quarter of 2024, this had risen to 41 per cent, of which the majority (68 per cent) were in hotels.[92] Whether in temporary, contingency or dispersed accommodation, the quality will, as a matter of policy choice, be of a low standard.

Since 2011, the provision of asylum accommodation has been outsourced by the Home Office to private contractors; in 2019 there were three: Clearsprings, Mears, and Serco. The private providers are looking for the cheapest accommodation possible. This will often be in some of the more run-down areas of the country where there is surplus housing and cheaper hotels; the distribution of asylum seekers per number of residents is far higher in the north-east and north-west of England than the south-east. For those housed in self-contained accommodation, the housing is often in a poor state of repair, often unhygienic.⁹³ The asylum seeker is given no choice over the accommodation, and rental agreements are with the private contractor, not those from whom the house is being rented, resulting, in effect, in no right of complaint when repairs are needed. As one participant with lived experience of asylum accommodation explained for a study conducted by the Institute for Public Policy Research (IPPR):

> So, I was like, 'Would you tell me, just look in my eyes, would you be able to live in this flat?' (Male, 18–24)⁹⁴

For those in hostels, hotels, and other large contingency sites awaiting dispersal accommodation, standards are often even worse. In recent years, there have been large numbers of reports of overcrowding, insanitary conditions, infestations, lack of cleanliness and hygiene, mould, unhealthy food, a lack of facilities for children, and concerns over shared rooms and isolation. Participants in the IPPR study outlined some of the problems:⁹⁵

> We will stay in the room [with] four in the room, just one room. No cleaning, no bedsheet, you will sleep on that bedsheet for a month. (Male, 25–34)

> There are no facilities nearby, there are no buses around either, so we felt really isolated. And the transportation is also a problem, to go to the hospital or GP or the pharmacy. (Male, 35–44)

> I was given the wrong period products and kept staining the bed. (Female, unknown age)

And at times, safety was compromised:

> I was sharing a room with a minor, so that was quite shocking to me, to share the room, the accommodation

with a minor person, and nothing was done to have him his own privacy as well as protection. Because I am an LGBT person, and there could be some kind of allegation of inappropriateness. Although the person is not homophobic that I am sharing with, but he, himself, needs to be protected, too. So, it was shocking for me to have a minor sharing the room. (Male, unknown age)

The accommodation is dirty, smelly and I don't feel protected staying there, because I get sexual harassment in there because they mix and match in that floor. (Female, unknown age)

The NGO Refugee and Asylum Participatory Action Research (RAPAR) has been challenging such conditions in hotels run by Serco in the Greater Manchester region.[96] They report of residents in one hotel facing a scabies outbreak, of rubbish being piled in corridors, and insects found in the food.[97] Other residents came forward voicing concerns that their school-age children were not receiving education, to which they have a statutory right, and others of safeguarding concerns. RAPAR reported their findings, denied by Serco, to the statutory authorities but despite the seriousness of the allegations, RAPAR found that 'no evidence of meaningful investigation by any implicated statutory authority, or their privatised subcontractors, into the human rights violation allegations asserted by hotel residents has been produced'.[98]

On top of these poor housing conditions, those seeking asylum have no financial independence. While awaiting a decision, those seeking asylum are not allowed to work, with some exceptions for those who have waited over a year and for which the delay is not their fault. For those in accommodation centres or in hotels or other contingency accommodations providing food, the government provides an allowance of around £9 a week to cover the purchase of other 'necessities'. For those in dispersed, that is, self-contained accommodation, there is an allowance of just under £50 a week to pay for food, clothing, and toiletries.

Such low amounts are designing destitution into the system.[99] Though asylum seekers form a small proportion of overall immigration (around 7 per cent in 2023), and over time are a tiny proportion of the UK population (around 0.6 per cent),[100] asylum seekers formed nearly one in ten of the overall numbers in destitution in the UK in 2022.[101]

At the same time, and as a direct result of the large overall caseload, the costs of operating the asylum system have been rising rapidly. In 2022/23, it was nearly £4 billion, up from around half a billion a year in the years up to 2015.[102] And much of this will go into the hands of the private contractors.

If there was a properly functioning asylum system, none of this would be necessary. Most people coming to this country seeking asylum are successful in their claim. Two-thirds of asylum applications submitted from 2018 to 2020 are estimated to have received a grant of asylum-related protection, either on initial decision or after appeal, by June 2022. The success rate varies by country with, for example, Syria, Eritrea, and Iran (along with Afghanistan) being high and Brazil, Albania, and India being low. This knowledge should enable a more streamlined and humane system that allows for bespoke routes to apply for asylum from outside the UK. For what we have at present is a system that takes an enormous psychological toll on those who have already faced tremendous trauma:

> There were times I think of suicidal thoughts, think of taking my life, but I had just one hope ... that I have a family. That was the only thing that was keeping me going. ... Up till now, I'm still battling with the trauma and the stress. Whenever I think of that life I've lived ... I feel so sad, I feel ashamed of myself. And the only

crime I committed was to come and seek asylum. That was the only crime I committed.[103] (Male, 25–34)

It was such vulnerable people that faced the baying mobs in August 2024, scenes to be repeated in anti-immigration riots in Northern Ireland in June 2025,[104] and in Epping, Essex, in September 2025, where residents of a local hotel housing asylum seekers were attacked by firecrackers and smoke bombs. While in Epping, the protesters' anger had been triggered by the arrest of one of the asylum seekers for sexual assault,[105] more generally it was migrants who were being blamed for the problems in the area: the breakdown of services, the lack of housing and jobs, and the decline in the civic fabric.

The cause of these problems is not asylum seekers, or immigration more generally, but the deliberate political choices that have left such communities behind and so many in the UK impoverished – and it is this, in turn, that has led to anti-migrant attitudes. As a large cross country EU study of attitudes to migration found, anti migration attitudes are strongest where there are low levels of migrations and 'those who feel politically disempowered, financially insecure and without social support are more likely to become extremely negative towards migrants'.[106] What are needed are solutions to the real and enduring problems of impoverishment – and these need to be found within the context of the climate crisis already upon us which, in itself, will increase global migration.

8

The interlocking challenges of climate change and poverty

As the UK welcomed in the new year of 2025, storms battered the country. Weather warnings were issued across the nation.[1] In Merseyside, the River Sankey broke its banks, flooding nearby properties in the Haydock area including that of Daniel Pownall, his partner and their two children who were woken in the early hours by neighbours screaming 'we are going under'.

'Just looking at the devastation downstairs from your microwave to your fridges floating in the front room', Mr Pownall told BBC Radio Merseyside, 'there was nothing we could do. It was like a scene from the *Titanic*.'[2] Only the Christmas tree in his living room was left standing.

Overall, the Environment Agency estimated that some 1,400 properties had been flooded in the first ten days of the year. What had previously been seen as 'once in a hundred year' events were becoming more and more frequent – consistent with what might be expected from climate change.[3]

Over the previous year, multiple weather records had been broken: in the south of England it had been the wettest February since 1836 and across England and Wales the warmest February on record, in May average mean temperatures across the UK were at a new high, in the autumn ten counties across south and central England experienced their wettest September on record, and by October and November, multiple storms and high winds were hitting the west of the country.[4] The year as a whole was the fourth warmest since mean temperature records began in 1884.[5] The Met Office, the UK's official and highly respected meteorological service not noted for its overstatement, concluded that climate statistics from the year showed that the UK was heading outside of the 'envelope of historical weather observations'.[6]

Across the world, the impact has been more severe.[7] In 2024, record-breaking high temperatures were reached across the globe, with temperatures just short of 50°C turning some cities, such as New Delhi, into life-threatening heat traps.[8] In 2024, for the first time, the amount by which average global temperatures were above pre-industrial levels exceeded 1.5°C,[9] the initial limit that had been set as the target to protect future generations. And with rising heat comes the risk of more frequent and more intense storms: devastating floods hit countries across the world, bringing catastrophic damage in their wake.[10]

The impacts of climate change were no longer just in the future – they were already beginning to be seen. Across the world, thousands died and millions were displaced. 'This is climate breakdown – in real time', the UN Secretary-General António Guterres observed in his 2025 New Year message.[11]

Questions as to how to integrate climate change policies with those aimed at social justice and poverty reduction are becoming ever more urgent.

Climate injustice

While the impact of global warming poses an existential threat to peoples across the world, it is not one that is equally shared. A special report in 2018 by the Intergovernmental Panel on Climate Change on the impacts of global warming of 1.5°C above pre-industrial levels concluded that global warming would disproportionately affect disadvantaged and vulnerable populations through food insecurity, higher food prices, income losses, lost livelihood opportunities, adverse health impacts and population displacements.[12] It estimated that 122 million additional people could experience extreme poverty, mainly due to higher food prices and declining health, with substantial income losses for the poorest 20 per cent across 92 countries.

But these impacts spill out globally with consequent disruptions to the world's economic systems. The Institute and Faculty for Actuaries, not known as a radical environmental campaigning body, has estimated that 'the global economy could face a 50 per cent loss in GDP between 2070 and 2090 unless immediate action on risks posed by the climate crisis in taken'.[13] The UK is not isolated from these wider impacts, in particular relating to trade, migration, and food security.

The UK imports about 40 per cent or so of the food it consumes, with the level of imports being particularly high for fruit – only 17 per cent of which is produced within the UK – and, to a lesser extent, for vegetables.[14] Of the fruit and vegetable imports, 3.8 per cent comes from countries highly vulnerable to climate change and 13.8 per cent from countries moderately vulnerable.[15] Combined with changing weather patterns also affecting UK agricultural production levels,[16] shortages become more likely – and this would be expected to push up prices making it harder for low-income households to maintain a healthy diet.

Climate change will increase global migration patterns as areas become less habitable due to droughts creating severe water shortages, crop failure resulting in famine and starvation, sea level rises threatening coastal areas, and natural disasters leaving people homeless and jobless. The extent of climate-induced migration to be expected in future years is difficult to estimate but is generally accepted to be in the hundreds of millions.[17]

The response of countries less affected by climate change, and therefore better placed to accept migrants, has been to increase border security and barriers to migration. Many of the world's biggest carbon emitters – countries responsible for almost half of the world's historic greenhouse gas emissions – spend more than twice as much on border and immigration enforcement as they spent on climate finance to help developing and vulnerable countries protect their people and economies against climate disasters.[18] But simply upping security, as seen in Chapter 7, will not stop people who are desperate and can no longer survive in their own countries from trying to move elsewhere. What is needed is far higher levels of finance for mitigation programmes within those countries – finance that so far has been inadequate[19] – as well as higher levels of international aid. Soon after taking over in January 2025, President Donald Trump decided instead to slash US funding for foreign humanitarian aid, despite the grave impacts that would follow. Although widely condemned by humanitarian organisations,[20] other Western countries followed suit. In May 2025, the Labour government decided to dramatically cut UK aid, a move that is not just inhumane but, particularly in the light of the impacts of climate change, shortsighted.[21]

There is a fundamental inequality at the heart the climate crisis for it is the richer countries, and richer people within those countries, that contribute by far most to the carbon dioxide (CO_2) emissions that drive global warming while its impacts are most severely felt by poorer countries and within all countries by those who are poorer.

The unequal impact of climate change in the UK

Overall, more deprived neighbourhoods are more likely to be affected by the impacts of climate change than richer ones, while at the same time being less able to cope.

Looking first at the impact of rising temperatures, the Met Office's climate modelling projects that in summer while all parts of the UK will get somewhat warmer, the greatest increases will be seen in the already-warmer south of England.[22] Within this overall pattern, cities, in particular, are more likely to be warmer than surrounding areas, simply because buildings retain heat and there is less green space, the 'urban heat island effect'. And, because many of the most deprived areas are in inner cities, this makes deprived communities, particularly in London, more vulnerable overall than others.

Excess heat can lead to heat exhaustion, heatstroke, increased strain on the heart and heart attacks and, if body temperature is highly elevated, damage multiple organs. At worst, it increases the risk of dying, starting at temperatures above 24°C and continuing to rise, with 28°C triggering public health alerts.[23] Looking at 2022, a year in which temperatures in the UK exceeded 40°C for the first time, the Office for National Statistics estimates that there were between 3,300 and 5,600 heat-related deaths across the year.[24] In the absence of new adaptation strategies, estimates suggest this could rise to up 13,000 by the 2050s,[25] with the highest risk for those who are older and poorer and who live in inner cities in the south of England.

Older people and the very young are most at risk from these health impacts and of increased mortality rates, so the impact of heat and the resultant pressure on public services and well-being will very much depend on the demographic profile of an area. In addition, deprived households are already likely to have higher rates of ill-health and heart and respiratory problems, illnesses which, in particular, increase the risk from excess heat. Moreover, poorer households are less likely to be able to afford to cool their home or to make adaptations to make the house cooler, especially if they are low-income tenants.

Global warming will also change rainfall patterns in the UK with the Met Office predicting drier summers and wetter winters, with heavier rainfall when it does rain.[26] Along with sea level rises and more intense storm surges, this will lead to a substantial increase in the risk of flooding along rivers and coastal estuaries with the areas already at the greatest risk – notably

Yorkshire, the Humber, and the East Midlands – being the most affected.[27] Within these areas, it is the more deprived areas that generally face the greatest risk. This is partly because, historically, working-class terraces were more likely to have been built on low-lying flat areas next to rivers as industrialisation first took place.[28]

However, houses continue to be built in flood risk areas, indeed at a faster rate than elsewhere. The Resolution Foundation estimates that building in areas where there is some risk of flooding have grown 50 per cent faster than in areas where there is no risk,[29] while Aviva, the UK's largest home insurer, finds that 8 per cent of homes completed in the last decade have been built in areas with the highest risk of flooding and reports that one in eight (13 per cent) new-build residents say their home has been affected by flooding inside. Since such properties are likely to be cheaper to buy or rent, they are more likely to be occupied by low-income families.

At the same time, metropolitan areas, again areas where more deprived communities are more likely to live, will become more vulnerable to surface flooding, that is when heavy rainfall overwhelms the drainage system and the ability of the ground to absorb the rain.

Overall, climate change could take the total number of properties in areas at risk of flooding from rivers and the sea, and of surface flooding, to around 8 million by the middle of the century, that's one in four properties in England.[30] Impacting most heavily on poorer communities,[31] this will widen inequality.[32]

Only one in three low-income households (those in the bottom three household income deciles) has home insurance, with about the same percentage wanting it but not being able to afford it; the remaining third, many of whom will be younger, seem happy to take the risk or have too few contents to be worried.[33] This means that poorer households are often unable to bounce back as they struggle to replace what they once had.

As flood risks increase and insurance premiums continue to rise, this problem will intensify.

Of particular concern are the large number of homes built after 2009 in high flood-risk areas. These properties, because they were built after 2009, are excluded from the flood reinsurance scheme (Flood Re), a pooled fund set up by insurance companies in 2016 to make insurance for houses in the highest flood-risk areas more affordable.[34] As a result, home insurance for these new homes is virtually impossible to obtain. This is a complete failure of regulation which has placed all the financial risks associated with flooding on future homeowners and residents while the those who profited from building the house will have long since gone. The Labour government are pushing hard for housing growth, with a plan for 1.5 million new homes in five years, and on past patterns, unless regulation is tightened, 100,000 of these could be expected to be built in high-risk flood zones.[35]

Dealing with the impacts of climate change cannot be left to the individual; higher insurance premiums to pick up the costs of flood damage, and more money spent on cooling the home are not the answer. What's needed is a wide range of collective action, at governmental or regional level, to mitigate the impacts of the new weather patterns.

These would include a further stepping up of flood protection measures beyond the current, and improved, plans.[36] In its autumn budget in 2024, the Labour government promised to increase spending to £1.2 billion a year for 2024–25 and 2025–26, not far short of the £1.5 billion a year recommended by the National Infrastructure Committee. However, the government added that 'significant funding pressures' meant that 'it is necessary to review these plans from 2025–26'.[37] This would be short-sighted. Experts estimate that every £1 invested in flood defences prevents around £8 of damage, including £3 of direct saving to the government from damage is to publicly owned infrastructure.[38]

There also need to be tighter controls on housebuilding to ensure new builds are not in areas of flood risk; and higher housebuilding standards to take account of extreme heat as well as cold. It needs investment in the current housing stock to ensure more resilience to extreme weathers and changes to urban planning to ensure soakaway paving to better cope with heavy rains and more green space and trees to help lower summer temperatures. Perhaps above all, it needs far better management of the water supply system to ensure an adequate and safe supply during the hotter summers, including for agriculture, and a sewage and drainage system that can cope with intense rainfall.

England's failed experiment in water privatisation

As the impact of climate change becomes more apparent, there are increasing concerns about the security of the water supply and possible shortages. This has been made more acute by the high levels of leakages from the supply system with almost a fifth (19 per cent) of water supplies lost by water companies before reaching customers' taps,[39] and the complete lack of investment in new reservoirs over the last 40 years. By mid-2025, following a particularly dry spring, four regions of the UK – the East and West Midlands, the north-west and Yorkshire – had already declared drought status.[40]

There are also increasing concerns about surface flooding. In London, where Thames Water are in charge, the combination of increasingly heavy storms, rainfall on large areas of impermeable ground, and outdated Victorian drainage has already resulted in a water drainage system increasingly unable to cope. Homes and streets underwater have become an increasingly common occurrence in parts of the capital.[41]

Many see these problems as stemming from the privatisation of the water system and subsequent decades of underinvestment in infrastructure.[42]

The interlocking challenges of climate change and poverty

When water utilities were privatised in England and Wales (though not Scotland) by the Thatcher government in 1989, all existing debt was written off and it was promised that privatisation would lead to improved efficiency and greater investment without drawing on the taxpayer or government borrowing. Over subsequent years, with the exception of Wales where Welsh Water (Dŵr Cymru) became a not-for-profit company in 2001 and Scotland where water was not privatised, water companies became largely owned by international investors and private equity companies whose main aim was to maximise returns on their monopoly holdings.

To provide some outside control, new regulators were established: OFWAT and, later, the Environment Agency and National Resources Wales. OFWAT's brief was not to protect consumers but to ensure that companies had sufficient profits to meet their investment needs. There has been a continuing revolving door between OFWAT executives and the privatised water companies ever since it was established.[43] The Environment Agency and National Resources Wales were supposed to oversee environmental sustainability but have in recent years, faced with reduced budgets, struggled to do anything of the kind.

The end result of privatisation and the lack of proper financial regulation has been a system which has prioritised profits for shareholders over investment for the future, enriching shareholders while consumers, particularly poorer consumers, have paid the price.[44]

The justification for privatisation is that it leads to capital injection by shareholders for which they are rewarded by dividend and interest payments. But while there has been investment (albeit insufficient) this has not come from shareholders, but from consumers, through their bills.[45] Research has found that in almost every year since privatisation, consumers' bills directly covered the capital expenditure of the water companies. The high levels of dividend payments to shareholders have come from extracting the profits made,[46] leaving none to reinvest in improvements, and from complex financial engineering to increase investor returns by taking on huge levels of debt.[47] By 2023, the total of these debts amounted to £64.4 billion,[48] and the financing of interest payments on these debts again fell on consumers. In London, Thames Water's debts swallow up as much as 28 per cent of consumer bills,[49] while South East Water spent more on dividends and servicing its debt than on infrastructure in the two years to March 2022, a period in which consumers were at times left without running water.[50]

In 2023, OFWAT were given new powers to fine companies that paid excessive dividends and, in 2024, Thames Water was subject to an £18 million fine for a £37.5 million dividend it paid in 2023 and a £158.3 million dividend in 2024, a relatively small fine compared to the dividends extracted and one that will, in effect, end up being paid by consumers. In 2025, OFWAT gave permission to water companies to raise their prices over the next five years by 36 per cent (before inflation, which will be added on top) with these increases being front loaded with households paying comparatively more in the first years, with smaller increases over the following years.[51] Permission for these price rises was given to cover future investment; investment that should have already have been made from past bills but was not.

Consumers are still effectively being held to ransom by monopoly suppliers who face inadequate oversight. This really matters for low-income households because the end result has been that consumer bills have soared. Since privatisation bills have risen at twice the rate of inflation.[52] This is particularly problematic for low-income households because these bills are not optional; you cannot choose to go without water. While water companies have been banned (since 1999) from disconnecting households, if you cannot afford the water bill, debts can mount and for those on benefits these debts can be taken from their benefit payments.

Moreover, water bills are in generally regressive, with the poor paying proportionately more of their overall income.

The interlocking challenges of climate change and poverty

This is partly because all households pay a standing charge and partly because of the pricing structure. For those on water meters, charges are calculated by how much they use with a flat rate charge for every litre used; though such households could in principle reduce their bills by cutting back, there is a limit to doing this without potential health implications. For those without a water meter, there is a set charge (whatever the usage) determined by the rateable value of the property; but rateable values are an outdated system (it has not been rebased since 1991), which results in properties of low value paying a disproportionate share compared to those of high value.[53]

Water companies are required to offer a 'social tariff' for certain (limited) types of vulnerable customers, but the system is neither fair nor consistent, varies from company to company resulting in a postcode lottery,[54] and is fully funded from other customers' bills.

A fairer system would be for everyone to be on water meters, with a small, or possibly non-existent standing charge (for first homes only, with a premium for second homes) and for the rate per unit to be lower for the first tranche of water used per year and progressively higher for those who used water excessively. This would ensure everyone had access to clean water at a reasonable price and would have the added advantage of encouraging all households to use water more efficiently and thereby match one of the problems coming down the road of drier summers.

But above all to keep costs to consumers under control while adapting to climate change, the way water companies are operated and owned needs to change away from the failed experiment in privatisation to some form of public ownership and control. This has widespread public support[55] though the current government has shown no inclination to take this step. For Thames Water, which has stumbled from crisis to crisis, the government tasked the businessman Varun Chandra – whose company, Hakluyt, had previously been paid £1 million by

Thames Water for strategic advice – with finding a private sector solution.[56]

The government argues that taking the water companies into public ownership would cost the Exchequer too much, quoting figures of some £90 billion based on a study commissioned by the water companies and carried out by the Social Market Foundation, a cross-party thinktank which describes its mission as enabling markets and governments to work together.[57] But these estimates have been widely disputed. Calculations for the *Financial Times* by Moody's, the rating agency, estimate that, based on the book value of the 15 English water companies' shareholder equity, the cost would be around £14.5 billion,[58] a sum potentially swiftly recouped from lower borrowing costs and the absence of shareholder dividends. We Own It, a campaigning group for public ownership, argues that this process could be kick started by the government taking shares, rather than fines from companies when they pollute.[59] If Thames Water was declared financially insolvent, the company could be taken over without any compensation to shareholders.

Ruling out such action, the government simply plans a new water ombudsman to be 'a consumer champion',[60] a move that hardly gets to the root of the problem.

These arguments about how to ensure that adapting to climate change is equitable apply equally to the need to move to a net-zero economy.

Moving to net zero

Since 2008, UK governments have committed to moving to a net-zero economy by 2050. The 2008 Climate Change Act[61] was the first binding mitigation target set by any country and required greenhouse gas emissions to be reduced by 80 per cent by 2050 compared to 1990 levels. In 2019[62] this target for the reduction of greenhouse gas emissions was tightened to 100 per cent by 2050 and is seen as a 'net-zero' target as remaining emissions would be required to be removed from the atmosphere through various forms of carbon capture.[63]

The UK has subsequently made considerable progress at reducing its carbon emissions, which are now less than half that in 1990. This has been largely achieved by the phasing out of coal and its replacement with renewable energy, but it is also partly because the UK's heavy industries (such as steel) have declined and imports replacing these products do not count towards emissions. Even so, current progress is too slow. The Climate Change Committee (CCC), set up in 2008 to monitor progress, reported in July 2024 that the 2030 targets were at risk, with credible plans covering only about a third of the reduction needed. The UK, the CCC concluded, is 'off track for net zero'.[64]

The need for action is now extremely urgent and must be embedded in all aspects of policy: transport, energy supply, housing, industry, waste disposal, and much else.[65] And it needs to be done in a way that keeps the public on side. In the UK at least, and unlike the US, action on climate change has high levels of public support, but to keep this, change needs to be done and to be seen to be done in a fair and equitable way.

To date, net-zero polices have been driven largely from an environmental and climate change perspective with the result that distributional questions have tended to take second place. Often the costs of these policies have been borne directly by consumers and often on goods and services used universally and relatively evenly, creating considerable unfairness with those least able paying as much as those far more able to do so. This needs to change, primarily because of questions of justice but also to keep public support for the targets set. Already, climate change deniers, notably the political party Reform UK, have broken the cross-party consensus on net zero, promising to scrap the target, arguing that the costs for households right now are too high to implement, a move subsequently followed by the Conservative Party under Kemi Badenoch.[66]

The discussion and policies need to be reframed and redesigned.

Energy use is a key area of household expenditure which is not just universal and critical but for which costs tend to be high, and higher as a proportion of spending for lower- than higher-income households. How could net-zero energy policies be combined with policies to alleviate poverty?

How consumers have borne the cost of the low-carbon energy transition

The main mechanism used to increase investment in renewable energy has been through various subsidies to UK suppliers of electricity through long-term, guaranteed-price support for electricity from renewable sources. The aim has been to provide certainty for investors as to the revenue they will receive and thereby stimulate investment.[67] The schemes have done this by collecting money from 'green levies' on energy bills to pay the generators of this new low-carbon electricity the difference between the wholesale market price and the set price.

In the long run, as the price of the technologies involved in wind and solar power (currently, the main sources of renewable energy) drop, such incentives may not be necessary but meanwhile these schemes are widely credited with having played a significant role in accelerating the pace at which renewable generation has developed.[68] The green levies have been primarily on household energy bills, mostly electricity bills rather than gas, which is in itself problematic. Moving to net zero requires a rebalancing of electricity and gas prices so that electricity, rather than being as it is currently more expensive, becomes relatively cheaper. There are also levies on business bills, though these rates have been much lower, and there is a reduced rate if the business is energy intensive. The UK Energy Research Centre estimate that in 2016 overall, £6.5 billion was raised from household energy bills (adding around £130 a year to household bills) and a further £1.8 billion from UK businesses, resulting in UK households contributing the majority (78 per cent) of the total money raised.[69]

The result of placing the cost burden primarily on household bills is that low-income households are disproportionately impacted. This is primarily because the poorest households spend around 10 per cent of their income on heat and power in their homes, whereas the richest households only spend 3 per cent,[70] but also because direct energy use in the home represents a much bigger share of total energy use for poorer households than richer households which, through their higher level of purchases, use more energy sourced outside the home.[71]

Renewable energy projects are bringing down the cost of electricity and will continue to do so as the projects become more cost efficient. It will also reduce the UK's current over-reliance on the volatile gas market for its energy supply which in turn affects electricity prices. This is partly because around 40 per cent of electricity is still generated from gas but is also because about two-fifths of electricity generated is sold on 'the spot market' at 'marginal cost pricing', that is it is sold at the price of the most expensive unit needed to meet demand at a particular moment in time. When gas prices are high, this will be gas-generated electricity.[72] Thus in 2022, when wholesale gas prices, following the end of lockdown and the Russian invasion of Ukraine,[73] reached record highs, it led to a rapid rise in energy prices across the board and, as seen in Chapter 4, this was a key driver of the cost-of-living crisis which so badly hit poorer households. The benefits to be gained from moving to renewables are therefore huge, and not just for the environment but also for people's living standards.

However, this does not reduce the short-term pain for poorer households from disproportionately bearing the cost of transition. Other ways of funding these schemes would be fairer. If funding was switched to general taxation, richer households would pay more while the poorest far less;[74] in 2022, the government did temporarily move these levies to general taxation in response to the energy crisis, subsequently returning to household bills. Finally, in the autumn budget of 2025, the Chancellor moved a portion of renewable-energy subsidies from bills to general taxation. An alternative approach could be to set up a specific fund – like Germany's Climate and Transformation Fund – which could be funded from other sources, including levies on carbon polluters such as oil companies or a more general carbon tax.

But to move to net-zero energy, more needs to be done.

The next stage of the revolution in energy generation

To achieve the next stage in the transition to renewable energy generation, many have argued that a new element needs to be introduced into how government gets new projects off the ground to ensure that the benefits of the transition are more fairly spread.[75] Until now the approach taken has been entirely dependent on stimulating private financing of renewable projects by insulating the private companies from the risks associated with new development. Thus, while some of the costs have been borne by the public (though their bills), all the profits made go the companies. The beneficiaries are large companies, largely foreign-owned, often by state-backed enterprises; the IPPR estimate that more than half of the subsidies that UK billpayers contributed through levies primarily benefited companies owned by foreign governments.[76] While this has delivered an impressive increase in renewable energy production, there is a growing argument that the benefits accruing from the next stage of the development needed to advance renewable technologies should be retained for public benefit. That is, that there needs to be a different system for the way energy is generated, namely one that incorporates forms of public or local ownership.[77]

The current Labour government has taken some of this argument on board and, as well as subsidising private companies to incentivise them to invest in current technologies for renewables energy, it has also established a new publicly owned company, Great British Energy, to develop new technologies.[78] Backed by £8.3 billion of direct government funding over the current parliament, GB Energy hopes to drive innovation and investment for the next generation of clean energy technologies – such as floating offshore wind, tidal, hydrogen generation and storage, and carbon capture – while ensuring that the supply chains developed for these technologies and the profit generated are kept in the UK.[79] As well as these innovative projects, GB Energy is looking to invest in community-owned energy generation.[80]

The Manchester-based Centre for Local Economic Strategies in conjunction with the Carbon Co-op have already been looking at ways in which the transition to net-zero energy could help local communities and address social inequalities along with reducing the UK's carbon footprint.[81] Some such projects are already underway, such as Oldham Community Power, where the council has brought together businesses and key institutions in the area to develop locally based renewable energy and a local energy market. Solar panels have been installed on a number of sites, including schools, and the electricity generated has been sold back to the local community at a discount.[82] Similar schemes are run by other councils, for example, Hackney Light and Power, run by Hackney Council.[83]

In more densely populated urban areas, district heating networks could also play a major role in both decarbonisation and reducing household costs. District heating distributes heating, or cooling, from a central source or sources to homes, offices, public buildings, and the like, thus avoiding the need for a heating system in every building and enabling access to other sources of energy such as deep underground heating or rivers. In other countries, district heating systems are common, for example, in Denmark around 64 per cent of homes are heated through such networks[84] with similar levels in Sweden. In the UK, collective heating schemes have taken a far smaller role and have generally been communal heating schemes rather than district schemes, distributing heat to just one building (for example a block of flats).[85] These communal schemes, often privately owned, have had a rather poor reputation. Many do not meter the individual tenants, meaning you pay the same however little you use, are generally fired by gas boilers, and are often expensive.

However, in some areas local councils have taken the initiative, investing in new district networks utilising the latest technologies and ensuring that benefits return to the community. In Gateshead, the council established Gateshead Energy Company in 2017, which is 100 per cent owned by the council though operated externally.[86] It's built a new district energy system installing a deep-mine-water heat pump, as well as using council land to develop a movable ground-mounted solar array in the town centre.[87] By keeping ownership and control of this new lost-cost, low-carbon energy, it's been able to offer 5 per cent discount to customers compared to market energy tariffs,[88] as well as return profits made to the council. A Gateshead Council officer explains their thinking: 'Every step you give away […] you'll give away profit margin that a private company is going to take, and it erodes the benefit that's left for the community and the Council.'[89]

These are innovative schemes that challenge the economic model of how energy is generated in a way that translates the principle of a just and equitable transition into reality. However, the government seems, at least to some extent, to have backed down on its commitment to these kinds of renewable projects. In its spring 2025 spending review, while the budget for GB Energy was maintained, the government, out of the blue, announced that effectively a third of its £8.3 billion budget would be diverted to funding the development of small nuclear reactors.[90] This is an untested, and relatively expensive, solution to moving to net zero. While investing in developing these future technologies may be worthwhile in the longer run, it is not a trade-off for investing in cheaper and proven solutions that bring immediate and transparent benefits, in particular helping bring energy bills down.

But more needs to be done to ensure that the transition to low-carbon energy is a bonus, not a burden, for low-income households.

Shifting the UK housing stock to net zero

The upgrading of Britain's housing stock to be more energy efficient is crucial for the transition to a low-carbon economy. The energy used in UK homes is responsible for some 16 per cent of the UK's greenhouse gas emissions,[91] largely through the use of gas for heating and cooking. The potential for improvement is enormous: the UK Energy Research Centre estimates that 'one half of the energy currently used in UK housing could be saved by investing in a mix of current technologies encompassing improved energy efficiency, heat pumps and heat networks'.[92]

Better-insulated homes would use less energy for heating, whether gas or electricity, and could enable a rebalancing of gas and electricity prices to make gas relatively more expensive (at present difficult as so many houses run on gas). This would help the transition from gas- to electricity-based heating by making heat pumps more cost-effective. Improving insulation would also improve key aspects of poor housing conditions (such as damp, condensation, and mould), would make houses easier to heat in winter, protecting against fuel poverty, and would keep them cooler in summer, protecting vulnerable households from excess heat.

Upgrading the energy efficiency of housing is a huge task in the UK, primarily because much of the UK's housing stock is old with the majority of UK houses being over 60 years old and one in five properties over 100 years.[93] Older properties are far less energy efficient than newer ones: in England only a fifth of houses over 100 years old meet the minimum energy efficiency target set by the government in 2017 (that is, with a rating of C or above) and less than half of those over 60 years old do,[94] with similar figures for the other UK nations.

Newer homes are more energy efficient, with around 83 per cent hitting the minimum target, but even here very few of even the most recently built homes meet the top energy rating categories.[95] This is because in 2015 the newly elected Conservative government, lobbied by the large construction companies (many of which were large donors to the party), abandoned the zero-carbon homes policy, first announced in 2006 by the then-chancellor Gordon Brown, that would have required higher energy efficiency standards for new builds from 2016. This was done on the grounds of 'reducing regulation for housebuilders'[96] and that it would have added to the cost of a new home but was, as ever, short sighted. It has been estimated that to incorporate higher standards into new builds while under construction would have cost £4,800, while it would cost an average of £26,300 to retrofit these homes, far more than installing the technology in the first place.[97]

Nevertheless, the priority for upgrading remains with older homes where there is most to be gained and, here, progress has in recent years been slow.

During the 2010s, the coalition and then Conservative governments introduced a variety of schemes to try to improve energy efficiency of UK housing, the large majority of which were funded through the green levies on household energy bills. The most significant of these schemes was the Energy Company Obligation (ECO), which aimed to deliver home energy improvements such as insulation to low-income households, and accounted for around 12 per cent of the money raised through green levies on bills.[98] The scheme itself was badly targeted. Though it was meant to help low-income households, only 35 per cent of those helped are fuel poor[99] with only half of the fuel-poor households in England being even eligible for help. Overall, the poorest households contribute more to the levy than they receive back through savings from reduction in energy use delivered by the ECO scheme.[100]

Although the scheme has funded around 2.5 million home improvements since its introduction in 2013, since 2015, as a result of the government's decision to reduce targets so as to lower energy bills, the rate of improvements has slowed down dramatically. While there were more than 80,000 improvements per month in early 2014, there were fewer than 20,000 per month (on average) from mid-2016 to mid-2020.[101]

Even taking account of other (much smaller) schemes that have been introduced, progress in the decade leading up to the energy crisis had plummeted.[102] The House of Commons Environmental Audit Committee described the results as 'woefully inadequate'[103] and the CCC as 'insufficient', 'slow', 'off track', and 'to lag behind' what's needed.[104] This failure has a direct impact on levels of fuel poverty. The New Economic Foundation (NEF) calculates that if the rate of progress had kept to its 2012 peak with better-targeted schemes, most fuel-poor households would already have met the decent energy efficiency standard, resulting in savings of, on average, £530 per upgraded household to their bills,[105] lifting many out of fuel poverty.

In March 2023, the Conservative government introduced the latest version of the ECO schemes, the 'Great British Insulation Scheme', to run to March 2026 and placing an additional £1 billion obligation on suppliers, to be funded from increases in the green levy, adding to the average household bill around £17 a year from 2024–26.[106] This scheme is aimed at helping around 300,000 houses, not just low-income households but more generally homes with low energy ratings, covers only one insulation type per property, and recipients can be required to pay for part of the cost. The scheme is off track, having completed only some 60,000 in its first two years, of which, moreover, many, like its predecessor scheme ECO 4, were found by the National Audit Office to be of such poor standard that they needed fixing, including some which posed an immediate risk to health and safety.[107]

In the meantime, in 2019, the government also announced plans to spend £6.6 billion between 2019 and 2024 and a further

£6 billion between 2025/26 and 2027/28 on energy efficiency programmes including solar panels, heat pumps, and the like, as well as insulation,[108] to be directly funded by the government (as opposed to funded from consumer bills). This was the first time since the coalition government ran down the publicly funded Warm Front scheme, first introduced in 2000, that a government was directly funding any energy efficiency scheme in England (the Scottish government, by contrast, had continued to fund some schemes directly). This was potentially a major investment and a step change in the approach taken to energy efficiency in housing. Unfortunately, little materialised. Analysis by the NEF found 'a massive gap between these targets and reality':[109] the two main directly funded schemes aimed at home insulation improvement – the Homes Upgrade Grants scheme and the Local Authority Delivery scheme, both aimed at low-income households – installed just 36,384 home upgrades between 2020 and 2023,[110] way below what was promised or needed.

In its election manifesto, the Labour Party promised to invest an extra £6.6 billion on top of the £6 billion already promised by the previous Conservative government, to be spent over the life of the next parliament. Some of this will be in grants – with the emphasis here on households in fuel poverty – and some through loans and the like, supported through the government's newly established National Wealth Fund. The overall aim is to upgrade five million homes in total at an average cost of around £2,600 per home, not just with insulation but also with solar panels, batteries, heat pumps and the like.[111] This is the kind of ambition needed, in terms of the number of houses targeted, to start to tackle the problem, though for a full upgrade more is likely to be needed; the CCC estimates that retrofitting homes (including installing heat pumps) would cost around £10,000 per home to achieve.[112]

The key question is who pays and how. It is generally agreed that for those living in social housing, the owner of the social housing (council or housing association) is responsible, for those living in rented accommodation it is the private landlord, and homeowners are primarily responsible for their own property, though for the latter incentives and some level of subsidy is generally seen as required.

The greatest progress in improving energy efficiency standards has been in social housing, types of tenure much more accessible to direct government policy and more likely to be targeted by policies aimed at low-income households. By 2022, 72 per cent of housing association properties and 67.5 per cent of council properties had reached the decent energy efficiency standard (that is with a rating of C or above).[113] Tackling the energy efficiency of social housing is where you make the biggest impact on poverty.

By contrast, progress in the private rented sector and owner-occupied sector has been much slower and has effectively stalled in recent years. Only 44.9 per cent of private rented and 43.3 per cent of owner-occupied property had reach the decent energy standard by 2022.[114] This failure to tackle energy efficiency in properties in the private rented and home-ownership sectors is not just problematic for net-zero targets but also for poverty reduction. For the private rented sector, the poverty rate, while lower than for those in social housing, is still high: 35 per cent are in relative income poverty compared to 43 per cent for social housing (Table 8.1). For the owner-occupied sector the rate is relatively low (12 per cent) but because the majority of people live in this sector, the numbers in poverty are high. As can be seen in Table 8.1 more people in poverty are owner-occupiers than any other tenure and it is these homes that are most likely to fail minimum energy standards.

The problem for many owner-occupiers is that the upfront costs are too high and the payback period from energy bill savings too long. This is especially true for lower-income homeowners and for many elderly homeowners. The last government trialled

Table 8.1: Poverty rates, number of people in poverty,* and percentage of dwellings below energy standards**, by tenure, 2022/23

Tenure	Poverty rate	Numbers in poverty	% of properties below energy standard
Owner-occupied	12%	5,200,000	56.7%
Private rented	35%	4,500,000	55.1%
Social housing	44%	4,800,000	29.7%

Note: * Relative income poverty after housing costs, ** Below energy efficiency rating band C

Source: HBAI 2022/23, income series, Table 3.6db and English Housing Survey 2022, Energy Performance, Table DA7101[115]

various schemes whereby government subsidies were provided to banks to provide cut-price mortgage rates to homeowners who undertook energy efficient improvements.[116] Others have called for stamp duty rebates for homes that are more energy efficient.[117] Such moves could improve incentives for homeowners especially those on current mortgages but seem unlikely to shift the dial significantly.

To do so would require more innovative thinking. This could include improved loan schemes for low-income households where, for example, the annual repayments matched the energy savings made for the payback period, with government subsidies to the lender for shortfalls if required. Or it could look to tougher rules on sales of below-standard homes which deduct from the sale the amount required to upgrade the home which is then released to the new homeowner solely for that purpose.

For those who own their home outright, their home is, of course, a substantial financial asset. This group now account for getting on for half of all homeowners but are more likely to be in income poverty than those buying their home with a mortgage (primarily because they are more likely to be retired). Ways of enabling access to this home equity for home energy improvement could make a substantial difference. Currently, home equity release schemes are commercially available but can be complex and not necessarily good value.

In South Korea, government-backed financial instruments – basically equity release schemes – are used to provide a monthly payout for low-income pensioners set against the value of their home. Being non-commercial, the government protects the homeowner from various risks, including any losses from a drop in the housing market, and ensures any excess on the death of the homeowner is passed on to their heirs. The scheme has been very successful in increasing the disposable income of low-income older adults by 20 per cent on average, and has reduced poverty rates by some ten percentage points.[118] This kind of approach could be adapted to help low-income, homeowning pensioners to have the resources to upgrade the energy standards of their homes as well additional income.

For the private rented sector, while there are a large number of people in poverty in energy inefficient rentals, there is little case for government subsidies and support as the main beneficiaries of the investment would be the landlords as the value of their property would rise. A more regulative approach is needed. In February 2025, the government announced new requirements for private rented tenancies which would mandate landlords to meet the minimum energy efficiency ratings (C and above) in their properties by 2030,[119] renewing requirements that had been abandoned by the previous Conservative government. The private rented sector has the highest proportion of extremely energy inefficient properties of all sectors, with 11.9 per cent rated E or below (by contrast, under 3 per cent of social housing has such low ratings) and the largest energy savings are to be found in moving from an energy rating of E to C, estimated at £748 annually.[120]

The key point here is that the challenge of decarbonisation can provide an opportunity for new thinking that would not just tackle how to reach net zero but also how to alleviate poverty.

As we turn to what an anti-poverty strategy for the future might look like, there is also a need to simultaneously require an anti-poverty policy to embed the urgent need to move to net zero.

9

Lowering the basic costs of living

At its heart, poverty is about people being unable to afford the necessities of life and, as seen in earlier chapters, the soaring cost of living is making this increasingly difficult for many households.

For some it means they are no longer really managing:[1]

> Food shopping is stressful. I never know if I'll have enough when I get to the till. My daughter has one pair of school trousers because I can't find any spare money. … My gas always runs out. My electric bill is high. Every day is a worry. (Female, 35–44, renting, employed)

> I have had to reduce my energy use, so my flat is often uncomfortably cold. And I avoid cooking meals in the oven and keep the lights off as much as possible. I also have had to reduce the number of times I pay for activities for my child like swimming, days out, cinema – and I can't afford to go on holiday. It has meant worrying about money each month. (Female, 45–54, renting, unemployed)

> Everything is going up. I'm struggling to feed my kids healthy meals without it costing too much. My bills

are going up, but our pay isn't. Choosing to buy food or pay bills is hard and even harder around this time of year. (Female, 25–34, renting, employed)

Some have been particularly badly hit by rising housing costs:

> For me, I now rent the spare room in a relative's house. I could no longer afford to privately rent on my own with the rising cost of rent, bills and food. (Female, 25–34, renting, employed)

> Rent increases of 40 per cent mean there's little disposable income left after buying essential items. (Female, 45–54, renting, employed)

> The end of my fixed-rate mortgage deal has caused my mortgage payments to increase dramatically. Whilst I am able to make all my commitments, there is no more wriggle room in the budget for any unexpected expenditure. (Male, 45–54, mortgage, employed)

While others are relying on their savings, making them more vulnerable in the future:

> I'm drawing on savings every month just to break even. (Male, 55–64, lifetime mortgage, unemployed)

> Our savings have been decimated keeping up with costs. (Male, 25–34, mortgage, employed)

To tackle these rising basic costs, anti-poverty policies have tended to concentrate on the adequacy of household income, supporting these incomes where necessary though the benefits system. But a wider view needs to be taken that goes back to basics and looks instead at how needs are best met.

Many will indeed be directly met through direct purchases of goods through household incomes. Here, the question is not just whether income is adequate to cover these purchases but how the costs are set in the first place. For many goods, this will be through a competitive market, but there are times when these prices need regulation, notably when the market is not competitive such as when there are monopolies or cartels, and when government wants to influence behaviour. Other needs will be best met through collectively provided services, some of these services will be free to all at the point of delivery, some will be free to some but not others, and some will be paid for. Here, there are questions as to which should be free and to whom, and, if paid for, the aims of the pricing structure.

The key point here is that when looking at how to fix poverty, it is not just income that is important but how the costs of the various necessities that make up a minimum standard of living are decided.

Going beyond income

Currently, success, or otherwise, of the impact of policies on poverty is largely judged by the level of household income. The most widely used measure is the proportion of households that fall below a threshold of 60 per cent of median household income (either before or after housing costs). As discussed in Chapter 1, this has advantages, but the level is arbitrary and at times of inflation, if median household incomes and those below all fail to keep up with inflation, the level of poverty appears unchanged even if poorer households are being particularly badly hit by the price rises.

Other measures of poverty – such as the MIS – also focus exclusively on household income. In the case of the MIS, this is done by setting a level of household income needed to meet household needs, consensually agreed through focus groups. While this overcomes the arbitrariness of the relative income measure, it has its problems when thinking about policy. By simply costing the items that form part of a minimum standard and translating them into a household budget, the solution to any shortfall between a household's actual income and the minimum income budget is more income, generally achieved through raised benefit levels.

Household income levels are critical but seeing anti-poverty simply in these terms can be limited and can distort the choices made. Publicly provided services free at the point of delivery – such as healthcare or education – constitute an important resource for households which otherwise would be paid for and are a key part of any conception of a minimum standard of living. Other services – such as water and sanitation, transport and electricity – are also widely considered to be essential, and while many pay for these services, they are free, or subsidised, for some. The question is not just whether such items are necessary but how they are provided, whether they should be free for all, or some, or none, and where there are charges how these charges are set. Similarly, for those aspects of a minimum standard of living where the price is set by the market, increasing prices tend to be simply translated into a need for higher minimum income levels rather than asking what it is that has driven the increase and how it can be controlled.

By simply focusing on income, measures such as the MIS essentially see individuals and households as separate economic entities, whose personal and household incomes should enable them to be self-sufficient in meeting their needs in a competitive market. If costs rise rapidly, as they have done for energy, water, and food, there is no challenge as to why, or questioning of what can be done to bring these costs down; it simply translates the rising prices into a higher minimum income. Similarly, if failures in universal services lead to an agreement that a minimum income should include money for the private purchase of the service, then it simply increases the MIS rather than focus on policies to improve the public service.

This can be seen in the 2024 MIS where an allowance has been included for the purchase of private medical care for things like occupational therapy or physiotherapy sessions.[2] But if people feel this service is essential and waits on the NHS are too long, the answer to this is not to make sure everyone has enough money to buy private treatment. That answer takes you down a route to a two-tier healthcare system where the costs of healthcare are pushed back on to individuals and their families. And if that is the route taken, it is the poorer households that will miss out – precisely the type of household that the MIS is set up to try to protect. The answer to NHS services being difficult to access is to work out how to improve the service and the resources needed for these improvements. Providing money to individuals to pay for an alternative private service takes resources away from this aim.

How material deprivation measures open up policy choices

As discussed in Chapter 1, there are alternatives to looking at poverty simply in terms of household income, namely, to look directly at deprivation. The consensual approach to measuring poverty (which, to declare an interest, I have played a part in developing), identifies what is called 'socially perceived necessities' based on what the majority of the public think is needed for a minimum acceptable way of life. It then identifies those who have 'an enforced lack' of these necessities, asking people who lack a necessity whether it is because they do not want it or because they cannot afford it and only classing people as deprived if the lack was because they couldn't afford it.[3] This subsequently formed the basis of the material deprivation index developed by the DWP, discussed in Chapter 1.

When the method was first developed in the UK back in the early 1980s, it primarily looked at material items purchased by the household rather than services, essentially establishing a material deprivation index based on goods and activities rather than one that takes account of the level of service provision. At that time healthcare and education (including degree-level education), were universally provided, free at the point of delivery. Other basic services like electricity, water and sanitation, buses, and trains were (almost) universally in public ownership and costs were relatively affordable. Council housing had not been sold off, the private rented sector had not yet boomed, and for low-income households, housing costs were relatively controlled. This is not to argue that this was some kind of golden age or that poverty levels then were acceptable. There was much that needed improvement; discrimination based on sex and race were high, pensioners fared badly, and the standard of much of the housing stock was low, for example.

In subsequent years, the cost of services in the UK has risen and the method has been adopted by a wide range of high-, mid, and low-income countries where universal services are not necessarily the norm, with the result that the approach has expanded to include questions about access to, quality of, and the affordability of services.[4] The approach now provides a comprehensive measure of poverty that has the advantage, when looking at policies to reduce poverty, of remaining open to the question as to whether this is best addressed by increasing incomes or controlling costs (or both), or providing universal free services.

In 2024 the DWP commissioned the Centre for Analysis of Social Exclusion at the London School of Economics, to update its material deprivation index so that it covered working-age adults as well as children and pensioners and continued to reflect public perceptions of necessities.[5] The review was comprehensive and thorough, and recommended an extensive updating of the measures, including a number of services in which availability as well as affordability were important. The items included, for example, questions on access to transport that is reliable, timely, safe, and affordable; on attending regular dental appointments; reliable access to the internet; and, for young children, attendance at a nursery or playgroup.[6]

The review also recommended that for some items, merely lacking the item was enough to be classed as deprived, and questions of affordability were not relevant. These items included having a damp-free home and being able to keep the home adequately warm in cold weather; for those living in rented accommodation where it is the landlord's responsibility to keep the home damp-free or ensure that it has an adequate, functioning heating system, items for which the lack is not necessarily directly related to the household income of the tenant but the behaviour of the landlord.[7]

From 2023/24, these items will be included in the Family Resources Survey, providing an official measure of material deprivation for these groups. In addition, as part of its Child Poverty Strategy, the government have committed to a new 'deep material poverty' measure based on those who lacked 4 of a subset of 13 of the 22 children's items, focused on those items indicating the severest levels of poverty.[8]

These are important developments and will provide alternative and complementary measures to looking at relative income poverty. Further developments could also be undertaken to develop a measure of service deprivation to be incorporated into this measure of material deprivation.[9] Supplementary questions on which services are essential for a minimum standard of living could be added and for those that are essential, questions not just about their affordability but also about the extent of their provision and adequacy. These service deprivation indicators, combined with the update and improved material deprivation indicators, would provide a comprehensive view of whose standards of living are below what is seen to be acceptable and why – whether it is lack of money or lack of adequate provision.

Focusing on needs and how and whether they are met, rather than just on income, is important as it enables a far more nuanced view of anti-poverty policies and a better assessment of their success, or otherwise.

This is not, for one moment, to say that household income is unimportant nor that relative income measures should be abandoned – relative income remains a key measure in that it can be easily tracked over time and tells us how many are falling behind compared to the median. Nor is it to say that the level of benefits is not crucial to combatting poverty; how to achieve this in a reformed benefits system will be examined in Chapter 11.

But it allows other important factors to become a focus of attention: controlling the price of essential goods and ensuring the provision and affordability of key services.

Drawing the line between purchasing and providing what we need

So where should the line lie between needs which are purchased individually and needs which are best provided through collective services. And where do these overlap to ensure levels of choice within that which is collectively provided?

The NEF has drawn up a framework to group the way basic necessities are met according to whether they are best met through free collective services, through some level of direct payments for collective services, or predominantly individual purchase met by direct payments.[10] Necessities predominantly met through services still need regulation and oversight to ensure standards while those met on an individual basis through purchases similarly need oversight – including possible subsidies and regulation – to ensure fair pricing, accessibility, and quality.

How different needs are best met depends, NEF argues, on a number of factors, including the scale of cost and risk to the individual, the risk to society, the extent to which the service is a monopoly, and historical and cultural norms.

Some necessities, such as those related to healthcare, can be quite unpredictable as to what will be needed in the future and their cost. At times these costs can be extremely high. If the individual or household has to pay for this, the risk of not being able to do so is high, even if insurance is affordable to offset such costs. Services such as healthcare are best provided collectively, sharing the risk, and free at point of use.

Other services are predictable in the sense that everyone participates at some point and their costs do not vary greatly between individuals. However, there is an overwhelming argument that the services should be provided free for all on the basis that the benefits do not just accrue to the individual but to society as a whole. Primary and secondary education – and increasingly nursery education – fall into this category; a well-educated workforce is essential for business and the economy, and a good education is key to each individual's future opportunities. There is a strong case that this applies to higher education as well.

In the UK, health and education up to secondary school level are (largely) provided for free to all who choose to use the NHS and state school system. The challenge here is to make sure that these services are provided to the highest standards for all regardless of income and background.

We will look at services best provided for free, or at least free for certain groups, in Chapter 10. Here will consider at necessities that are purchased.

Many basic utilities are monopolies simply because of the nature of the service provided and the infrastructure required to provide that service. For essential services such as water supply, sewage, and energy, there is no real way of introducing an alternative infrastructure for the supply to the household, meaning that competition at the consumer level for water is non-existent and for energy limited. Such services are essential, and everyone needs access to them, while the way in which these services are run also has far wider social impacts and, particularly in the face of rapid climate change, on the environment. Many (as argued in Chapter 8) are best provided through publicly accountable enterprises rather than private ones so that public interest is prioritised rather than private profit. But whatever the ownership structures, there needs to be a fair pricing system.

While such services are essential for all, in a resource-restricted world they cannot be free however much you use; at some level, they need to be paid for to discourage overuse. Therefore, costs need to be carefully controlled and structured. In Chapter 8, we looked at the failure of the privatised water system and argued that for such monopoly services, collective ownership would ensure a better public service and that private profits were not being extracted at the expense of costs to consumers. We also looked at how the pricing system of water and sewerage could be restructured so that there would be a reduced rate for a set level of use to ensure everyone has access, but higher rates for higher levels of use to ensure resources were not wasted. This would be a far better approach than extending 'social tariffs' for low-income and vulnerable customers which largely simply extends means testing by another name to the provision of essential services.

Similar reforms are needed for energy.

Reforming the energy retail system

Since the privatisation of energy retail in the late 1980s and early 1990s, the vast majority of the distribution of energy into people's homes has been via private companies. As seen in Chapter 8, the way that energy prices are determined meant that following the record-high gas prices resulting from Russia's invasion of Ukraine, energy prices (including electricity) soared and were a key driver of the resulting cost-of-living crisis.

Lowering the basic costs of living

But even before the energy crisis of 2022, deep structural flaws in the way it was operating had emerged.[11] Bills were rising, fuel poverty was rising, and there was no incentive for the companies to improve the energy efficiency of their customers (quite the reverse). Some of these problems are inherent in the privatised system but some had been made far worse by changes to the way it was regulated.

During the 2010s the government regulator, OFGEM, introduced a series of reforms to increase competition by making it easier to set up a company to supply households with energy; the number of companies surged from 12 in 2010 to more than 70 in 2018, with new suppliers undergoing relatively little financial scrutiny.

This system was fragile and with the huge rise in gas prices in 2021, many of these new entrants collapsed. They had not 'hedged' against future price rises (by buying future energy at a set price ahead of time) as this has to be paid upfront and they did not have the reserves to do so. Faced with soaring consumer bills, OFGEM introduced a price cap in 2019, and these companies were caught between rising wholesale costs and the price cap.

When a supplier collapses, generally a new supplier is appointed by OFGEM to take on its customers and compensated for the costs from a levy paid by all suppliers, who pass this levy to customers in their bills. So, all customers of other companies pay when a supplier of other customers collapses. Citizens Advice estimated the collapse of these companies added an additional £94 (on top of other increases from rising gas prices) to customers' bills from April 2022, paid through the standing charge.[12]

Then Bulb Energy collapsed. It had once been Britain's fastest-growing energy company, rising from a 2015 startup to 1.5 million customers by 2022 and had enabled its two founders to cash in £4 million each in 2018. Eventually, Bulb was sold to Octopus Energy with Octopus's costs potentially being picked up by the levy.[13]

What is clear is that this system is inherently unstable, regulation has been ineffective, and customers have picked up the costs through their bills. With almost a quarter of a household's average energy bill taken in profit, a different system of energy retail, including of public ownership and local ownership, would provide a more effective way of helping customers reduce their bills.[14]

At the same time, there needs to be a fairer system of pricing energy that protects low-income customers, discourages profligate use, and incentivises energy saving. This could be done, as I argued for water, by removing, or at least substantially reducing the standing charge for first (but not second) homes and by the rate per unit being lower for the first tranche of energy used per year and progressively higher for those who use excessively.

The Trade Union Congress (TUC), the collective body representing 47 member unions, go one step further arguing for a free band of energy to every household to cover basic lighting, heating, and cooking needs like keeping the lights on, keeping warm, and running a fridge, paid for by charging for energy used beyond a certain high-usage threshold at a significantly higher rate.[15] In this sort of system, there would need to be protection for those who require higher-than-average electricity consumption for medical reasons, such as those on dialysis. Consultation on who would need exemptions along with regulation and oversight should be able to ensure this.

As for water, such a pricing structure would encourage more efficient use of a limited resource through energy-saving measures, such as insulation, and for those with higher energy use it would incentivise the installation of home solar panels and battery storage. Overall, such measures would be redistributive with higher-income households, who use more electricity, paying proportionately more of their income than low-income households.

But most importantly from the perspective of fixing poverty, these kinds of reforms to the pricing structure would go a long way to ending fuel poverty. This, in turn, would lift pressure on the benefits system. If the government, instead of means-testing the winter fuel allowance for pensioners, had first introduced a fairer pricing structure, they might well have been able to remove the winter fuel allowance altogether rather than be caught in a humiliating U-turn on the extent of means-testing.

A similar approach could apply to internet services with a basic, free rate and a premium rate for faster services and higher use. An investigation by the Communications and Digital Committee of the House of Lords in 2023 found that around 1.7 million households have no mobile or broadband internet at home.[16] Up to a million people had had to cut back or cancelled internet packages over the previous year as a result of the rising cost of living.

With so many services now almost entirely dependent on digital access – housing, health, banking, and the benefits system for example – and with good and fast access to the internet being increasingly vital for education, this digital exclusion has severe consequences. While some of this problem needs to be tackled through improved services in certain parts of the country and some through basic training in digital skills, the current cost of services is an important factor.

For many goods and services seen as essential, how far they could or should be socially provided relates strongly to cultural values and historical norms.

Controlling the cost of housing

Housing is an example where relative levels of homeownership, renting and public housing vary enormously by country. In the UK, a high value is placed on homeownership and over the last 40 years policy has largely been directed towards supporting this aspiration. But this has failed and resulted in levels of homeownership that are back at the level of the 1980s, with the shift instead being from social housing to private renting.

The UK system – and its failures – has resulted in extraordinarily high housing costs, averaging 44 per cent more than the OECD average.[17] While other countries and cities successfully run very different systems with higher levels of renting and lower costs, the cultural and historical attachment in the UK to homeownership makes such a shift unlikely. Therefore, policy needs to address ways of enabling homeownership without feeding the ever-rising price of housing, while at the same time ensuring that there is adequate social housing for all who qualify for it and controlling the private rented sector.

As seen in Chapter 6, the government has invested heavily in the Affordable Homes Programme with a promised £39 billion investment over the next decade.[18] This is the biggest boost to affordable housing for decades with an ambition to build 300,000 social and affordable home of which 180,000 homes would be for social rent and the remainder being for other tenures including shared ownership, affordable rent, and intermediate rent.[19] Although this is a significant increase in social housing, it remains well below the estimated 90,000 social homes a year for the next ten years estimated to be needed to solve the social housing crisis.[20] There will need to be substantially more investment to deliver this level of increase.

In 2024, Shelter commissioned the global engineering, planning, and sustainable development firm, Arup, to model the level of funding needed to deliver social housing at the necessary scale. This suggested that around £6.2 billion in grant funding would be needed for social housing a year, with an additional £6.2 billion from other sources such as loans.[21]

Though a challenge, this is not impossible. With further increases to direct funding for councils and housing associations, changes in the rules by which public bodies can borrow, and by using some monies to renovate and acquire existing unoccupied housing, the numbers of social houses available could reach the levels needed. This would produce enormous savings.

Shelter estimate that one year of building 90,000 social rented homes would result over 30 years in significant direct savings to the government, including: £4.5 billion savings on housing benefit (as private tenants move into social rented homes where rents are on average a third of private rents), £5.2 billion savings to the NHS from current harms being done to people's health from living in poor rental accommodation and temporary housing, and £4.5 billion from a reduction in homelessness, currently being spent on temporary accommodation.[22] There would also be a huge economic impact from the employment generated in the construction of the homes. Including these wider economic benefits, the research estimates that the upfront investment would pay back in a few years and would generate some £51 billion in benefits to the economy over 30 years.[23]

But this all requires the government to rethink both its spending plans and its fiscal rules to unlock the finance needed. Doing this would, arguably, be the single most significant policy to reduce poverty in the long term.

In the meantime, those in low-income households in private rental accommodation will continue to face high rental costs. While the government has introduced a Renters' Rights Bill[24] that will give greater security and stability to private rented tenants, it does relatively little to reduce the high rents being paid. While tenants would be given the right to appeal against rents above market rates, landlords will still be able to increase rents to market price for their properties, with an independent tribunal making a judgement on this, if needed. To make private rental more affordable, more would need to be done. Many countries have rent control of one form or another,[25] particularly in areas of high rental pressure such as London. While any form of rent control would meet strong resistance, in particular from landlords who argue that it would result in a collapse of the rental sector,[26] exploring where this would be beneficial and how to achieve it would be an important step to controlling – and bringing down – the high costs of private renting and its role as a driver of poverty.[27]

The final key factor driving high housing costs is the surge in house prices, which have risen twice as fast as earnings over the last 30 years.[28] This has put homeownership out of reach of many younger adults, turning them towards private renting, thereby pushing up private rental costs too. For those who get their foot on the ladder, this has resulted in higher mortgages, resulting in higher monthly outgoings and greater vulnerability to varying interest rates. At the lower-income end, this can push families with mortgages into severe financial difficulties.

The government's plan – or hope – is that the increase in new homes being built will lead to a fall in price, as supply meets demand. Many of the promised 1.5 million new homes will be built by the private sector for sale at market prices with private builders being encouraged and enabled to build more through changes in planning rules. Government research suggests that a 1 per cent increase in housing stock lowers prices by 2 per cent if nothing else changes. Given the housing stock is around 30 million, a 1.5 million increase to the stock could, in theory, lead to a price drop of 10 per cent.[29] However, the research also suggests that a 1 per cent rise in real incomes increases prices by 2 per cent (knocking out the gain from more housing) while lower interest rates also increase house prices which, while helping existing mortgage holders, makes it yet more difficult for first-time buyers. Building more homes for sale, while important, is, on its own, unlikely to be a game changer.

What is needed is a way to reverse the shift that has taken place from housing primarily being about a safe and secure place to live to being a financial investment. Since the 1980s, the liberalisation of mortgage credit markets, along with historically low real interest rates and the entry of financial investors into the housing market, had, by the time of the global financial crisis, led to a quadrupling of mortgage credit from around 20 per cent of GDP to 80 per cent.[30] It is this above all that drove the five-fold increase in real house prices during this period. UK housing has, put simply, become a magnet for foreign investors, buy-to-let purchases, and investment for high-income households, in particular through the rapid increase in second homes. No wonder low-income households struggle with their mortgage costs.

What is needed is far bolder policies that break the attractiveness of housing as an investment. This could include an annual property tax, replacing stamp duty and council tax.[31] This would make property a less-attractive investment, while those on lower incomes who own high-value housing could be helped through government-backed equity release schemes or be allowed to defer payments until the property is sold. Other moves could include restricting foreign investment in housing and increasing the cost of second-home ownership by introducing a surcharge on such properties or significantly raising capital gains tax.

What is needed is new thinking, both regarding renting and homeownership, as to how to control the market price of housing. And this question as how to influence market prices applies to many other necessities that are purchased at an individual or household level, goods such as food and clothing or leisure and social activities.

Controlling the market costs of essential goods

The economic theory behind relying on markets to set prices is the idea that a strong and competitive market will bring down costs to the consumer. But this only works if consumers have clear information on costs and quality, can make informed choices, and where there is actually competition rather than a small number of large companies essentially setting the price for their own, and not the consumer's, benefit. In the UK, the main way through which this is regulated is by the Competition and Markets Authority (CMA), the principal authority responsible for consumer protection. Its 2024/25 'Annual Plan' sets out as one of its priorities being to 'have particular regard to consumers who need help the most'.[32]

An example of this in practice is well illustrated by their 2025 ruling on baby formula milk. It is an area where there is very limited competition with three companies – Danone, Nestlé, and Kendal – accounting for more than 90 per cent of the market and just two of these – Danone and Nestlé – for 85 per cent. In addition, it is an area where research indicates that those least able to afford formula are more likely to be reliant on it.

Formula milk prices have soared recently with the average price of a pack of powdered cow's milk-based infant formula rising by over 25 per cent between March 2021 and April 2023.[33] For new parents dependent on formula milk – either because mothers are unable to breast feed, or have been advised not to, or through choice – this put added strain on their often already-stretched budgets, with potential additional costs of up to £500 in the first year of a child's life.[34] In 2018, the All-Party Parliamentary Group on Infant Feeding and Inequalities found that, even before the current sharp price rise, the cost of infant formula was 'having a negative impact on some family budgets', and that this might lead to 'unsafe practices to feed their baby' or that it might limit their own food intake or that of other children.[35]

In response, the CMA made a number of recommendations aimed at finding a balance between excessive pricing and the overall health recommendation for breastfeeding where possible. The resultant package of measures proposed standardising infant formula packaging, enhancing nutritional information, extending the advertising ban to include follow-on formula, and removing a restriction on parents using loyalty points and vouchers to buy baby milk in supermarkets.[36] If this package of measures did not achieve price reductions in a 'reasonable' timeframe, the CMA offered, as a 'backstop', the option of introducing a price cap.[37]

These proposals were widely welcomed by food poverty campaigners[38] though others felt that the CMA should have gone further by proposing a price cap, with UNICEF describing such a cap as 'essential to protect families in the long term from unjustified price increases'.[39] Though the ruling could have been stricter, overall it demonstrates the importance of strong regulation in controlling costs and the impact this has on living standards.

It is very odd, therefore, to see the Prime Minister, Keir Starmer, accuse the CMA of stifling growth[40] and the Chancellor, Rachel Reeves, launching an all-out attack on regulation, calling for 'watchdog bosses to tear down regulatory barriers'.[41] This has all the appearance of simply shooing 'growth' into every announcement, and into areas into which it not appropriate and even dangerous to do so. It echoes the language and aims of the most powerful monopolies and the libertarian, pro-market right. It will backfire on its own terms – clear, strong, and predictable regulation attracts investment, while a free-for-all market with ever-lower standards and highly concentrated market power in the hands of a few firms reduces growth.[42]

In particular, it will backfire on the poorest. The CMA is the strongest protection that the UK has against monopoly power, and now the UK is outside the European Union, it is ever more important. It is abundantly clear that monopoly power pushes up prices. This can be seen clearly in the actions of Amazon; as it has increased its monopoly power, the advertising fees that independent sellers must pay to be seen by customers on their website saw a nearly 17-fold rise from 2017 to 2022.[43] This left Amazon taking more than half of sellers' revenue fees.[44] Moreover, Amazon uses its economic muscle to ensure that sellers do not undercut their prices when selling the item outside of Amazon. And thus starts a vicious circle with sellers putting up their prices to stay afloat. In effect, it becomes a fee on consumers paid to Amazon and its CEO, Jeff Bezos.

It seems a particularly bad omen, therefore, that within six months or so of coming to power, the government effectively sacked the existing chair of the CMA, Marcus Bokkerink, following complaints from big business, and replaced him with a former Amazon UK head, Doug Gurr.[45] While a poacher can turn gamekeeper, it comes at a time when there were cuts to staffing levels at the CMA and instructions from the prime minister to the CMA 'to prioritise growth, investment, and innovation' by removing 'needless regulation'.[46]

Far from less regulation, there needs to be stronger regulation. And far from prioritising a misplaced growth agenda onto the CMA, the government should be emphasising the importance of the CMA's existing responsibility for the more vulnerable consumer and its 'regard to consumers who need help the most'. This would help keep the price of essential goods down. Additionally, this would directly impact people's living standards and, in doing so, take pressure off low-income households in particular.

It is time to turn to services and how they can be a key part of an anti-poverty strategy.

10

Renewing public services

Since the 2010s, policies that enable poverty to be tackled at the root through services and support have been, as seen in Chapter 5, devasted by the years of austerity. This has impacted on everyone's lives but particularly on the poorest, with some of the severest cuts being in the most deprived areas. Such services provided a crucial lifeline.

In 2024, *The Guardian* newspaper interviewed families who had had access to Sure Start when it was up and running and the participants described the transformative impact it had had on them and their mental health.[1]

> I was full of anxiety about being a mum. I was spiralling into postnatal depression, and my health visitor directed me to a Sure Start centre. I went to a baby massage class and while I am not sure whether the massage did anything for my baby, the advice and support I got from the staff and the other mums really helped my precarious mental health. We started to call the group 'Is this normal?' as that's what we asked each other most weeks. I will be eternally grateful. (Rebecca Lever, 51-year-old marketing director from Cardiff)

Emma Speake a single mother, then on benefits and with no qualifications, ended up volunteering as a breastfeeding supporter, 'Sure Start helped me build confidence and believe that life could be different.' Emma went back into education and obtained two degrees, 'Thank you for the gift of hope and confidence', she said.

Across the board, good public services can provide similar transformative experiences. Ben, interviewed for a research project on youth work at the University of Edinburgh, attended a local youth club. He felt the support he received and the friendships he made had contributed to his pathway to college: 'It is so hard to describe, that's the thing. I was slowly taking on volunteer roles. It has made a tonne of difference to me. But overall, all the little bits of support, they are all the little bits of the jigsaw. I now feel that whatever path I take, I'll get to my destination.'[2]

Similarly, severe cuts to the bus network in parts of the UK outside London have left people isolated and struggling as interviews for Transport for the North found: 'I'm losing my sight and rely on taxis for everything. Leaves me little money. I have to limit what I spend on household items. I don't go out,' explained one participant. 'I'm late for work almost every day, without it being my fault. I even set off earlier – at 6am – and I'm still late for work at 9am. It impacts my mental health,' explained another.[3]

In recent years there has been increasing interest in developing and expanding the provision of free or subsidised services as a way of tackling inequality and of ensuring that everyone's basic needs are met in a way that fosters social cohesion rather than division. It has been termed a Universal Basic Services (UBS) guarantee.[4]

The redistributive impact of public services

While the primary purpose of public services is to fulfil a wide variety of social, economic, and environmental aims, such services are intrinsically highly redistributive. This is partly because higher-income households contribute more through the taxation; this is the case even if taxation is not progressive and broadly proportionate to income, simply because their incomes are larger. It is also partly because the value of the services received is a higher proportion of the incomes of low-income households than high-income households, even if their use of the services is the same.

Furthermore, the Institute for Fiscal Studies have found that spending per person is higher in cash terms for low-income households than for richer households,[5] making such services even more redistributive. Similarly, the OECD have found that, looking at all types of public services across member countries, the value of these services accounts for a much higher share of disposable income among lower-income than among higher-income households: 76 per cent of disposable income for the poorest 20 per cent and only 14 per cent for the top 20 per cent.[6] So, in terms of tackling inequality, public services are extremely effective in that they redistribute resources while, at the same time, because they are freely available to all, having a high level of public buy-in.

Additionally, public services, because they benefit all income groups rather than just the poorest and because their provision is not (with some exceptions such as prescriptions) based on income level, have very limited, if any, impact on incentives to work or to increase earnings at work. Indeed, for many services the provision of that service enables people to work. This is important not just, or even primarily, for the economy and growth, but for people's sense of well-being.[7]

Unlike income-based approaches to solving poverty, UBS is rooted in a more collective view of needs and responsibility and aims to strengthen the bonds within a community and participation in it, as well as enabling people to meet their needs. The concept is intrinsically linked to how those services are provided and seeks more collective ways of doing so than one based on consumer sovereignty and the market. Its ideas fit and link in with those developed to renew what is seen as the 'foundational economy', the network of services and provisions, generally relatively sheltered from international competition, that underpin our everyday lives.[8]

Moving towards a more service-based provision for meeting needs does not mean that all, or most, services are provided on a national basis. While some services are best provided at a national level, others are not. There could be a wide variety of models, including state ownership, collective ownership, third sector non-profit provision, registered charities, community and neighbourhood groups, or, for some sectors, where high levels of investment in infrastructure is needed, such as transport, subcontracted private provision. But the state – whether central, regional, or local government – would ensure the provision of such services, guarantee the funding either directly from taxation or from enabling borrowing, and, importantly, provide the oversight and regulation of standards.

Re-emphasising services as part of an anti-poverty strategy could provide an alternative way of meeting certain needs. Additionally, because such services are the equivalent of a 'social wage', replacing what would otherwise need to be paid for, it would lower the level of financial income needed to meet a minimum standard of living. And this could reduce the need for higher levels of cash transfers to low-income households through the benefits system.

On coming to power, the Labour government had two key priorities for rebuilding the social fabric of the UK: ushering in a new era of social housing (discussed in Chapter 9) and fixing the NHS. Both of these publicly provided services, though very different in their reach, are deeply intertwined with poverty.

Rebuilding the NHS

In July 2024, in the incoming Labour government commissioned Lord Darzi, Professor of Surgery and Director of the Institute of Global Health Innovation at Imperial College, London, to carry out an independent report into the NHS in England. The report published in the autumn that year concluded that, despite a depth of clinical talent within the service, the NHS was in 'serious trouble'.[9] Over the previous decade, the service had come under ever-increasing pressure with the result that people were struggling to see their GP and waiting lists were too long, particularly for community and mental health services, but also in other areas such as routine surgery, as well as cancer and cardiac services. While overall the quality of care provided was high, there were some areas where it was not always up to standard.

Lord Darzi attributed these problems to a range of factors but among the most prominent was an overall lack of spending during the 2010s, with 'unrealistically low spending settlements', resulting in that period being 'the most austere decade since the NHS was founded'.[10] There was chronic capital underinvestment in both facilities and technology,[11] and too little spent on community care and mental health services[12] with the result that more people than necessary ended up in hospital. The underinvestment and spending were exacerbated by an ageing population. On top of this, the nation's health, particularly that of lower-income groups, had started to deteriorate in recent years, itself closely tied into the austerity of the previous decade.[13] This had left the NHS stretched even before COVID-19, so when the pandemic arrived its impact was particularly damaging and long-lasting.[14]

The Labour government has promised to 'transform' the NHS to make it 'fit for the future'.[15] It has produced a 'ten-year plan' to do so with the long-term priorities of bringing 'three big shifts' in the NHS, from hospital to community, analogue to digital and sickness to prevention.[16] Additional investment has been made, with an additional £26 billion NHS funding in the first budget and a £40 million funding pot for NHS trusts who make the biggest improvements in cutting waiting lists.[17] These are important aims, and the additional funding has been welcomed.[18]

While an analysis of what needs to be done to transform the NHS is well outside the scope of this book, it is worth noting that there remain substantial concerns. The first concern centres not so much on whether the additional funding will produce some improvement, indeed in the first five months of the new government some 2 million additional elective care appointments had been delivered compared to the same period in the previous year,[19] but whether enough will be achieved. The promised extra funding is widely seen to be insufficient[20] or at best tight.[21]

The second concern centres on the way the funding will be used to achieve these improvements. To tackle its short-term priorities the government has decided to outsource some operations on the waiting list to the private sector. In doing so the government insists that it is just being 'pragmatic'.[22] But there is strong evidence that outsourcing does not effectively reduce waiting lists; the same pool of doctors perform the operation whether privately (for the NHS) or directly for and in the NHS; if they were not being paid to do the operations privately they would, otherwise, be available to work directly for the NHS with the difference being that the cost to the NHS is higher when these operations take place in private hospitals.[23]

It runs counter to the Labour Party's stated pre-election aims which recognised the dangers of outsourcing key public services.[24] And it risks further embedding the private sector into the NHS, a process that has been underway since the coalition government introduced the 2012 Health and Social Care Act, an act described by Lord Darzi's report as a 'calamity without international comparison'.[25] The act claimed to be 'liberating the NHS,'[26] and opened the way to the outsourcing of services to private companies, leading to a significant proportion of health service contracts being awarded to the private sector.[27]

There is a sense in which, from the patient's point of view, it does not matter who is providing the operation as long as it is done quickly and safely, or who is providing healthcare, as long as it is reliable and accessible. But for the long-term future and cost of the NHS it really matters. The British Medical Association warns it 'could lead to a decline in standards and poor value for money, fragmentation and destabilisation of services putting staff and patients at risk'.[28] It risks costs to the public purse escalating, not just because profit is being extracted but also because market-based systems tend to lead to mergers and acquisitions and to large (often international) companies with increasing monopoly power over overall health expenditure. The result is a waste of public money which otherwise could be spent on improving people's health.

Moreover, a consumer-based market system tends to be wasteful, partly because it tends to encourage overconsumption. This is particularly important when trying to, at the same time as all else, achieve net-zero goals. In the US, the privatised medical care system not only fails to deliver adequate healthcare to poorer households but also does so with an annual per-head carbon footprint twice that of the UK.[29] While there are many ways the NHS could improve, it has reduced its carbon footprint by 29 per cent compared to the 1990 baseline (despite expanded provision) and has committed to become the world's first net-zero-carbon health system.[30]

The incoming Labour government recognised the dangers of a privatised system and was clear about its mission to end outsourcing.[31] In its long-term plan for the NHS, the government needs to set out clearly how it will reverse this damaging shift to outsourcing public services to the private sector.

Throughout the book it has been argued that outsourcing the provision of core public services to the private sector over the last 30 years, whether childcare and nurseries, child and adult social care, or bus services, has been costly and inefficient and has often lacked in accountability. It has led to provision being increasingly provided by large, international, investor-led companies seeking to maximise profit. If, as argued, free or affordable public services should be at the heart of an anti-poverty strategy, then this needs to be addressed.

Reversing this will be difficult. It would be potentially costly in the short term particularly if, or when, compensation to private providers was legally required. As contracts expire, services could return to being provided in-house, possibly through collaboration between neighbouring local authorities or by non-profit organisations. In the meantime, there need to be far stricter rules as to who can run such services and far more regulation as to standards. And this needs to be tackled urgently.

There are two areas, both vital to any anti-poverty strategy, where this is clearly the case: social care and childcare. In Chapter 4, we saw how the lack of adequate support for carers was pushing unpaid carers into poverty and in Chapter 5, we saw how the means-tested social care system now dominated by private companies has resulted in a fragmented, costly, and unstable system.

Similarly, in Chapter 4, we saw how the expansion of childcare through the government subsidising free childcare for a set number of hours for working parents has created an explosion of private childcare providers, with 84 per cent of provision now delivered by for-profit providers. This lightly regulated, market-based system, with underfunded subsidies per hour, has resulted in low-paid and underqualified staff, variable quality in provision, and an unevenly distributed network of providers with more deprived areas in particular lacking sufficient provision and with inadequate provision for children with disabilities.

What needs to be done? First, there needs to be a new model for social care.

Establishing a National Care Service

In its manifesto for the 2024 election, the Labour Party promised a new National Care Service,[32] including a 'fair pay agreement' to set pay, terms, and conditions, along with training standards. Establishing a National Care Service on par and working with the NHS, and ensuring that everyone has access to quality care which is fair and affordable for all is the right approach. It would need to tackle the fragmentation and privatisation of the system, discussed in Chapter 5, and would need to ensure that costs were not borne, as is currently the case, by those unlucky enough to need care but be above the means-tested limit, but be fairly shared. All this would need additional funding, though there could be savings from changes to how the system is run and the use of large private chains.

However, no details were attached as to how a National Care Service would work or how it would be funded, and the promise was widely seen as at best 'a plan to come up with a plan'[33] or 'so vague it looks like a tick box exercise'.[34] What has resulted from this is a commission into social care in England, the third in three decades, this time headed by the ex-civil servant and go-to trouble shooter, Lousie Casey.[35] Her report is not due until 2028, meaning that it will be the early 2030s before any such plan comes into place and older people and their families benefit. It all feels like kicking the can down the road. There needs to be a swifter timescale and a swifter plan, especially given that much of the evidence and many of the options have already been investigated in previous inquiries and reports.[36]

In 2023, UNISON, as part of their campaign for a National Care Service,[37] commissioned the Fabian Society to research and flesh out what a National Care Service might look like and how it could be implemented. The resultant report, Support Guaranteed,[38] set out how a system of end-to-end support for everyone in need of care could be provided to ensure that everyone has access to the services they need, in a way they wish, regardless of means and in a wide variety of ways. The report proposes that charges should be reformed, starting with some immediate steps, which could include making short-term care free (or at a minimum uprating means-testing thresholds); providing free support for certain groups, starting with, for example, people disabled before adulthood and those with 'very significant support and clinical needs'; limiting the total amount for which anyone would be liable with a lifetime cap on the amount expected to be spent; and a 'modest universal contribution to everyone's care costs'.[39] Over time, further charging reforms would be progressively introduced to ensure a fair sharing of the costs required to meet needs.

The report envisages a diversity of providers, with greater emphasis on home care, and a 'new settlement' with private providers requiring licensing of those providing a service with 'robust requirements regarding the quality of care, ethical workforce practice and financial standards'.[40] All licensed providers would offer national pay, terms and conditions for all care workers, and a proper workforce plan underpinned by a national framework and tight financial regulation to ensure that money was being spent for high-quality service. These would be first steps with the aim of non-profit care organisations playing a larger role – whether housing associations, charities, employee mutuals, or cooperatives controlled by people drawing on services – and, over the longer-term, public provision and insourcing playing a larger role. Local authorities would decide the balance between different providers, according to local need.

The government have taken some steps in this direction announcing, in September 2025, a new negotiating body of employers and unions to introduce fair pay agreements for the adult social care sector in England.[41] The aim is to have a fair pay agreement in place by 2028, with an initial £500 million put aside to fund the resultant pay increases. Though more money will be needed, it is a step in the right direction. It will improve the pay and conditions of care workers, helping lift many out of poverty, and potentially tackle the shortfall of workers, currently filled by migrant workers on work visas.

Moving to a new and universal childcare system

The challenges in creating a universal childcare system are similar, in that current provision is dominated by private providers. If you could start with a clean slate, rather than the under-regulated market system inherited from the coalition and Conservative years, the aim would be to build a publicly commissioned system, running from early-years care to nursery and primary schools, free for all and provided by non-profit organisations and local authorities so as to prioritise child welfare and education rather than the bottom line. As it is, the government are pouring billions – after the latest expansion about £8 billion a year – into a system which is not fit for purpose and increasingly dominated by big international chains.

In its 2024 manifesto, Labour essentially made two promises. The first was to ensure that the promise made in 2023 by the previous government to provide, from September 2025, 30 hours a week of free childcare for children from the age of nine months to two years during term time was delivered. The second was to provide over 3,000 new nursery classes across England by converting spare school classrooms into spaces for nurseries, to be financed from ending the charitable status tax break of private schools.[42] As the first step towards fulfilling this promise, in the autumn of 2024, Bridget Phillipson, the Education Secretary, launched a call for applications for schools with empty classroom spaces to be converted into state nurseries, with the aim of 300 new nurseries opening by the following September.[43] New childcare providers would be encouraged to set up in these locations, with funding rates that are substantially higher than current rates.

The plan would create around 100,000 new nursery places which would go a long way to filling the gap between existing provision and what is needed to meet the expansion of extra free hours promised.[44] It should also help the government target the areas where new provision is created, helping tackle the gaps left by the current system in more disadvantaged areas. It could help drive up standards with an emphasis on education as well as care and offer the chance for an evidence-based assessment of the next steps to take.

These changes nudge the system in a different direction but, on their own, would not make a substantial difference overall. For that, there needs to be a major shift in how the existing system is controlled and run. The evidence, across a wide range of public services is that depending on the market to provide for a 'public good' (that is things we collectively agree are needed) does not work.[45] Over time, it leads to a few large suppliers dominating the market as smaller suppliers, less able to take on shortfalls and debts, are priced out, and, as a consequence, it results in lower standards, lower wages, and shortages of provision in certain areas. It is poor value for government and ends up decreasing choice as smaller and non-profit suppliers are bought out.[46]

To tackle this there needs to be a shift from a market-led system to a commissioning-led system. That is, the system should move away from one where private providers receive large sums of public money (through subsidised free hours) yet decide where to set up and what form provision will take based on market demand. Instead, the public money should be used to commission the provision of places on the basis of need either by establishing new provision or by procuring services from existing suppliers chosen on the basis of quality, not just cost. Funding for existing providers would be dependent on new and more stringent conditions including standards of care and education provided, pay levels with properly qualified staff, and strict financial regulation so that profits and company structure were clear and transparent. In essence, this would set up a licensing system for providers; indeed, in Scotland, private providers already operate through a social licensing model, with standards including financial and fair work requirements set nationally and the provider commissioned locally. Though the system in Scotland needs strengthening, it provides an initial model.[47]

In return, funding should increase from its current level, where funding is not adequate to cover unit costs and providers cross-subsidise free places with paid places, to one that is adequate to cover core costs. The underfunding of the existing system has, in itself, contributed to the increasing dominance of larger private providers and chains who are more able to redistribute the losses from underfunded free places and better placed to use private equity money to fill gaps in support.[48] In addition, extra funding for provision that is more expensive to provide, in particular for children with disabilities, would also be needed.[49]

Further, the provision of free places needs, as it was originally, to be available for all whether in work or not, rather than, as currently, being dependent on being in work for at least 16 hours. This can act as a disincentive to move into full-time work from part-time work, or, indeed, to move into work at all if the work was insecure and as a result your childcare place moved from being funded to being unfunded. There is strong international evidence that making eligibility for free hours dependent on number of hours worked is likely to result in the children who most need access to early learning and care not getting it,[50] and that universal access greatly improves employment levels among women, contributing to reduced gender inequalities in income over the life course.[51]

Moreover, the current 30-hour limit to the total number of free hours does not, in practice, cover all the hours needed for parents in full-time work and could mean that parents are reluctant to move into full-time work, especially if their hours are uncertain. There is a strong case that free hours should at least equal the number of hours normally worked in a week. Moving to a more universal service with more extended hours would require a further expansion of places. This would provide the opportunity to shift the balance of providers to local authority-run nurseries and smaller, more local non-profit providers.

With these sorts of steps, as with the proposed new National Care Service, a new universal childcare and education service for all could start to be created. This would give parents more choice than the current market system; parents would still be able to choose between different providers according to their child's needs and they would be able to choose to take up provision or not, if, for a wide variety of reasons (see Chapter 4) they prioritised time spent with their children over work.

Of course, this would cost money and more than currently allocated. But government money is already being poured into the system in such a way that there are gaps, risks of extractive exploitation from a decreasing number of providers and variable quality. These reforms should create better value for money with tighter financial regulation ensuring profits are ploughed back into the system. In addition, as provision is expanded, some of this could be funded from the tax-free childcare currently provided above the free hours,[52] largely benefitting the better paid, which would no longer be needed, and from reduced benefits payments as more women enter the workforce and are able to do so at higher salary levels. The Women's Budget Group found that a similar reform package aimed at ensuring a universal high-quality system with well-paid staff, free at the point of use would have an initial investment cost of 0.7 per cent of GDP (£18 billion in 2022 levels), but 61 per cent of that would be recouped through positive impacts on the wider economy.[53]

In December 2024, the Labour Party published its Plan for Change which emphasised the importance of early years and committed to driving up the proportion of children 'ready to learn' when starting school from 67.7 per cent to 75 per cent reaching the set development goals.[54] This renewed focus on early years is welcome and in July 2025 the Education Secretary Bridget Phillipson announced the launch of Best Start Family Hubs to give parents advice and help and support children's early-years development and language – basically a successor to Sure Start.[55] In its initial phase, the government planned to invest £500 million to create a network of up to 1,000 Best Start Family Hubs across every local authority in England by 2028. It is a significant step but to make a real difference it needs to be just the start.

At the end of the day, if you want higher standards, you need a better qualified and paid workforce to bring up standards, proper provision across the country and an ability to meet varying needs, and if you want to do this in a way the ensures low-income households have access through a universal service, then it needs to be paid for with higher initial investment. But the long-term benefits for society of providing a universal service for pre-school children, including very young children and infants, are huge; it is crucial to improving children's educational outcomes and life chances, especially those from more disadvantaged backgrounds,[56] and it would substantially help families to lift themselves out of poverty and thereby have a substantial impact on levels of child poverty.

Another step would be to remove the means-testing that currently applies to the provision of some services for children.

Making school meals free for all

Free school meals are currently available to primary school pupils for year two and under – an initiative of the coalition government back in 2014.[57] After that age, free school meals for primary school pupils and all secondary school pupils are – with some exceptions in some areas – means-tested, so that only the poorest households receive them.

In 2018 the then-Conservative government tightened the rules for children receiving means-tested free school meals so that, rather than all families on UC qualifying, the children of those in work earning more than £7,400 were no longer eligible.[58] It left some 280,000 low-income working families in England being worse off overall and made it even harder to move out of poverty. For those earning just under the £7,400 limit, taking on extra hours or getting a pay rise could make them worse off as they would lose the free school meal entitlement and those just above the limit would need to earn £3,500 more before they recouped the loss.[59]

In June 2025 the new Labour government returned entitlement to free school meals to all children in households on UC – a move, the government estimated, that would lift 100,000 children out of poverty.[60] While clearly good news for the families affected, it was hardly the 'historic' expansion the government claimed, maintaining the means-tested system with a somewhat higher household income cutoff.

There are, however, deep problems with means-testing school meals which are well documented and range from embedding the poverty trap, to covering only a small proportion of those in poverty, to being highly stigmatising for the children receiving the meals.[61] Moreover, research into the impact of providing universal free school meals for 5- to 7-year-olds has found that it has improved the health and attainment of all children, but more for the children who always had qualified for free school meals when it was means-tested than the newly qualified group.[62] In other words, if you want to help the life chances of the poorest children, it is more effective to do so through a universal system.

The move to make free school meals available to all is gaining traction[63] and moreover, becoming policy in certain areas. Since September 2023, the London Mayor, Sadiq Khan, has funded free school meals for *all* primary school pupils in the region. Similarly, free school meals are provided in Scotland by the Scottish Parliament for primary school pupils up to 9 years old (Primary 5), while in Wales, from 2023 the Welsh Assembly started to roll out free primary school meals starting with the youngest age groups.

In London, to assess the impact of providing the free school meals in primary schools, the Mayoral Office commissioned Impact on Urban Health to carry out an independent evaluation. The report found the policy popular with parents and valued highly by those working in schools, that it had helped to address the problems of hidden hunger and food insecurity, and improved access to nutritious school food of greater variety. The study found widespread examples of parents, school staff, and children noticing positive shifts in behaviour, concentration, and energy levels during the school day 'with children talking about feeling "stronger and healthier" and having "more energy"'.[64] The children valued being able to sit and eat together, sharing an equal lunchtime experience and for some children it shifted how they felt about school, contributing to feelings of greater fairness, belonging, and community. Overall, the findings strongly suggested the policy had improved pupils' sense of well-being. And for the families the introduction of free school meals had helped alleviate financial hardship; 84 per cent of parents surveyed said it had helped or significantly helped household finances and a third reported that they had less debt as a result.

A good place to start in expanding universal basic services would then be to make free school meals available to all state primary school children in the UK. There is also a strong case for making free school meals universally available for all pupils, secondary as well as primary. PricewaterhouseCoopers (PwC) estimated, in an analysis for Impact on Urban Health, that if this policy was applied across England then for every £1 invested there would be a return of £1.71 in core benefits, by which is meant those benefits resulting directly from the policy as opposed to also including secondary benefits impacting the wider economy.[65]

The government has taken a step in the direction of universal provision with trials of free universal breakfast clubs in a selected 750 primary schools,[66] echoing a similar scheme already run by the Welsh government for primary schools in Wales.[67] The long-term aim is to roll out free and universal breakfast clubs to all schools in England, replacing the National School Breakfast Club Programme, a subsidised scheme for schools with at least 40 per cent of pupils from income-deprived areas.

Critics of universalism will say that these sorts of policies are just middle-class perks[68] and what's needed is tightly targeted means-tested help, primarily on the basis that it costs less. But this is to completely misunderstand how means-testing works and how it results, definitionally, in exclusion. And it misunderstands the wider benefits of universal services and how they can help develop cohesion and equality. And, as a result, it misunderstands how in the long run universalism is more cost-effective. PwC estimates that the financial return on means-tested free school meals that included only those on universal benefit would be at £1.38 for every £1 invested compared to the £1.78 return for the universal system.[69] The upfront costs of more universal policies are higher but the long-term benefits are far greater.

For other services there could be different approaches to reaching a more universal system.

Expanding free or discounted public transport to new groups

Some services are currently free for certain groups but not others and these discounted or free services could be expanded to other groups. Throughout the UK, senior citizens qualify for a free bus pass once they reach retirement age and in certain areas (London, Scotland, and Northern Ireland, for example), once they reach the age of 60. In most parts of the UK, there are also free (or concessionary) bus passes for those with a registered disability, though, as is typically the case with senior citizen bus passes, the hours within which it can be used are often limited to off-peak services. In some areas there are free bus passes for young people (under 22 in Scotland and under 18 in London, for example) and other concessionary rates. And, to drive up usage after COVID-19, price caps were introduced on certain routes, currently extended to the end of 2025.

A first step towards ensuring the affordability of bus services would be to extend the best practices (such as in London and Scotland) across the country. The next steps could be to make bus services – and where relevant other local transport services such as tube, tram, or local overground – free for other groups (carers or parents of young children for example) or free for all on certain routes (to hospitals, schools, or areas with a high concentration of jobs, for example) or certain areas (where congestion is high, for example). A key advantage of the kind of franchising system operated in London and Manchester (and being expanded by the Labour government, see Chapter 5) is that it allows these kinds of decisions on how to operate the bus system to be made on the basis of public gain rather than private profit and in a way that reflects local needs.

A final step could be making buses free for all. The Institute for Global Prosperity at UCL has modelled the cost of moving to free local bus services to be around £5–10 billion, depending on the extent to which demand increases,[70] and that a universal bus service would also be broadly progressive as poorer households tend to use buses far more than richer households. There would, in addition, be other significant social and environmental benefits, such as tackling isolation and reducing particulate pollution.

Focusing on local communities

The implementation of any scheme for improving and expanding services as part of an anti-poverty strategy depends on strong and robust local government. The general principle behind such a strategy is that power should be devolved to the lowest democratically accountable level appropriate for that service. This could be central government, regional, or metropolitan authorities, or district and local councils so, for example, transport might be best operated at a regional level while various support services might be better at a more local level where they would be more accountable to the people who use them and better able to draw on the experience of users of those services. Within these areas, responsibility for aspects of each service could be devolved further to more locally based organisations.

In this approach, various tiers of government in an area work with other locally based and rooted organisations both private and public – what are called 'anchor' institutions in that they cannot readily or easily move out of the area – and collectively leverage their resources to support and benefit their local communities in 'anchor' networks.[71] This approach was pioneered in Preston, Lancashire, where the city council pulled together key institutions in the area to harness their spending and supply chains for greater local economic benefit.[72] The impact was significant, with spending on procurement retained within Preston rising from £38.2 million in 2012/13 to £112.3 million in 2016/17, and within Lancashire (including Preston) from £288.7 million to £488.7 million.[73] The extra money being spent in the area helped local business and increased the numbers of people employed locally, which in turn helped the area's well-being and health.

Other areas have subsequently established such networks. In 2019, the Birmingham Anchor network was established, involving the city council and other large local employers. During the COVID-19 pandemic, it launched its pilot 'Hospitality to Health' employment programme to connect and help those made redundant in the hospitality sector move into care work. This was followed by the 'I Can' recruitment programme, which aimed to deliver health and social care employment opportunities for unemployed and young people across Birmingham and Solihull, specifically targeting residents in the most economically disadvantaged areas.[74] As seen in Chapter 7, Oldham Council used a similar initiative to establish Oldham Community Power to develop locally based renewable energy. And the Greater Manchester Combined Authority has coordinated councils in the area to build its GM full fibre network, lowering costs and providing fast internet services to schools and public bodies throughout the area.[75]

In Worcester, Worcestershire County Council and the University of Worcester have worked together to create a new city centre library, history, and advice centre for students and the public, the Hive.[76] Driven by an ethos of inclusivity, the new library is Europe's first fully integrated university and public library. It is an imaginative centre of learning for people of all ages, for example offering the university's strong collection of resources for primary school teaching, including books for children, to local residents to borrow.

These kinds of innovative schemes show the ways that services could be re-imagined. Others provide different ways of tackling food poverty.

Community food hubs

In Flintshire, the county council has teamed up with Clwyd Alyn Housing Association and the social enterprise Can Cook to launch Well Fed.[77] Since Well Fed was established in 2019, it has distributed over 60,000 meals to vulnerable households, has launched a meal box service for local residents whereby households receive a meal box containing recipe cards and fresh ingredients at discounted prices, and set up MealVend and MealLocker,[78] refrigerated vending outlets to improve access to food for isolated communities where it is a struggle to access food. The aim is to source as much of the food as possible locally, thereby supporting local farmers and reducing air miles. It is an innovative scheme looking at helping tackle food poverty, encouraging healthier eating, and the acquisition of essential cooking skills.

Similar schemes have been tried elsewhere, such as the BRITE box (Building Resilience in Today's Environment) scheme which started in Kingston-upon-Thames, London, and has spread to seven neighbouring boroughs. Funded by grants and fundraising from the local authorities, free weekly recipe boxes with pre-weighed ingredients are provided to children and families during school terms to take home for their evening meal.[79] The provision of the boxes is run (largely) by volunteers with ingredients sourced where possible from local suppliers, while the choice of families receiving the boxes is left to the school.

Other schemes have involved using surplus food to 'recycle' into ready-made meals. In Richmond-on-Thames, London, The Real Junk Food Project obtains food from local supermarkets, independent shops, and allotments and turns the produce into ready-made meals distributed at various sites on a pay-as-you-feel model, allowing clients to donate but without the obligation to do so.[80] Researchers from Kingston University, London, investigating the impact of the scheme, found that as surplus food was used, clients accessing the café and food hubs were not all necessarily food insecure. And this had advantages in that it 'meant that people who would not normally meet each other had an opportunity to mix in a safe and welcoming space, which was inclusive and non-judgemental, but also potentially reduced stigma since reasons for attending could be environmental rather than financial'.[81]

More generally, food aid that takes the form of community food hubs, rather than handing out food parcels, can have similar advantages. Studies of males attending food aid sites in Middlesbrough found that participants would describe attending these sites out of loneliness and isolation and 'as a source of informal support and friendship', particularly important for single men who were not receiving this support from a relationship or through family networks.[82]

Traditional food banks have been much criticised for their use of referral systems requiring proof of need and the resultant stigma and shame attached to being a recipient. They are essentially a shadow welfare system picking up the pieces of a failed benefit system – leaving the real problem of the inadequacy of benefits unaddressed. Clients can feel devalued by having no possibility of making a financial contribution while their lack of food choices at many food banks embeds an idea that poor people don't care about the aesthetics of food,[83] or its quality or taste; food becomes just a matter of nutritional value and calories.

To some extent, some of the schemes outlined above overcome some of these criticisms, but not all. While the volunteers were highly motivated and keen to help their local community, the line between voluntary community action and government responsibility remained blurred. Moving forward there needs to be an approach that builds on the community strengths of such schemes while not substituting for the government's responsibility to provide adequate incomes.

Taking devolved government seriously

In the government's provisional settlement for local government finance for 2025/26, there was some increase to funding levels; England saw a rise of 3.8 per cent in real terms,[84] after accounting for forecast economy-wide inflation, with a slightly larger increase of 4.3 per cent for Scotland[85] and Wales.[86] This is composed of a number of elements, some of which, in particular a new 'recovery' grant, were highly targeted at councils serving deprived areas. Overall, the Institute for Fiscal Studies calculates that there was an increase of 5.8 per cent of core spending power in the most deprived tenth of council areas, but just 0.3 per cent in the least deprived.

This extra funding, especially in the more deprived areas, will help councils meet some of the additional pressures they are under – but by no means all. Just to tread water, the Local Government Association estimates that the combination of increases in demand and above-inflation increases in costs for key services requires this kind of level of extra funding. To re-establish the kinds of preventative services of the past that tackled poverty and deprivation at root, such as youth clubs, it needs a return to the funding levels of the past; a small increase does nothing to reverse the impact of austerity. To implement the kinds of transformation outlined above would need additional funding to that of past levels, though, in the longer term, especially if accompanied by a return to insourcing services, there would be savings. A stabilisation of the reduced funding after years of austerity simply does not match what is needed.

The government has allowed councils to raise council tax bills by 3 per cent, and those with social care responsibilities by a further 2 per cent, without a local referendum, with some councils in financial difficulties allowed some further increases. But council tax is an extraordinarily unfair tax. Based on the value of properties in 1991, it fails to reflect huge changes in property wealth over the past three decades. It has a limited level of bands above which all pay the same, however many millions the property is worth. The Resolution Foundation estimates that the poorest fifth of households spend around 4.8 per cent of their gross household income on the tax, up from 2.9 per cent in 2002–03 and compared to 1.5 per cent paid by the richest fifth.[87] It also strongly favours local authorities in richer areas, whose residents are more able to pay higher levels of council tax.

Council tax is in urgent need of reform. Some kind of properly graduated property tax based on current property values, with a proportion going nationally for redistribution so that richer and poorer areas could be evened up and a proportion locally so that residents could decide the level they wanted, would be a way of sorting this. There are, no doubt, other approaches to restructuring council tax. But no government seems ready to take this on.

To fill gaps in funding for young people, the government has launched a Better Futures Fund, backed by £500 million of government funding over ten years and with the aim of raising a further £500 million from local government, social investors, and philanthropists. The scheme aims to bring together various local bodies from local government, charities, social enterprises, businesses, and private funders to support projects to help children 'struggling with exclusion, mental health or crime'.[88] Any extra investment to help vulnerable young people is welcome and bringing together a network of organisations and partnerships can improve the way support is delivered. But the level of cuts has been such that in 2024 around £1.2 billion (adjusted for inflation) less was spent on youth services than in 2010.[89] To think this is a 'major step',[90] as claimed, is overstating the case.

To kickstart the kinds of changes looked at in this chapter, there needs to be a commitment to a substantial increase in spending on services, to bring both the existing services up to standard and creating new ones that will help tackle poverty. In the long run, this would improve people's quality of life across the board and help lift vulnerable groups out of poverty, but it also has the potential to create long-term savings. Chapter 12 will look at how this investment in the future could be achieved.

It is now time to look at the final key element of a serious anti-poverty strategy – household income.

11

Income security for all

The devastating impact that the current inadequacy of many people's household incomes has on their lives is clear. While the Labour government has introduced a raft of measures to try to improve both job security and pay (see Chapter 4), its plans to 'reform' the benefit system backfired (see Chapter 3). Many would agree that the current benefits system is just not working. It is inadequate to live off and it fails to provide a route out of poverty. Just reversing the policies of the last decade, important as much of this is, would not be enough.

There needs to be *both* a recovery from the current damage imposed on the benefits system and a remodelling of how it works. This needs to ensure adequate household income for those unable to work so that they have a fulfilling life while at the same time enabling those who are able to work to move into jobs that set a path for future opportunities. What then needs to be done, both in the short and long term?

Short-term fixes

People who experience poverty best understand first-hand the inadequacies and failures of the current social security system and without listening to these voices, policy changes risk being ineffective by misunderstanding people's lives, the problems and barriers they face and their aspirations and motivations.[1] And the priorities of those on benefits is clear.

In the run up to the general election of 2025, the Changing Realities participatory project[2] identified four for families. These are: increasing the value of all benefits, regular payments rather than temporary measures, ending the two-child limit and the benefit cap, and increasing child benefit.[3] Not surprisingly, these priorities fit closely with evidence presented in earlier chapters of failings in the current system and echo very similar priorities to that of all the main anti-poverty campaigning groups including the TUC,[4] Child Poverty Action Group,[5] and the Fabian Society.[6]

Of these, the incoming Labour government has indicated its intention to take action on only the two-child limit, and that belatedly. While removing the two child limit would provide a significant boost (of around 13%) to larger families on UC (some 660,000 households), it is not, on its own, a magic bullet. For 70,000 of the poorest families affected, the gains are partially or fully wiped out by the benefit cap.[7] And although child poverty rates would drop, by about 3 to 4 percentage points, rates would remain high and without other measures to lift the economy would be likely to rise over time. Of other potential short-term fixes, increasing the value of UC would, of course, make an immediate impact on the living standards of poorer households. And for this reason, given the extremely low living standards currently faced, it is worth doing. But it would potentially decrease incentives to move into full-time work and would need to be done with the kind of changes outlined subsequently.

The Scottish government has introduced various additional payments to families with children on means-tested benefits including 'top-up' child payments for all children under 16 living in low-income households, grants to help with the costs of pregnancy and having a new baby, a payment to households with two- and three-year-olds to help with their learning, and another when they start school.[8] Early evidence suggests this is having some effect on reducing child poverty levels[9] but such moves add to both the complexity and the disincentive effects of means testing and there are other more service based solutions that could have a similar impact (see Chapter 10).

The rent cap continues to cause intense problems for low-income families in high-rent areas. And while the housebuilding target and reforms to private renting introduced by the Labour government (see Chapter 9) should have an impact in the longer term on rental prices, in the short term, the housing element of UC needs to be increased in line with local housing rental values.[10]

Another change needs to focus on the conditionality placed on means-tested benefits and the resultant sanctions. These have been largely counter-productive, pushing people away from work. While it might be necessary, after a certain length of time, to introduce a level of conditionality, this should come after a period in which people can search for a better job that suits their potential and aspirations, rather than being forced into any dead-end job that comes around.

There needs to be more emphasis in the benefits system on helping people gain the skills and confidence to move into work. This is an approach the government has adopted, announcing in March 2025 plans to bring in 1,000 work coaches to help the long-term unemployed into work.[11] This is a start but not enough and needs to be done in conjunction with moves to rejig the local economy to make sure suitable jobs are available.

At the same time, most migrants are excluded by the NRPF rules from claiming UC, a situation which extending the wait before gaining citizenship will make far worse. Removing the exclusion of migrants from claiming UC would have a sharp impact on poverty levels and in particular destitution levels. To do this, the government would need to make a clear case as to the value migration brings to the country and the decision-making process as to which potential migrants are given the right to live and work in the UK. But it should be a matter of principle that everyone who has the right to live in the UK should have access to public funds. Their exclusion should not be used as a tool of immigration policy.

Reforming in-work benefit transfers

There is a strong case for supporting household income for those where one or more household members are in work (see Chapter 4), a role now undertaken by UC. But, as seen, there are problems with the way it works. It does not provide a long-term route out of poverty and disincentivises savings. It needs restructuring. First, the disincentives to save need to be removed by lifting the savings thresholds at which benefits received are deducted. And the way it operates needs to provide a better path into full-time work.

The Institute for Fiscal Studies has done some interesting work on how this could be achieved, looking at the relative long-term impacts of increasing the threshold at which withdrawal of the benefit starts (work allowances) and the rate at which it is withdrawn as incomes increase (the taper rate).[12] On the surface, both seem similar in that they put more money into the pockets of households where someone moves from being out of work into work. However, while both reforms get people into work, increasing the work allowance incentivises moving from unemployment into part-time work, while lowering the taper rate also incentivises moving into full-time work, because benefits are reduced more slowly as earnings increase. It is thus more effective at increasing the numbers in full-time work and hourly rates of pay across a lifetime,[13] and is more successful at moving households out of poverty. It also, as a result, boosts tax revenues in the long term.

Lowering the taper rate would result in Working Tax Credit going to households with higher incomes and indeed many in the upper half of the income distribution. This goes against the grain of most government reforms of recent years which have increasingly tightened means-tested benefits so that more of the money is spent on the lowest-income households where, it is argued, it is most needed. While this saves government money in the short term, these studies suggest that you need to look also at the impact in the longer run. And if this is taken into account, tighter means-testing of work-related benefits could well be counter-productive in terms of making work a more effective route out of poverty. An approach to UC that withdraws it gradually would turn the benefit into a sort of household earned-income support scheme, as opposed to a means-tested benefit that keeps households on a minimum income level.

The need to row back from means-testing

When the modern welfare state was introduced by the 1945 Labour government, the UK's social security system, following the 1942 Beveridge Report, aimed to cover people's basic income needs from 'cradle to grave' through a system of National Insurance, paid without recourse to means-testing which was seen to be demeaning, to penalise savings, to discourage work, and to encourage fraud. It was also a contributory system with benefits paid in return for contributions paid through National Insurance rather than given as a right and paid for from general taxation. This was seen to encourage a sense of responsibility, a 'something for something' deal.[14]

The scheme started well with the numbers claiming means-tested benefits dropping dramatically.[15] But society started to change, often in ways not foreseen, the most significant of which were the rise in divorce and the numbers of single parents, the increasing recognition of the additional costs of living with a disability, the rise in rents, and the increase in low-paid jobs. As a result, new benefits were introduced such as single-parent benefit, housing benefit, and various disability benefits. To limit costs these were often means-tested, and increasingly aggressively with lower savings limits and sharper cutoffs.

At the same time, the purpose of the contributory element was watered down. This was primarily because the contributory element was increasingly seen to be excluding certain groups who had not been able to keep up their contributions. This was particularly likely for women, who often took time off paid employment to look after children and for other caring responsibilities, and thereby failed to make sufficient contributions to gain full levels of benefit. This has gradually changed so that now if someone is ill, disabled, on maternity pay, or on Carer's Allowance, for example, they can receive National Insurance 'credit' as if they had paid their contributions, thereby maintaining the value of their state pension.[16] These changes are important in terms of inclusivity. Women who had spent long periods out of the labour market caring for children saw substantial increases to their pension.

The shift to means-testing also undermined contributory benefits. For example, payments made under the National Insurance element of unemployment benefit are deducted from UC payments pound for pound, making it worthless to those who become unemployed and live in low-income households.[17] Not surprisingly, relatively few people out of work claim it, around 88,000 in August 2023.[18]

For those of working age, the result of these trends is that the share of expenditure on working-age benefits going to means-tested payments has risen from under 25 per cent of all benefit payments in the early 1980s to over 60 per cent in recent years. Over the same period, the share going on contributory benefits has fallen from just under 50 per cent to around 9 per cent, with the share taken by non-contributory, non-means-tested benefits such as PIPs, remaining fairly constant at about 25 per cent.[19]

As a result, the aim of the benefit system for working-age people has become primarily focused on providing a minimum household income rather than supporting households across the income range against unpredictable life events and for the times during life when there are additional needs and costs. It is a minimalist view of social security, limited to the relief of poverty rather than the collective sharing of risk in an uncertain world. Its focus is on alleviating poverty (even if it is unsuccessful in doing so) rather than preventing poverty in the first place by protecting incomes that unpredictably fall so that the poverty line is not reached or by providing a long-term route out of poverty. It means that the stake that those who are more middle class, or on somewhat higher household incomes, have in social security is low – perhaps explaining its lower levels of overall public support than for the NHS and state education.[20]

And it increases financial insecurity by discouraging saving. Once savings (outside pension schemes) reach a certain level (currently around £6,000), the savings are taken into account when assessing benefit levels with money deducted for every pound saved above the level. For those on means-tested benefits there is little point in saving.

But most concerningly it has not worked.

Essentially, a means-tested minimum income support for those out of work is designed to produce a lower household income than that which can be obtained from work, primarily to incentivise work. This means that in an economy where wage levels are low, providing a decent level of living for those out of work is difficult. One way of solving this is to provide support for those in work, to maintain incentives to work. But even with such support for those in work, in an economy where wages are stagnating and inadequate, means-tested benefits for those out of work will tend to be inadequate.

Across Europe, means-tested minimum income schemes have become increasingly widespread. Yet despite European Union Council recommendations to member states to adapt their minimum income schemes and make them more adequate, there is little evidence this has happened.[21] Even in member states with historically more generous welfare systems, such as the Netherlands, means-tested minimum income supports have remained inadequate.[22]

Means-tested benefits aimed, as currently structured, at providing a bare minimum of support to just the poorest households need to be replaced by a system of household income support that is adequate when there are no other sources of income, is independent of savings, and is gradually withdrawn as household incomes increase. This would be far more effective in enabling people to move out of poverty on a long-term and sustainable basis.

Creating a modern insurance-based system

For most people, losing your job in the UK leads to a large income loss, and a loss much higher than in most other countries. While for some this might not result in an immediate risk of poverty, the lack of financial support when out of work means that many end up taking any job available, with no prospects, thereby stepping onto a downward spiral. This is, of course, bad for the person involved and their dependents but it is also bad for the economy. Most economists think it creates a less dynamic economy over time, as people are reluctant to move jobs or change the course of their work or to relocate. This, in turn, leads to lower productivity and an economy stagnating rather than growing.[23] Enabling people to retrain and move jobs could become increasingly important as the impact of artificial intelligence on jobs becomes more apparent.

Many European countries operate a much more contributory, insurance-based system for people of working-age than that in the UK[24] and pay far more generous unemployment benefits. In Denmark, insurance unemployment benefit is paid at 90 per cent of previous salary, in Sweden; it's paid at 80 per cent dropping to 70 per cent after nine months; in Netherlands at 75 per cent dropping to 70 per cent after two months; in Belgium,

65 per cent, Austria and Canada at 55 per cent and so on for many other countries that all have higher rates.[25]

The Resolution Foundation has looked at the impact paying those who had been in employment for the past year unemployment insurance at 65 per cent of previous salary (capped at median earnings), bringing it in line with most advanced economies and far higher than current JSA rates.[26] On their proposals, this would run for three months before dropping in level, on the basis that many will have found employment in that time, and you need to keep up incentives to find alternative work. The Resolution Foundation estimates that, as long as unemployment remains relatively low, the cost would be relatively small. If these assumptions turned out to be less than optimal for encouraging people back into high-quality work, other choices could be made; in some countries (such as South Korea) the length of time payments are made increases during economic downturns when unemployment is high.

Most importantly benefits paid under the proposed scheme would not, as is the case for contributory JSA, be deducted pound for pound from UC. Instead it would be treated by UC as if it was earned income with UC tapering away. For some, the payment would be enough to take them out of the UC system altogether.

In the shake-up of the benefits system announced in March 2025, the Work and Pensions Secretary, Liz Kendall, proposed to consult on the introduction of a time-limited unemployment insurance paid at a higher rate. This could be a step in the right direction though the details have remained unclear.[27]

These sorts of proposals would help prevent people dropping into poverty in the first place. It would be hoped that they also had economic benefits in turning the UK into a higher-paid, more-productive economy but even if that was not the case it should enable those out of work enough time and security to look for better-quality jobs with long-term prospects.

Such moves could help households through the uncertainties of working life. What else could be done?

Is there a case for a Universal Basic Income?

Universal Basic Income (UBI) is an idea that has gained increasing attention in recent years; indeed, much of the debate around rethinking the social security system has been dominated by it.[28] For some it seems an idea whose time has come.[29] In essence, it is simple: a regular cash payment to every individual regardless of their income and wealth and without any conditions attached. It is worth clarifying this as there is some confusion as to what counts as a UBI scheme. Some proposals include regular non-means-tested and non-conditional payments to specific groups (such as care leavers) in UBI[30] rather than what these actually are, which is a non-means-tested payment to a particular group with particular needs. These could be seen as a basic income for certain groups but not as a *universal* basic income.

In its universality, UBI's proponents see it as a way of providing better economic security for all and reducing the stigmatising effects of means-tested systems while providing individual autonomy as to how it is spent. Many also see it as an answer to growing insecurity in the labour market and to the spectre of artificial intelligence creating a new wave of technological job losses.[31] In its simplicity it is attractive and at times is offered as a one-stop solution to *all* the problems of the social security system. In reality, its implementation would be far from simple with its impact on poverty, and its overall cost, dependent on the level at which payments are set, its overall design in relation to other benefits, and the way in which taxes are adjusted to pay for it.

Howard Reed, of Landman Economics, and academic colleagues have modelled various options, increasing in levels of generosity.[32] The most basic scheme would offer an unconditional, guaranteed UBI of £63 a week per adult between 18 and 64, £190 per adult aged 65 and over, and £41 per child, while its most generous scheme would offer £230 per adult aged 18 or over and £95 per child. The most basic scheme would not keep those currently at risk of poverty out of poverty and is supplemented by additional means-tested payments paid through UC, and while the most generous scheme would eliminate many payments under UC, additional housing and childcare payments as well as most disability payments would still be needed. For all schemes there would be some losers in the lower-income groups, though all would reduce overall poverty levels.

Additional taxation would be needed to pay for the additional expenditures. For the most basic scheme, an extra 3p on income tax rates and a reduction in the personal allowance to £750 would be required, while the most generous scheme would raise income tax rates to 65p (basic), 85p (higher), and 95p (additional), though employee and self-employed National Insurance contributions would be abolished. The high level of tax rises in the more generous schemes make them, the authors admit, 'potentially politically challenging'[33] to implement, a statement which, as Donald Hirsch of Loughborough University comments on reviewing the schemes, 'makes a good candidate for academic understatement of the year'.[34]

The least generous scheme is more feasible – Reed and colleagues describe it as 'affordable, feasible and highly progressive'[35] – but the problem here is it retains much of the problems of the current means-tested system of UC. Those modelling similar potential UBI schemes have come up with similar findings, though their interpretation of the implications is somewhat different. The Institute for Policy Research at Bath University concluded from their models that 'an affordable UBI would be inadequate, and an adequate UBI would be unaffordable'.[36]

By framing the policy as a public health measure, its proponents argue that these costs could be funded in part through significant (future) savings to the NHS through the reduction in poverty and increase in physical and mental well-being. Though these potential savings on health expenditure would apply to other proposals to reduce poverty, UBI has the potential to provide greater feelings of income security if set a high enough level.

Its proponents argue that there could be other advantages to UBI; for example, that it would increase entrepreneurship.[37] However, there are equally reasons to think that its impact on work incentives might be negative. For the least generous schemes marginal tax rates are at times high as different elements are withdrawn at different rates and at different thresholds,[38] while for the most generous schemes it is not clear why at least some people would feel that it was necessary to work given many of their needs are met by UBI. The problem is it is all rather untested, not surprisingly, as, though partial basic income schemes have been tried, full blown UBI schemes, paid to all, have not.

These reservations are reinforced by extensive work done in British Columbia, Canada, where the state government funded a generous research project tasked with examining the viability of a basic income in the province and whether elements could be used to enhance current provision.[39] The study found that far from simplifying the system, a basic income would not provide a replacement for most benefits and thereby would add complexity to the system and concluded that in each case studied a basic income 'might have positive effects but there was an alternative, more targeted, policy that was better'.[40] These were not always cash transfer policies. Looking at women on low wages and in poverty, often women from minority communities, the researchers argue that a more direct way of helping would be to concentrate on tightening labour market regulations. And this would apply in many other areas.

There is also concern that the high level of resources that a UBI would require at anything other than a token level, would mean that improvements in other areas could take second place. Public Services International, a global trade union federation for workers in public services, worries, for example, that UBI could threaten 'existing targeted programs such as public housing, public subsidies to childcare, public transport and public health'[41] and that it could strengthen the hand of those who simply want to cut public services who would argue that the state's obligations had been met by providing a universal income. While this is not the position of most proponents of UBI, there are those on the libertarian right and prominent proponents in Silicon Valley[42] who would like to see the state play a minimal role and who see limited cash payments as laying the way to this. With President Trump and his allies in control in the White House, and the rise of the far-right elsewhere, such concerns should not be taken idly.

Nevertheless, proponents of UBI have directed attention to important, and often overlooked, aspects of the debate about how to tackle poverty.

Replacing the personal tax allowance with a cash payment

The debate on tackling poverty tends to be focused on benefits – usually that spending on benefits is too high or out of control[43] – while the wide variety of tax allowances are presented as a deserved break for the 'hard-working taxpayer'. Increasing both tax allowances and benefits puts money into households' pockets with the difference being who benefits the most. With tax allowance it is generally better-off households that benefit far more from any increase than lower-income households, while benefits tend to be more concentrated on low-income households. The financial support provided to households by the tax-free allowances in the income tax system can been seen as a 'shadow welfare' system, supporting household incomes. Over the last decade or so there has been a huge shift from benefit spending to increasing tax allowances.

Most UBI schemes propose scrapping, or at least cutting, the basic tax allowance and redirecting this money to fund a UBI. For most schemes, doing this on its own does not cover the cost, and certainly not for the more generous schemes. But nevertheless, shifting the way households are supported from tax allowance towards a weekly cash payment might make sense.

The NEF calculates that removing the personal tax-free allowance, worth more than £100 billion in 2019/20, and replacing it with a weekly cash payment for adults of £2,500 per year, paid to everyone outside the richest 1 per cent and treated as earned income for those on UC, and upping child benefit back to its 2010 level, would not cost the Treasury anything but would be both highly redistributive and help lift families out of poverty.[44] For most households in the middle of the income range the gains and losses would balance out but for the poorest there would be gains, while for richer households there would be losses with these losses being concentrated in the top 10 per cent, a group which has seen the biggest gains in recent years.[45]

The NEF reckons that overall, about 200,000 families would be lifted out of income poverty, while the non-conditionality of the payment might help people search for the right job with better prospects rather than take any job. If such a move had these positive impacts, the weekly cash payment could be gradually increased.

Targeted basic income

So, what else could be done to shift the benefits system away from its current emphasis on means-testing? Currently, there are a number of benefits that target those with specific needs, providing a benefit to all in that group, regardless of wealth and income. These benefits are quite different in their conception and purpose to UBI schemes. Whereas a UBI would go to everyone regardless of their ability to work or otherwise and regardless of any specific requirement, these benefits are aimed at times in one's life when there are specific needs to be met or when work is not a viable way of achieving income.

One of the most vulnerable groups in society are those who leave care. In the UK, care leavers find that on reaching the age of 18, there is an abrupt end to much of the support available to them as looked after children with a resultant huge drop in how they feel about their well-being.[46] Many report deep financial problems and a lack of support[47] and levels of homelessness are high and growing.[48]

Here, direct cash support might be part of the answer, along with other support including housing and being part of a community who will stay in their lives.[49] In Wales, the Welsh government have run a trial, which started in 2022, in which those who leave care receive a basic income payment of £1,600 a month before tax (£1,280 per month, after tax) for 24 months from the month after their 18th birthday.[50] This is an important trial and could be an important part of a way forward to helping care leavers find their feet. Similar cash payments could be a way forward to helping those who are homeless and there have been proposals for trials in Manchester.[51]

Such initiatives could help fill in gaps in support for some of the most vulnerable. But the most important actions, and the ones that would have the most widespread impact, would be to build on those universal benefits already in place.

Guaranteeing the future of the state pension

Across the board the state pension provides nearly half of the income of pensioners.[52] It is by far the single most important source of income for all pensioners in the bottom third, many of whom receive no private pension income.[53] Even for higher-income pensioners the state pension is a substantial part of their overall income, accounting for around a quarter of income for the top 20 per cent.[54] And unlike other benefits, the state pension was protected throughout the years of austerity through the triple lock.

This, along with the rise in private pensions, has meant that overall, pensioners have never been as well off as they are today. Unlike working-age incomes, overall pension incomes have continued to rise since 2010, particularly sharply for higher-income pensioners but low-income pensioners have also benefitted.

In addition, the gap in the provision for men and women has closed substantially. This is partly because women have been more engaged in the workforce and more have been receiving both the state pension and some private pension, though the gender gap for private pensions remains large. It is also because there have been far more comprehensive credits for time spent not in paid work, resulting in most women, on reaching pension age, receiving the full state pension.

As pensioners have got better off, there has been a sharp fall in the numbers receiving pension credit.[55] Going forward, this trend is likely to continue. The new state pension (to which pensioners who retired after April 2016 have been entitled) is notably higher than the old state pension and is worth more than the standard rate of pension credit.[56] This means that for those on the new state pension only those eligible for a higher award of pension credit – due to having a dependent child or eligibility for a disability premium or eligible for housing benefit – receive pension credit. This is important as increases in the state pension do not get passed on in full to those on pension credit; the state pension counts as income with resultant deductions in the amount of pension credit received.

The increase in the new state pension level, and the ways it has turned into being a benefit for all regardless of insurance contributions, provides a secure base of income for future generations of pensioners on which to build with private pensions (work-based or otherwise). It encourages saving for the future since savings are not deducted from your state pension, as is the case when applying for means-tested benefits. But there remain both some problems and some future challenges.

The ability of low-income earners to build a private pension is low; they simply do not have the spare financial resources to save. Automatic enrolment into private pension schemes for those in work has pushed up the rate but moves to increase this further will come up against the relatively high levels of in-work poverty. The government has announced a new review into pensions to look into how to encourage higher levels of savings into private pension schemes[57] but attempts to increase this further will need to be matched by moves to increase employment incomes for the lower paid.[58]

Furthermore, the increase in state pension has been enabled by raising the state pension age to pay for it. It is currently 66, with an increase to 67 planned between 2026 and 2028 and a further increase to 68 between 2044 and 2046. The increase in state pension age has already left increasing numbers of older people finding they are no longer able to work up until retirement and, as a result, in financial difficulties.[59] This has hit women particularly hard, where the rise in retirement age has been sharpest, and those in certain types of manual occupations who find they are no longer able to work. For these groups there may need to be some phasing in of support coming up to the state retirement age, which might include phased access to some level of pension for those unable to work, or greater flexibility at work in the years coming up to retirement, including a phased reduction in the number of hours worked.[60]

The next question relates to housing. Most pensioners are owner-occupiers, with almost three-quarters owning their home outright and for this group the new state pension, on its own, is now high enough for the household income of pensioner couples to be above the relative income poverty levels after housing costs and similarly for the large majority of single pensioners.[61] The next group, some 17 per cent, are in social housing, and most of this group are also above the relative income level after housing costs. A small minority (around 5 per cent) are private renters and within this group those with just the new state pension who live in the south of England, are more likely to find the new state pension inadequate. Moving forward, there needs to be more thought as to how to support pensioners who do not own their home with the cost of rent, especially as a lower percentage of future pensioners are set to own their own house outright. Options could include enabling those who are in social rents to make additional contributions while they are in work to cover payments at a later date.

Then there are the biggest, most controversial, questions. The point of the triple lock has been to raise pension levels relative to household incomes for those of working age so that pensioners did not continue to get left behind and to ensure an adequate household income in old age. It has done much of this work, in particular for those who have retired since 2016. There will need to be a decision as to when the new state pension has reached that level and then how to update it to keep it at that level. The new state pension should be high enough to cover the basic needs of pensioners, thus ensuring there is no need for pension credit and, in addition, maintain a certain percentage of median full-time earnings so that pensioners do not fall behind the rest of society.

And then there is the question of an aging population and the resultant rising cost of the state pension. It would be very difficult, and potentially very unfair, to raise the pension age yet again or to bring the planned increases forward though there are concerns this is what the government has in mind.[62] This would be quite unjustifiable in a time when life expectancy is falling for low-income groups and in particular healthy life expectancy is falling. Money to pay for this cannot be found from an endless raising of the pension age and therefore would need to be paid for in other ways.

Focusing, instead, on increasing taxes on richer, wealthier pensioners who have gained greatly over recent years would be a better way forward (discussed in Chapter 12).

Re-investing in child benefit

When child benefit was introduced in 1977, it transformed the existing family allowance and Child Tax Credit into a new, simple, flat-rate amount for each child in the family, paid to the main carer, regardless of household income. It was easy to claim, with no stigma attached, parents just had to register once, when a child was born, and then payments continued until the child was 16 or, if in education or training, 18. The rate of uptake, at 96 per cent, was high and it provided a stable and reliable base on which families could build to provide for their children. The benefit was aimed at supporting parents with the cost of raising a child on the basis that investing in the life chances of the next generation benefits us all, that raising a child contributes to the good of society. And it recognises that families with children are at greater risk of poverty than the population as a whole.

But these principles have been undermined. In the 2000s, the then-Labour government introduced Child Tax Credit (see Chapter 4), now the child element of UC. This was aimed at providing a means-tested boost to the incomes of low-income families with children.

The universality of child benefit was further undermined in 2013, when the coalition government introduced the High Income Child Benefit Charge (HICBC). This gradually withdrew child benefit from families where there was an earner on an annual salary of over £50,000, increased to £60,000 in 2024/25. It was further undermined by the benefit cap as child benefit was included in the benefits that counted towards the cap. At the same time, successive years of below-inflation uprating and outright freezes under the coalition and then Conservative governments led to a decline in its value, falling by 20 per cent in real terms between 2010/11 and 2022/23.[63]

The effect of these changes has been, in the long run, to undermine the fight against child poverty, and, in particular, child poverty among households in work which, as seen in Chapter 4, has soared. This is partly because levels of financial support overall (whether child benefit or through means-tested UC) are just so low. This, in itself, is connected with the shift towards means-testing as it is generally easier to target cuts on means-tested policies which generally have lower levels of support than those that benefit across the income range.

But it is also, and importantly, because the way the support has shifted from being pro-child (that is for all children) to pro-poor (that is for those on low incomes). Research at the University of Malaga, Spain, looking at transfers across 30 European countries, finds that the form of targeting matters in reducing child poverty, concluding that a country's intent to target children matters even more than their intent to target lower incomes, in terms of reducing child poverty.[64] While policies targeting those on lower incomes is associated with lower child poverty levels, policies targeting children directly are more effective at reducing child poverty, even after controlling for other factors.

Furthermore, the HICBC is a peculiarly bad system. It results in high marginal tax rates for those above the limit, for some up to 70 per cent depending on the number of children; for those repaying student loans, the rate will be even higher.[65] It is also deeply unfair to single-earner families who are anyway more likely to fall into poverty; they start to lose their child benefit from the level of the cap, while two-earner households with both earners just below the cap would still keep the benefit.[66] The HICBC needs to be removed, it is unfair, ineffective, and damages work incentives.

Many other countries in Europe – Germany and Finland for example – have much higher rates of universal child benefit with consequent higher reductions in child poverty.[67] The UK needs to return to the principle of universality and to increase the rates. The Women's Budget Group (WBG) proposes increasing child benefit to £50 a week (a small real-term increase on its level in 2010) and paying it at the same rate for all children. For a family with two children that would mean a guaranteed payment of £100 a week thus providing not just a significant contribution to family finances but, as importantly, a guaranteed security.

The WBG calculate that their proposals would lift nearly a million children out of poverty and would cost an additional

£14.2 billion annually, or 0.5 per cent of GDP. This investment is significant but would have a significant payback in terms of improved childhood health, education, and development, which in turn would lead to better employment prospects and lifetime health. There is room for discussion as to the balance between the level of payments for the first and subsequent children (the costs of a first child are generally higher)[68] or whether there should be different rates for different ages (excluding childcare, older children cost more) or whether there should be a higher rate for single parents (whose costs are higher overall) but the principle of the need for universality and the need for a significant increase in the rates would be the same.

Those who favour a means-tested approach to tackling poverty will argue that such sums are better spent targeting those who are poor but, perhaps counterintuitively, this is not the case. Policies that succeed in compensating for a high share of the costs of childrearing for all families largely tend to succeed in reducing the poverty gap as well.[69] This is partly because children are largely located in the lower part of the income distribution, so a pro-child policy is also a pro-poor policy, but it is also because universal policies provide a better springboard from which to improve future earnings by removing all the disincentives and poverty traps associated with means-testing.

Very similar arguments apply to how to support people with long-term disabilities.

Turning disability benefits into a right

People with disabilities and ill health face higher costs just to get by. Quite simply, life costs more if you are disabled. The non-means-tested PIP is aimed at covering these additional costs and the principle of PIP is important: that everyone, regardless of means, should be supported with the extra costs of disability and ill health so that the financial burden of covering these costs is not borne by the disabled person themselves and their families.

That these payments have nothing to do with whether people work or don't work, or whether they could or should work, is right: they are simply compensation for additional costs. The benefit should be a foundation on which to build further support to enable different pathways for people with disabilities to fully participate in society.

However, PIP has flaws. It is not flexible enough to cover everyone's additional costs, and, in these circumstances, conditions often worsen as a result. And the process of being assessed is stressful, demeaning, often inaccurate and aimed at being exclusionary rather than inclusive. The tighter rules that had been proposed by the government before their U-turn would have made this worse (see Chapter 3).

It does need to be reformed, just not in a way driven by attempts to cut the benefits bill. There needs to be a reduction in the number of assessments, an increase to the award length so that there are not constant reassessments, and assessments only being required when other evidence (from doctors, for example) is lacking – and it needs to recognise a wider range of additional costs.[70] It might be the case that some of the increase in diagnosis in recent years, in particular of mental health conditions, has had potential harms (internalising stigma for example) and that such people themselves might be better off outside the disability benefit system. But this would need to be shown through evidence. There may need to be changes to the criteria for assessing benefit and benefit levels, but this would need to be done working with people with disabilities, disability charities, and experts rather than simply being made to save money. Indeed, it might well cost more.

It should be based on a positive vision based on what people could do if provided with the right assistance and support rather than the current, and ever more, minimalist approach. Those whose disabilities limit, or deter them from, work should be recognised and supported even if their disabilities do not require a high level of additional payments for day-to-day living.

Such changes to the benefits system need to go hand in hand with improvements to personal support services (see Chapter 5) and better support from the community. Manchester's Live Well initiative is a good starting place for the kind of integrated change needed.[71] This scheme brings together all the different organisations that support people's health and social care, so that services can join up and act faster when people need support. It starts from the individual and looks across all aspects of their lives to bring coordinated improvements.

There are, in addition, ways in which the benefits system could be improved to help people with disabilities into work. Currently, the system can deter people from looking for work, with a fear of losing their PIP entitlement because their health is assumed to have improved being high on the list of concerns.[72] The government has promised a 'right to try' work for disabled people, meaning moving into work would not lead to a benefit reassessment. This is a step in the right direction. But there need to be further guarantees as to how long this lasts for and that there would be no benefit loss if it did not work out.[73] In addition, there need to be tougher requirements on employers to provide flexible working options and support for people with disabilities.[74]

A guaranteed benefit for those with disabilities and ill health who are out of work set at a level to provide an adequate standard of living would reduce levels of means-testing and help people move forward out of poverty. For those receiving PIP, it would be in addition to PIP (which is compensating for additional costs of a disability, not providing living costs). It would also be available for those who do not qualify for PIP but whose disabilities prevent them from working (or working full-time) or for whom the transition to work is difficult; it would be essentially a recognition of the problems that people with disabilities have in finding suitable work. To qualify for this, there would need to be a separate assessment process and this should be provided by properly qualified professionals. Such out-of-work benefits for those with disabilities should not be based on conditionality and sanctions; this is largely counterproductive. Instead, those who receive the benefits should be provided with support to help move into work where this would be beneficial for the individual concerned. And there would need to be a phased reduction of these benefits as people move into work (that is, a long taper rate).

This approach would need to be time limited so that after a certain period of time, dependent on the claimant's condition, there would need to be reassessment for those who remained on these out-of-work disability benefits to ensure that people had not been taking advantage of the system. If so, there may be a case at that point for a reduced level of benefit and a return to the basic rate of UC.

For some with the most serious disabilities, whose condition is not likely to improve, this out-of-work element of their benefit should not be time limited. Options such as volunteering should be allowed, without risking benefit reductions. This would enable people to feel more valued and could prepare a path, if circumstances changed, to paid work. The aim would be to help people lead a more fulfilling life, including, if possible and desirable, paid work, but recognising that this might not be possible for all. None of this is the direction the government is moving in (see Chapter 3); instead, out-of-work benefits for those with disabilities are being reduced and tightened.

Similar principles to those outlined could also be applied to those who undertake caring roles. Replacing the outdated and inadequate carers allowance is a matter of urgency. As seen in Chapter 4, the current Carer's Allowance is vastly inadequate and extraordinarily punitive for those who try to do some paid work alongside their caring role. This system needs to be reformed into a universal, non-means-tested benefit that provides a level of support for carers on which they can build, and which recognises their enormous contribution to society.

If you get these basics right, overall financial costs would be likely to come down as people with disabilities would be in a better position to participate in society and to work. But improving people's lives, rather than a short-term cutting of social security budget, should be the driver of change.

Choosing to improve lives over benefits cuts

Each stage of the reforms outlined would need to be assessed to see what else was needed and if it was working – and improved and adjusted as a result. But over time, such an approach should start to move the benefits system back to being a support system for everyone at different stages of their lives and with different needs. And this would have a big impact on poverty levels.

At the end of the day, it is a choice as to whether to make the benefits system work better for everyone or not, whether to provide a more generous system that supports people through their lives or not. To do so would require a redistribution of resources across people's lives but also across income levels.

The case for this needs to be made but if the system, as proposed, became based on the principle of universality and meeting everyone's needs during their lives rather than tight means-testing helping just the poorest, it is more likely to gain support. It would be less easy to dismiss as just encouraging idleness and scrounging as currently has been the case and easier to defend as an inclusive system that offers everyone security throughout their lives and the foundations on which to build a better life.

As with reforms to services, it would cost money and require investment, but the UK remains a wealthy society overall. There are plenty of sources of money.

If you want a well-funded state, it needs to be paid for.

12

Making change happen

To kickstart the kinds of changes needed to end the impoverishment of the UK, there needs to be a commitment to a substantial increase in spending on services and benefits. Existing services need to be brought up to standard and new ones created. There need to be changes to the benefit system to guarantee that everyone has an adequate income throughout their lifetimes. In the long run, this would improve people's quality of life across the board and have a substantial impact on poverty levels. It also has the potential to create long-term savings to the Exchequer through better health, higher levels of employment and work intensity, improved career prospects, and a more dynamic economy.

In its manifesto, the Labour government, however, tied its hands by promising to stick to the fiscal rules it inherited while at the same time to not raising taxes on 'working people'.[1] As a result, its promises on public spending were 'tiny, going on trivial' according to the Institute for Fiscal Studies, described by its director, Paul Johnson, as a promise 'not to do things'.[2]

Fiscal rules were first introduced by the last Labour government in 1997 and are essentially not really rules but targets a government sets itself to constrain its own decisions on spending, taxes and levels of government debt. These rules have frequently been changed.[3] And could be again. The NEF argues that the rules are outdated and should be replaced by a 'more flexible, accountable, and forward-looking framework'.[4] The OECD[5] and the IMF[6] have called on the government to be more flexible so as to enable greater investment and avoid spending cuts.

In its autumn budget of 2024, the Treasury tweaked them so that instead of targeting overall borrowing, the government reverted to previous rules that targeted current spending and only allowed borrowing for capital investment. This meant that while the current spending budget was required to be in balance – with day-to-day costs met by revenue – there was more room for capital spending. The definition of public debt was also slightly tweaked to give a greater allowance for public assets though the overall aim to reduce debt remained, indeed the timetable for doing was to be gradually reduced from five to three years.[7] This has allowed the government to make some significant increases in capital spending projects – on transport and nuclear energy, for example.

Nevertheless, the government's increase to public investment on taking office did little more than cancel out the cuts planned by the previous government, maintaining public investment at around 2.5 per cent of GDP over the next five years, still far short of the OECD average of 3.7 per cent over the past 25 years. The increases in public investment, while welcome, are far from sufficient to drive the kind of renewal of public services needed, as leading economists have argued.[8] And the constraints on current spending make it impossible to renew public services in the ways needed. Indeed, departmental budgets – the money that goes to day-to-day spending – will grow more slowly than under the last government.[9] And the bulk of the additional spending will go on health, education and defence, leaving other areas really struggling.

Though the fiscal rules gain the most attention, the management of government finances goes beyond this. The Bank of England, for example, is currently selling the bonds it created to keep the financial services sector running after the financial crash of 2008. The creation of the bonds is known as quantitative easing and the current moves are the reverse, quantitative tightening. In doing so, the Bank of England is making a loss and the Treasury is picking up the bill. This, along with interest rates that the Bank of England is paying to commercial banks for money they hold at the Bank, is costing the Exchequer about £40 billion a year.[10] This is, in effect, the Treasury handing over huge sums of public money to commercial banks, not a sector that is in need of government subsidy. This payback could be deferred.

However, while further changes to the government's fiscal rules could allow more leeway, the government still faces constraints on borrowing, especially given the poor state of government finances it inherited and the high costs in interest payments of doing so. Substantial savings could, as discussed previously, be made by reversing the moves toward privatisation of services and returning to services being insourced, but to set the country on a different path there needs to be more revenue coming into the Exchequer. In her first budget, Chancellor Rachel Reeves raised around an additional £36 billion from tax revenues, most controversially by increasing employers' National Insurance rates.[11] In her second in November 2025, she raised a further £26 billion through a package of measures skewed towards raising more from those with higher incomes and wealth.[12] While some of this funded a number of significant steps, much of the increase was to create 'headroom' for meeting her fiscal rules.[13]

Taxes need to rise further, and this needs to be done in a way that is redistributive. Those most able to pay, need to pay the most.

Increasing taxes on income

The simplest and most direct way of increasing revenue would be to raise more from income taxes. Income taxes, unlike purchase taxes, are generally progressive with higher earners paying more. This, however, is generally regarded as a no-go area and the government are of the belief that voters see taxes on working people as too high. Certainly, increasing numbers of people in work are finding it difficult to make ends meet.

But the situation is rather more complex. The basic rate of income tax has not risen for many years. Indeed, what economists call the tax wedge – the proportion of labour cost paid in tax for the average worker – is no higher than it was in the 1990s and far lower than most other high-income countries. Out of the ten largest European economies and Canada and the US, only Canada and the US have a smaller proportion of average wages going towards taxes than the UK.[14] The situation does vary across households, with the tax wedge for single earners in the UK being particularly low. Nevertheless, as seen in earlier chapters, marginal tax rates (the amount taken for every pound earned) can be high – this is particularly true for graduates as their student loan repayment kick in.[15] Given the squeeze on household living standards at the bottom end, simply increasing the basic rate (currently 20 per cent on incomes between £12,571 and £50,270) would be difficult, though there may well be a case for new, more graduated, tax rates between the basic, the higher (currently 40 per cent on incomes from £50,270 to £125,140) and highest rate (currently 45 per cent on income above £125,140) and for an additional higher tax band on even higher incomes. That would make the system more progressive while softening the cliff-edges between tax bands.

However, there are other ways of changing the income tax system to raise more money and to make it fairer – namely tackling the large number of tax allowances currently available to better-off earners. During the years of the coalition and Conservative governments, the tax and benefits system shifted dramatically in favour of the better off. The Fabian Society calculates that between 2010/11 and 2022/23, at a time when inflation increased by 30 per cent, the cash value of tax-free allowances grew by 117 per cent while basic working-age benefits by grew by 18 per cent.[16] To make the system fairer and raise revenue, a number of changes could be made.

Firstly, the tax relief given for pension contributions could be limited to the basic rate of tax. Currently, higher income earners paying tax at higher rates get relief at those rates. This is deeply regressive, and while such a move would need to be done in a way that does not draw those currently on basic tax rates into the higher bands, it has the potential to raise large sums. Richard Murphy, Professor of Accounting Practice at the University of Sheffield Management School and author of the Taxing Wealth reports,[17] estimates that limiting tax relief on pension contributions to the basic rate would raise £12.5 billion while Demos, a cross-party thinktank, estimate it would be getting on for £13 billion.[18]

There is a plethora of further tax reliefs that could be targeted from capping the rate at which tax relief is given on charitable donations under Gift Aid (currently at the higher rate of income tax for higher earners) to capping tax relief on ISA contributions over a lifetime. These could raise further revenue while at the same time being redistributive. But most importantly, there needs to be an alignment of taxes on income from different sources. Currently taxes on earned income are taxed more heavily than taxes on unearned income. This deeply favours those who have wealth. While the chancellor made some small tweaks in the October 2024 budget and raised tax on dividend income in the 2025 budget, far more could be done. A package of measures to equalise capital gains and income tax rates could raise between £12 billion and £15 billion a year.[19]

Reducing the amount money that can be taken out of pension pots tax-free (which is effectively income) should be reduced. Currently, 25 per cent of a pension pot can be withdrawn tax-free, up to a limit on pension pots of £1 million. That is, for those with large pension pots, a withdrawal of over £250,000 tax-free. While there is a case for allowing some withdrawal tax-free to encourage pension saving, the way it currently works is far more beneficial to wealthy pensioners than others. There is a strong case for lowering this limit. The IFS calculates that if the tax-free withdrawal allowed was limited to £100,000 that would affect one in five retirees with a pension pot but would mean that about 40 per cent of pension *wealth* lost the benefit of the tax-free component, just showing how concentrated the perk is to the wealthiest. This would raise about £2 billion a year.[20]

Then there is National Insurance (NI). Some have argued that NI should simply be abolished and replaced by increases in income tax on the basis that the benefits paid out no longer bear much relationship to payments made.[21] But this would be a step in the wrong direction. It would take away the link between employers and their responsibilities to their employees. However, it does need reforming. In her 2025 budget, the Chancellor capped, from 2029, NI contributions relief on salary sacrifice into pension schemes to the first £2,000 of pension contributions. But more could be done to make it fairer.

Currently (2025/26), National Insurance payments kick in for employees at incomes over £12,570 a year, are paid at a rate of 8 per cent on earnings up to around £50,000 and then paid at 2 per cent on earnings above this level. Those who are self-employed pay a lower rate whatever their income, while those whose income is from unearned sources (such as dividends) or pensions do not pay National Insurance. Simply, increasing the employee National Insurance rates of those earning over £50,000 to that paid below that level would raise around £10–12 billion a year[22] while introducing National Insurance on income from investments could raise a further £8 billion.[23] If similar changes were made on payments by the self-employed a further £1.5 billion could be raised.

Raising taxes on wealth

To raise yet more money, we need to look at wealth, for this is where inequalities are greatest. According the ONS, the wealth held by the top 10 per cent of households is around five times greater than the wealth of those in the bottom half of all households combined[24] and while wealth inequality fell during most of the last century, it has, since 1980, been rising.[25] The government has made some changes, for example abolishing the exemptions allowing those living in the UK but claiming their permanent home is abroad (non-dom status) to avoid tax on foreign investments and increasing tax rates on property income. However, taxes on various forms of wealth remain low.

The first area to look at here is taxes on inherited wealth. Currently inheritance tax kicks in if the value of the estate is over £350,000, though there are so many exemptions and ways of getting around this that the total revenue raised from inheritance tax is tiny. In 2020/21, under 4 per cent of all estates were subject to inheritance tax.[26] Any move to tighten and widen inheritance tax would be likely to be highly controversial, as witnessed by the uproar with which the government's proposed change to inheritance tax on farms was met.[27] This doesn't make it wrong but the argument that inherited wealth brings unfair advantages to those who receive it needs to be better made.

There could, for example, be room to remove some of the exemptions (excluding where there is a surviving spouse) from inheritance tax of money in pension funds on death. There could be a case for reducing the property value at which inheritance tax kicks in, which currently allow homeowners an additional £500,000 to their tax-free threshold if their property is worth less than £2 million, though any such change would no doubt be met by outrage from homeowners. A better approach could be to charge capital gains tax on the final sale of a property on the death of the last partner. This would need to be done alongside abolishing stamp duty – a tax that clogs up the housing market by disincentivising moving – and reforming council tax – a deeply outdated and regressive tax – with an annual tax on property. Such a tax would need to be progressive, with properties of high value for an area taxed more heavily, allow for regional variations in property value so that those living in areas with high property values are not unfairly hit, and enable those who are income poor but have a high value property to defer payments.[28] Such moves would create a more coherent and fair approach to taxing property. In her 2025 budget, the Chancellor introduced a high value property surcharge, starting at £2,500 per year for properties worth over £2 million and rising to £7,500 for those worth over £5 million.[29] This is a positive step but not the wholesale reform needed.

And, finally, there are the calls, increasingly widespread on the left of politics, for a wealth tax, that is a single tax on all forms of wealth. In 2020, the Wealth Tax Commission was set up by a group of academic institutions and research bodies to bring together a wide range of experts to look at the merits, or otherwise, of a wealth tax. Their final report,[30] suggested that an annual wealth tax might be difficult to implement, costly to administer, limited in how much it could raise because of liquidity concerns surrounding assets such as the family home, and likely to produce behavioural change that would limit its effectiveness. While the sums raised could potentially be significant, a 0.6 per cent tax on wealth over £2 million could raise around £10 billion a year, similar sums could be raised by improving existing taxes on various aspects of wealth (as discussed). By contrast, the Commission did recommend a one-off wealth tax. Such a tax would be economically efficient as it is raised against past gains and would not affect current behaviour. If the assessment date was the day it was announced, it would be difficult to avoid as it would be based on wealth that had already accumulated, while those who were asset-rich but cash-poor could defer their payments. Dependent on the level of wealth at which it started and how progressive the rate imposed was, how many were affected and by how much would vary. But it has the potential to raise eye-catching sums. For example, a one-off tax on individuals with a wealth over £1 million at 4 per cent spread over 5 years (that is an annual rate of 0.8 per cent) rising to 15 per cent (an annual rate of 3 per cent) for those worth over £10 million would raise £260 billion.

Any such major redistribution of wealth would be met by howls of protest from those who would lose out. An argument would need to be made that the scale of the problems the UK faces – from climate change to rising world tensions, from decades of underfunding to stagnating growth – requires a reset in which the wealthiest need to play their part.

Making different choices

There are plenty of options to raise money. And there is a wide range of policies that could be introduced that would make a difference to people's lives. Some of the suggestions made might work better than others. There may be others.

But if we want to fix Britain's poverty problem, we need to make different choices. Across a whole range of areas, there needs to be a rethink and a change in direction. This will be difficult, requiring political will and determination. It would require a challenge to established economic thinking and for a fairer distribution of resources. It needs the argument to be made that ending the impoverishment of the UK benefits us all as well as those at the sharp end of poverty. There would be strong and fierce oppostion. But, as seen throughout this book, it could be done.

We owe it to those living in poverty to try to do so. For many the situation is so dire that change cannot come swiftly enough. As Gemma, a disabled, single mother with three children, writes, echoing the experiences of those in poverty over the years, 'I sometimes find it difficult to imagine how my situation can get better, but it really has to because life should not be this hard.'[31]

Notes

Dedication
1. *Breadline Britain* 1983, see https://www.poverty.ac.uk/living-poverty/breadline-britain-1983-2013, accessed September 2025, for transcripts of the series.

Introduction
1. https://foodfoundation.org.uk/initiatives/food-insecurity-tracking#tabs/Round-14, accessed July 2025; https://www.ons.gov.uk/peoplepopulationandcommunity/personalandhouseholdfinances/expenditure/articles/impactofincreasedcostoflivingonadultsacrossgreatbritain/julytooctober2023, accessed July 2025
2. https://ifs.org.uk/publications/living-standards-last-election, accessed July 2025
3. https://labour.org.uk/change/first-steps-for-change/, accessed July 2025
4. https://www.gov.uk/government/speeches/chancellor-vows-to-go-further-and-faster-to-kickstart-economic-growth, accessed July 2025; https://www.gov.uk/government/news/chancellor-unveils-plan-to-turbocharge-investment-across-the-uk, accessed July 2025
5. https://labour.org.uk/change/break-down-barriers-to-opportunity/, accessed July 2025
6. https://www.gov.uk/government/news/ministerial-taskforce-launched-to-kickstart-work-on-child-poverty-strategy, accessed July 2025
7. For examples, see: https://www.theguardian.com/commentisfree/article/2024/jul/11/labour-will-it-scrap-two-child-benefit-cap, accessed July 2025; https://social-policy.org.uk/50-for-50/two-child-policy/, accessed July 2025; https://endchildpoverty.org.uk/about/allkidscount/, accessed July 2025
8. https://www.theguardian.com/society/article/2024/jun/17/campaigners-hope-labour-will-scrap-two-child-benefit-cap-once-in-no-10, accessed July 2025
9. https://ifs.org.uk/articles/two-child-limit-poverty-incentives-and-cost, accessed October 2025

[10] https://www.theguardian.com/politics/article/2024/jul/23/labour-mps-vote-to-scrap-two-child-benefit-cap-in-first-rebellion-for-starmer, accessed July 2025; https://www.theguardian.com/commentisfree/article/2024/jul/24/the-guardian-view-on-labours-rebellion-removing-the-whip-is-a-step-too-far?, accessed July 2025

[11] https://cpag.org.uk/news/things-will-only-get-worse-why-two-child-limit-must-go

[12] https://ifs.org.uk/articles/two-child-limit-poverty-incentives-and-cost, accessed July 2025

[13] https://www.theguardian.com/politics/article/2024/jul/29/hospital-and-road-projects-face-cuts-to-plug-22bn-fiscal-hole-reeves-says, accessed July 2025

[14] https://www.theguardian.com/society/article/2024/jul/29/up-to-2m-pensioners-will-struggle-without-winter-fuel-help-say-campaigners, accessed July 2025; https://www.ageuk.org.uk/our-impact/campaigning/save-the-winter-fuel-payment/, accessed July 2025

[15] https://ifs.org.uk/articles/definitions-debt-and-new-governments-fiscal-rules, accessed July 2025

[16] https://www.instituteforgovernment.org.uk/comment/rachel-reeves-welcome-changes-fiscal-rules, accessed July 2025

[17] https://commonslibrary.parliament.uk/research-briefings/sn06852/, accessed July 2025

[18] https://assets.publishing.service.gov.uk/media/67211bf34da1c0d41942a8bf/A_strong_fiscal_framework.pdf, accessed July 2025

[19] https://www.disabilityrightsuk.org/news/open-letter-liz-kendall-don%E2%80%99t-continue-wca-cuts, accessed July 2025

[20] https://dpac.uk.net/2024/12/disabled-activist-takes-dwp-to-court-over-disingenuous-consultation-on-tightening-work-capability-assessment/, accessed July 2025

[21] https://www.itv.com/news/2025-03-07/government-to-make-6bn-welfare-savings-with-benefits-shake-up, accessed July 2025

[22] https://www.itv.com/news/2025-02-06/too-many-people-taking-the-mickey-with-benefits-work-secretary-says, accessed July 2025

[23] https://www.theguardian.com/politics/2025/mar/07/dont-punish-the-vulnerable-labour-mp-uneasy-over-planned-welfare-cuts, accessed July 2025

[24] https://www.gov.uk/government/news/welfare-bill-will-protect-the-most-vulnerable-and-help-households-with-income-boost, accessed July 2025

[25] These percentages on welfare spending as a percentage of GDP are for Great Britain and cover all welfare spending including that administered

Notes

by HMRC (such as child and tax credits), as well as that administered by the DWP. See https://view.officeapps.live.com/op/view.aspx?src=https%3A%2F%2Fassets.publishing.service.gov.uk%2Fmedia%2F67c84ee68247839c255ae30d%2Foutturn-and-forecast-tables-autumn-budget-2024.ods&wdOrigin=BROWSELINK, 'GB welfare', rows 31–37, accessed September 2025. Total welfare spending data for the UK only goes back to 2013/14 and is slightly higher as a percentage of GDP as it includes spending by the devolved administrations. For UK spending on benefits administered by the DWP alone see 'Benefit summary' table, rows 35–42. This is slightly lower as a percentage of GDP as it excludes non DWP benefits.

[26] https://www.resolutionfoundation.org/press-releases/green-paper-delivers-tiny-income-gains-for-up-to-four-million-households-at-cost-of-major-income-losses-for-those-who-are-too-ill-to-work-or-no-longer-qualify-for-disability-benefit-support/, accessed July 2025

[27] https://www.theguardian.com/world/2025/may/12/uk-risks-becoming-island-of-strangers-without-more-immigration-curbs-starmer-says, accessed July 2025

[28] https://www.bbc.co.uk/news/articles/cj3rxrg2pnjo, accessed July 2025

[29] https://assets.publishing.service.gov.uk/media/6821f334ced319d02c906103/restoring-control-over-the-immigration-system-web-optimised.pdf, accessed July 2025

[30] https://migrationobservatory.ox.ac.uk/resources/commentaries/changes-to-settlement-what-do-they-mean/, accessed July 2025

[31] https://www.ippr.org/articles/citizenship-a-race-to-the-bottom, accessed July 2025

[32] https://www.theguardian.com/politics/2025/may/25/the-charts-that-show-just-how-worried-labour-should-be-about-the-polls, accessed July 2025

[33] https://www.bbc.co.uk/news/articles/cd925jk27k0o, accessed July 2025

[34] https://www.bbc.co.uk/news/articles/cp8jdr900r7o, accessed July 2025

[35] https://www.instituteforgovernment.org.uk/comment/reeves-starmer-winter-fuel-allowance-u-turn, accessed July 2025

[36] https://www.bbc.co.uk/news/live/c5yxvdl4d0pt, accessed July 2025

[37] https://ifs.org.uk/articles/expanding-eligibility-winter-fuel-payment, accessed July 2025

[38] https://www.theguardian.com/politics/live/2025/jun/09/labour-spending-review-end-austerity-home-office-conservatives-keir-starmer-uk-politics-live-news, accessed July 2025

[39] https://www.instituteforgovernment.org.uk/comment/reeves-starmer-winter-fuel-allowance-u-turn, accessed July 2025

40. https://assets.publishing.service.gov.uk/media/67e667fe4a226ab6c41b1fe2/spring-statement-2025-health-and-disability-benefit-reforms-impacts.pdf, p 9, accessed July 2025
41. https://www.gov.uk/government/news/welfare-bill-will-protect-the-most-vulnerable-and-help-households-with-income-boost, accessed July 2025
42. https://www.resolutionfoundation.org/publications/no-workaround/, accessed July 2025
43. https://researchbriefings.files.parliament.uk/documents/CBP-10283/CBP-10283.pdf, p 47, accessed September 2025
44. https://www.gov.uk/government/publications/spring-statement-social-security-changes-updated-impact-on-poverty-levels-in-great-britain-july-2025/spring-statement-social-security-changes-updated-impact-on-poverty-levels-in-great-britain-july-2025, accessed July 2025
45. https://www.benefitsandwork.co.uk/news/labour%E2%80%99s-poverty-lie-%E2%80%93-changes-will-still-push-100,000-into-poverty, accessed July 2025
46. https://www.resolutionfoundation.org/publications/no-half-measures/, accessed November 2025
47. https://www.gov.uk/government/speeches/budget-2025-speech, accessed November 2025
48. https://assets.publishing.service.gov.uk/media/6931e272502f392086ee8c5d/child-poverty-strategy.pdf, accessed December 2025
49. https://www.gov.uk/government/publications/spending-review-2025-document/spending-review-2025-html#executive-summary, accessed July 2025
50. https://www.jrf.org.uk/sites/default/files/pdfs/a-decade-of-falling-incomes-jrf-s-pre-budget-assessment-of-living-standards-9bc2961deee33529c46352f318e50cd9.pdf, figure 2, p7, accessed October 2025
51. https://www.resolutionfoundation.org/app/uploads/2025/06/LivingStandardsOutlook2025.pdf, p 29 (accessed October 2025).

Chapter 1

1. https://www.ons.gov.uk/peoplepopulationandcommunity/personalandhouseholdfinances/expenditure/articles/impactofincreasedcostoflivingonadultsacrossgreatbritain/julytooctober2023, accessed July 2025
2. https://changingrealities.org/about, accessed July 2025
3. All quotes from: (Jordan, Patrick, Power, Pybus, & Kaufman, 2025)
4. (Marmot, Allen, Boyce, Goldblatt, & Morrison, 2020), Table 2.1, p 21
5. https://ncdrisc.org/data-downloads-height.html, accessed July 2025
6. https://foodfoundation.org.uk/publicationeglected-generation-reversing-decline-childrens-health, accessed July 2025

Notes

7. (Watson, et al, 2024)
8. https://www.gov.uk/government/publications/how-low-income-is-measured/text-only-how-low-income-is-measured, accessed July 2025
9. The FRS uses the OECD modified equivalence scale: https://www.gov.uk/government/statistics/households-below-average-income-for-financial-years-ending-1995-to-2023/households-below-average-income-series-quality-and-methodology-information-report-fye-2023#equivalisation-1, accessed July 2025
10. https://www.gov.uk/government/statistics/households-below-average-income-for-financial-years-ending-1995-to-2023, accessed July 2025
11. https://ifs.org.uk/living-standards-poverty-andinequality-uk#incomes-overtime, accessed July 2025
12. See (Atkinson, 2015), pp 16–21
13. (Ray-Chaudhuri, Waters, Wernham, & Xu, 2023), p 14
14. https://ifs.org.uk/living-standards-poverty-andinequality-uk#incomes-over-time, accessed July 2025
15. (Brewer, Browne, Joyce, & Sibieta, 2010), Table 5.1, p 26
16. https://ifs.org.uk/living-standards-poverty-andinequality-uk#incomes-over-time, accessed July 2025
17. (Hills, 2013), p 10
18. (Brewer, Browne, Joyce, & Sibieta, 2010), pp 25–6
19. (Brewer, Browne, Joyce, & Sibieta, 2010), pp 25–6
20. The research into the MIS is carried out by the Centre for Research in Social Policy, Loughborough University. A full description of the procedures used to set the MIS budgets can be found in (Davis, Hirsch, Padley, & Marshall, 2015)
21. https://www.jrf.org.uk/households-livingbelow-a-minimum-income-standard-2008-2023, accessed July 2025
22. Details can be found in (Padley, Stone, & Robinson, 2024), Appendix 2
23. For further discussion see (Mack, 2018)
24. See https://www.gov.uk/government/statistics/households-below-average-income-for-financial-years-ending-1995-to-2023/households-below-average-income-series-quality-and-methodology-information-report-fye-2023#combined-low-income-and-child-material-deprivation for further details, accessed July 2025
25. https://ifs.org.uk/publications/living-standardslast-election, figure 6; accessed July 2025
26. https://www.bankofengland.co.uk/monetary-policy-report/2023/august-2023, accessed July 2025
27. https://assets.publishing.service.gov.uk/media/65f81 47da f6a0 d6b9 b90d 511/hbai- 2223-ods-table-pack.zip, accessed July 2025
28. (Francis-Devine, 2024), p 8

[29] Trussell Trust, End of year stats, https://www.trussell.org.uk/news-and-research/latest-stats/end-of-year-stats, accessed July 2025
[30] https://www.gov.uk/government/statistics/households-below-average-income-for-financial-years-ending-1995-to-2023, Tables 9.1 and 9.4, accessed July 2025
[31] (Garthwaite, 2016)
[32] This widely used definition stems from (Anderson, 1990). See also (Dowler, 2003)
[33] https://www.gov.uk/government/statistics/family-resources-survey-financial-year-2019-to-2020/family-resources-survey-background-information-and-methodology#frs-changes-in-year-2019-to-2020, Section 6, accessed July 2025
[34] https://www.gov.uk/government/statistics/households-below-average-income-for-financial-yearsending-1995-to-2024, accessed July 2025
[35] https://foodfoundation.org.uk/initiatives/food-insecurity-tracking#tabs/Round-16, accessed July 2025
[36] (The Food Foundation, 2025), p 28
[37] https://www.nhs.uk/live-well/eat-well/food-guidelines-and-food-labels/the-eatwell-guide/, accessed July 2025
[38] (The Food Foundation, 2025), p 30
[39] https://www.fca.org.uk/publication/financial-lives/financial-lives-survey-2024-key-findings.pdf, pp 54–5
[40] All quotes are from (Financial Conduct Authority, 2024)
[41] For data tables see https://www.fca.org.uk/financial-lives, accessed July 2025
[42] (Bramley & Fitzpatrick, 2023)
[43] For full details of the method used see (Bramley, Fitzpatrick, Sosenko, & Littlewood, 2016)
[44] (Fitzpatrick, et al, 2015), (Fitzpatrick, Bramley, Sosenko, & Blenkinsopp, 2018), (Fitzpatrick, et al, 2023a)
[45] (Fitzpatrick, et al, 2023a)
[46] All quotes are from (Fitzpatrick, et al, 2023a)

Chapter 2

[1] (House of Commons Work and Pensions Committee, 2019a), p 3
[2] (House of Commons Work and Pensions Committee, 2016), p 3
[3] (House of Commons Work and Pensions Committee, 2019a), p 43
[4] (House of Commons Work and Pensions Committee, 2019a), p 45
[5] (Alston, 2018), p 12
[6] (Alston, 2018), p 2
[7] (Alston, 2018), p 3

Notes

[8] For a short discussion of the goods included in the RPI and CPI and the different formulas used to calculate the indices see: https://www.incomesdataresearch.co.uk/resources/insights/which-inflation-measure-cpi-cpih-or-rpi, accessed July 2025; (Plunkett, 2011)

[9] (Hills, 2015), p 15

[10] (House of Commons Work and Pensions Committee, 2019a), p 37

[11] See https://view.officeapps.live.com/op/view.aspx?src=https%3A%2F%2Fassets.publishing.service.gov.uk%2Fmedia%2F67c84ee68247839c255ae30d%2Foutturn-and-forecast-tables-autumn-budget-2024.ods&wdOrigin=BROWSELINK, 'GB welfare', rows 31–37, accessed September 2025.

[12] (Hills, 2013), pp 13–14, Table A1, p 46

[13] https://www.legislation.gov.uk/ukpga/2016/7/section/11/enacted, accessed July 2025

[14] (Kennedy, Honeysett, Mackley, Francis-Devine, & McInnnes, 2019), pp 29–30

[15] https://www.jrf.org.uk/social-security/end-the-benefit-freeze-to-stop-people-being-swept-into-poverty, accessed July 2025

[16] https://www.jrf.org.uk/social-security/end-the-benefit-freeze-to-stop-people-being-swept-into-poverty, accessed July 2025

[17] https://www.gov.uk/government/statistics/abstract-of-dwp-benefit-rate-statistics-2022, accessed July 2025

[18] There is a similar decline on value if CPI is used to rebase the value each year rather than RPI, though less steep.

[19] (Cribb, Henry, & Karjalainen, 2024), p 13

[20] (Cribb, Henry, & Karjalainen, 2024), p 2

[21] https://www.appgpoverty.org.uk/home-page/appg-publishes-report-on-inadequacy-of-social-security/, accessed July 2025

[22] (Brewer & Murphy, 2023), p 4

[23] (Hoynes, Joyce, & Waters, 2023), p 30

[24] https://www.gov.uk/government/news/national-introduction-of-benefit-cap-begins, accessed July 2025

[25] The benefit cap was not introduced in Northern Ireland until 2016 and there were some discretionary payments made available to mitigate its effect.

[26] https://ifs.org.uk/articles/two-child-limit-poverty-incentives-and-cost, accessed July 2025

[27] https://www.parliament.uk/globalassets/documents/impact-assessments/IA15-006E.pdf, accessed July 2025

[28] (Patrick, Anderson, Reader, Reeves, & Stewart, 2023), p 8

[29] https://ifs.org.uk/articles/two-child-limit-poverty-incentives-and-cost, accessed July 2025

[30] https://social-policy.org.uk/50-for-50/two-child-policy/, accessed July 2025
[31] (Wilson & Hobson, 2021), p 16
[32] (Crisis, 2019), p 15
[33] (Hoynes, Joyce, & Waters, 2023), p 47
[34] The impact of the housing benefit changes and whether it is borne by landlords or tenants is explored in detail in (Brewer, Browne, Emmerson, Hood, & Joyce, 2019)
[35] https://www.gov.uk/government/statistics/english-housing-survey-2021-to-2022-private-rented-sector/english-housing-survey-2021-to-2022-private-rented-sector, accessed July 2025
[36] All quotes are from (Crisis, 2019), pp 17, 29
[37] (Crisis, 2019), pp 15–16
[38] https://www.gov.uk/government/publications/benefit-expenditure-and-caseload-tables-2022#full-publication-update-history, accessed July 2025
[39] (Hoynes, Joyce, & Waters, 2023), p 1
[40] (Wilson & Hobson, 2021), p 14
[41] https://www.theguardian.com/commentisfree/article/2024/jun/05/14-years-tory-housing-benefit-homelessness-poor-cities?, accessed July 2025
[42] https://www.jrf.org.uk/sites/default/files/pdfs/stop-the-freeze-permanently-re-link-housing-benefits-to-private-rents-faa7691b627d78fae601ea1fdc252fb1.pdf, p 10, accessed July 2025
[43] https://www.insidehousing.co.uk/news/homelessness-charities-extremely-disappointed-by-governments-failure-to-unfreeze-lha-89159, accessed July 2025
[44] https://www.jrf.org.uk/sites/default/files/pdfs/stop-the-freeze-permanently-re-link-housing-benefits-to-private-rents-faa7691b627d78fae601ea1fdc252fb1.pdf, Table 1, pp 14–15, accessed July 2025
[45] https://www.jrf.org.uk/sites/default/files/pdfs/stop-the-freeze-permanently-re-link-housing-benefits-to-private-rents-faa7691b627d78fae601ea1fdc252fb1.pdf, Figure 4, p 16, accessed July 2025
[46] https://assets.publishing.service.gov.uk/media/6694e486a3c2a28abb50cf1b/FA3101_demographic_and_economic_characteristics_of_social_and_privately_renting_households.ods, accessed July 2025
[47] https://www.localgov.co.uk/Suicide-victim-was-worried-about-bedroom-tax-coroner-finds/36973, accessed July 2025
[48] https://blogs.lse.ac.uk/politicsandpolicy/a-policy-that-kills-the-bedroom-tax-is-an-affront-to-basic-rights/, accessed July 2025
[49] (Wilcox, 2014), p 5
[50] https://www.theguardian.com/commentisfree/2014/jan/14/bedroom-tax-death-leveller, accessed July 2025
[51] (Wilcox, 2014), pp 21–8
[52] (Wilcox, 2014), p 23

Notes

53. (Wilcox, 2014), p 25
54. https://askcpag.org.uk/content/200088/the-bedroom-tax-limps-on, accessed July 2025
55. https://www.theguardian.com/commentisfree/2019/oct/31/bedroom-tax-victims-forgotten-welfare-reform, accessed July 2025
56. https://www.itv.com/news/2023-07-27/ten-years-on-and-no-plans-to-axe-the-bedroom-tax, accessed July 2025
57. https://www.theguardian.com/politics/2023/jul/19/rachel-reeves-labour-bedroom-tax-child-benefit-cap; https://www.partyof.wales/cost_of_living, accessed July 2025
58. https://www.parallelparliament.co.uk/lord/baroness-bennett-of-manor-castle/dept/DWP/writtenanswers: to question from Baroness Bennett, accessed July 2025
59. (Howard & Bennett, 2021), p 16
60. (Hoynes, Joyce, & Waters, 2023), p 48
61. (Comptroller and Auditor General, 2018), p 8
62. https://publications.parliament.uk/pa/cm201719/cmselect/cmpubacc/1183/118307.htm#footnote-063, accessed July 2025
63. https://www.civilserviceworld.com/professions/article/dwp-criticised-as-study-claims-food-bank-hikes-linked-to-universal-credit-rollout, accessed July 2025
64. (StepChange, 2020)
65. (Comptroller and Auditor General, 2018), p 42
66. (Edmiston, 2024), p 3
67. (Clegg, 2024), p 37
68. (Edmiston, 2024), p 3
69. (Edmiston, 2024), p 8
70. (StepChange, 2020), p 13
71. (Edmiston, 2024), p 14
72. https://www.gov.uk/government/statistics/benefit-uprating-estimated-number-and-type-of-families-and-individuals-in-families-benefitting-from-the-uprating-of-benefits-in-2025-to-2026/estimated-number-and-type-of-gb-families-and-individuals-in-families-benefitting-from-the-uprating-of-benefits-in-2025-to-2026-and-the-fair-repayment, accessed July 2025
73. https://covidrealities.org/about, accessed July 2025
74. Quotes are from (Patrick, 2023), p 8
75. (Centre for Social Justice, 2009)
76. (Brewer & Handscomb, 2020), pp 19–20
77. This project is now https://changingrealities.org/about, accessed July 2025
78. (Patrick, et al, 2022), p 18
79. (Brewer & Handscomb, 2020), pp 57–8

80 https://www.gov.uk/government/publications/covid-winter-grant-scheme/covid-winter-grant-scheme-guidance-for-local-councils; https://www.gov.uk/government/publications/covid-local-support-grant-guidance-for-local-councils/covid-local-support-grant-extension-21-june-to-30-september-2021-guidance, accessed July 2025
81 (Meers, 2019)
82 (Comptroller and Auditor General, 2016), p 5
83 (Comptroller and Auditor General, 2016), p 7
84 (Meers, 2019), p 55
85 https://www.jrf.org.uk/social-security/keepthelifeline-urging-the-government-not-to-cut-universal-credit, accessed July 2025
86 (Meers, Colliver, Hudson, & Lunt, 2024)
87 (Meers, Colliver, Hudson, & Lunt, 2024), p 27
88 https://www.gov.uk/government/publications/household-support-fund-guidance-for-local-councils/1-april-2025-to-31-march-2026-household-support-fund-guidance-for-county-councils-and-unitary-authorities-in-england, accessed July 2025
89 https://www.bbc.co.uk/news/articles/cwyx7z4ynr5o, accessed July 2025
90 (Meers, Colliver, Hudson, & Lunt, 2024), p 33
91 (Edmiston, et al, 2022), p 778
92 https://www.theguardian.com/politics/article/2024/aug/20/how-england-came-to-rely-on-a-sticking-plaster-crisis-fund, accessed July 2025
93 (Edmiston, et al, 2022), p 783
94 (Middleton, Mehta, McNaughton, & Booth, 2018), p 707
95 HBAI, Table 5.11ts, 2022/23 figures, https://www.gov.uk/government/statistics/households-below-average-income-for-financial-years-ending-1995-to-2023, accessed July 2025

Chapter 3

1 https://www.itv.com/news/2025-02-06/too-many-people-taking-the-mickey-with-benefits-work-secretary-says, accessed July 2025
2 https://politicaladvertising.co.uk/2010/04/21/conservative-poster-cut-benefits-for-those-who-refuse-work/, accessed July 2025
3 See in particular, (Morrison, 2019) and (Golding, 2023)
4 (Brewer & Murphy, 2023), p 8
5 (House of Commons Work and Pensions Committee, 2018), pp 6–10
6 (Patrick, 2023), p 12
7 https://www.gov.uk/government/statistics/benefit-sanctions-statistics-to-november-2024/benefit-sanctions-statistics-to-november-2024, accessed July 2025

Notes

8. https://www.gov.uk/government/statistics/benefit-sanctions-statistics-to-november-2023-official-statistics-in-development/benefit-sanctions-statistics-to-november-2023-official-statistics-in-development, accessed July 2025
9. (Vizard & Hills, 2021), p 103
10. (House of Commons Work and Pensions Committee, 2018), pp 19–22
11. All quotes are from evidence and submission to the House of Commons Work and Pensions Committee, (House of Commons Work and Pensions Committee, 2018), pp 19–22
12. (Wright, Robertson, Gawlewicz, Bailey, & Katikiteddi, 2020)
13. All quotes are from (Wright, Robertson, Gawlewicz, Bailey, & Katikiteddi, 2020)
14. The Welfare Conditionality Project was funded by the Economic and Social Research Council (ESRC) and run by a team from six UK universities: http://www.welfareconditionality.ac.uk/, accessed July 2025
15. (Wright, et al, 2018), p 1; all following quotes are from (Wright, et al, 2018), pp 6–7
16. See also (House of Commons Work and Pensions Committee, 2018)
17. This has been studied in detail by the Institute for Fiscal Studies, see (Codreanu & Waters, 2023)
18. (Codreanu & Waters, 2023), pp 15–17
19. (Codreanu & Waters, 2023), pp 21–2
20. As measured of those in households below 60 per cent median income BHC, see https://ifs.org.uk/articles/pre-pandemic-relative-poverty-rate-children-lone-parents-almost-double-children-living-two, accessed July 2025
21. See, for examples, https://www.disabilitynewsservice.com/heartless-reforms-to-disability-benefits-defy-logic/, accessed July 2025; (Pring, 2017); and (Ryan, 2019)
22. (Hood & Keiller, 2016), pp 57–9.
23. https://www.scope.org.uk/campaigns/disability-price-tag, accessed July 2025
24. All quotes from (Wright, Field, Moss, Frounk, & Veruete-McKay, 2024)
25. Though these savings never materialised due to a rise in the number of claimants (Hood & Keiller, 2016), p 60
26. In Scotland, PIP is to be replaced by an Adult Living Allowance, though quite what form this will take is under discussion as of July 2025, see (Heap, 2024)
27. (Comptroller and Auditor General, 2016), p 13
28. (House of Commons Work and Pensions Committee, 2023), pp 126–32
29. Citizens Advice submission to the House of Commons Work and Pensions committee inquiry on health assessments for benefits, p 2: https://committees.parliament.uk/writtenevidence/40727/pdf/, accessed July 2025; see also (Negri & Cavanagh, 2024), pp 84–5

[30] (House of Commons Work and Pensions Committee, 2023), p 50
[31] All quotes are from the experiences claimants reported to the select committee: https://publications.parliament.uk/pa/cm201719/cmselect/cmworpen/355/35504.htm, accessed July 2025
[32] (House of Commons Work and Pensions Committee, 2023), pp 57–63 and https://committees.parliament.uk/writtenevidence/40716/html/, accessed July 2025
[33] (Hoynes, Joyce, & Waters, 2023), pp 9–10
[34] (Clegg, 2024), p 5
[35] (Clegg, 2024), p 4
[36] (Clegg, 2024), pp 18–19
[37] (Clegg, 2024), p 24
[38] HBAI 2023 data tables, Table 7.3ts: https://www.gov.uk/government/statistics/households-below-average-income-for-financial-years-ending-1995-to-2023, accessed July 2025
[39] (Banks, Karjalainen, & Waters, 2023), p 22
[40] (Joseph Rowntree Foundation, 2024), pp 12–13
[41] (Fitzpatrick, et al, 2023a), p 29
[42] (Heap, 2024), p 171
[43] https://www.gov.scot/binaries/content/documents/govscot/publications/consultation-paper/2023/01/adult-disability-payment-consultation-mobility-component/documents/adult-disability-payment-consultation-mobility-component/adult-disability-payment-consultation-mobility-component/govscot%3Adocument/adult-disability-payment-consultation-mobility-component.pdf, accessed July 2025
[44] (Heap, 2024), pp 171–4
[45] https://commonslibrary.parliament.uk/local-authority-data-adult-disability-payment/, accessed July 2025
[46] (Heap, 2024), p 177
[47] (Banks, Karjalainen, & Waters, 2023), pp 27–9
[48] (Negri & Cavanagh, 2024), pp 61–5
[49] https://www.disabilityrightsuk.org/resources/access-work, accessed July 2025
[50] (Emmerson, Joyce, & Sturrock, 2017), pp 183–4
[51] (Ray-Chaudhuri & Waters, 2024), p 2
[52] (British Medical Association, 2022)
[53] (Marmot, Allen, Boyce, Goldblatt, & Morrison, 2020), Table 2.1, p 21
[54] (Latimer, Pflanz, & Waters, 2024), pp 16–18
[55] https://www.bbc.co.uk/news/articles/cd7ejvr3y0zo, accessed July 2025
[56] https://www.rethink.org/news-and-stories/news-and-views/2025/our-response-to-the-health-secretary-s-claim-that-mental-illnesses-are-being-overdiagnosed/, accessed July 2025

Notes

57 https://www.rethink.org/news-and-stories/news-and-views/2025/our-message-to-the-government-ahead-of-planned-cuts-to-the-social-security-system, accessed July 2025

58 https://neweconomics.org/2025/05/whats-behind-the-rise-in-disability-benefit-claims, Figure 1, accessed July 2025

59 https://ifs.org.uk/data-items/annual-spendingworking-age-benefits-2024-25-prices, accessed July 2025

60 (Latimer, Pflanz, & Waters, 2024), p 2

61 (Ray-Chaudhuri, Waters, Wernham, & Xu, 2023), p 2

62 https://www.disabilityrightsuk.org/news/open-letter-liz-kendall-don%E2%80%99t-continue-wca-cuts, accessed July 2025

63 https://www.theguardian.com/politics/2025/mar/06/liz-kendall-says-getting-people-into-work-is-best-way-to-cut-benefits-bill, accessed July 2025

64 https://news.sky.com/story/ministers-determined-to-fix-broken-benefits-system-as-welfare-cuts-expected-13327905, accessed July 2025

65 https://www.theguardian.com/politics/2025/mar/06/liz-kendall-says-getting-people-into-work-is-best-way-to-cut-benefits-bill, accessed July 2025

66 https://www.gov.uk/government/consultations/pathways-to-work-reforming-benefits-and-support-to-get-britain-working-green-paper, accessed July 2025

67 https://www.gov.uk/government/news/biggest-shake-up-to-welfare-system-in-a-generation-to-get-britain-working, accessed July 2025

68 https://ifs.org.uk/articles/ifs-response-announced-reforms-disability-and-incapacity-benefits, accessed July 2025

69 https://www.theguardian.com/world/2025/jun/24/keir-starmer-says-government-will-stand-firm-on-disability-welfare-overhaul, accessed July 2025

70 https://www.theguardian.com/politics/2025/jun/15/labour-has-made-me-feel-like-a-scrounger-disabled-people-urge-welfare-cuts-rethink, accessed July 2025

71 https://www.citizensadvice.org.uk/policy/publications/pathways-to-poverty-how-planned-cuts-to-disability-benefits-will-impact-the, accessed July 2025

72 https://www.mind.org.uk/news-campaigns/news/mind-reacts-to-uk-government-green-paper-on-benefit-reform/, accessed July 2025

73 https://www.resolutionfoundation.org/press-releases/green-paper-delivers-tiny-income-gains-for-up-to-four-million-households-at-cost-of-major-income-losses-for-those-who-are-too-ill-to-work-or-no-longer-qualify-for-disability-benefit-support/, accessed July 2025

74 https://www.gov.uk/government/news/welfare-bill-will-protect-the-most-vulnerable-and-help-households-with-income-boost, accessed July 2025

[75] https://ifs.org.uk/articles/ifs-response-announced-reforms-disability-and-incapacity-benefits, accessed July 2025
[76] https://neweconomics.org/2025/03/benefits-cuts-driven-by-need-to-meet-fiscal-rules-rather-than-support-for-ill-and-disabled-nef-warns, accessed July 2025
[77] https://www.scope.org.uk/campaigns/open-letter-to-the-chancellor-the-cost-of-cuts-to-disability-benefits, accessed July 2025
[78] https://www.theguardian.com/politics/2025/jul/02/disabled-people-react-watered-down-welfare-reform-bill-passes, accessed July 2025
[79] https://www.benefitsandwork.co.uk/news/will-new-dwp-boss-mcfadden-be-worse-than-kendall-for-claimants, accessed July 2025
[80] https://www.theguardian.com/commentisfree/2025/mar/10/disabled-people-labour-benefits-system, accessed July 2025

Chapter 4

[1] https://www.gov.uk/government/news/chancellor-we-will-build-a-britain-where-those-who-can-work-will-work, accessed July 2025
[2] Quotes from evidence to the All-Party Parliamentary Group on Poverty, 2021/22 (All-Party Parliamentary Group on Poverty, 2022), p 3
[3] https://assets.publishing.service.gov.uk/media/6836dae29411f0341f323689/HBAI_2324odstable_pack.zip, accessed September 2025
[4] https://assets.publishing.service.gov.uk/media/6836dae29411f0341f323689/HBAI_2324odstable_pack.zip, accessed September 2025
[5] https://assets.publishing.service.gov.uk/media/6836dae29411f0341f323689/HBAI_2324_ods_table_pack.zip, and https://assets.publishing.service.gov.uk/media/6836dae29411f0341f323689/HBAI_2324_ods_table_pack.zip, accessed September 2025
[6] https://assets.publishing.service.gov.uk/media/6836dae29411f0341f323689/HBAI_2324odstable_pack.zip, accessed September 2025
[7] https://minimumwage.blog.gov.uk/2023/05/05/how-we-calculate-a-path-for-the-national-living-wages-target-of-two-thirds-of-median-wages-in-2024/, accessed July 2025
[8] https://www.theguardian.com/uk-news/2015/jul/08/budget-2015-uk-gdp-other-rich-nations-george-osborne, accessed July 2025
[9] https://www.gov.uk/government/news/new-national-living-wage-to-give-living-standards-boost-to-over-a-million-workers, accessed July 2025
[10] (Cominetti & Sloughter, 2024), p 4
[11] (Hoynes, Joyce, & Waters, 2023), p 31
[12] (Cribb, et al, 2021), Figure 2
[13] (Cribb, et al, 2021), pp 28–34
[14] (Hick & Lanau, 2017), p 3

Notes

15. https://www.gov.uk/government/news/chancellor-chooses-a-budget-to-rebuild-britain, accessed July 2025
16. https://www.gov.uk/government/speeches/budget-2025-speech, accessed November 2025
17. (Giupponi & Machin, 2024), pp i886–7
18. (Farquharson, McNally, & Tahir, 2022), p 21
19. (Farquharson, McNally, & Tahir, 2022), p 22
20. (Giupponi & Machin, 2024), pp i899–900
21. (Giupponi & Machin, 2024), p i885
22. https://highpaycentre.org/ceo-to-worker-pay-gaps-in-the-ftse-350-five-years-of-pay-ratio-disclosures-2/, accessed July 2025; https://blogs.lse.ac.uk/businessreview/2025/06/25/british-ceos-earn-100-times-what-they-pay-employees/, accessed July 2025
23. (Giupponi & Machin, 2024), p i893
24. (Giupponi & Machin, 2024), p i893
25. See for examples: https://www.bsg.ox.ac.uk/sites/default/files/2018-05/BSG-WP-2016-014.pdf; https://www.theguardian.com/politics/ng-interactive/2024/jun/28/how-the-unforced-error-of-tory-austerity-wrecked-britain; https://www.theguardian.com/commentisfree/article/2024/sep/04/keir-starmer-rachel-reeves-austerity, all accessed July 2025
26. https://mainlymacro.blogspot.com/2018/03/the-economic-and-political-cost-of-uk.html, accessed July 2025
27. https://www.resolutionfoundation.org/data/median-employee-earnings/, accessed July 2025
28. https://www.niesr.ac.uk/wp-content/uploads/2023/11/JC760-NIESR-Outlook-Autumn-2023-Global-Topical-Feature-v2.pdf?, accessed July 2025
29. https://cepr.org/voxeu/columns/impact-brexit-uk-economy-reviewing-evidence, accessed July 2025
30. https://www.gov.uk/government/statistics/coronavirus-job-retention-scheme-statistics-3-june-2021/coronavirus-job-retention-scheme-statistics-3-june-2021#employments-on-furlough-over-time, accessed July 2025
31. (Tomlinson, 2021), Figure 5
32. (Tomlinson, 2021)
33. https://www.ons.gov.uk/employmentandlabourmarket/peopleinwork/earningsandworkinghours/bulletins/lowandhighpayuk/2020, accessed July 2025
34. https://www.gov.uk/government/publications/the-self-employment-income-support-scheme-final-evaluation/the-self-employment-income-support-scheme-final-evaluation#chapter-6-final-evaluation-conclusions, accessed July 2025

[35] https://ifs.org.uk/articles/government-publishes-new-evidence-impacts-income-and-job-protection-schemes-during, accessed July 2025
[36] (Stuart, Spencer, MacLachan, & Forde, 2021), Table 2, p 6
[37] (Blundell, Costa Dias, Joyce, & Xu, 2020), pp 298–9
[38] https://www.ons.gov.uk/peoplepopulationandcommunity/personalandhouseholdfinances/expenditure/articles/impactofincreasedcostoflivingonadultsacrossgreatbritain/februarytomay2023, Figure 1, accessed July 2025
[39] (Harari, Francis-Devine, Bolton, & Keep, 2023), pp 48–9
[40] https://www.ons.gov.uk/economy/inflationandpriceindices/bulletins/householdcostsindicesforukhouseholdgroups/april2024tojune2024/pdf, accessed July 2025
[41] https://www.ons.gov.uk/peoplepopulationandcommunity/personalandhouseholdfinances/expenditure/compendium/variationintheinflationexperienceofukhouseholds/2014-12-15/chapter4democraticindices/pdf, accessed July 2025
[42] https://www.ons.gov.uk/economy/inflationandpriceindices/bulletins/householdcostsindicesforukhouseholdgroups/january2022toseptember2023#strengths-and-limitations, Table 1 and Figure 3, accessed July 2025
[43] https://www.ons.gov.uk/economy/inflationandpriceindices/bulletins/householdcostsindicesforukhouseholdgroups/october2023todecember2023#household-costs-indices-data, Figure 1, accessed July 2025
[44] https://www.niesr.ac.uk/blog/truss-kwarteng-mini-budget-one-year, accessed July 2025
[45] https://www.opendemocracy.net/en/liz-truss-conservative-party-housing-crisis-rent/, accessed July 2025
[46] https://www.politico.eu/article/beaten-by-a-lettuce-44-glorious-days-of-liz-truss/, accessed July 2025
[47] (Joseph Rowntree Foundation, 2024), p 153
[48] (Labour Party, 2024)
[49] (Labour Party, 2024), p 3
[50] https://publications.parliament.uk/pa/bills/cbill/59-01/0011/240011.pdf, accessed July 2025
[51] https://www.gov.uk/government/news/public-services-back-on-track-as-strikes-act-to-be-repealed, accessed July 2025
[52] (UK Government, 2024), p 64
[53] https://news.sky.com/story/unions-demand-no-retreat-on-workers-rights-after-rayner-quits-13426073, accessed September 2025
[54] https://www.tuc.org.uk/blogs/employment-rights-bill-potential-game changer, accessed July 2025
[55] (Brewer, Browne, Joyce, & Sibieta, 2010), p 30

Notes

56 https://www.gov.uk/government/speeches/chancellor-george-osbornes-summer-budget-2015-speech, accessed July 2025
57 (Brewer, Handscomb, & Try, 2021), p 2
58 (Hoynes, Joyce, & Waters, 2023), pp 21–2
59 https://www.gov.uk/government/speeches/we-have-to-invest-in-good-work-theresa-mays-speech-at-taylor-review-launch, accessed July 2025
60 (Britton, Farquharson, & Sibieta, 2019), p 7
61 See (Coleman, Dali-Chaouch, & Harding, 2020), p 9, for full details of entitlements
62 (Reis & Stephens, 2022), p 2
63 (Farquharson & Olorenshaw, 2022), pp 16–17
64 (Simon, et al, 2021), p 13
65 (Reis & Stephens, 2022), p 6
66 (Simon, et al, 2021), p 13
67 https://www.theguardian.com/money/2023/aug/04/childcare-sector-england-not-playground-private-equity-experts-say, accessed July 2025
68 (Simon, et al, 2021), pp 9–10
69 https://assets.publishing.service.gov.uk/government/uploads/system/uploads/attachment_data/file/1039675/Main_summary_survey_of_childcare_and_early_years_providers_2021.pdf, pp 13, 15, Figure 6; accessed September 2025
70 (Simon, et al, 2021), p 9
71 (Reis & Stephens, 2022), p 4
72 (Coleman, Dali-Chaouch, & Harding, 2020), pp 20–1
73 (Reis & Stephens, 2022), p 8
74 https://www.health.org.uk/publications/long-reads/understanding-unpaid-carers-and-their-access-to-support, accessed July 2025
75 https://www.carersuk.org/media/bgolg5u2/cuk-carers-rights-day-research-report-2022-web.pdf, p 16; accessed July 2025
76 https://www.benefitsandwork.co.uk/news/no-genuine-co-production-for-timms-review, accessed September 2025
77 (Gulland, 2024), p 102
78 https://www.theguardian.com/society/2018/oct/07/uk-carers-face-prosecutions-and-fines-due-to-overpaid-benefit, accessed July 2025
79 (House of Commons Work and Pensions Committee, 2019b), pp 11–12
80 https://www.theguardian.com/society/2024/apr/07/unpaid-carers-allowance-payment-prosecution-earnings-rules, accessed July 2025
81 All quotes from (House of Commons Work and Pensions Committee, 2019b), p 16
82 https://www.theguardian.com/uk-news/2024/oct/15/labour-to-set-up-review-after-carers-allowance-overpayments-scandal, accessed July 2025

[83] https://www.gov.uk/government/publications/review-of-carers-allowance-overpayments, accessed November 2025
[84] (Thompson, Jitendra, & Woodruff, 2023), p 4
[85] (Joseph Rowntree Foundation, 2024), p 70
[86] (Joseph Rowntree Foundation, 2024), pp 69–70
[87] (Hoynes, Joyce, & Waters, 2023), Table 3, p 21, and Table A1, p 60

Chapter 5

[1] https://www.theguardian.com/commentisfree/2024/nov/17/britain-austerity-labour-uk-economy-councils, accessed July 2025
[2] (Ogden & Phillips, 2024), p 8
[3] (Sandford, 2023)
[4] (Ogden & Phillips, 2024), p 8
[5] (Ifan & Sion, 2019)
[6] (Phillips, 2021), p 12
[7] https://www.instituteforgovernment.org.uk/publication/fixing-public-services-labour-government/local-government, accessed July 2025
[8] (Davenport & Zaranko, 2020), pp 321–4
[9] https://www.instituteforgovernment.org.uk/publication/fixing-public-services-labour-government/local-government, accessed July 2025
[10] See the Index of Multiple Deprivation small area mapping for more details: https://data.cdrc.ac.uk/dataset/index-multiple-deprivation-imd, accessed July 2025
[11] https://www.gov.uk/government/speeches/boris-johnsons-first-speech-as-prime-minister-24-july-2019, accessed July 2025
[12] (Farquharson, Heath Milsom, Tahir, Upton, & Vyas, 2024), p 2
[13] (Marmot, Allen, Boyce, Goldblatt, & Morrison, 2020), Table 2.1, p 21
[14] (Marmot, Allen, Boyce, Goldblatt, & Morrison, 2020), p 22
[15] https://www.kingsfund.org.uk/insight-and-analysis/data-and-charts/key-facts-figures-adult-social-care, accessed July 2025
[16] (Carers UK, 2023), p 13
[17] https://www.kingsfund.org.uk/insight-and-analysis/long-reads/social-care-360, accessed July 2025
[18] https://www.kingsfund.org.uk/insight-and-analysis/data-and-charts/key-facts-figures-adult-social-care, accessed July 2025
[19] (Hoddinott, Rowland, Davies, Kim, & Nye, 2024), p 41
[20] https://www.kingsfund.org.uk/insight-and-analysis/long-reads/social-care-360-access#1.-requests-for-support, accessed July 2025
[21] (Carers UK, 2023), p 15
[22] (Bach-Mortensen, Degli Esposti, Corlet Walker, & Barlow, 2024), p 6
[23] (Hoddinott, Davies, Fright, Nye, & Richards, 2023), pp 146–9

Notes

[24] (MacAlister, 2022), pp 19–20
[25] (Bach-Mortensen, Degli Esposti, Corlet Walker, & Barlow, 2024), p 22
[26] (Bach-Mortensen, Degli Esposti, Corlet Walker, & Barlow, 2024), p 19
[27] https://www.cqc.org.uk/press-release/combination-cost-living-crisis-and-workforce-pressures-risks-unfair-care-longer-waits, accessed July 2025
[28] https://www.theguardian.com/business/2011/jul/16/southern-cross-incurable-sick-business-model, accessed July 2025
[29] https://www.theguardian.com/business/2011/jun/01/rise-and-fall-of-southern-cross, accessed July 2025
[30] https://hansard.parliament.uk/Commons/2011-07-19/debates/11071985000034/SouthernCross, accessed July 2025
[31] https://blogs.lse.ac.uk/politicsandpolicy/corporate-care-homes/, accessed July 2025
[32] https://www.wbs.ac.uk/news/uk-care-home-sector-in-trouble/, accessed July 2025
[33] https://www.wbs.ac.uk/news/uk-care-home-sector-bailed-out-but-burned-out-after-covid-19-pandemic/, accessed July 2025
[34] https://www.theguardian.com/society/2022/jul/24/uk-private-care-providers-profit-rise-covid-report, accessed July 2025
[35] https://www.ox.ac.uk/news/2024-10-07-new-report-profit-social-care-provision-has-drastically-increased-despite-concerns., accessed July 2025
[36] https://www.itv.com/news/2025-03-03/disabled-man-left-to-eat-from-bin-itv-news-exposes-appalling-neglect, accessed July 2025
[37] (Competitions and Markets Authority, 2022), p 5
[38] (Competitions and Markets Authority, 2022), p 9
[39] https://www.theguardian.com/society/2024/mar/02/profiteering-off-children-care-firms-in-england-accused-of-squeezing-cash-from-councils, accessed July 2025
[40] https://www.instituteforgovernment.org.uk/publication/fixing-public-services-labour-government/local-government, accessed July 2025
[41] (MacAlister, 2022), p 50
[42] (Chazan, Laing, Cox, Jackson, & Lloyd, 1976) and subsequent studies. See also https://social-mobility.data.gov.uk/intermediate_outcomes/compulsory_school_age_(5_to_16_years)/attainment_at_age_16/latest.
[43] (Black, 1980) and subsequent studies (e.g., Marmot, Allen, Boyce, Goldblatt, & Morrison, 2020)
[44] https://cls.ucl.ac.uk/wp-content/uploads/2017/05/13_briefing_web.pdf, Figure 1, accessed July 2025
[45] (Cattan, Conti, Farquharson, & Ginja, 2019), pp 17–21
[46] (Hall & Stephens, 2020), p 7

47 https://www.newstatesman.com/thestaggers/2023/02/replacing-lost-sure-start-centres-is-a-tacit-admission-of-austeritys-failure, accessed July 2025
48 (Hall & Stephens, 2020), p 7
49 (Sammons, Hall, Smees, & Goff, 2015), p 122
50 (Smith, Sylva, Smith, Sammons, & Omonigho, 2018), p 5
51 (Sammons, Hall, Smees, & Goff, 2015), p 132
52 https://www.instituteforgovernment.org.uk/publication/performance-tracker-2023/childrens-social-care, accessed July 2025
53 (Cattan, Conti, Farquharson, & Ginja, 2019)
54 (Cattan, Conti, Farquharson, & Ginja, 2019), p 7
55 (Carneiro, Cattan, & Ridpath, 2024)
56 (Carneiro, Cattan, & Ridpath, 2024), pp 19–21
57 https://www.unison.org.uk/at-work/local-government/key-issues/cuts-to-local%20services, accessed July 2025
58 https://www.ukyouth.org/wp-content/uploads/2021/08/Benefits-of-youth-work-to-current-govt-priorities.pdf; https://www.ukyouth.org/wp-content/uploads/2022/09/Economic-Value-of-Youth-Work-Final-260822-STC-clean75-1.pdf, accessed July 2025
59 (Villa, 2024)
60 (Campaign for Better Transport, 2019), pp 6–7
61 https://www.gov.uk/government/statistical-data-sets/bus-statistics-data-tables, accessed July 2025
62 https://www.southyorkshire-ca.gov.uk/getmedia/2b2b8b2d-718d-485d-8c81-179535fbf335/Bus-Review-Report-June-2020.pdf, p 11, accessed July 2025
63 (Department of Transport, 2021), p 47
64 (Campaign for Better Transport, 2020)
65 (Lucas, Stokes, Bastiaanssen, & Burkinshaw, 2019), p 23
66 (Alston, Khawaja, & Riddell, 2021), p 22
67 https://bettertransport.org.uk/wp-content/uploads/legacy-files/research-files/Young_People_and_Buses_FINAL_forweb_0.pdf, accessed July 2025
68 https://www.its.leeds.ac.uk/fileadmin/user_upload/Events/DJ_Comp_Cities_Workshop.pdf, slide 24, accessed July 2025
69 https://www.its.leeds.ac.uk/fileadmin/user_upload/Events/DJ_Comp_Cities_Workshop.pdf, slide 21, accessed July 2025
70 (Alston, Khawaja, & Riddell, 2021), p 23
71 https://publications.parliament.uk/pa/cm201719/cmselect/cmtrans/1425/142505.htm, accessed July 2025
72 (Department of Transport, 2021), p 59
73 https://www.bankofengland.co.uk/monetary-policy/inflation/inflation-calculator, accessed July 2025

Notes

[74] (Alston, Khawaja, & Riddell, 2021), p 21
[75] https://www.gov.uk/government/news/over-1-billion-to-boost-bus-services-across-the-country-as-bus-fares-capped-at-3, accessed July 2025
[76] (Alston, Khawaja, & Riddell, 2021), p 7
[77] (Alston, Khawaja, & Riddell, 2021), p 9
[78] (Lucas, Stokes, Bastiaanssen, & Burkinshaw, 2019), pp 9–10
[79] https://news.tfgm.com/press-releases/4755e95a-fc9f-40a6-bb71-7416ce1b4605/pioneering-bee-network-marks-one-year-anniversary-with-record-numbers-of-people-travelling-on-cheaper-cleaner-more-reliable-buses, accessed July 2025
[80] (Department of Transport, 2021), p 4
[81] https://www.theguardian.com/politics/2022/jan/23/boris-johnsons-bus-back-better-red-wall-levelling-up-treasury-cuts-funding, accessed July 2025
[82] (Campaign for Better Transport, 2022), p 6
[83] https://www.gov.uk/government/news/transport-secretary-sets-the-wheels-in-motion-on-biggest-overhaul-to-buses-in-a-generation, accessed July 2025
[84] https://www.gov.uk/government/consultations/proposed-changes-to-bus-franchising-guidance/outcome/proposed-changes-to-bus-franchising-guidance-consultation-outcome, accessed July 2025
[85] https://www.gov.uk/government/news/over-1-billion-to-boost-bus-services-across-the-country-as-bus-fares-capped-at-3, accessed July 2025
[86] https://www.newstatesman.com/spotlight/2018/06/municipal-bus-companies-can-public-ownership-be-profitable, accessed July 2025
[87] (KPMG, 2024), p 18

Chapter 6

[1] https://www.ons.gov.uk/economy/inflationandpriceindices/bulletins/privaterentandhousepricesuk/latest#private-rent-prices-by-country, accessed July 2025
[2] (Joyce, Mitchell, & Keiller, 2017), Figure 3.2 and Figure 3.11, pp 13, 26
[3] All quotes from (Crisis, 2019), pp 17, 29
[4] (Joyce, Mitchell, & Keiller, 2017), pp 35–8
[5] (Cribb, Wernham, & Xu, 2023), Figures 4 and 5, p 8
[6] See for examples: (Diner, 2023), pp 17–21; https://neweconomics.org/2022/05/the-damaging-legacy-of-right-to-buy; https://www.theguardian.com/society/2022/jun/29/how-right-to-buy-ruined-british-housing; https://www.cih.org/news/uk-housing-review-2022-shows-england-s-right-to-buy-is-a-strategic-failure-and-will-exacerbate-inequalities-if-left-unchecked, all accessed July 2025

[7] https://lordslibrary.parliament.uk/right-to-buy-past-present-and-future/#:~:text=1.2%20Housing%20Act%201980,-In%201980%2C%20the&text=The%20manifesto%20said%20that%20helping,mortgage%20from%20their%20local%20authority, accessed July 2025

[8] https://www.historyandpolicy.org/policy-papers/papers/the-right-to-buy-history-and-prospect, accessed July 2025

[9] https://view.officeapps.live.com/op/view.aspx?src=https%3A%2F%2Fassets.publishing.service.gov.uk%2Fgovernment%2Fuploads%2Fsystem%2Fuploads%2Fattachment_data%2Ffile%2F850392%2FLT_671_-_discontinued.xlsx&wdOrigin=BROWSELINK, accessed July 2025

[10] https://www.insidehousing.co.uk/news/affordable-rent-costs-double-the-equivalent-social-rent-in-parts-of-england-81195, accessed July 2025; https://commonslibrary.parliament.uk/research-briefings/cbp-8963/, accessed July 2025

[11] https://www.insidehousing.co.uk/insight/10-years-of-affordable-rent-73711#:~:text=2011%20was%20a%20key%20year,reform%2C%20will%20be%20published%20tomorrow, accessed July 2025

[12] https://commonslibrary.parliament.uk/research-briefings/cbp-8963/, accessed July 2025

[13] https://www.resolutionfoundation.org/app/uploads/2021/12/Housing-Outlook-Q4-2021.pdf, accessed July 2025

[14] (Hoynes, et al, 2023), p 25

[15] For a discussion of the evolution of this idea, see https://www.democraticaudit.com/2017/07/26/who-invented-the-british-dream-of-a-property-owning-democracy/, accessed July 2025

[16] https://lordslibrary.parliament.uk/right-to-buy-past-present-and-future/#:~:text=1.2%20Housing%20Act%201980,-In%201980%2C%20the&text=The%20manifesto%20said%20that%20helping,mortgage%20from%20their%20local%20authority, accessed July 2025

[17] (Hoynes, et al, 2023), p 25

[18] (Grayston, et al, 2024), p 4

[19] https://www.ons.gov.uk/economy/inflationandpriceindices/articles/ukprivaterentedsector/2018#:~:text=The%20number%20of%20households%20living,consistent%20at%2017.7%20million%20households, accessed July 2025

[20] (Grayston, et al, 2024), pp 8–9

[21] https://commonslibrary.parliament.uk/constituency-data-housing-tenure/#:~:text=On%20average%20across%20the%20UK,Explore%20constituency%20data, accessed July 2025

[22] https://england.shelter.org.uk/media/press_release/living_in_a_social_home_is_over_60_more_affordable_than_private_renting_#:~:text=Living%20in%20a%20social%20home,renting%20%2D%20Shelter%20England%20%2D%20Shelter%20England, accessed July 2025

Notes

[23] (Fitzpatrick, et al, 2023b), Figure 5.1, p 92
[24] https://assets.ctfassets.net/6sxvmndnpn0s/ZhlMP1aeh1mOBzBDX2z1H/58b3122b8d18585a6b57c7cd693601ad/Homelessness_HRA17_Implementation_Briefing_FINAL.pdf, accessed July 2025
[25] (Comptroller and Auditor General, 2024), p 34
[26] (Comptroller and Auditor General, 2024), pp 16–17
[27] https://www.theguardian.com/money/article/2024/sep/06/labour-moves-to-end-no-fault-evictions-within-months, accessed July 2025; https://www.gov.uk/government/news/landmark-reforms-to-give-greater-security-for-11-million-renters, accessed September 2025
[28] (Comptroller and Auditor General, 2024), p 8
[29] (Fitzpatrick, et al, 2023b), p 90
[30] https://www.gov.uk/government/statisticaldata-sets/live-tables-on-homelessness, accessed July 2025
[31] (Fitzpatrick, et al, 2023b), pp 92–3
[32] https://www.crisis.org.uk/ending-homelessness/homelessness-knowledge-hub/homelessness-monitor/about/the-homelessness-monitor-great-britain-2022/, accessed July 2025
[33] https://trustforlondon.org.uk/news/how-the-temporary-accommodation-crisis-is-affecting-londoners-health-and-wellbeing/#:~:text=Temporary%20accommodation%20has%20a%20detrimental,are%20often%20more%20expensive.%E2%80%8B, accessed July 2025
[34] (Procter, Pratt, & Wise-Martin, 2023), p 12
[35] All quotes from (Procter, Pratt, & Wise-Martin, 2023), pp 12–18
[36] https://www.gov.uk/government/statisticaldata-sets/live-tables-on-homelessness, accessed July 2025
[37] Quotes from (Procter, Pratt, & Wise-Martin, 2023), p 15
[38] (Comptroller and Auditor General, 2024), p 4
[39] (Fitzpatrick, et al, 2023b), p 110
[40] (Comptroller and Auditor General, 2024), p 39
[41] https://www.lewes-eastbourne.gov.uk/article/2875/Council-leader-warns-of-forced-service-cuts-due-to-homelessness-crisis; https://www.theguardian.com/society/2023/oct/30/englands-broken-housing-system-is-now-a-problem-no-council-can-avoid, accessed July 2025
[42] (Comptroller and Auditor General, 2024), pp 24–6
[43] https://www.hbf.co.uk/news/housing-horizons-new-analysis-shows-true-scale-of-how-uk-housing-is-falling-behind-international-counterparts, accessed July 2025
[44] https://www.gov.uk/government/statistics/chapters-for-english-housing-survey-2022-to-2023-headline-report/chapter-4-dwelling-condition, accessed July 2025

[45] https://www.gov.uk/government/statistics/english-housing-survey-2022-to-2023-housing-quality-and-condition/english-housing-survey-2022-to-2023-housing-quality-and-condition#introduction-and-main-findings, accessed July 2025

[46] https://phw.nhs.wales/news/the-cost-of-poor-housing-in-wales/the-full-cost-of-poor-housing-in-wales/, accessed July 2025

[47] https://www.gov.uk/government/statistics/chapters-for-english-housing-survey-2022-to-2023-headline-report/chapter-4-dwelling-condition, Figure 4.5, accessed July 2025

[48] https://www.gov.uk/government/statistics/english-housing-survey-2022-to-2023-housing-quality-and-condition, accessed July 2025

[49] https://www.health.org.uk/publications/long-reads/moving-to-healthy-homes, accessed July 2025

[50] https://www.cieh.org/ehn/housing-and-community/2023/november/damp-rented-homes-are-increasing-children-s-risk-of-ill-health, accessed July 2025

[51] https://www.judiciary.uk/wp-content/uploads/2022/11/Awaab-Ishak-Prevention-of-future-deaths-report-2022-0365_Published.pdf, accessed July 2025

[52] https://www.gov.uk/government/statistics/english-housing-survey-2022-to-2023-housing-quality-and-condition, accessed July 2025

[53] https://www.theguardian.com/uk-news/2023/nov/13/loophole-adds-to-shameful-rental-conditions-in-england-says-housing-chief, accessed July 2025

[54] https://www.nrla.org.uk/news/councils-are-failling-to-inspect-potentially-hazardous-housing, accessed July 2025

[55] https://committees.parliament.uk/publications/9608/documents/163793/default/, p 9, accessed July 2025

[56] https://committees.parliament.uk/publications/9608/documents/163793/default/, p 9, accessed July 2025

[57] https://www.nrla.org.uk/news/councils-are-failling-to-inspect-potentially-hazardous-housing, accessed July 2025

[58] https://www.london.gov.uk/mayor-london-calls-national-action-new-analysis-reveals-private-landlords-receiving-billions-pounds, accessed July 2025

[59] https://www.bettersocialhousingreview.org.uk/, accessed July 2025

[60] (Ejiogu & Denedo, 2021)

[61] https://www.bbc.co.uk/news/uk-40291372, accessed July 2025

[62] https://www.bbc.co.uk/news/uk-40301289, accessed July 2025

[63] https://www.grenfelltowerinquiry.org.uk/, accessed July 2025

Notes

64 https://www.theguardian.com/uk-news/article/2024/sep/05/grenfell-tower-the-fire-the-findings-whos-to-blame-and-what-happens-next, accessed July 2025
65 (Moore-Bick, Akbor, & Istephan, 2024), p 16, pt 2.58
66 https://www.bbc.co.uk/news/articles/c62305qx946o, accessed July 2025
67 https://theconversation.com/what-the-grenfell-report-gets-wrong-structural-racism-is-evident-in-access-to-safe-social-housing-238377, accessed July 2025
68 For a summary of the regulatory failures see https://www.constructionnews.co.uk/buildings/building-safety/serious-and-longstanding-failures-the-role-of-government-and-regulators-in-grenfell-fire-04-09-2024/, accessed July 2025
69 https://www.gov.uk/government/publications/building-safety-remediation-monthly-data-release-may-2024/building-safety-remediation-monthly-data-release-31-may-2024, accessed July 2025
70 (Savills, 2023), p 1
71 (Southwark Council, 2024), p 15
72 (Southwark Council, 2024), p 8
73 (Southwark Council, 2024), p 9
74 https://yieldinvesting.co.uk/how-is-social-housing-funded-in-the-uk/, accessed July 2025
75 https://www.insidehousing.co.uk/insight/thirty-years-on-how-the-housing-act-changed-everything-59821, accessed July 2025
76 https://www.housing.org.uk/our-work/quality/better-social-housing-review/, accessed July 2025
77 https://www.gov.uk/government/statistics/english-housing-survey-2022-to-2023-housing-quality-and-condition/english-housing-survey-2022-to-2023-housing-quality-and-condition#cost-to-make-decent, accessed July 2025
78 https://labour.org.uk/wp-content/uploads/2024/06/Change-Labour-Party-Manifesto-2024-large-print.pdf, p 38, accessed July 2025
79 https://www.gov.uk/government/news/cma-finds-fundamental-concerns-in-housebuilding-market, accessed July 2025
80 (Galarza, et al, 2024), p 7; (Metcalfe, 2024), pp 33–5
81 https://www.gov.uk/government/news/cma-finds-fundamental-concerns-in-housebuilding-market, accessed July 2025
82 https://commonslibrary.parliament.uk/affordable-housing-in-england/, accessed July 2025
83 (Galarza, et al, 2024), pp 4–5
84 https://www.gov.uk/government/news/housing-targets-increased-to-get-britain-building-again, accessed October 2025

[85] https://www.gov.uk/government/news/planning-overhaul-to-reach-15-million-new-homes, accessed October 2025; https://www.gov.uk/government/news/housing-targets-increased-to-get-britain-building-again, accessed October 2025

[86] https://www.theguardian.com/society/2025/feb/12/up-to-12-new-towns-will-be-under-construction-in-england-by-next-election-says-starmer, accessed July 2025

[87] For a full list of the eight major builders see https://www.gov.uk/government/news/cma-finds-fundamental-concerns-in-housebuilding-market, accessed July 2025

[88] (Metcalfe, 2024), p 28

[89] https://england.shelter.org.uk/what_we_do/updates_insights_and_impact/a_needed_win_for_social_rent_homes, accessed July 2025

[90] https://england.shelter.org.uk/what_we_do/updates_insights_and_impact/a_needed_win_for_social_rent_homes, accessed July 2025

[91] https://lordslibrary.parliament.uk/meeting-housing-demand-built-environment-committee-report/, accessed July 2025

[92] https://www.housing.org.uk/news-and-blogs/news/government-to-miss-1.5m-homes-target-by-half-a-million-homes-without-funding-and-policy-intervention-industry-bodies-warn/; https://www.savills.co.uk/research_articles/229130/366981-0, accessed July 2025

[93] https://lordslibrary.parliament.uk/supply-of-affordable-housing/#heading-12, accessed July 2025

[94] https://www.gov.uk/government/statistics/social-housing-lettings-in-england-april-2024-to-march-2025/social-housing-lettings-in-england-tenancies-april-2024-to-march-2025#rents-of-new-lettings, accessed November 2025

[95] https://www.gov.uk/government/news/chancellor-to-unlock-housing-in-first-budget, accessed July 2025

[96] https://www.gov.uk/government/statistical-data-sets/live-tables-on-affordable-housing-supply, accessed July 2025

[97] https://www.gov.uk/government/publications/letter-from-housing-minister-to-registered-providers-of-social-housing-spending-review-2025/letter-from-housing-minister-to-registered-providers-of-social-housing-spending-review-2025, accessed July 2025

[98] https://www.gov.uk/government/news/hundreds-of-thousands-to-get-secure-roof-over-their-heads, accessed July 2025

Chapter 7

[1] https://www.liverpoolecho.co.uk/news/liverpool-news/we-prayed-wouldnt-inside-terrifying-29688669, accessed July 2025

Notes

2. https://hopenothate.org.uk/2024/07/31/the-far-right-and-the-southport-riot-what-we-know-so-far/, accessed July 2025
3. https://www.bbc.co.uk/news/articles/c6p2yrg3pvpo, accessed July 2025
4. https://www.liverpoolecho.co.uk/news/liverpool-news/police-condemn-sickening-scenes-southport-29646018, accessed July 2025
5. https://www.liverpoolecho.co.uk/news/liverpool-news/distressing-scenes-mosque-targeted-during-29646287, accessed July 2025
6. https://www.liverpoolecho.co.uk/news/liverpool-news/thug-shouted-shouses-punched-police-29678959, accessed July 2025
7. https://www.liverpoolecho.co.uk/news/liverpool-news/distressing-scenes-mosque-targeted-during-29646287, accessed July 2025
8. https://metro.co.uk/2024/08/05/rioters-set-race-checkpoint-ask-drivers-white-english-21360645/, accessed July 2025
9. https://www.nursingtimes.net/leadership/filipino-nurses-attacked-as-nhs-community-condemns-racist-riots-05-08-2024/, accessed July 2025
10. https://www.gettyimages.co.uk/detail/news-photo/an-anti-immigration-protester-holds-up-a-sign-reading-news-photo/2167259980, accessed July 2025
11. https://www.birminghammail.co.uk/news/uk-news/chaos-tamworth-far-right-protesters-29676720, accessed July 2025
12. https://www.theguardian.com/uk-news/article/2024/aug/04/rioters-try-to-torch-rotherham-asylum-seeker-hotel-amid-far-right-violence, accessed July 2025
13. https://www.liverpoolecho.co.uk/news/liverpool-news/we-prayed-wouldnt-inside-terrifying-29688669, accessed July 2025
14. https://www.theguardian.com/uk-news/article/2024/aug/03/love-will-prevail-how-a-far-right-rally-in-liverpool-was-defused, accessed July 2025
15. https://www.theguardian.com/commentisfree/article/2024/aug/11/extremism-in-all-its-forms-has-been-ignored-for-too-long-by-british-politicians; https://www.lrb.co.uk/blog/2024/august/this-time-it-s-worse, accessed July 2025
16. https://www.theguardian.com/politics/2024/sep/27/sayeeda-warsi-on-leaving-the-tories-you-have-to-recognise-when-a-relationship-is-toxic, accessed July 2025
17. (Taylor, 2018), p 2
18. (Åhlberg & Granada, 2022), p 127
19. (Taylor, 2018), p 8
20. (Åhlberg & Granada, 2022), pp 127–8
21. (Taylor, 2018), p 13
22. (Jones, et al, 2015), p 3

[23] https://www.ohchr.org/en/statements/2018/05/end-mission-statement-special-rapporteur-contemporary-forms-racism-racial?LangID=E&NewsID=23073, pt 34, accessed July 2025
[24] https://www.ohchr.org/en/statements/2018/05/end-mission-statement-special-rapporteur-contemporary-forms-racism-racial?LangID=E&NewsID=23073, pt 38, accessed July 2025
[25] (Gentleman, 2020)
[26] https://jcwi.org.uk/reportsbriefings/windrush-scandal-explained/, accessed July 2025
[27] (Williams, 2020), p 10
[28] https://www.theguardian.com/uk-news/article/2024/jun/22/yvette-cooper-promises-labour-would-turn-the-page-on-windrush-scandal, accessed July 2025
[29] https://www.gov.uk/government/news/home-office-smashes-targets-with-mass-surge-in-migrant-removals, accessed July 2025
[30] https://www.gov.uk/government/publications/asylum-and-returns-policy-statement/restoring-order-and-control-a-statement-on-the-governments-asylum-and-returns-policy, accessed November 2025
[31] https://www.theguardian.com/commentisfree/2025/may/09/labour-asylum-seekers-policy-reform-voters-refugees-government, accessed July 2025
[32] (Goodwin & Milazzo, 2017)
[33] https://migrationobservatory.ox.ac.uk/resources/briefings/eu-migration-to-and-from-the-uk/, accessed July 2025
[34] (McKinney, Kennedy, Gower, & Sturge, 2024), p 5
[35] https://migrationobservatory.ox.ac.uk/resources/commentaries/between-a-rock-and-a-hard-place-the-covid-19-crisis-and-migrants-with-no-recourse-to-public-funds-nrpf/, accessed July 2025
[36] (Smith, O'Reilly, Rumpel, & White, 2021), p 6
[37] (Pemberton, Phillimore, & Robinson, 2014), p 8
[38] https://www.gov.uk/government/publications/the-uks-points-based-immigration-system-policy-statement/the-uks-points-based-immigration-system-policy-statement, accessed July 2025
[39] https://www.ons.gov.uk/peoplepopulationandcommunity/populationandmigration/internationalmigration/bulletins/longterminternationalmigrationprovisional/yearendingdecember2024, accessed July 2025
[40] https://www.brunel.ac.uk/news-and-events/news/articles/Post-Brexit-UK-migration-trends-and-the-all-time-highs, accessed July 2025
[41] https://migrationobservatory.ox.ac.uk/resources/reports/how-is-the-end-of-free-movement-affecting-the-low-wage-labour-force-in-the-uk/, accessed July 2025

Notes

42. https://neweconomics.org/2016/09/restricting-immigration-wont-pay-for-working-people-2, accessed July 2025
43. (Åhlberg & Granada, 2022), pp 129–30
44. https://www.gla.gov.uk/whats-new/press-release-archive/21122021-couple-arrested-after-glaa-discovers-care-workers-sleeping-on-floor-mattresses, accessed July 2025
45. https://www.gla.gov.uk/whats-new/press-release-archive/21122021-couple-arrested-after-glaa-discovers-care-workers-sleeping-on-floor-mattresses, accessed July 2025
46. https://www.independent.co.uk/voices/modern-slavery-asylum-immigration-human-trafficking-sex-workers-jobs-a8859931.html, accessed July 2025
47. https://labourexploitation.org/app/uploads/2024/02/The-continuum-of-exploitation-report-2024-.pdf, pp 12–13, accessed July 2025
48. (Mayer & Bridgen, 2022), p 12
49. https://www.lgcplus.com/services/health-and-care/hundreds-of-thousands-more-care-workers-needed-amid-recruitment-crisis-18-07-2024/, accessed July 2025
50. (Smith, O'Reilly, Rumpel, & White, 2021)
51. (Smith, O'Reilly, Rumpel, & White, 2021), pp 14–20
52. (Smith, O'Reilly, Rumpel, & White, 2021), p 15
53. (Smith, O'Reilly, Rumpel, & White, 2021), p 18
54. (Mayer & Bridgen, 2022)
55. (Mayer & Bridgen, 2022), Tables 2 and 3
56. (Smith, O'Reilly, Rumpel, & White, 2021), pp 24–6
57. (Fitzpatrick, et al, 2023a), p 2
58. (Fitzpatrick, et al, 2023a), Figure 10, p 30
59. https://commonslibrary.parliament.uk/research-briefings/cbp-10267/, accessed July 2025
60. https://static1.squarespace.com/static/5d91f87725049149378fce82/t/63ffbfb2388bca477efd5620/1677705140309/10_year_route_March23.pdf, accessed July 2025
61. https://migrationobservatory.ox.ac.uk/resources/commentaries/changes-to-settlement-what-do-they-mean/, accessed July 2025
62. https://migrationobservatory.ox.ac.uk/resources/commentaries/labours-pledges-on-migration-the-data/, accessed July 2025
63. https://www.unhcr.org/uk/about-unhcr/overview/1951-refugee-convention, accessed July 2025
64. https://www.unhcr.org/uk/publications/global-amnesia-refugee-convention-after-70-years, accessed July 2025
65. https://homeofficemedia.blog.gov.uk/2023/08/24/safe-and-legal-routes-factsheet-august-2023/, accessed July 2025

[66] (Benson, Sigona, & Zambelli, 2024), p 4
[67] (Benson, Sigona, & Zambelli, 2024), p 5
[68] https://www.gov.uk/government/statistics/immigration-system-statistics-year-ending-june-2024/safe-and-legal-humanitarian-routes-to-the-uk, accessed July 2025
[69] (Machin, 2023), p 302
[70] https://www.gov.uk/government/statistics/immigration-system-statistics-year-ending-june-2024/safe-and-legal-humanitarian-routes-to-the-uk, accessed July 2025
[71] https://justice.org.uk/justice-launches-report-calling-on-government-to-double-down-on-efforts-to-relocate-afghans-who-supported-britain/, accessed July 2025
[72] https://migrationobservatory.ox.ac.uk/wp-content/uploads/2023/10/2024-Briefing-Afghan-asylum-seekers-and-refugees-in-the-UK.pdf, pp 5–6, accessed July 2025
[73] https://migrationobservatory.ox.ac.uk/wp-content/uploads/2023/10/2024-Briefing-Afghan-asylum-seekers-and-refugees-in-the-UK.pdf, pp 6–7, accessed July 2025
[74] https://migrationobservatory.ox.ac.uk/wp-content/uploads/2023/10/2024-Briefing-Afghan-asylum-seekers-and-refugees-in-the-UK.pdf, pp 8–10, accessed July 2025
[75] https://migrationobservatory.ox.ac.uk/resources/briefings/people-crossing-the-english-channel-in-small-boats/, Figure 6, accessed July 2025
[76] https://migrationobservatory.ox.ac.uk/resources/briefings/migration-to-the-uk-asylum/, accessed July 2025
[77] (Sturge, 2024), p 16, accessed July 2025
[78] https://www.gov.uk/government/news/prime-minister-outlines-his-five-key-priorities-for-2023#full-publication-update-history, accessed July 2025
[79] https://www.gov.uk/government/collections/illegal-migration-bill, accessed July 2025
[80] For examples see https://www.ippr.org/articles/what-would-the-illegal-migration-bill-mean-in-practice; https://www.refugeecouncil.org.uk/wp-content/uploads/2023/03/Refugee-Council-Asylum-Bill-impact-assessement.pdf; https://migrationobservatory.ox.ac.uk/resources/commentaries/uk-policies-to-deter-people-from-claiming-asylum/; and https://freemovement.org.uk/wp-content/uploads/2022/11/Annex-A-Sovereign-Borders-International-Asylum-Comparisons-Report-Section-1-Drivers-and-impact-on-asylum-migration-journeys.pdf, all accessed July 2025

Notes

[81] https://www.independent.co.uk/news/uk/politics/starmer-asylum-seekers-albania-meloni-italy-b2612898.html, accessed July 2025

[82] https://www.politico.eu/article/albania-keir-starmer-pm-uk-pushto-asylum-seekers-third-countries/, accessed September 2025

[83] https://www.theguardian.com/commentisfree/2024/sep/23/italy-migrant-pact-albania-keir-starmer-britain-giorgia-meloni, accessed July 2025

[84] https://www.gov.uk/government/news/prime-minister-unveils-game-changing-investment-to-tackle-national-security-threat-from-people-smuggling-gangs#:~:text=He%20will%20also%20set%20out,on%20international%20organised%20crime%20cases, accessed July 2025

[85] https://www.refugeecouncil.org.uk/press-office/media-centre/governments-asylum-policies-projected-to-make-big-cuts-to-backlog-and-costs/, accessed July 2025

[86] https://migrationobservatory.ox.ac.uk/resources/briefings/the-uks-asylum-backlog/, accessed July 2025

[87] https://www.bbc.co.uk/news/live/ckg6x4g6gg6t, accessed July 2025

[88] https://www.refugeecouncil.org.uk/press-office/media-centre/nearly-150-charities-and-faith-leaders-unite-against-refugee-citizenship-ban/, accessed July 2025

[89] https://www.gov.uk/government/publications/asylum-and-returns-policy-statement/restoring-order-and-control-a-statement-on-the-governments-asylum-and-returns-policy, accessed November 2025

[90] https://www.theguardian.com/commentisfree/2025/nov/17/labour-asylum-reform-britain-ice-raid-refugees; https://gmiau.org/nov-25-changes-to-the-uk-asylum-system-what-we-know-so-far/, both accessed November 2025

[91] For examples of coverage of asylum seekers, see https://www.thesun.co.uk/news/20305829/migrants-five-star-hotels-housing/; https://www.dailymail.co.uk/news/article-14090253/Were-worried-weve-kept-dark-inside-story-leafy-Cheshire-town-convulsed-fear-suspicion-300-young-male-migrants-arrived-hotel-dead-night.html; https://www.express.co.uk/news/uk/1870268/uk-town-asylum-seeker-hotels, all accessed July 2025. For government attitudes see: https://www.gov.uk/government/publications/asylum-and-returns-policy-statement/restoring-order-and-control-a-statement-on-the-governments-asylum-and-returns-policy, accessed November 2025

[92] https://migrationobservatory.ox.ac.uk/resources/briefings/migration-to-the-uk-asylum/, Figure 10, accessed July 2025

[93] (Brown, Gill, & Halsall, 2024), pp 257–9

[94] (Mort & Morris, 2024), p 24
[95] Quotes from (Mort & Morris, 2024), p 24–9
[96] (Moran & McMahon, 2023)
[97] https://www.rapar.co.uk/rapar-updates/on-the-bbc-stockport-council-and-rapar-speak-out-about-scabies-outbreak-rubbish-in-corridors-and-inhumane-treatment-in-serco-run-asylum-hotel, accessed July 2025
[98] (Moran & McMahon, 2023), p 306
[99] https://www.jrf.org.uk/deep-poverty-and-destitution/its-wrong-that-uk-immigration-and-asylum-systems-make-people-destitute, accessed July 2025
[100] https://migrationobservatory.ox.ac.uk/resources/briefings/migration-to-the-uk-asylum/, accessed July 2025
[101] (Fitzpatrick, et al, 2023a), p 30
[102] https://migrationobservatory.ox.ac.uk/resources/briefings/migration-to-the-uk-asylum/, accessed July 2025
[103] (Mort & Morris, 2024), p 30
[104] https://www.psni.police.uk/latest-news/disorder-arrests-stand-31-riot-accused-court-today, accessed July 2025
[105] https://www.thurrockgazette.co.uk/news/25446520.epping-asylum-seeker-hotel-resident-attacked-protest/, accessed September 2025
[106] (Messing & Ságvári, 2019), p 37–38

Chapter 8

[1] https://www.gov.uk/government/news/environment-agency-urges-caution-ahead-of-new-year-celebrations, accessed July 2025
[2] https://www.bbc.co.uk/news/articles/c5y7ewwynl4o, accessed July 2025
[3] https://www.bbc.co.uk/news/articles/c4g2vy3jr1jo, accessed July 2025
[4] https://www.metoffice.gov.uk/blog/2024/review-of-2024-multiple-records-broken-in-a-year-of-mixed-weather, accessed July 2025
[5] https://www.metoffice.gov.uk/about-us/news-and-media/media-centre/weather-and-climate-news/2025/2024-provisionally-the-fourth-warmest-year-on-record-for-the-uk, accessed July 2025
[6] https://www.metoffice.gov.uk/about-us/news-and-media/media-centre/weather-and-climate-news/2025/2024-provisionally-the-fourth-warmest-year-on-record-for-the-uk, accessed July 2025
[7] https://www.worldweatherattribution.org/when-risks-become-reality-extreme-weather-in-2024/, accessed July 2025

Notes

8. https://www.reuters.com/world/india/unrelenting-heatwave-kills-five-indian-capital-2024-06-19/, accessed July 2025
9. https://unfccc.int/process-and-meetings/the-paris-agreement, accessed July 2025
10. https://www.bbc.co.uk/weather/articles/c1el8z2d7v8o, accessed July 2025
11. https://news.un.org/en/story/2024/12/1158611, accessed July 2025
12. (Joyashree, Tschakert, & Waisman, 2018)
13. https://actuaries.org.uk/news-and-media-releases/news-articles/2025/jan/16-jan-25-planetary-solvency-finding-our-balance-with-nature/, accessed July 2025
14. https://www.gov.uk/government/publications/uk-food-security-index-2024/uk-food-security-index-2024, accessed July 2025
15. (Parliamentary Office of Science and Technology, 2019), p 2
16. (Parliamentary Office of Science and Technology, 2019), p 2
17. https://interactive.carbonbrief.org/climate-migration/index.html, accessed July 2025
18. https://interactive.carbonbrief.org/climate-migration/index.html, accessed July 2025
19. https://www.carbonbrief.org/cop29-key-outcomes-agreed-at-the-un-climate-talks-in-baku/, accessed July 2025
20. https://www.oxfamamerica.org/explore/issues/making-foreign-aid-work/what-do-trumps-proposed-foreign-aid-cuts-mean/, accessed July 2025
21. https://www.independent.co.uk/voices/foreign-aid-budget-uk-spending-review-reeves-b2768098.html, accessed July 2025
22. https://www.bbc.co.uk/news/resources/idt-d6338d9f-8789-4bc2-b6d7-3691c0e7d138, accessed July 2025
23. (Parliamentary Office of Science and Technology, 2024), pp 3–4
24. (Parliamentary Office of Science and Technology, 2024), p 4
25. (Munro, Boyce, & Marmot, 2020), p 8
26. https://www.bbc.co.uk/news/resources/idt-d6338d9f-8789-4bc2-b6d7-3691c0e7d138, accessed July 2025
27. (Environment Agency, 2024), pp 21–2
28. (Houston, et al, 2011), p 8
29. (Judge & Marshall, 2022), p 1
30. (Environment Agency, 2024), p 30
31. (Environment Agency, 2022), p iv
32. https://www.mccip.org.uk/coastal-flooding, accessed July 2025
33. (Judge & Marshall, 2022), p 5
34. https://www.aviva.com/newsroom/news-releases/2024/01/one-in-thirteen-new-homes-built-in-flood-zone/, accessed July 2025

[35] https://www.theguardian.com/environment/2025/feb/08/more-than-100000-homes-in-england-could-be-built-in-highest-risk-flood-zones, accessed July 2025
[36] https://www.gov.uk/government/publications/national-flood-and-coastal-erosion-risk-management-strategy-for-england--2, accessed July 2025
[37] https://commonslibrary.parliament.uk/research-briefings/cbp-7514/, accessed July 2025
[38] https://www.theguardian.com/environment/2025/mar/20/flood-defences-spending-warning, accessed July 2025
[39] https://www.gov.uk/government/news/more-action-needed-to-protect-future-water-resources, accessed July 2025
[40] https://www.gov.uk/government/news/yorkshire-second-region-in-england-to-move-into-drought-status; https://www.theguardian.com/environment/2025/jul/15/four-areas-of-england-now-in-drought-as-hot-weather-threatens-wildlife-and-crops, accessed July 2025
[41] https://www.mylondon.news/news/nostalgia/london-flooding-shocking-pictures-show-21143654, accessed July 2025
[42] https://www.ft.com/content/b2314ae0-9e17-425d-8e3f-066270388331, accessed July 2025
[43] https://www.telegraph.co.uk/news/2022/09/03/water-watchdogs-independence-question-revolving-door-polluting/, accessed July 2025
[44] https://www.spectator.co.uk/article/water-woes-whos-to-blame-for-the-shortages/; https://www.newstatesman.com/new-statesman-view/2024/04/sold-down-the-river; https://www.gre.ac.uk/news/articles/public-relations/2018/privatised-water-failure, all accessed July 2025
[45] (Hall, 2022), pp 13–14
[46] (Helm, 2018), p 11
[47] https://www.ft.com/content/b2314ae0-9e17-425d-8e3f-066270388331, accessed July 2025
[48] (Public Services International Research Unit [PSIRU], 2024), pp 14–15
[49] https://www.theguardian.com/environment/ng-interactive/2023/dec/18/how-much-of-your-water-bill-is-swallowed-up-by-company-debt-interactive, accessed July 2025
[50] https://www.economist.com/by-invitation/2023/07/10/mathew-lawrence-on-why-privatisation-has-been-a-costly-failure-in-britain, accessed July 2025
[51] https://www.theguardian.com/money/2024/dec/19/water-bills-for-households-in-england-and-wales-to-rise, accessed July 2025
[52] (Public Services International Research Unit [PSIRU], 2024), p 16
[53] https://ifs.org.uk/articles/council-tax-needs-urgent-reform-not-being-frozen-time-1991, accessed July 2025

Notes

[54] https://www.independentage.org/sites/default/files/2024-12/Water_Single_Social_Tariff_Report_web.pdf, accessed July 2025
[55] https://www.ipsos.com/en-uk/3-in-5-britons-would-prefer-utilities-to-be-publicly-owned-and-operated, accessed July 2025
[56] https://www.theguardian.com/business/2025/sep/13/thames-water-paid-1m-plus-to-corporate-spooks-firm-part-owned-by-starmer-adviser, accessed September 2025.
[57] https://www.theguardian.com/business/2024/sep/29/labour-water-industry-analysis-argue-against-nationalisation, accessed September 2025
[58] https://www.ft.com/content/8ee5d48a-6103-11e9-a27a-fdd51850994c, accessed September 2025
[59] https://weownit.org.uk/public-ownership/water, accessed September 2025
[60] https://www.gov.uk/government/news/powerful-water-ombudsman-to-support-customers-with-complaints, accessed July 2025
[61] https://www.legislation.gov.uk/ukpga/2008/27/section/1, accessed July 2025
[62] https://www.legislation.gov.uk/uksi/2019/1056/article/2/made, accessed July 2025
[63] (Burnett, Hinson, & Stewart, 2024), p 9
[64] https://www.theccc.org.uk/2024/07/18/uk-off-track-for-net-zero-say-countrys-climate-advisors/, accessed July 2025
[65] (Climate Change Committee, 2023)
[66] https://www.bbc.co.uk/news/articles/c62k75qp1edo; https://www.bbc.co.uk/news/articles/cly3pnjyzp4o, accessed October 2025
[67] (Watson & Bolton, 2024), pp 1–6
[68] (Ason & Dal Poz, 2024), p 8
[69] (Owen & Barrett, 2020), p 1199
[70] (Barrett, Owen, & Taylor, 2018), p 4
[71] (Barrett, Owen, & Taylor, 2018), p 4
[72] https://commonslibrary.parliament.uk/why-is-cheap-renewable-electricity-so-expensive
[73] https://www.iea.org/topics/global-energy-crisis, accessed July 2025
[74] (Barrett, Owen, & Taylor, 2018), p 5
[75] https://www.common-wealth.org/publications/power-to-the-people-the-case-for-a-publicly-owned-generation-company, accessed July 2025; (Garman & Aldridge, 2015), pp 21–5
[76] (Garman & Aldridge, 2015), p 16
[77] https://www.common-wealth.org/publications/power-ahead-an-energy-system-fit-for-the-future, accessed July 2025
[78] https://researchbriefings.files.parliament.uk/documents/CBP-10088/CBP-10088.pdf, accessed July 2025

79. https://assets.publishing.service.gov.uk/media/66a235daab418ab055592d27/great-british-energy-founding-statement.pdf, p 4, accessed July 2025
80. https://assets.publishing.service.gov.uk/media/66a235daab418ab055592d27/great-british-energy-founding-statement.pdf, p 12, accessed July 2025
81. https://cles.org.uk/wp-content/uploads/2021/11/Front-page-FINAL.pdf, accessed July 2025
82. https://cles.org.uk/wp-content/uploads/2021/11/Part-4-FINAL-v2.pdf, pp 7–12, accessed July 2025
83. https://hackney.gov.uk/hackney-light-and-power, accessed July 2025
84. https://www.gatesheadenergycompany.co.uk/article/29152/About-us, accessed July 2025
85. https://www.heattrust.org/about-heat-networks, accessed July 2025
86. https://cles.org.uk/wp-content/uploads/2021/10/Part-3-FINAL.pdf, p 22, accessed July 2025
87. https://www.gatesheadenergycompany.co.uk/article/29152/About-us, accessed July 2025
88. https://www.gateshead.gov.uk/article/2993/Gateshead-District-Energy-Scheme, accessed July 2025
89. https://cles.org.uk/wp-content/uploads/2021/10/Part-3-FINAL.pdf, p 22, accessed July 2025
90. https://green-alliance.org.uk/wp-content/uploads/2025/06/Was-the-spending-review-good-for-environmental-priorities.pdf, accessed July 2025
91. https://assets.publishing.service.gov.uk/media/63e131afe90e07626c86856c/emissions-statistics-summary-2021.pdf, accessed July 2025
92. https://d2e1qxpsswcpgz.cloudfront.net/uploads/2020/03/ukerc_cied_policy-briefing_unlocking-britains-first-fuel.pdf, p 1, accessed July 2025
93. (Bolton, 2024), p 7
94. (Bolton, 2024), p 19
95. (Bolton, 2024), p 21
96. https://assets.publishing.service.gov.uk/government/uploads/system/uploads/attachment_data/file/443897/Productivity_Plan_print.pdf, p 43, accessed July 2025
97. https://www.theguardian.com/environment/2021/jan/23/buyers-of-brand-new-homes-face-20000-bill-to-make-them-greener, accessed July 2025
98. (Owen & Barrett, 2020), p 1199
99. https://www.energysavingtrust.org.uk/sites/default/files/reports/ERP2_The%20Clean%20Growth%20Plan_Tackling%20Fuel%20Poverty.pdf, accessed July 2025
100. (Owen & Barrett, 2020), p 1194
101. (Bolton, 2024), pp 5, 12–13

Notes

[102] https://neweconomics.org/2024/02/over-a-decade-of-cold-and-draughty-homes, accessed July 2025

[103] https://committees.parliament.uk/work/309/energy-efficiency-of-existing-homes/news/152918/net-zero-impossible-unless-urgent-action-taken-on-energy-efficiency-this-decade/, accessed July 2025

[104] https://www.theccc.org.uk/wp-content/uploads/2023/06/Progress-in-reducing-UK-emissions-2023-Report-to-Parliament-1.pdf, pp 138–44, accessed July 2025

[105] (Jaccarini, Yunda, & Kumar, 2022), p 2

[106] https://www.gov.uk/government/statistics/great-british-insulation-scheme-release-january-2024/summary-of-the-great-british-insulation-scheme-january-2024, accessed July 2025

[107] https://www.nao.org.uk/press-releases/weak-controls-and-oversight-blamed-for-faulty-home-installations-under-energy-efficiency-scheme/, accessed October 2025

[108] https://assets.publishing.service.gov.uk/media/63761099d3bf7f720cfc0040/CCS1022065440-001_SECURE_HMT_Autumn_Statement_November_2022_Web_accessible__1_.pdf, p 48, accessed July 2025

[109] https://neweconomics.org/2024/02/over-a-decade-of-cold-and-draughty-homes, accessed July 2025

[110] https://neweconomics.org/2024/02/over-a-decade-of-cold-and-draughty-homes, Figure 1, accessed July 2025

[111] https://labour.org.uk/change/make-britain-a-clean-energy-superpower/#warm-homes, accessed July 2025

[112] https://www.theccc.org.uk/wp-content/uploads/2020/12/The-Sixth-Carbon-Budget-The-UKs-path-to-Net-Zero.pdf, p 120, accessed July 2025

[113] https://www.gov.uk/government/statistical-data-sets/energy-performance, Table DA7101 (SST7.1): Energy performance – dwellings, 2022, accessed July 2025

[114] https://www.gov.uk/government/statistical-data-sets/energy-performance, Table DA7101 (SST7.1): Energy performance – dwellings, 2022, accessed July 2025

[115] https://www.gov.uk/government/statistics/households-below-average-income-for-financial-years-ending-1995-to-2023 and https://www.gov.uk/government/statistical-data-sets/energyperformance, both accessed September 2025

[116] https://www.gov.uk/government/news/mortgage-rate-cut-for-energy-efficient-homes-under-government-backed-trials, accessed July 2025

[117] https://www.insidehousing.co.uk/news/major-bank-urges-government-to-scale-up-retrofit-support-for-households-86280, accessed July 2025

[118] (Choi, Noh, & Baek, 2022)
[119] https://www.gov.uk/government/news/warm-homes-and-cheaper-bills-as-government-accelerates-plan-for-change, accessed July 2025
[120] https://assets.publishing.service.gov.uk/media/67a4e511baccec3af36b3c70/improving-the-energy-performance-of-prs-homes-consultation-document.pdf, p 45, accessed July 2025

Chapter 9

[1] All quotes from (Financial Services Authority, 2024)
[2] (Davies, et al, 2024), p 60
[3] (Mack & Lansley, 1985), pp 37–48
[4] For examples, see https://www.poverty.ac.uk/world, accessed July 2025
[5] (McKnight, Bucelli, Burchardt, & Karagiannaki, 2024)
[6] (McKnight, Bucelli, Burchart, & Karagiannaki, 2024), pp 131–2
[7] (McKnight, Bucelli, Burchart, & Karagiannaki, 2024), pp 116–17, 149
[8] https://www.gov.uk/government/statistics/deep-material-poverty-financial-year-ending-2024/deep-material-poverty-financial-year-ending-2024, accessed December 2025
[9] For a detailed account of how this might be done see (Lanau, Mack, & Nandy, 2020)
[10] See (Button & Coote, 2021), pp 14–16
[11] https://www.ft.com/content/a14fb3c0-a665-4320-8980-2b5c2156269c, accessed July 2025
[12] (Citizens Advice, 2021), p 5
[13] https://publications.parliament.uk/pa/cm5803/cmselect/cmpubacc/1232/summary.html, accessed July 2025
[14] https://www.common-wealth.org/interactive/who-owns-britain/data-dashboard/tabs/energy, accessed September 2025
[15] (TUC, 2022), p 6
[16] (Communications and Digital Committee, House of Lords, 2023)
[17] https://www.resolutionfoundation.org/publications/whose-price-is-it-anyway/, accessed July 2025
[18] https://www.gov.uk/government/news/hundreds-of-thousands-to-get-secure-roof-over-their-heads, accessed July 2025
[19] https://www.gov.uk/government/publications/delivering-a-decade-of-renewal-for-social-and-affordable-housing/delivering-a-decade-of-renewal-for-social-and-affordable-housing, accessed July 2025
[20] https://commonslibrary.parliament.uk/affordable-housing-in-england/, accessed July 2025
[21] (Galarza, et al, 2024), p 43
[22] (Galarza, et al, 2024), p 13

Notes

23. (CEBR, 2024), pp 5–6
24. https://www.gov.uk/government/publications/guide-to-the-renters-rights-bill/guide-to-the-renters-rights-bill, accessed July 2025
25. https://blogs.lse.ac.uk/politicsandpolicy/rent-controls-in-london/, accessed July 2025
26. https://www.nrla.org.uk/news/rent-controls-would-be-a-disaster-for-tenants, accessed July 2025
27. https://www.london.gov.uk/sites/default/files/2025-02/Zo%C3%AB%20Garbett%20Rent%20Commission%20Report_Feb_2025_compressed.pdf, accessed July 2025
28. https://www.ons.gov.uk/peoplepopulationandcommunity/housing/bulletins/housingaffordabilityinenglandandwales/2024/pdf, accessed September 2025
29. (Ministry of Housing, Communities and Local Government, 2018), pp 2–3
30. (Ryan-Collins, 2024), p 17
31. (Ryan-Collins, 2024), pp 48–9
32. (Competition and Markets Authority, 2024), p 14
33. (Competition and Markets Authority, 2025), p 8
34. https://www.theguardian.com/business/2023/nov/29/leading-grocery-brands-fuelling-greedflation-uk-regulator-finds, accessed July 2025
35. http://www.infantfeedingappg.uk/wp-content/uploads/2018/11/APPGIFI-Inquiry-Report-cost-of-infant-formula.pdf, p 1, accessed July 2025
36. (Competition and Markets Authority, 2025), pp 141–74
37. (Competition and Markets Authority, 2025), p 142
38. https://foodfoundation.org.uk/news/our-response-cma-infant-formula-prices-report, accessed July 2025
39. https://www.unicef.org.uk/babyfriendly/baby-friendlys-response-to-cma-report/, accessed July 2025
40. https://www.ft.com/content/1346c70e-3a0f-471f-adb1-de204a41b89b, accessed July 2025
41. https://www.gov.uk/government/news/chancellor-calls-on-watchdog-bosses-to-tear-down-regulatory-barriers-that-hold-back-growth, accessed July 2025
42. (Hearn, 2024)
43. https://www.theguardian.com/commentisfree/2025/jan/25/labours-decision-to-muzzle-regulators-in-the-name-of-growth-will-backfire-horribly, accessed July 2025
44. https://www.marketplacepulse.com/articles/amazon-takes-a-50-cut-of-sellers-revenue, accessed July 2025
45. https://www.ft.com/content/2d6b74e6-f5dd-4aaa-af19-91225272c423, accessed July 2025

[46] https://www.gov.uk/government/news/major-investment-deals-set-to-be-announced-at-governments-inaugural-international-investment-summit-as-pm-vows-to-remove-needless-regulation-declar, accessed July 2025

Chapter 10

[1] https://www.theguardian.com/society/2024/apr/10/sure-start-centres-early-years-support-families, accessed July 2025
[2] Quoted in (Davidson, 2024), p 14
[3] https://www.transportforthenorth.com/wp-content/uploads/TRSEintheNorth-2023-2024.pdf, accessed July 2025, pp 21, 30
[4] (Portes, Reed, & Percy, 2017); (Button & Coote, 2021)
[5] (Ogden & Phillips, 2023), pp 1–2
[6] (Verbist, Förster, & Vaalavuo, 2012), p 36
[7] (Portes, Reed, & Percy, 2017), p 22
[8] https://foundationaleconomy.com/introduction/, accessed July 2025; (Calafati, Froud, Haslam, Johal, & Williams, 2023)
[9] (Lord Darzi, 2024), p 1
[10] (Lord Darzi, 2024), pp 6–7
[11] (Lord Darzi, 2024), pp 113–14
[12] (Lord Darzi, 2024), pp 83–9
[13] (Marmot, Allen, Boyce, Goldblatt, & Morrison, 2020), p 5
[14] (Lord Darzi, 2024), pp 9, 106–10
[15] https://www.gov.uk/missions/nhs, accessed July 2025
[16] https://change.nhs.uk/en-GB/, accessed July 2025
[17] https://www.gov.uk/government/news/over-two-million-extra-nhs-appointments-delivered-early-as-trusts-handed-40-million-to-go-further-and-faster, accessed July 2025
[18] https://www.nhsconfed.org/publications/autumn-budget-2024-what-you-need-know, accessed July 2025
[19] https://www.gov.uk/government/news/over-two-million-extra-nhs-appointments-delivered-early-as-trusts-handed-40-million-to-go-further-and-faster, accessed July 2025
[20] https://www.health.org.uk/reports-and-analysis/briefings/labour-s-10-year-plan-for-the-nhs-in-england-what-should-it-look, accessed July 2025
[21] https://www.nuffieldtrust.org.uk/news-item/what-did-the-autumn-budget-do-for-the-nhs-s-financial-health, accessed July 2025
[22] https://www.theguardian.com/society/2025/jan/10/wes-streeting-defends-nhs-use-private-sector-but-pull-its-weight, accessed July 2025
[23] https://www.bma.org.uk/media/fy3czsaf/bma-nhs-outsourcing-report-september-2024.pdf, accessed July 2025

Notes

24. https://labourlist.org/2021/02/its-time-to-take-back-control-of-public-services-rachel-reeves-full-speech/, accessed July 2025
25. (Lord Darzi, 2024), p 10
26. https://www.gov.uk/government/publications/liberating-the-nhs-white-paper, accessed July 2025
27. (Roderick & Pollock, 2022), p 472
28. (British Medical Association, 2022), p 2
29. (Gough, 2020), pp 5–6
30. (Button & Coote, 2021), p 23
31. https://labourlist.org/2021/02/its-time-to-take-back-control-of-public-services-rachel-reeves-full-speech/; https://www.newstatesman.com/politics/preparing-for-power/2023/03/wes-streeting-interview-nhs-privatisation-politics-values-aims, accessed July 2025
32. https://labour.org.uk/change/build-an-nhs-fit-for-the-future/#social-care, accessed July 2025
33. https://www.communitycare.co.uk/2024/06/14/no-funded-social-care-commitments-in-labour-manifesto/, accessed July 2025
34. https://news.liverpool.ac.uk/2024/06/17/labours-enticing-plan-for-a-national-care-service-is-so-vague-it-looks-like-a-tick-box-exercise/, accessed July 2025
35. https://www.gov.uk/government/news/new-reforms-and-independent-commission-to-transform-social-care, accessed July 2025
36. https://www.communitycare.co.uk/2025/01/03/commission-on-adult-social-care-reform-announced-by-government/, accessed July 2025
37. https://www.unison.org.uk/our-campaigns/lets-make-care-work/, accessed July 2025
38. (Cooper & Harrop, 2023)
39. (Cooper & Harrop, 2023), p 8
40. (Cooper & Harrop, 2023), p 28
41. https://www.gov.uk/government/consultations/fair-pay-agreement-process-in-adult-social-care/fair-pay-agreement-process-in-adult-social-care-consultation-document, accessed October 2025
42. https://labour.org.uk/updates/stories/labours-plan-for-childcare-and-early-education/, accessed July 2025
43. https://www.bbc.co.uk/news/articles/cw4489zllkvo, accessed July 2025
44. https://ifs.org.uk/articles/labours-plans-build-childcare-spaces-schools-will-nudge-market-different-direction-not, accessed July 2025
45. https://www.jrf.org.uk/care/believing-market-competition-will-improve-care-services-is-a-false-hope, accessed July 2025
46. (Jitendra, 2024), pp 11–12
47. (Jitendra, 2024), p 27

48. (Jitendra, 2024), p 15
49. (De-Freitas, Ville, & Azad, 2024), p 10
50. (De-Freitas, Ville, & Azad, 2024), p 9
51. (De Henau, 2022), p 3
52. https://www.gov.uk/tax-free-childcare, accessed July 2025
53. https://www.wbg.org.uk/publication/wbg-finds-government-funding-for-early-education-and-childcare-falls-short-by-5-2bn/, accessed July 2025; see also (De Henau, 2022), scenario 2, for detailed calculations as to the costings
54. https://assets.publishing.service.gov.uk/media/6751af4719e0c816d18d1df3/Plan_for_Change.pdf, pp 35–8, accessed July 2025
55. https://educationhub.blog.gov.uk/2025/07/best-start-family-hubs-what-parents-need-to-know/, accessed July 2025
56. (De Henau, 2022), p 3
57. https://www.gov.uk/government/news/deputy-prime-minister-launches-free-school-meals
58. https://www.gov.uk/apply-free-school-meals, accessed July 2025
59. https://www.childrenssociety.org.uk/sites/default/files/2020-10/fsm-poverty-trap-tcs-cpag.pdf, accessed July 2025
60. https://www.gov.uk/government/news/over-half-a-million-more-children-to-get-free-school-meals
61. https://cpag.org.uk/sites/default/files/2024-01/Discretion%20dignity%20and%20choice%20free%20school%20meals.pdf; https://cpag.org.uk/sites/default/files/2024-05/The%20Cost%20of%20Missing%20Lunchtime%20-%20a%20Briefing%20on%20Free%20School%20Meals%20in%20the%20North%20East%20of%20England.pdf, all accessed July 2025
62. (Holford & Rabe, 2020), p 4
63. https://www.tuc.org.uk/blogs/no-child-left-behind-free-school-meals-all; https://foodfoundation.org.uk/news/feed-future-campaign; https://freeschoolmealsforall.org.uk/about/the-campaign, all accessed July 2025
64. (Impact on Urban Health, 2024), p 5
65. (Impact on Urban Health, 2022), p 3
66. https://educationhub.blog.gov.uk/2024/11/free-school-breakfast-clubs/, accessed July 2025
67. https://www.gov.wales/sites/default/files/publications/2018-12/free-breakfast-in-primary-schools-statutory-guidance-for-local-authorities-and-governing-bodies.pdf, accessed July 2025
68. https://magazine.newstatesman.com/2025/02/14/when-will-labour-tell-the-truth-about-scotland/content.html, accessed July 2025
69. (Impact on Urban Health, 2022), p 6
70. (Portes, Reed, & Percy, 2017), pp 25–6

Notes

71. https://cles.org.uk/blog/5-things-you-always-wanted-to-know-about-anchor-networks/, accessed July 2025
72. (Preston City Council, 2019), p 10
73. (Preston City Council, 2019), p 12
74. https://cles.org.uk/blog/anchor-networks-sow-the-seeds-of-change/, accessed July 2025
75. https://www.ciscolive.com/c/dam/r/ciscolive/emea/docs/2024/pdf/CSSENS-1816.pdf, accessed July 2025
76. https://www.thehiveworcester.org/creating-the-hive.html, accessed July 2025
77. https://www.cancook.co.uk/about-well-fed/, accessed July 2025
78. https://www.flintshire.gov.uk/en/Business/Shared-Prosperity-Fund/Success-Stories/North-Wales-Growth-Vision-Well-Fed.aspx, accessed July 2025
79. (Mulrooney & Ranta, 2024)
80. (Mulrooney & Ranta, 2024)
81. (Mulrooney & Ranta, 2024), p 351
82. (Machray & Haddow, 2024), p 390
83. For an interesting discussion of this, see (Swan, Hussain, Miah, & Yip, 2024)
84. https://ifs.org.uk/articles/2025-26-english-local-government-finance-settlement-explained, accessed July 2025
85. https://commonslibrary.parliament.uk/research-briefings/cbp-10184/, accessed July 2025
86. https://www.gov.wales/written-statement-provisional-local-government-settlement-2025-26, accessed July 2025
87. (Try, 2025), pp 5–6
88. https://www.gov.uk/government/news/largest-fund-of-its-kind-to-support-vulnerable-kids-families, accessed July 2025
89. https://ymca.org.uk/wp-content/uploads/2025/01/ymca-youth-services-beyond-the-brink.pdf, p 6, accessed October 2024
90. https://www.gov.uk/government/news/largest-fund-of-its-kind-to-support-vulnerable-kids-families, accessed July 2025

Chapter 11

1. (Bennett, 2024), p 481
2. https://changingrealities.org/about, accessed July 2025
3. (Jordan, Patrick, Power, Pybus, & Kaufman, 2025), pp 213–14
4. (Klair, 2022)
5. (Child Poverty Action Group, 2024)
6. (Harrop & Cooper, 2019)

[7] https://ifs.org.uk/news/abolishing-two-child-limit-would-be-cost-effective-way-reducing-child-poverty-no-silver-bullet; accessed October 2025
[8] https://opfs.org.uk/support-and-advice/having-a-baby/best-start-grant-best-start-foods-and-the-baby-box/, accessed July 2025
[9] https://cpag.org.uk/sites/default/files/2024-07/CPAG%20Strengthening%20Social%20Security%20Scotland%20-%20briefing.pdf, accessed July 2025
[10] https://www.citizensadvice.org.uk/policy/publications/uprating-local-housing-allowance-briefing-note/, accessed July 2025
[11] https://www.bbc.co.uk/news/articles/cx2898n721yo, accessed July 2025
[12] (Hoynes, Joyce, & Waters, 2023), pp 38–40; for full details see (Goll, Joyce, & Waters, 2023), pp 18–20
[13] (Goll, Joyce, & Waters, 2023), pp 18–20
[14] (Timmins, 2023), pp 1–2
[15] (Timmins, 2023), p 4
[16] https://www.litrg.org.uk/tax-nic/national-insurance/national-insurance-credits, accessed July 2025
[17] (Brewer & Murphy, 2023), p 5
[18] https://www.gov.uk/government/statistics/dwp-benefits-statistics-february-2024/dwp-benefits-statistics-february-2024#other-working-age-benefits, accessed July 2025
[19] https://commonslibrary.parliament.uk/contributory-benefits-and-social-insurance-in-the-uk/, accessed July 2025
[20] (Timmins, 2023), p 3
[21] (Pereirinha & Pereira, 2025)
[22] (Goderis, 2025)
[23] (Brewer & Murphy, 2023), pp 13–16
[24] (Brewer & Murphy, 2023), p 20
[25] (Brewer & Murphy, 2023), p 20
[26] (Brewer & Murphy, 2023), pp 5–6
[27] https://www.theguardian.com/politics/2025/mar/18/key-changes-uk-benefits-cuts-disability-pip-labour, accessed July 2025
[28] (Mack & Pomati, 2023); (Harrop, 2016), pp 131–2
[29] (Martinelli, 2017), pp 19–20; (Johnson, et al, 2025)
[30] (Reed, et al, 2023), p 150
[31] (Martinelli, 2017), pp 27–9
[32] (Reed, et al, 2023)
[33] (Reed, et al, 2023), p 159
[34] (Hirsch, 2023), p 164
[35] (Reed, et al, 2023), p 158
[36] (Martinelli, 2017), Executive Summary
[37] (Johnson, et al, 2025)

Notes

[38] (Martinelli, 2017), p 62
[39] (Green & Tedds, 2024); for full details of the research see https://bcbasicincomepanel.ca/, accessed July 2025
[40] (Green & Tedds, 2024), p 476
[41] (Coote & Yazici, 2019), p 4
[42] (Coote & Yazici, 2019), pp 21, 26
[43] https://news.sky.com/story/sir-keir-starmer-says-welfare-bill-is-indefensible-so-what-cuts-could-be-announced-13326286, accessed July 2025
[44] (Stirling & Arnold, 2019)
[45] (Stirling & Arnold, 2019), pp 14–15
[46] (Briheim-Crookall, et al, 2020)
[47] (Fitzpatrick, et al, 2023a)
[48] https://www.bbc.co.uk/news/articles/cj4dyy9kgrro, accessed July 2025
[49] (Green & Tedds, 2024), pp 476–7
[50] https://www.gov.wales/basic-income-pilot-care-leavers, accessed July 2025
[51] https://www.bigissue.com/news/social-justice/universal-basic-income-manchester-poverty-homeless-people/, accessed July 2025
[52] (Cribb, Henry, & Karjalainen, 2024), p 20
[53] (Cribb, Henry, & Karjalainen, 2024), Figure 4A4, pp 34, 39; (Cribb, Karjalainen, & O'Brien, 2024), p 6
[54] (Cribb, Henry, & Karjalainen, 2024), Figure 4A5, p 40; (Cribb, Karjalainen, & O'Brien, 2024), p 6
[55] (Cribb, Henry, & Karjalainen, 2024), Figure 4A7, p 42
[56] (Cribb, Emmerson, Johnson, & Karjalainen, 2023), p 20, Figures 2.1 and 2.2
[57] https://www.gov.uk/government/news/government-revives-landmark-pensions-commission-to-confront-retirement-crisis-that-risks-tomorrows-pensioners-being-poorer-than-todays, accessed July 2025
[58] (Cribb, Karjalainen, & O'Brien, 2024), pp 11–12
[59] (Cribb & O'Brien, 2022)
[60] (Otto, 2024), pp 11–12
[61] (Cribb, Henry, & Karjalainen, 2024), p 4
[62] https://www.itv.com/news/2025-07-21/government-announces-review-into-the-pension-age-what-does-it-mean-for-you, accessed July 2025
[63] (Child Poverty Action Group, 2023), p 4
[64] (Bárcena-Martín, Blanco-Arana, & Pérez-Moreno, 2018), p 753
[65] (Brewer, Handscomb, & Kelly, 2022), p 3
[66] (Women's Budget Group, 2024)
[67] (Women's Budget Group, 2024), p 5
[68] https://cpag.org.uk/sites/default/files/2025-02/COAC_2024_age_chart.pdf, accessed July 2025

[69] (Verbist & Van Lancker, 2016); (Bárcena-Martín, Blanco-Arana, & Pérez-Moreno, 2018)
[70] https://www.mind.org.uk/news-campaigns/campaigns/benefits/pip/; https://www.scope.org.uk/campaigns/making-benefits-work-report, all accessed July 2025
[71] https://gmintegratedcare.org.uk/livewell/, accessed July 2025
[72] (Porter, 2024), Section 5
[73] (Porter, 2024), Section 7
[74] https://www.scope.org.uk/campaigns/making-benefits-work-report, accessed July 2025

Chapter 12

[1] https://labour.org.uk/updates/stories/labour-manifesto-2024-sign-up/, accessed July 2025
[2] https://ifs.org.uk/articles/labour-party-manifesto-initial-response, accessed July 2025
[3] https://www.instituteforgovernment.org.uk/explainer/fiscal-rules-history, accessed July 2025
[4] https://neweconomics.org/2024/09/calling-time-on-fiscal-rules, accessed July 2025
[5] https://www.thetimes.com/business-money/companies/article/stop-focusing-on-the-debt-oecd-tells-rachel-reeves-v9mnlb03n, accessed July 2025
[6] https://www.theguardian.com/business/2025/may/27/rachel-reeves-should-ease-fiscal-rules-to-prevent-emergency-spending-cuts-imf-says, accessed July 2025
[7] https://www.instituteforgovernment.org.uk/explainer/current-fiscal-rules, accessed July 2025
[8] Letter: A plea to the chancellor to avoid more spending cuts, https://www.ft.com/content/4b0d4ec3-cfb8-44fa-93a6-4474866dc917, accessed July 2025
[9] https://ifs.org.uk/sites/default/files/2025-06/IFS%202025%20Spending%20Review%20opening%20remarks.pdf, accessed 25 July 2025
[10] https://www.theguardian.com/commentisfree/2025/jun/29/labour-raising-taxes-austerity-amnesia-keir-starmer-rachel-reeves; https://neweconomics.org/2025/02/the-bank-of-england-is-costing-us-billions, both accessed July 2025
[11] https://lordslibrary.parliament.uk/autumn-budget-2024-key-announcements-and-analysis/#heading-3, accessed September 2025
[12] https://ifs.org.uk/articles/autumn-budget-2025-initial-response, accessed November 2025

Notes

13. https://www.jrf.org.uk/news/jrf-responds-to-autumn-budget-2025; https://www.instituteforgovernment.org.uk/live-blog/autumn-budget-2025?p=lc-10596239-74850, both accessed December 2025
14. https://taxpolicy.org.uk/2025/06/27/uk-workers-tax-wedge-infographics/, accessed July 2025
15. https://www.ucu.org.uk/media/8649/doc/pdf/LE_-_Impact_of_student_loan_repayments_on_graduate_taxation_July_17_-_embargo.pdf, accessed July 2025
16. (Harrop, 2022), p 3
17. https://taxingwealth.uk/, accessed July 2025
18. (Murphy, 2024), pp 60– 70; (Glover & Seaford, 2020), p 63
19. (Murphy, 2024), pp 129–38; https://taxjustice.uk/blog/how-to-raise-60-billion-for-public-services-our-ten-tax-reforms/, accessed July 2025
20. https://ifs.org.uk/articles/raising-revenue-reforms-pensions-taxation, accessed July 2025
21. https://www.newstatesman.com/politics/economy/2025/07/just-raise-tax, accessed July 2025
22. (Murphy, 2024), p 123
23. https://taxjustice.uk/blog/six-wealth-tax-policies-that-could-raise-50-billion/, accessed July 2025
24. https://www.ons.gov.uk/peoplepopulationandcommunity/personalandhouseholdfinances/incomeandwealth/bulletins/wealthingreatbritainwave5/2014to2016, accessed July 2025
25. https://www.resolutionfoundation.org/app/uploads/2020/12/The-UKs-wealth-distribution.pdf, Figure 1, p 12; accessed July 2025
26. (Murphy, 2024), p 198
27. https://www.nfuonline.com/updates-and-information/apr-case-studies/, accessed July 2025
28. For various versions of a property tax see https://www.ippr.org/articles/pulling-down-the-ladder; https://www.jrf.org.uk/housing/after-the-council-tax-impacts-of-property-tax-reform-on-people-places-and-house-prices; https://www.resolutionfoundation.org/publications/home-affairs-options-for-reforming-property-taxation/, all accessed November 2025
29. https://www.instituteforgovernment.org.uk/live-blog/autumn-budget-2025?p=lc-10596239-74850, accessed, November 2025
30. (Advani, Chamberlain, & Summers, 2020)
31. https://www.theguardian.com/commentisfree/2025/jan/14/cold-weather-fuel-poverty-bills, accessed July 2025

Bibliography

Advani, A., Chamberlain, E., & Summers, A. (2020). *A wealth tax for the UK: Executive summary*. London: The Wealth Tax Commission. Retrieved from https://www.wealthandpolicy.com/wp/WealthTaxFinalReport.pdf, accessed July 2025

All-Party Parliamentary Group on Poverty. (2022). *In-work poverty*. London: House of Commons.

Alston, P. (2018). *Statement on visit to the United Kingdom*. Geneva: United Nations.

Alston, P., Khawaja, B., & Riddell, R. (2021). *Public transport, private profit: The human cost of privatizing bus services in the United Kingdom*. New York: New York University School of Law.

Anderson, S. A. (1990). Core indicators of nutritional state for difficult-to-sample populations. *Journal of Nutrition*, *120*(11), 1555–600.

Ason, A., & Dal Poz, J. (2024). *Contracts for difference: The instrument of choice for the energy transition*. Oxford: The Oxford Institute for Energy Studies. Retrieved from https://www.oxfordenergy.org/wpcms/wp-content/uploads/2024/04/ET34-Contracts-for-Difference.pdf, accessed July 2025

Atkinson, A. (2015). *Inequality*. Cambridge, MA: Harvard University Press.

Bach-Mortensen, A. G., Degli Esposti, M., Corlet Walker, C., & Barlow, J. (2024). *Evidencing the outsourcing of social care provision in England*. Oxford: University of Oxford.

Banks, J., Karjalainen, H., & Waters, T. (2023). *Inequalities in disability, IFS Deaton review of inequality*. London: Institute for Fiscal Studies.

Bárcena-Martín, E., Blanco-Arana, M. C., & Pérez-Moreno, S. (2018). Social transfers and child poverty in European countries: Pro-poor targeting or pro-child targeting? *Journal of Social Policy*, *47*(4), 739–58. doi: https://doi.org/10.1017/S0047279418000090

Bibliography

Barrett, J., Owen, A., & Taylor, P. (2018). *Funding a low carbon energy system: A fairer approach*. London: UK Energy Research Centre. Retrieved from https://d2e1qxpsswcpgz.cloudfront.net/uploads/2020/03/ukerc_funding_a_low_cost_energy_system.pdf, accessed July 2025

Bennett, F. (2024). The merging of knowledge? Lived experience of poverty and its place in public debate. *Journal of Poverty and Social Justice, 32*(3), 480–6. doi: https://doi.org/10.1332/17598273Y2024D000000019

Benson, M., Sigona, N., & Zambelli, E. (2024). *Humanitarian visas in a hostile environment: Historical legacies, geopolitical ties and everyday experiences*. Birmingham and Lancaster: MIGZEN. doi: https://doi.org/10.5281/zenodo.10571433

Black, D. (1980). *Inequalities in health*. London: Department of Health and Social Security.

Blumenthal, D., Gumas, E. D., Shah, A., Gunja, M. Z., & Williams II, R. D. (2024). *Mirror, mirror 2024: A portrait of the failing U.S. health system – comparing performance in 10 nations*. New York: The Commonwealth Fund. Retrieved from https://www.commonwealthfund.org/sites/default/files/2024-10/Blumenthal_mirror_mirror_2024_final_v4.pdf, accessed July 2025

Blundell, R., Costa Dias, M., Joyce, R., & Xu, X. (2020). Covid 19 and inequalities. *Fiscal Studies, 41*(2), 291–319. doi: https://doi.org/10.1111/1475-5890.12232

Bolton, P. (2024). *Energy efficiency of UK homes*. London: House of Commons. Retrieved from https://researchbriefings.files.parliament.uk/documents/CBP-9889/CBP-9889.pdf, accessed July 2025

Bramley, G., & Fitzpatrick, S. (2023). Capturing the neglected extremes of UK poverty: A composite modelling approach to destitution and food bank usage. *Journal of Poverty and Social Justice, 31*(1), 5–26. doi: https://doi.org/10.1332/175982721X16649700901023

Bramley, G., Fitzpatrick, S., Sosenko, F., & Littlewood, M. (2016). *Destitution in the UK – technical report*. Edinburgh: Heriot-Watt University.

Brewer, M., & Handscomb, K. (2020). *This time it's different – Universal Credit's first recession*. London: Resolution Foundation.

Brewer, M., & Murphy, L. (2023). *From safety net to springboard*. London: Resolution Foundation.

Brewer, M., Browne, J., Emmerson, C., Hood, A., & Joyce, R. (2019). The curious incidence of rent subsidies: Evidence of heterogeneity from administrative data. *Urban Economics*, *114*. doi: https://doi.org/10.1016/j.jue.2019.103198

Brewer, M., Browne, J., Joyce, R., & Sibieta, L. (2010). *Child poverty in the UK since 1998–99: Lessons from the last decade*. London: Institute for Fiscal Studies.

Brewer, M., Handscomb, K., & Kelly, G. (2022). *Inconsistent incentives: How the overlap between Universal Credit and the High Income Child Benefit Charge limits work incentives*. London: Resolution Foundation. Retrieved from https://www.resolutionfoundation.org/app/uploads/2022/12/Inconsistent-Incentives.pdf, accessed July 2025

Brewer, M., Handscomb, K., & Try, L. (2021). *Taper cut: Analysis of the Autumn Budget changes to Universal Credit*. London: Resolution Foundation.

Briheim-Crookall, L., Michelmore, O., Baker, C., Oni, O., Taylor, S., & Selwyn, J. (2020). *What makes life good: Care leavers' views on their well-being*. London: Coram Voice. Retrieved from https://www.coram.org.uk/wp-content/uploads/2023/01/1883-CV-What-Makes-Life-Good-Report-final.pdf, accessed July 2025

British Medical Association. (2022). *The country is getting sicker*. London: BMA.

Britton, J., Farquharson, C., & Sibieta, L. (2019). *2019 annual report on education*. London: Institute for Fiscal Studies.

Brown, P., Gill, S., & Halsall, J. P. (2024). The impact of housing on refugees: An evidence synthesis. *Housing Studies*, *39*(1), 227–71. doi: https://doi.org/10.1080/02673037.2022.2045007

Burnett, N., Hinson, S., & Stewart, I. (2024). *The UK's plans and progress to reach net zero by 2050*. London: House of Commons.

Button, D., & Coote, A. (2021). *A social guarantee: The case of universal services*. London: New Economics Foundation.

Calafati, L., Froud, J., Haslam, C., Johal, S., & Williams, K. (2023). *When nothing works: From cost of living to foundational liveability*. Manchester: Manchester University Press.

Campaign for Better Transport. (2019). *The future of the bus*. London: Campaign for Better Transport. Retrieved from https://bettertransport.org.uk/research/future-bus-future-funding-arrangements-october-2019/, accessed July 2025

Bibliography

Campaign for Better Transport. (2020). *Transport deserts*. London: Campaign for the Protection of Rural England.

Campaign for Better Transport. (2022). *Funding local bus services in England*. London: Campaign for Better Transport.

Carers UK. (2023). *State of caring 2023*. London: Carers UK.

Carneiro, P., Cattan, S., & Ridpath, N. (2024). *The short- and medium-term impacts of Sure Start on educational outcomes*. London: Institute for Fiscal Studies.

Cattan, S., Conti, G., Farquharson, C., & Ginja, R. (2019). *The health effects of Sure Start*. London: Institute for Fiscal Studies.

CEBR. (2024). *The economic impact of social housing*. London: Centre for Economic and Business Research.

Centre for Social Justice. (2009). *Dynamic benefits*. London: Centre for Social Justice. Retrieved from https://www.centreforsocialjustice.org.uk/library/dynamic-benefits-towards-welfare-that-works, accessed July 2025

Chazan, M., Laing, A., Cox, T., Jackson, S., & Lloyd, G. (1976). *Deprivation and school progress*. London: Schools Council.

Child Poverty Action Group. (2023). *Money well spent – Why we should recognise and reinvest in child benefit*. London: Child Poverty Action Group. Retrieved from https://cpag.org.uk/sites/default/files/2023-10/Money%20Well%20Spent.pdf, accessed July 2025

Child Poverty Action Group. (2024). *Universal Credit: A three-step plan*. London: Child Poverty Action Group. Retrieved from https://cpag.org.uk/sites/default/files/2024-05/Universal_credit_three_steps.pdf, accessed July 2025

Choi, K.-J., Noh, S., & Baek, I. (2022). Does home equity liquidation reduce older adults' poverty rate? Evidence from South Korea. *Journal of Poverty and Social Justice*, *30*(1), 59–76. doi: https://doi.org/10.1332/175982721X16385307728468

Citizens Advice. (2021). *Market meltdown: How regulatory failures landed us with a multi-billion pound bill*. London: Citizens Advice. Retrieved from https://assets.ctfassets.net/mfz4nbgura3g/2ff4kuJXzi19vdSQSfQHZB/c5f67860a0270106a188364ce48bbc3e/Market_20Meltdown_20-_20Dec_202021_v2_20_1_.pdf, accessed July 2025

Clegg, A. (2024). *In credit? Assessing where Universal Credit's long roll-out has left the benefits system and the country*. London: Resolution Foundation.

Climate Change Committee. (2023). *Progress in reducing emissions*. London: Climate Change Committee. Retrieved from https://www.theccc.org.uk/wp-content/uploads/2023/06/Progress-in-reducing-UK-emissions-2023-Report-to-Parliament-1.pdf, accessed July 2025

Codreanu, M., & Waters, T. (2023). *Do work search requirements work: Evidence from a UK reform targeting single parents*. London: Institute for Fiscal Studies.

Coleman, L., Dali-Chaouch, M., & Harding, C. (2020). *Childcare survey 2020*. London: Coram Family and Childcare. Retrieved from https://bit.ly/2MASdrg, accessed July 2025

Cominetti, N., & Sloughter, H. (2024). *The RF labour market outlook, Q2, 2024*. London: Resolution Foundation.

Communications and Digital Committee, House of Lords. (2023). *Digital exclusion*. London: House of Lords.

Competition and Markets Authority. (2024). *Competition and Markets Authority annual plan 2024/25*. 2024: Competition and Markets Authority. Retrieved from https://assets.publishing.service.gov.uk/media/65f1a6f5981227a772f61377/CMA_Annual_Plan_2024-25.pdf, accessed July 2025

Competition and Markets Authority. (2025). *Infant formula and follow-on formula market study*. London: Competition and Markets Authority. Retrieved from https://assets.publishing.service.gov.uk/media/67b5b9cad15c152ea555bf8e/____Final_report_.pdf, accessed July 2025

Competitions and Markets Authority. (2022). *Children's social care market study*. London: Competitions and Markets Authority.

Comptroller and Auditor General. (2016). *Contracted-out health and disability assessments*. London: National Audit Office.

Comptroller and Auditor General. (2016). *Local welfare provision*. London: National Audit Office. Retrieved from https://www.nao.org.uk/wp-content/uploads/2016/01/Local-welfare-provision.pdf, accessed July 2025

Comptroller and Auditor General. (2018). *Rolling out Universal Credit*. London: National Audit Office.

Comptroller and Auditor General. (2024). *The effectiveness of government in tackling homelessness*. London: National Audit Office.

Bibliography

Cooper, B., & Harrop, A. (2023). *Support guaranteed: The roadmap to a National Care Service*. London: Fabian Society. Retrieved from https://fabians.org.uk/wp-content/uploads/2023/06/Fabians-Support-Guaranteed-Report-WEB.pdf, accessed July 2025

Coote, A., & Yazici, E. (2019). *Universal Basic Income: A union Perspective*. Geneva: Public Services International. Retrieved from http://tankona.free.fr/ubiunion19.pdf, accessed July 2025

Cribb, J., & O'Brien, L. (2022). *How did increasing the state pension age from 65 to 66 affect household incomes?* London: Institute for Fiscal Studies. Retrieved from https://ifs.org.uk/sites/default/files/output_url_files/R211-How-did-increasing-the-state-pension-age-affect-household-incomes.pdf, accessed July 2025

Cribb, J., Emmerson, C., Johnson, P., & Karjalainen, H. (2023). *The future of the State Pension*. London: Institute for Fiscal Studies.

Cribb, J., Giupponi, G., Joyce, R., Lindner, A., Waters, T., Wernham, T., & Xu, X. (2021). *The distributional and employment impacts of nationwide minimum wage changes*. London: Institute for Fiscal Studies. Retrieved from https://ifs.org.uk/publications/distributional-and-employment-impacts-nationwide-minimum-wage-changes, accessed July 2025

Cribb, J., Henry, A., & Karjalainen, H. (2024). *How have pensioner incomes and poverty changed in recent years?* London: Institute for Fiscal Studies.

Cribb, J., Karjalainen, H., & O'Brien, L. (2024). *Pensions: Five key decisions for the next government*. London: Institute for Fiscal Studies. Retrieved from https://ifs.org.uk/publications/pensions-five-key-decisions-next-government, accessed July 2025

Cribb, J., Wernham, T., & Xu, X. (2023). *Housing costs and income inequality in the UK*. London: Institute for Fiscal Studies.

Crisis. (2019). *Cover the cost: Restoring the Local Housing Allowance rates to prevent homelessness*. London: Crisis.

Darzi, A., Lord (2024). *Independent investigation of the National Health Service in England*. London: Department of Health and Social Care.

Davenport, A., & Zaranko, B. (2020). *Levelling up: Where and how?* London: Institute for Fiscal Studies.

Davidson, E. (2024). *The power of youth work: A longitudinal biographical study*. Edinburgh: Centre for Research on Families and Relationships, University of Edinburgh. Retrieved from https://binks-hub.ed.ac.uk/wp-content/uploads/2024/12/Power-of-youth-work_study-report_final-1.pdf, accessed July 2025

Davies, A., Blackwell, C., Ellis, W., Padley, M., Stone, J., & Balchin. (2024). *A minimum income standard for the United Kingdom in 2024*. York: Joseph Rowntree Foundation. Retrieved from https://www.jrf.org.uk/sites/default/files/pdfs/a-minimum-income-standard-for-the-united-kingdom-in-2024-e116516af2e648270033450aeaf18412.pdf, accessed July 2025

Davis, A., Hirsch, D., Padley, M., & Marshall, L. (2015). *How much is enough?: Reaching social consensus on minimum household needs*. Loughborough: Loughborough University.

De Henau, J. (2022). Simulating employment and fiscal effects of public investment in high-quality universal childcare in the UK. *International Journal of Childcare and Education Policy*, *16*(3), 1–27. doi: https://doi.org/10.1186/s40723-022-00096-y

De-Freitas, A., Ville, L., & Azad, Z. (2024). *Transforming early childhood education and care: Sharing international learning: Part 2*. London: Fawcett Society. Retrieved from https://www.fawcettsociety.org.uk/Handlers/Download.ashx?IDMF=1d7b54f1-3931-486f-aeb5-1afaf350ee78, accessed July 2025

Department of Transport. (2021). *Bus back better*. London: Department of Transport.

Diner, A. (2023). *Beyond new build*. London: New Economics Foundation. Retrieved from https://neweconomics.org/uploads/files/NEF_Beyond-new-build.pdf, accessed July 2025

Dowler, E. (2003). Food and poverty: Insights from the 'North'. *Development Policy Review*, *21*(5–6), 569–80.

Edmiston, D. (2024). Indentured: Benefit deductions, debt recovery and welfare disciplining. *Social Policy Administration*, 1–16. doi: https://doi.org/10.1111/spol.13021

Bibliography

Edmiston, D., Robertshaw, D., Young, D., Ingold, J., Gibbons, A., Summers, K., ... de Vries, R. (2022). Mediating the claim? How 'local ecosystems of support' shape the operation and experience of UK social security. *Social Policy Administration, 56*(5), 775–90. doi: https://doi.org/10.1111/spol.12803

Ejiogu, A., & Denedo, M. (2021). *Stigma and social housing in England*. Durham: Durham University/University of Leicester.

Emmerson, C., Joyce, R., & Sturrock, D. (2017). Working-age incapacity and disability benefits. In C. Emmerson, P. Johnson, & R. Joyce, *The IFS green budget* (pp 177–202). London: Institute for Fiscal Studies.

Environment Agency. (2022). *Social deprivation and the likelihood of flooding*. London: Environment Agency. Retrieved from https://assets.publishing.service.gov.uk/media/6270fe448fa8f57a3cdbbeb9/Social_deprivation_and_the_likelihood_of_flooding_-_report_2.1.pdf, accessed July 2025

Environment Agency. (2024). *National assessment of flood and coastal erosion in England*. London: Environment Agency. Retrieved from https://assets.publishing.service.gov.uk/media/675c362898302e574b91536e/E03253099_EA_Flood_Coastal_Erosion_Risk_Assessment_accessible.pdf, accessed July 2025

Farquharson, C., & Olorenshaw, H. (2022). *The changing costs of childcare*. London: Institute for Fiscal Studies.

Farquharson, C., Heath Milsom, L., Tahir, I., Upton, B., & Vyas, G. (2024). *How do the last five years measure up on levelling up?* London: Institute for Fiscal Studies.

Farquharson, C., McNally, S., & Tahir, I. (2022). *Education inequalities, IFS Deaton Review of Inequalities*. London: Institute for Fiscal Studies.

Financial Conduct Authority. (2024). *Financial lives cost of living Jan 2024 (recontact survey)*. London: Financial Conduct Authority.

Fitzpatrick, S., Bramley, G., Blenkinsopp, J., Johnsen, S., Littlewood, M., Netto, G., & Watts, B. (2015). *Destitution in the UK: An interim report*. York: Joseph Rowntree Foundation.

Fitzpatrick, S., Bramley, G., Sosenko, F., & Blenkinsopp, J. (2018). *Destitution in the UK, 2018*. York: Joseph Rowntree Foundation.

Fitzpatrick, S., Bramley, G., Treanor, M., Blenkinsopp, J., McIntyre, J., Johnsen, S., & McMordie, L. (2023a). *Destitution in the UK, 2023*. York: Joseph Rowntree Foundation.

Fitzpatrick, S., Bramley, G., McMordie, L., Pawson, H., Watts-Cobb, B., & Young, G. (2023b). *The homelessness monitor: England 2023*. London: Crisis.

Francis-Devine, B. (2024). *Food banks in the UK*. London: House of Commons.

Galarza, V., Rich, H., Trew, C., Bloomer, S., Berry, C., & Matthews, W. (2024). *Brick by brick: A plan to deliver the social homes we need*. London: Shelter. Retrieved from https://downloads.ctfassets.net/6sxvmndnpn0s/3gKsteftNszu0ttpNdSdkO/4e5e1107d5236a579c164d46bcc49695/2024-07-11_-_Brick_By_Brick_Report_-_Single_Spread.pdf, accessed July 2025

Garman, J., & Aldridge, J. (2015). *When the levy breaks*. London: Institute for Public Policy Research. Retrieved from https://ippr-org.files.svdcdn.com/production/Downloads/when-the-levy-breaks_Jun2015.pdf, accessed July 2025

Garthwaite, K. (2016). *Hunger pains: Life inside foodbank Britain*. Bristol: Policy Press.

Gentleman, A. (2020). *The Windrush betrayal: Exposing the hostile environment*. London: Guardian Faber.

Giupponi, G., & Machin, S. (2024). Labour market inequality. *Oxford Open Economics*, *3*(1), 1884–1905. doi: https://doi.org/10.1093/ooec/odad039

Glover, B., & Seaford, C. (2020). *A people's budget: How the public would raise taxes*. London: Demos. Retrieved from https://demos.co.uk/wp-content/uploads/2020/12/A-Peoples-Budget-Sept-2020-v5.pdf, accessed July 2025

Goderis, B. (2025). Safety net of last resort: The evolution, determinants and adequacy of Dutch minimum income support. *Journal of Poverty and Social Justice*, *33*(1), 8–29. doi: https://doi.org/10.1332/17598273Y2024D000000033

Goll, D., Joyce, R., & Waters, T. (2023). *Intensive margin labour supply and the dynamic effects of in-work transfers*. London: Institute for Fiscal Studies.

Goodwin, M., & Milazzo, C. (2017). Taking back control? Investigating the role of immigration in the 2016 vote for Brexit. *British Journal of Politics and International Relations*, *19*(3), 450–64. doi: https://journals.sagepub.com/doi/10.1177/1369148117710799

Bibliography

Gough, I. (2020). The case for universal basic services. *LSE Public Policy Review, 1*(2), 6: 1–9. doi: https://doi.org/10.31389/lseppr.12

Grayston, R., Hudson, N., & Lloyd, T. (2024). *Is the private-rented sector shrinking?* York: Joseph Rowntree Foundation. Retrieved from https://www.jrf.org.uk/housing/is-the-private-rented-sector-shrinking, accessed July 2025

Green, D. A., & Tedds, L. M. (2024). The place of a basic income in the search for a more just society: A comment on '"Covering all the [welfare] basics": a critical policy study of the Expert Panel on Basic Income report in British Columbia, Canada' by Tracy Carrier-Smith et al. *Journal of Poverty and Social Justice, 32*(3), 472–9. doi: https://doi.org/10.1332/17598273Y2024D000000029

Gulland, J. (2024). How does Carer's Allowance in the UK construct family carers? History and recent developments. *Journal of Care and Caring, 8*(1), 98–113. doi: https://doi.org/10.1332/239788221X16716339335353

Hall, D. (2022). *Water and sewerage company finances 2021.* London: University of Greenwich. Retrieved from https://gala.gre.ac.uk/id/eprint/34274/, accessed July 2025

Hall, M., & Stephens, L. (2020). *Quality childcare for all.* London: New Economics Foundation.

Harari, D., Francis-Devine, B., Bolton, P., & Keep, M. (2023). *Rising cost of living in the UK.* London: House of Commons Library. Retrieved from https://researchbriefings.files.parliament.uk/documents/CBP-9428/CBP-9428.pdf, accessed July 2025

Harrop, A. (2016). *For us all: Redesigning social security, for the 2020s.* London: Fabian Society.

Harrop, A. (2022). *In the shadows: How 'shadow welfare' has overtaken social security.* London: Fabian Society. Retrieved from https://fabians.org.uk/wp-content/uploads/2022/03/In-the-Shadows-Fabian-Society.pdf, accessed July 2025

Harrop, A., & Cooper, B. (2019). *Where next? Reforming social security over the next 10 years.* London: Fabian Society. Retrieved from https://fabians.org.uk/wp-content/uploads/2019/11/Fabians-Where-Next-Report-WEB.pdf, accessed July 2025

Heap, D. (2024). Goodbye to PIP, but hello to what? Disability, social security, devolution and policy change in Scotland. *Journal for Poverty and Social Justice*, *32*(1), 170–80. doi: https://doi.org/10.1332/17598273Y2023D000000011

Hearn, D. (2024). *Harms from concentrated industries: A primer*. New York: Columbia Centre on Sustainable Investment. Retrieved from https://ccsi.columbia.edu/sites/default/files/content/docs/ccsi-harms-from-concentrated-industries.pdf, accessed July 2025

Helm, D. (2018). *The dividend puzzle*. Retrieved from https://dieterhelm.co.uk/wp-content/uploads/assets/secure/documents/XFN-The-Dividend-Puzzle.pdf, accessed July 2025

Hick, R., & Lanau, A. (2017). *In-work poverty in the UK*. Cardiff: Cardiff University.

Hills, J. (2013). *Labour's record on cash transfers, poverty, inequality and the lifecycle, 1997 to 2010*. London: London School of Economics. Retrieved from https://sticerd.lse.ac.uk/dps/case/spcc/wp05.pdf, accessed July 2025

Hills, J. (2015). *The coalition's record on cash transfers, poverty and inequality, 2010–2015*. London: London School of Economics.

Hirsch, D. (2023). The big tax hikes that make UBI 'affordable' could be used to cut poverty in more targeted ways: A reply to 'Universal Basic Income is affordable and feasible: Evidence from UK economic microsimulation modelling' by Howard Robert Reed et al. *Journal of Poverty and Social Justice*, *31*(1), 163–5. doi: https://doi.org/10.1332/175982721X16702576055509

Hoddinott, S., Davies, N., Fright, M., Nye, P., & Richards, G. (2023). *Performance tracker 2023*. London: Institute for Government.

Hoddinott, S., Rowland, C., Davies, N., Kim, D., & Nye, P. (2024). *Fixing public services: Priorities for the new Labour government*. London: Institute for Government.

Holford, A., & Rabe, B. (2020). *Impact of the Universal Infant Free School Meal policy*. Colchester: Institute for Social and Economic Research, University of Essex. Retrieved from https://www.iser.essex.ac.uk/wp-content/uploads/files/misoc/reports/Impact_of_the_Universal_Infant_Free_School_Meal_policy.pdf, accessed July 2025

Hood, A., & Keiller, A. N. (2016). *A survey of the UK benefit system*. London: Institute for Fiscal Studies.

House of Commons Work and Pensions Committee. (2016). *The local welfare safety net*. London: House of Commons.

Bibliography

House of Commons Work and Pensions Committee. (2018). *Benefit sanctions*. London: House of Commons.

House of Commons Work and Pensions Committee. (2019a). *Welfare safety net*. London: House of Commons.

House of Commons Work and Pensions Committee. (2019b). *Overpayments of Carers' Allowance*. London: House of Commons.

House of Commons Work and Pensions Committee. (2023). *Health assessments for benefits*. London: House of Commons.

Houston, D., Werritty, A., Bassett, D., Geddes, A., Hoolachan, A., & McMillan, M. (2011). *Pluvial (rain-related) flooding in urban areas: The invisible hazard*. York: Joseph Rowntree Foundation.

Howard, M., & Bennett, F. (2021). *Distribution of money within the household and current social security issues for couples in the UK*. London: Women's Budget Groups.

Hoynes, H., Joyce, R., & Waters, T. (2023). *Benefits and tax credits*. London: Institute for Fiscal Studies.

Ifan, G., & Sion, C. (2019). *Cut to the bone?* Cardiff: Cardiff University/Prifysgol Caerdydd.

Impact on Urban Health. (2022). *Investing in children's future: A cost benefit analysis of free school meal provision expansion*. London: Impact on Urban Health. Retrieved from https://urbanhealth.org.uk/wp-content/uploads/2022/10/FSM-Executive-Summary.pdf, accessed July 2025

Impact on Urban Health. (2024). *More than a meal: An independent evaluation of universal primary free school meals for children in London*. London: Impact on Urban Health. Retrieved from https://urbanhealth.org.uk/wp-content/uploads/2024/11/IoUH-Executive-Summary-Free-School-Meals-Report.pdf, accessed July 2025

Jaccarini, C., Yunda, P., & Kumar, C. (2022). *An emergency insulation to cut bills this winter*. London: New Economics Foundation.

Jitendra, A. (2024). *A new social contract in the childcare system*. York: Joseph Rowntree Foundation. Retrieved from https://www.jrf.org.uk/sites/default/files/pdfs/a-new-social-contract-in-the-childcare-system-4259b42658a72fdd8c82b5bce215cfe9.pdf, accessed July 2025

Johnson, M., Pickett, K., Nettle, D., Reed, H., Johnson, E., & Robson, I. (2025). *Basic income: The policy that changes everything*. Bristol: Policy Press.

Jones, H., Bhattacharyya, G., Davies, W., Dhaliwal, S., Forkert, K., Gunaratnam, Y., ... Saltus, R. (2015). *Go home: Mapping the unfolding controversy of the Home Office immigration campaigns.* Warwick: University of Warwick.

Jordan, U., Patrick, R., Power, M., Pybus, K., & Kaufman, J. (2025). 'The scales never seem to balance': Exploring the lived realities of poverty during the UK 'cost-of-living crisis' through participatory research. *Journal of Poverty and Social Justice, 33*(2), 199–220. doi: https://doi.org/10.1332/17598273Y2025D000000041

Joseph Rowntree Foundation. (2024). *UK Poverty 2024.* York: Joseph Rowntree Foundation.

Joyce, R., Mitchell, M., & Keiller, A. N. (2017). *The cost of housing for low-income renters.* London: Institute for Fiscal Studies.

Judge, L., & Marshall, J. (2022). *The Resolution Foundation housing outlook, Q2, 2022.* London: Resolution Foundation. Retrieved from https://www.resolutionfoundation.org/app/uploads/2022/04/Housing-Outlook-Q2-2022.pdf, accessed July 2025

Kennedy, S., Honeysett, L., Mackley, A., Francis-Devine, B., & McInnnes, R. (2019). *Spending of the Department for Work and Pensions.* London: House of Commons. Retrieved from https://researchbriefings.files.parliament.uk/documents/CDP-2019-0173/CDP-2019-0173.pdf, accessed July 2025

Klair, A. (2022). *A replacement for Universal Credit.* London: Trades Union Congress. Retrieved from https://www.tuc.org.uk/research-analysis/reports/replacement-universal-credit

KPMG (2024). *The economic impact of local bus services.* London: KPMG

Labour Party. (2024). *Labour's plan to make work pay: Delivering a new deal for working people.* London: The Labour Party.

Lanau, A., Mack, J., & Nandy, S. (2020). Including services in multidimensional poverty measurement for SDGs: modifications to the consensual approach. *Journal of Poverty and Social Justice, 28*(2), 149–68. doi: https://doi.org/10.1332/175982720X15850580703755

Latimer, E., Pflanz, F., & Waters, T. (2024). *Health-related benefit claims post-pandemic: UK trends and global context.* London: Institute for Fiscal Studies.

Bibliography

Lucas, K., Stokes, G., Bastiaanssen, J., & Burkinshaw, J. (2019). *Inequalities in mobility and access in the UK transport system*. London: Government Office for Science. Retrieved from https://assets.publishing.service.gov.uk/governm ent/uploads/system/uploads/attachment_data/file/784685/future_of_mobi lity_access.pdf, accessed July 2025

MacAlister, J. (2022). *The independent review of social care: Final report*. London: Department of Education.

Machin, R. (2023). The UK – a home for Ukrainians? An analysis of social security and housing policy. *Journal of Poverty and Social Justice, 31*(2), 298–305. doi: https://doi.org/10.1332/175982723X16770921278736

Machray, K., & Haddow, K. (2024). 'Lads are daft though, aren't they?' Exploring men's narratives of mitigating food insecurity and navigating food aid. *Journal of Poverty and Social Justice, 32*(3), 382–97. doi: https://doi.org/ 10.1332/17598273Y2024D000000022

Mack, J. (2018). Fifty years of poverty in the UK. In G. Bramley, & N. Bailey, *Poverty and social exclusion in the UK, Volume 2 – The dimension of disadvantage* (pp 27–55). Bristol: Policy Press.

Mack, J., & Lansley, S. (1985). *Poor Britain*. London: George, Allen and Unwin.

Mack, J., & Pomati, M. (2023). Universal basic income: The debate. *Journal of Poverty and Social Justice*, 3–4. doi: https://doi.org/10.1332/175982721 X16704285585313

Marmot, M., Allen, J., Boyce, T., Goldblatt, P., & Morrison, J. (2020). *Health equity in England: The Marmot review ten years on*. London: Institute of Health Equity.

Martinelli, L. (2017). *Assessing the case for a universal basic income in the UK*. Bath: Institute for Policy Research, University if Bath. Retrieved from https://www.bath.ac.uk/publications/assessing-the-case-for-a-universal-basic-income-in-the-uk/attachments/ipr-assessing-the-case-for-a-univer sal-basic-income-in-the-uk.pdf, accessed July 2025

Mayer, T., & Bridgen, P. (2022). Open for the childless skilled only: The poverty risks of migrant workers with children under the UK points-based immigration system. *Journal of Poverty and Social Justice, 30*(1), 9–36. doi: https://doi.org/10.1332/175982721X16389693442869

McKinney, C., Kennedy, S., Gower, M., & Sturge, G. (2024). *No recourse to public funds*. London: House of Commons.

McKnight, A., Bucelli, I., Burchardt, T., & Karagiannaki, E. (2024). *Review of UK material deprivation measures*. London: Department for Work and Pensions.

Meers, J. (2019). Discretion as blame avoidance: Passing the buck to local authorities in 'welfare reform'. *Journal of Poverty and Social Justice*, *27*(1), 41–60. doi: https://doi.org/10.1332/175982718X15451305440442

Meers, J., Colliver, K., Hudson, J., & Lunt, N. (2024). Sticking plaster support: The Household Support Fund and localised assistance in the UK welfare state. *Journal of Poverty and Social Justice*, *32*(1), 26–46. doi: https://doi.org/10.1332/17598273Y2023D000000008

Messing, V., & Ságvári, B. (2019). *Still divided but more open*. Budapest: Friedrich-Ebert-Stiftung. Retrieved from https://library.fes.de/pdf-files/bueros/budapest/15322-20190505.pdf, accessed November 2025

Metcalfe, S. (2024). *From the ground up: How the government can build more homes*. London: Institute for Government. Retrieved from https://www.instituteforgovernment.org.uk/sites/default/files/2024-08/How-government-can-build-more-homes_0.pdf, accessed July 2025

Middleton, G., Mehta, K., McNaughton, D., & Booth, S. (2018). The experiences and perceptions of food banks amongst users in high-income countries: An international scoping review. *Appetite*, *120*, 698–708. doi: https://doi.org/10.1016/j.appet.2017.10.029

Ministry of Housing, Communities, and Local Government. (2018). *Analysis of the determinants of house price changes*. London: Ministry of Housing, Communities and Local Government. Retrieved from https://assets.publishing.service.gov.uk/media/5ad0a75ee5274a76be66c25c/OFF_SEN_Ad_Hoc_SFR_House_prices_v_PDF.pdf, accessed July 2025

Moore-Bick, T. R., Akbor, A., & Istephan, T. (2024). *Grenfell Tower inquiry: Phase 2 report overview*. London: Grenfell Inquiry.

Moran, R. A., & McMahon, G. (2023). Where does the buck stop? UK Home Office and other statutory body responses to allegations of human rights violations in two Serco-run hotels housing people seeking asylum. *Journal of Poverty and Social Justice*, *31*(2), 306–14. doi: https://doi.org/10.1332/175982721X16806944627654

Bibliography

Morrison, J. (2019). *Scroungers: Moral panics and media myths*. London: Zed.

Mort, L., & Morris, M. (2024). *Transforming asylum accommodation*. London: Institute for Public Policy Research.

Mulrooney, H., & Ranta, R. (2024). Contradictions, dilemmas, views and motivations of volunteers in two community food support schemes in two London boroughs. *Journal of Poverty and Social Justice, 32*(3), 343–70. doi: https://doi.org/10.1332/17598273Y2024D000000017

Munro, A., Boyce, T., & Marmot, M. (2020). *Sustainable health equity: Achieving a net-zero UK*. London: Institute of Health Equity.

Murphy, R. (2024). *The taxing wealth report 2024: The full edition*. Ely: Finance for the Future LLP. Retrieved from https://taxingwealth.uk/wp-content/uploads/2024/04/Taxing-Wealth-Report-2024-Full.pdf, accessed July 2025

Negri, O., & Cavanagh, H. (2024). *Making benefits work: Improving support for disabled people*. London: Scope. Retrieved from https://www.scope.org.uk/campaigns/making-benefits-work

Ogden, K., & Phillips, D. (2023). *The distribution of public service spending: The IFS Deaton review of inequality*. London: Institute for Fiscal Studies. Retrieved from https://ifs.org.uk/inequality/the-distribution-of-public-service-spending/, accessed July 2025

Ogden, K., & Phillips, D. (2024). *How have English councils' funding and spending changed? 2010 to 2024*. London: Institute for Fiscal Studies.

Otto, S. (2024). *When I'm 64: A strategy to tackle poverty before state pension age, summary report*. London: Fabian Society. Retrieved from https://fabians.org.uk/wp-content/uploads/2024/04/Fabian-Society-When-Im-64-WEB-3-2.pdf, accessed July 2025

Owen, A., & Barrett, J. (2020). Reducing inequality resulting from UK low-carbon policy. *Climate Policy, 20*(10), 1193–208. doi: https://doi.org/10.1080/14693062.2020.1773754

Padley, M., Stone, J., & Robinson, E. (2024). *Households living below minimum income standards: 2008–2022*. York: Joseph Rowntree Foundation.

Parliamentary Office of Science and Technology. (2019). *Climate change and agriculture*. London: House of Commons.

Parliamentary Office of Science and Technology. (2024). *Public Health Impacts of Heat*. London: House of Commons.

Patrick, R. (2023). *Living at the sharp end of socio-economic inequality: Everyday experiences of poverty and social security receipt*. London: Institute of Fiscal Studies.

Patrick, R., Anderson, K., Reader, M., Reeves, A., & Stewart, K. (2023). *Needs and entitlements: Welfare reform and larger families*. London: Nuffield Foundation.

Patrick, R., Garthwaite, K., Power, M., Kaufman, J., Page, G., Pybus, K., ... Howes, S. (2022). *Covid realities: Documenting life on a low income during the pandemic*. London: Nuffield Foundation.

Pemberton, S., Phillimore, J., & Robinson, D. (2014). *Causes and experiences of poverty among of economic migrants in the UK*. Birmingham: Institute for Research into Superdiversity, University of Birmingham.

Pereirinha, J. A., & Pereira, E. (2025). Regimes of social minima in Europe: A wide view of policy changes. *Journal of Poverty and Social Justice*, *33*(1), 2–7. doi: https://doi.org/10.1332/17598273Y2025D000000039

Phillips, D. (2021). *How and why has the Scottish Government's funding changed in recent years?* London: Institute for Fiscal Studies.

Plunkett, J. (2011). The coalition's £11bn stealth cut: Switching from RPI to CPI. *New Statesman*, 11 September. Retrieved from https://www.newstatesman.com/business/economics/2011/09/cpi-rpi-lower-cut-chancellor, accessed July 2025

Porter, I. (2024). *Unlocking benefits: Tackling barriers for disabled people wanting to work*. London: Joseph Rowntree Foundation. Retrieved from https://www.jrf.org.uk/work/unlocking-benefits-tackling-barriers-for-disabled-people-wanting-to-work, accessed July 2025

Portes, J., Reed, H., & Percy, A. (2017). *Social prosperity for the future: A proposal for universal basic services*. London: University College London. Retrieved from https://www.ucl.ac.uk/bartlett/igp/sites/bartlett/files/universal_basic_services_-_the_institute_for_global_prosperity_.pdf, accessed July 2025

Preston City Council. (2019). *How we built community wealth in Preston*. Manchester/Preston: Centre for Local Economic Strategies and Preston City Council. Retrieved from https://www.preston.gov.uk/media/1792/How-we-built-community-wealth-in-Preston/pdf/CLES_Preston_Document_WEB_AW.pdf?m=1563809932893, accessed July 2025

Pring, J. (2017). Welfare reforms and the attack on disabled people. In V. Cooper, & D. Whyte, *The violence of austerity* (pp 51–8). London: Pluto Press.

Bibliography

Procter, A., Pratt, S., & Wise-Martin, I. (2023). *APPG for Households in Temporary Accommodation: Call for evidence findings: Summary, analysis of themes and call to action*. London: All-Party Parliamentary Group, House of Commons. Retrieved from https://householdsintemporaryaccommodation.co.uk/wp-content/uploads/2023/01/APPG-Call-For-Evidence-Findings-Report.pdf, accessed July 2025

Public Services International Research Unit (PSIRU). (2024). *Clean water: A case for public ownership*. London: Unison.

Ray-Chaudhuri, S., & Waters, T. (2024). *Recent trends in and the outlook for health-related benefits*. London: Institute for Fiscal Studies.

Ray-Chaudhuri, S., Waters, T., & Wernham, T. (2024). *Living standards since the last election*. London: Institute of Fiscal Studies.

Ray-Chaudhuri, S., Waters, T., Wernham, T., & Xu, X. (2023). *Living standards, poverty and inequality in the UK: 2023*. London: Institute of Fiscal Studies.

Reed, H. R., Johnson, M. T., Lansley, S., Johnson, E. A., Stark, G., & Pickett, K. E. (2023). Universal basic income is affordable and feasible: Evidence from UK economic microsimulation modelling. *Journal of Poverty and Social Justice*, *31*(1), 146–62. doi: https://doi.org/10.1332/175982721X16702368352393

Reis, S., & Stephens, L. (2022). *Childcare and gender*. London: Women's Budget Group.

Roderick, P., & Pollock, A. M. (2022). Dismantling the National Health Service in England. *International Journal of Social Determinants of Health and Health Services*, *52*(4), 470–9. doi: https://doi.org/10.1177/00207314221114540

Ryan, F. (2019). *Crippled: Austerity and the demonization of disabled people*. London: Verso.

Ryan-Collins, J. (2024). *The demand for housing as an investment*. London: Institute for Innovation and Public Purpose, University College London. Retrieved from https://www.ucl.ac.uk/bartlett/publications/2024/oct/demand-housing-investment, accessed July 2025

Sammons, P., Hall, J., Smees, R., & Goff, J. (2015). *The impact of children's centres: Studying the effects of children's centres in promoting better outcomes for young children and their families*. London: Department for Education.

Sandford, M. (2023). *Council tax: Local referendums*. London: House of Commons Library.

Savills. (2023). *Research into expenditure within the Housing Revenue Account*. London: Local Government Association. Retrieved from https://www.local.gov.uk/sites/default/files/documents/5.151%20LGA%20arch%20nfa%20-%20expenditure%20research%20-%20RA.pdf, accessed July 2025

Simon, A., Pen, H., Shah, A., Owen, C., Lloyd, E., Hollingworth, K., & Kuy, K. (2021). *Acquisitions, mergers and debt: The new language of childcare*. London: UCL Social Research Institute, University College London.

Smith, C., O'Reilly, P., Rumpel, R., & White, R. (2021). *How do I survive now? The impact of living with no recourse to public funds*. London: Citizens Advice.

Smith, G., Sylva, K., Smith, T., Sammons, P., & Omonigho, A. (2018). *Stop start*. London: Sutton Trust.

Southwark Council. (2024). *Securing the future of council housing*. London: Southwark Council. https://www.southwark.gov.uk/sites/default/files/2024-10/Securing%20the%20Future%20of%20Council%20Housing%20-%20Interim%20Report.pdf, accessed July 2025

StepChange. (2020). *Problem debt and the social security system*. Leeds: StepChange. Retrieved from https://www.stepchange.org/Portals/0/assets/pdf/social-security-mini-brief-report.pdf, accessed July 2025

Stirling, A., & Arnold, S. (2019). *Nothing personal: Replacing the personal tax allowance with a weekly national allowance*. London: New Economics Foundation. Retrieved from https://neweconomics.org/uploads/files/NEF_WeeklyNationalAllowance_2019.pdf, accessed July 2025

Stuart, M., Spencer, D. A., MacLachan, C. J., & Forde, C. (2021). *Employers' use of furlough and job retention support in the UK during the COVID-19 pandemic*. Geneva: International Labour Organization. Retrieved from https://www.ilo.org/media/85591/download, accessed July 2025

Sturge, G. (2024). *Asylum statistics*. London: House of Commons Library.

Swan, E., Hussain, S., Miah, S., & Yip, J. (2024). The fragrance of ghee: Food aesthetics, food insecurity and policy dreams. *Journal of Poverty and Social Justice*, *32*(3), 371–81. doi: https://doi.org/10.1332/17598273Y2024D000000025

Bibliography

Taylor, R. (2018). *Impact of 'hostile environment' policy: Debate on 14 June 2018: Library briefing*. London: House of Lords.

The Food Foundation. (2025). *The broken plate: The state of the nation's food system*. London: The Food Foundation. Retrieved from https://foodfoundation.org.uk/sites/default/files/2025-01/TFF_The%20Broken%20Plate%202005%20FINAL%20DIGITAL.pdf, accessed July 2025

Thompson, S., Jitendra, A., & Woodruff, L. (2023). *The caring penalty*. York: Joseph Rowntree Foundation.

Timmins, N. (2023). *Why has the UK's social security system become so means-tested?, IFS Deaton Review of Inequalities*. London: Institute for Fiscal Studies. Retrieved from https://ifs.org.uk/inequality/why-has-the-uks-social-security-system-become-so-means-tested/, accessed July 2025

Tomlinson, D. (2021). *Job well done: Eighteen months of the Coronavirus job retention scheme*. London: Resolution Foundation.

Try, L. (2025). *Money, money, money: The shifting mix of income sources for poorer households over the last thirty years*. London: Resolution Foundation.

TUC. (2022). *A fairer energy for families and the climate*. London: Trades Union Congress. Retrieved from https://www.tuc.org.uk/sites/default/files/2022-07/Public%20energy%20public%20paper%20-%20web.pdf, accessed July 2025

UK Government. (2024). *Employment Rights Bill: Economic analysis*. London: UK Government.

Verbist, G., & Van Lancker, W. (2016). Horizontal and Vertical equity objectives of child benefit systems: An empirical assessment for European countries. *Social Indicators Research, 128*(3), 1299–318. Retrieved from https://repository.uantwerpen.be/docman/irua/b6a2e8/129617.pdf, accessed July 2025

Verbist, G., Förster, M., & Vaalavuo, M. (2012). *The impact of publicly provided services on the distribution of resources: Review of new results and methods*. Paris: OECD. doi: https://dx.doi.org/10.1787/5k9h363c5szq-en

Villa, C. (2024). *The effects of youth clubs on education and crime*. Warwick: Warwick University. Retrieved from https://warwick.ac.uk/fac/soc/economics/staff/cvillallera/carmenvilla-jmp_compressed.pdf, accessed July 2025

Vizard, P., & Hills, J. (2021). *The Conservative government's record on social policy from May 2015 to pre-COVID 2020: Policies, spending and outcomes*. London: London School of Economics.

Watson, N., & Bolton, P. (2024). *Contracts for difference*. London: House of Commons. Retrieved from https://researchbriefings.files.parliament.uk/documents/CBP-9871/CBP-9871.pdf, accessed July 2025

Wilcox, S. (2014). *Housing benefit size criteria: Impacts for social sector tenants and options for reform*. York: Joseph Rowntree Foundation.

Williams, W. (2020). *Windrush: Lessons learned review*. London: House of Commons.

Wilson, W., & Hobson, F. (2021). *The rent safety net: Changes since 2010*. London: House of Commons Library.

Women's Budget Group. (2024, February). *Child benefit briefing*. Retrieved from Women's Budget Group: https://wbg.org.uk/wp-content/uploads/2024/02/Child-Benefit-Briefing_Final-1.pdf, accessed July 2025

Wright, S., Dwyer, P., Jones, K., McNeill, J., Scullion, L., & Stewart, A. (2018). *Universal credit: Final findings*. York: University of York.

Wright, S., Field, S., Moss, C., Frounk, A., & Veruete-McKay, L. (2024). *Disability price tag 2024*. London: Scope. Retrieved from https://www.scope.org.uk/campaigns/disability-price-tag, accessed July 2025

Wright, S., Robertson, L., Gawlewicz, A., Bailey, N., & Katikiteddi, V. (2020). *Mental health, welfare conditionality and employment support*. Glasgow: University of Glasgow.

Index

References to figures appear in *italic* type; those in **bold** type refer to tables. References to endnotes show both the page number and the note number (231n3).

A

Achiume, Tendayi 167–8
All-Party Parliamentary Group for Households in Temporary Accommodation 146–8
All-Party Parliamentary Group on Infant Feeding and Inequalities 232
All-Party Parliamentary Group on Poverty 88–9
Alston, Philip 36–7
Amazon 233
anti-poverty strategies 9, 216
  childcare: universal system 244–9
  community food hubs 255–6
  cost of living 217
  energy retail system reform 224–7
  essential goods costs 222, 231–4
  focusing on needs and how/whether they are met 216, 222, 238
  free/discounted public transport 252–3
  free school meals 249–52
  going beyond income measure 217–19
  household income adequacy 216–17, 222, 237, 259, 284
  housing costs control 227–31
  local communities 253–4
  local councils 256–8
  making different choices 292
  material deprivation measures and policy choices 219–22
  National Care Service 242–4, 247
  NHS 238–42
  poverty prevention *vs* poverty alleviation 265
  public services 220, 222–7, 236, 237–8, 241, 250, 252, 254, 258, 284, 286
  spending in services and benefits 284–6
  taxes 276, 286–91
  work as route out of poverty 88, 94, 105, 107, 108–9, 112, 263
  see also benefits and anti-poverty strategies
artificial intelligence 266, 268
Arup 160, 228
asylum seeking 169, 178–88
  Afghanistan 179, 180–1, 187
  asylum claim, lack of legal routes to 178–9, 181–2
  asylum claims backlog 179, 181, 182, 184, 187
  'asylum shopping' 169
  Hong Kong 179
  housing 184–6
  'no recourse to public funds' (NRPF) 179

offshoring asylum seekers (Rwanda, Albania) 182
'one in one out' deal 182–3
poverty 179, 183, 184–8
refugee status 180, 183
success of claims 187
Ukraine 179–80
UN Refugee Convention (1951) 178, 179
visa requirements 179
see also immigration system: negative impact on people
austerity 1, 26
benefit cuts 10, 19, 38
coalition government 40, 45, 98, 118
Conservative government 38, 40
differential impact of 39–42, 119–21
Labour government 5
services 235
Austria 267
Aviva 194

B

Badenoch, Kemi 201
Bank of England 285–6
Bath University: Institute for Policy Research 269
Belgium 266
benefits
 benefit cap 42–3, 277, 299n24
 benefit policies targeting larger families 42–5
 benefits cuts 4, 5, 6, 36, 82–6
 benefits cuts and poverty 7, 8, 19, 36, 39, 44, 48
 child poverty and 17–19, 43, 44–5, 277–8
 disability benefits 4–5, 6, 69–70, 80–6, *81*, 263, 279–83
 failures of benefits system 43–5, 46–8, 53, 54, 58, 59, 60, 256, 259
 housing benefit 45–9, 50, 107, 139, 140, 154, 229, 263
 low value of 41, 56, 259

migrants/asylum seekers: lack of benefits 6, 165–6, 170–1, 174–5, 177
motivating into work as aim of benefit reforms 62–3, 109
overpayments 52, 114–15
pensioner benefits 16
removing the link between household's actual costs and 43, 45
RPI value in 2022 prices 40–1, *40*
uprating 37–8, 39
see also child benefit; two-child benefit limit; unemployment/out of work benefits; welfare system; working-age benefits
benefits: means-tested 3, 6–7, 42, 70, 95, 106, 260, 268
 contributory benefits 264
 free school meals 249–52
 need to row back from 265–6, 272, 283
 shift to 263–4, 277–8
 social care 121, 123
 see also two-child benefit limit; UC; Working Tax Credit
benefits: non-means-tested 5, 37, 70, 113, 264, 279–80
benefits and anti-poverty strategies 216, 222, 284
 child benefit 277–9
 child poverty 2, 260–1, 278–9
 conditionality regimes 261
 disability benefits 279–83
 improving lives over benefits cuts 283
 in-work benefit transfers 262–3
 means-testing, need to row back from 265–6, 272, 283
 modern insurance-based system 266–7
 replacing personal tax allowance with cash payment 271–2
 short-term fixes 259–62
 state pension 264, 273–6
 targeted basic income 272–3

Index

UC 260, 261, 263, 269
see also anti-poverty strategies; Universal Basic Income
Beveridge Report (1942) 37, 263
Bezos, Jeff 233
Birmingham Anchor network 254
blaming the vulnerable 5, 62, 80, 188
  prosecution of claimants 114–15
  punitive measures against claimants 62, 64
Bokkerink, Marcus 233
Bolt, David 166
Bradshaw, Jonathan 45
Brexit 98–9, 169–70, 233
British Medical Association 241
Brown, Gordon 208
Bulb Energy 225
Burnham, Andy 137

C

Canada 266, 270, 287
Carbon Co-op 205
Care Quality Commission 125, 126, 127
carers 115
  Carer's Allowance 7, 77, 113–15, 116, 264, 282
  COVID-19 pandemic 126
  destitution 69
  financial penalty 116
  undervaluing of care 113–16
  unpaid/informal care 112–13, 116, 123, 242
  women 113, 264
care services
  adult social care 117, 121–4, 126–7, 241, 244
  care sector reform 174
  child social care 124, 127
  labour shortage in 173, 174
  local councils and 116, 118, 121–2, 123, 125, 244, 257
  National Care Service 242–4, 247
  private/for-profit providers 124–9, 242, 243, 244

residential care 122, 124, 126–7
social care crisis 116, 121–4
Support Guaranteed report 243–4
Carers UK 122
Casey, Lousie 243
cash payments/transfers 38, 57, 60, 238, 268, 271–2, 273
Centre for Economic Policy Research 99
Centre for Local Economic Strategies 205
Centre for Social Justice: *Dynamic Benefits* report 55
Chandra, Varun 199–200
Chancellor (of Exchequer) 3, 4, 38, 47, 48, 53, 59, 82, 83, 88, 94, 96, 102, 103, 106, 112, 115, 203, 208, 233, 286, 288, 289, 291
Changing Realities project 11–12, 260
child benefit 2, 6, 276–7
  erosion of value of 41, 277
  as frozen 37, 38, 277
  High Income Child Benefit Charge (HICBC) 277, 278
  increase in 18, 260, 278–9
  universality of 277, 278
childcare
  childcare gap 109–13, 245, 248
  children with disabilities 112, 242, 247
  Coram Childcare Survey 112
  costs of 22, 36, 109, 110
  funding 246–7
  government investment in 110–11, 245, 248
  local authorities and 111, 112, 245, 247
  non-profit providers 245, 246, 247
  private/for-profit providers 111–12, 242, 244–5, 246–7
  shift from market-led to commissioning-led system 246
  subsidies 112, 242, 246
  Sure Start 129–32, 235–6, 248

universal childcare system 244–9
women 264
child poverty 1, 3, 8, 9, *18*, 27
  benefits system and 17–19, 43, 44–5, 277–8
  child benefit and 2, 260–1, 278–9
  child deprivation 23–6, *25*, 129, 221
  Child Poverty Strategy 221
  education and 129, 248
  in-work poverty 89–90, *91*, 92, *92*
  pro-child *vs* pro-poor policies 278, 279
  reduction of 2, 105, 106, 250
  relative poverty 18, 19, 69, 89
  two-child benefit limit and 44–5, 260
  UC uplift and 58
Child Poverty Action Group 11, 260
children
  benefits, impact on children 43, 44–5
  Best Start Family Hubs 248
  children's services 127–32, *128*, 130, *131*
  child social care 124, 127
  early years provision 132
  education 129, 132, 248, 249
  health 12, 129, 130–2, 151
  poor housing conditions 151–2, *152*
  Sure Start 129–32, 235–6, 248
  see also families with children; two-child benefit limit
Child Tax Credit 18, 19, 43, 50, 105–6, 107, 276–7
  see also tax credits
Citizens Advice 59–60, 174–5, 225
Clifford, Ellen 86
climate change
  Climate Change Act (2008) 200
  Climate Change Committee (CCC) 201, 209, 210
  climate crisis 9, 188, 191, 192
  climate-induced migration 191

climate injustice 190–2
deniers of 201
droughts 191, 196
extreme weather 189–90
flooding and storms 189, 190, 193–5, 196
global warming 190–1, 192, 193
impact of 190, 193
poverty and 191
public support for action on 201
unequal impact of 192–6
water privatisation 196–200, 224
see also energy sector; greenhouse gas emissions
Clwyd Alyn Housing Association 255
coalition government (2010–15)
  austerity 40, 45, 98, 118
  benefits system 37, 42, 287
  child benefit 277
  childcare 245
  conditionality regimes 64, 65
  free school meals 249
  housing policies 46, 48–9, 141–2, 156
  NHS 240
  responsibility transfer from central to local government 57
  UC 50, 55
  UK housing: energy efficiency 208, 210
  welfare spending cap/cuts 4, 36, 98
Competitions and Markets Authority (CMA) 127, 231–4
conditionality regimes 63–9
  anti-poverty strategies 261
  counter-productive outcomes of 67–8, 69
  COVID-19 pandemic 55, 65
  disabled people 64, 70, 85, 282
  sanctions 63, 64, 65–9, 261
  single-parents 64, 68–9, 109–10
  UC 55, 64–5, 67, 68
  Working Tax Credit 64
Conservative government 4
  austerity 38, 40

Index

benefits system and 2, 36, 38, 42, 287
'black hole' in finances 3
child benefit 277
childcare 245
conditionality regimes 64, 65
free school meals 249
housing policies 46, 140–1, 156
immigration policies 165–6, 168–9, 179, 181–2
'levelling up' agenda 118, 121, 137
material deprivation during 23–4, *24*
minimum wage policy 94–6
UK housing: energy efficiency 208, 209–10
zero-carbon homes policy 208
Conservative Party 62, 201
Consumer Price Index (CPI) 37–8, 39–40, 41, 102
cost of living 80
anti-poverty strategies and 217
cost-of-living crisis (2012–23) 11–12, 20, 25, 29–31, 36, 203, 224
costs of living with a disability 70–1, 263, 279–80
rising cost of living 30, 215–16, 227, 263
COVID-19 pandemic 12, 19, 55, 65
care home residents and staff 126
Coronavirus Job Retention Scheme/furlough (CJRS) 55, 100, 176
COVID Local Support Grant 56–8
COVID Winter Grant Scheme 56–8
disabled people 79
economic impact of 100, 101
employment 55, 79, 100–1, 254
homelessness 144
local councils and 56–8, 118–19
Local Housing Allowance (LHA) 47

lockdowns 20, 54, 55, 58, 100, 203
migrants 176
NHS 239
Self-Employment Income Support Scheme 55, 101
UC 55–6, 85
unemployment 55, 100, 101
Covid Realities 54–5, 56
crises
climate crisis 9, 188, 191, 192
cost-of-living crisis (2012–23) 11–12, 20, 25, 29–31, 36, 203, 224
crisis funds, dependence on 59
energy crisis 203, 209, 225
financial crises 36
financial crisis (2008) 20, 38, 98, 125, 230
homelessness crisis 143–6, *145*
local councils crisis 117
rolling crises 1, 31, 98–9
social care crisis 116, 121–4
voluntary groups/charities as "last safety net" during crises 59–60
Crisis (charity) 47, 167
Homelessness Monitor 145, 148–9

D

Darzi, Ara (Lord) 238–9, 240
debt 31, *32*, 48, 50
conditionality and sanctions 65
COVID-19 pandemic and 101
debt deductions 52, 53–4
government 4, 284
migrants and 175, 177
poverty and 52, 53, 54
UC and 52, 54
unauthorised lenders and loan sharks 52–3
Demos 288
Denmark 205, 266
Department of Health and Social Care 122
Department of Work and Pensions (DWP) 27, 55, 72, 114

Family Resources Survey 23, 27, 221
material deprivation index 23–6, 25, 219–21
deprivation 13, 22–6, 138
  children 23–6, 25, 129, 221
  Conservative government and 23–4, 24
  deprived areas 12, 117, 120, 121, 125, 132, 193, 194, 235, 242, 251, 257
  DWP: material deprivation index 23–6, 25, 219–21
  low income households 23–4
  rise in 33
  service deprivation indicators 221
destitution 1, 34–5, 65–6
  definition and measure of 32
  disabled people 35, 69, 77
  migrants and asylum seekers 6, 165, 167, 176–7, 187
  rise of 31–5, 48
Disabled People Against Cuts 86
disabled people
  Adult Disability Payment (ADP) 77, 78
  anti-poverty strategies 279–83
  assessment for benefits entitlement 71–5, 78, 280
  'bedroom tax' 49, 50
  benefits 4–5, 6, 69–70, 80–6, 81, 263, 279–83
  childcare 112, 242, 247
  Child Disability Payment 113
  conditionality regimes 64, 70, 85, 282
  costs of living with a disability 70–1, 263, 279–80
  COVID-19 pandemic 79
  destitution 35, 69, 77
  Disabled Living Allowance (DLA) 71
  employment issues 78–9, 82–3, 85–6, 281, 282
  Employment Support Allowance (ESA) 64, 70, 76
  free/concessionary bus passes 252

out-of-work benefits 280, 281–2
Personal Independence Payments (PIP) 5, 7–8, 71, 72, 77, 78, 83–4, 86, 113, 279–80, 281
poverty 5, 76–7, 94
punitive targeting of 69–75
Severe Disability Premium 76
support group/services 70, 281
temporary accommodation 148
UC and 75–7, 84, 85, 86
Universal Credit and Personal Independence Bill 7–8
volunteering 282
Work Capability Assessment (WCA) 70, 72, 85
Duncan Smith, Iain 42, 55

E

Economic and Social Research Council (ESRC) 67, 68
economy
  Brexit's impact on 98–9
  climate change and 191
  COVID-19 pandemic and 100, 101
  economic growth 2, 16, 97, 98, 267, 233, 234
  'foundational economy' 238
  gig economy 97
  low-carbon/net-zero economy 200, 207
  migrants and 165, 261
  price setting 231
  stagnation of 9, 266
education
  child poverty and 129, 248
  children 129, 132, 248, 249
  earnings inequality and 96–7
  free provision of 22, 218, 220, 223, 245
  nursery 110, 221, 223, 245
  Worcester: the Hive 254
  young people 132, 135
employment/labour
  barriers to 44, 115
  benefit policies failures and 53
  career progression 108, 109

Index

COVID-19 pandemic 55, 79, 100–1, 254
disabled people 78–9, 82–3, 85–6, 281, 282
'Employment Rights Bill' 104–5
Employment Support Allowance (ESA) 64, 70, 76
Fair Work Agency 105
fire and rehire practices 104
free public services as incentive to work 237
full-time work 94, 108, 109, 247, 260, 262
getting parents into work 109, 112, 132, 247
job security 8, 97, 259
labour shortages and migrant labour 173, 174, 244
migrants, exploitation of 166–7, 173–4
Modern Slavery Act (2015) 174
motivating into work as aim of benefit reforms 62–3
'A New Deal for Working People' 104
on-call/temporary workers 97
part-time work 69, 98, 115, 247, 262
part-time work and poverty 94, 98, 108
self-employment 97, 98, 101, 269, 289
Strikes Act 105
transport and 135–6
UC and insecure work 51–2
universal childcare system and 247
women 109, 110, 247
work coaches 83, 261
zero-hours contracts 51, 97–8, 104
see also in-work poverty
Energy Company Obligation schemes (ECO) 208–9
energy sector 8–9
anti-poverty strategies and 224–7
coal 201
consumers and costs of low-carbon energy transition 201, 202–4
energy costs 22, 24, 30, 31, 35, 54, 102, 202, 203, 215, 224–5
energy crisis 203–4, 209, 225
energy efficiency 207–14, *212*, 225
fair pricing structure 226–7
free band of energy to all 226
fuel poverty 207, 208, 209, 210, 225, 227
gas-generated electricity 203
green levies 202, 204, 208, 209
inflation 102
nuclear energy 206, 285
privatisation of 224–5
regulation 225, 226
renewable energy 201, 202, 203–7, 210, 226, 254
subsidies 202, 204, 211, 212, 213
see also climate change; greenhouse gas emissions; heating
England
adult social care 121–2, 124, 244
childcare 110
extreme weather 189–90
free school meals 249, 251
homelessness 144, *145*, 146
housing and accommodation 141, 142, 149, 150, 151–2, *151*, *152*, 158
local councils 118, 119, *119*, 256–7
racist riots 163–4
temporary accommodation 146
transport 133–4, *134*, 137
water privatisation 196–200, 224
English Household Survey 157
Environment Agency 189, 197
European Union Council 265
Exchequer 75, 112, 200, 284, 286, 287

F

Fabian Society 243–4, 260, 287
families with children 18, 19, 43, 106
benefit policies targeting larger families 42–5

food, lack of 1, 12, 25, 26, 30
heating 25, 26
poverty and 23, 61, 93, 94, 175, 176, 277
far right politics 5, 163–4, 165, 169, 178, 183, 184, 271
finances 36, 41, 50
  COVID-19 pandemic and 56, 100, 101
  financial insecurity 29–31, 265
  government finances, poor state of 285, 286
  public finances, 'black hole' in 3, 156
  see also debt
Financial Conduct Authority: 'Financial Lives' survey 29–31
Financial Times (newspaper) 200
Finland 278
fiscal rules 3–4, 86, 229, 284–6
Flintshire 255
food
  BRITE box scheme 255
  climate change and 191
  community food hubs 255–6
  Eatwell Guide 29
  Flintshire: Well Fed 255
  food aid sites 256
  food inflation 102, 191
  food insecurity 26–9, *28*, 191
  food poverty 26, 215–16, 232, 254, 255
  formula milk prices 232–3
  'free breakfast clubs' (primary schools) 2, 251
  free school meals 249–52
  lack of 1, 12, 25, 26, 30, 31, 35, 175
  quality of food and ability to access a healthy diet 29, 124
  Real Junk Food Project 255–6
food banks 1, 34, 65–6, 256
  rise in number and use of 11, 26–7, 51
The Food Foundation 29

G

Gangmasters 173
Gateshead Energy Company 206
GB Energy 204–5, 206
Germany 204, 278
greenhouse gas emissions 192, 207
  moving to net zero 200–2
  NHS, net-zero goals 241
  UK as 'off track for net zero' 201
  see also climate change; energy sector
Guardian (newspaper) 84, 86, 168, 235
Guterres, António 190

H

Hackney Light and Power 205
healthcare
  free provision of 22, 218, 220, 223
  Health and Social Care Act (2012) 240
  migrants and 166, 170, 171, 177, 179
  MIS (2024) and private medical care 219
  see also National Health Service
health-related issues 12, 53, 193
  children 12, 129, 130–2, 151
  poor housing conditions and 151
  see also mental health
heating 31, 35, 207
  district/communal heating schemes 205–6
  families with children 25, 26
  heat pumps 206, 207, 210
  insulation 207, 208, 209, 210, 226
  unaffordable heating 11, 12, 29, 30, 123, 203, 215
  winter fuel allowance for pensioners 3, 6–7, 227
  see also energy sector
Hewitt, Daniel 126–7
Hirsch, Donald 269
homelessness 35, 48, 229, 273
  'core homelessness' 145–6

Index

crisis of 143–6, *145*
'Homelessness Reduction Act' 143–4
local councils and 144, 149
temporary accommodation 146, *147*
homeownership 142–3, 158, 227, 228, 231
'affordable' homeownership 161
energy efficiency 211–13, **212**
'Help to Buy' 160
home equity release schemes 213
house prices surge 139, 142, 230–1
housing as investment 156–7, 230, 231
inheritance tax and 290
mortgage 11, 30, 103, 143, 213, 216, 230, 231
pensioners 275–6
poverty and **212**, 213
Right to Buy 140–1, 142, 156
shared ownership 159, 161, 228
see also housing
housebuilding 158–61, 261
Affordable Homes Programme 161–2, *162*, 228
in flood risk areas 194–5, 196
Green Belt 159
housebuilding market 158, 230
National Planning Policy Framework (NPPR) 159
social housing 142, 158–60, 161–2, 228–9
'viability assessments' 159
zero-carbon homes policy 208
Household Costs Index (HCI) 102
Household Support Fund (HSF) 58–9
House of Commons 7–8
Environmental Audit Committee 209
Home Affairs Committee 166
Public Accounts Committee 153
Work and Pensions Committee 36, 65, 114–15
House of Lords 57, 160, 227

housing
'affordable housing' 141–2, 157, 158, 159, 160, 161, 228
'affordable rent' 141–2, 161, 229–30
'bedroom tax' 48–50
council housing, sale of 140–1, 142
COVID-19 pandemic 47
Discretionary Housing Payments 59
energy efficiency 207–14, **212**
evictions 125, 139, 144, 150, 153
high cost of 139–40, 216, 228, 230
Housing Act (1988) 156
housing benefit 45–9, 50, 107, 139, 140, 154, 229, 263
housing costs control 227–31
Housing Revenue Account (HRA) 156
local councils and 139, 143, 149, 153, 155–6, 158, 161
Local Housing Allowance (LHA) 45–8, 49, 50, 59
migrants and 167, 170, 175
policies failures 46–8, 49–50
poverty and 139, 140, **212**
private tenants/rents 49, 50, 103, 139–40, 143, 150, 152, 211, 213, 227, 229–30
targeting of low-income private renters 45–8
temporary accommodation 146–9, *147*
tenants with disabilities 49, 50
UC housing component 48, 50, 51, 107, 261
see also homelessness; homeownership; housebuilding; social housing
housing: poor conditions 140, 146–8, 149–53, *151*, *152*, 207, 229
asylum seekers 184–6
Decent Home Standard 150, 152, 155

Grenfell Tower fire 154–5
health and 151
Housing Health and Safety Rating System 150
regulation failure 153–7
social housing 154–6, 157
housing associations 141, 155, 156–7, 161, 211, 228, 244
Hunt, Jeremy 47, 82, 103, 112

I

immigration/migrants
  border and immigration enforcement 166, 192
  climate-induced migration 191
  COVID-19 pandemic 176
  EU/non-EU migrants 170, 173
  failed policies 172–3
  far right and 5, 163–4, 165, 169, 178, 183
  Home Office and 5–6, 165–6, 168–9, 183
  Illegal Immigration Act (2023) 181–2
  illegal/undocumented migrants 166, 168, 169, 173, 178, 181
  Immigration Acts (2014, 2016) 166
  immigration system: limiting immigration as aim 165, 172, 178
  Immigration White Paper (2025) 174, 177–8
  labour shortages and migrant labour 173, 174, 244
  low-paid migrant workers 171, 172, 173, 174, 176, 177, 178
  rise of immigration, 172, *172*, 178
  UC and 175, 261
  UK economy and 165, 261
  visa requirements 170, 171–2, 173, 174, 177
  see also asylum seeking
immigration system: negative impact on people
  anti-migrant attitudes 165, 166, 169, 188
  benefits, lack of 6, 165–6, 170–1, 174–5, 177
  Brexit and poverty risks for migrants 169–74
  citizenship/right to remain 6, 171, 177, 179, 180, 183, 261
  debt 175, 177
  deportation 168, 169, 181, 182
  destitution 6, 165, 167, 176–7, 187
  detention 168, 182
  discrimination 167, 168, 179
  exploitation of migrant labour 166–7, 173–4
  healthcare 166, 170, 171, 177, 179
  hostile environment 165–9
  housing 167, 170, 175
  human rights violations 168
  human trafficking 174, 179
  'no recourse to public funds' (NRPF) 170, 171, 174–8, 261–2
  policy rhetoric and anti-migrant attitudes 165, 169
  poverty 5, 165, 167, 171, 174–6
  racism and anti immigration riots 163–5, 169, 184, 188
  Windrush scandal 168–9
  see also asylum seeking
Impact on Urban Health 250–1
impoverishment 11, 12–13, 117
  causes 9–10, 188
  end of 284, 292
income 1
  household income adequacy 216–17, 222, 237, 259, 284
  pension incomes 273–4
  see also low income families; poverty, measures of; wages
inequality 16, 96–8, 165, 237
  earnings inequality 96–8, 106
  income gender inequalities 247
  income inequality and prospects for children 129
  racial inequalities 154–5

Index

regional inequalities 120–1
wealth inequality 290
inflation 29, 119, 191, 217
  2021–23 inflation 22, 24, 41, 58, 101–2, *103*, 176, 287
  long-term legacy of 101–4
Institute and Faculty for Actuaries 191
Institute for Fiscal Studies (IFS) 82, 95, 97, 110, 121, 130–1, 237, 257, 262, 284, 289
Institute for Public Policy Research (IPPR) 185, 204
Institute for Transport Studies (ITS) 135–6
Intergovernmental Panel on Climate Change 190–1
International Monetary Fund (IMF) 285
internet services 22, 221, 227, 254
in-work poverty 88–9
  adults 89, *90*, 91–4, *92*, *93*
  children 89–90, *91*, 92, *92*
  COVID-19 pandemic and aftermath 100–1
  families with children 93, 94
  inflation 101–4
  part-time work 94, 98
  private pension and 274–5
  rising importance of 89–94
  single-parent families 94
  see also wages
Ishak, Awaab 151, 156
Islamophobia 163
ITV News 126–7

J

Johnson, Boris 118, 121, 137
Johnson, Paul 284
Joseph Rowntree Foundation (JRF) 20, 31–2, 48, 77, 116, 176–7

K

Kendall, Liz 5, 7, 62, 82, 83, 86, 267
Khan, Sadiq 250

Kingston University 255–6
Kwarteng, Kwasi 102

L

labour *see* employment/labour
Labour Abuse Authority 173
Labour government (1945) 263
Labour government (1997–2010)
  anti-poverty policies 16, 18
  child poverty 17–19, 106
  conditionality regimes 63–4
  fiscal rules and 284
  housing policies 141, 155, 161
  Sure Start 129–30
  tax credits 106
  Working Tax Credit 105
Labour government (2024–present)
  anti-poverty policies and inaction 2–7, 8, 50, 284
  austerity 5
  budget (2024) 4, 48, 53, 96, 115, 285, 286, 288
  budget (2025) 8, 203–4, 286, 288, 289, 291
  capital spending projects 285
  childcare 245, 248
  child poverty 2, 3, 8, 9, 221
  economic growth 2, 233, 234
  employment 8, 9, 104–5, 259
  energy sector 8–9, 204, 206, 213
  fiscal rules and 3–4, 86, 229, 284, 285–6
  free school meals 249–50
  housing policies 8, 158–9, 161–2, 195, 228, 238, 261
  immigration policies 5–6, 169, 174, 177–8, 182–3
  long term policies and investments 8–9
  NHS 9, 238, 239, 240, 241
  public debt and 3–4, 285
  public disappointment on 3, 6, 45, 48
  two-child benefit limit 3, 6, 8, 260
  welfare spending cuts 4–5, 82
Labour Party
  'change' promise 2, 3

general election and manifesto (2024) 1, 2, 104, 157, 210, 240, 242, 245, 284
local elections (2025) 6
Plan for Change (2024) 248
Landman Economics 268–70
left politics 291
libertarian right 233, 271
Lister, Ruth 57
living standards 1, 9, 13, 238
  COVID-19 pandemic and 101
  income as proxy for 13, 19
  low living standards 1, 23, 260, 287
  Minimum Income Standard (MIS) 20–2, 217–18, 219
  survival standard 13
local councils
  'anchor' institutions and networks 253–4
  anti-poverty strategies 253–4, 256–8
  austerity, differential impact of 119–21
  childcare and 111, 112, 245, 247
  children's services 127–32, *128*, *131*
  clean energy and 205, 206
  council tax 118, 120, 170, 231, 257–8, 290
  COVID-19 pandemic and 56–8, 118–19
  crisis in 117
  education and 245, 248
  funding and spending cuts 9, 57, 60, 117–19, *119*, 123, 130–2, 155, 256–7
  homelessness and 144, 149
  housing and accommodation 139, 143, 149, 153, 155–6, 158, 161
  inflation and 119
  preventative services 127–9, 257
  responsibility transfer from central to local government 48, 57–9
  social care and 116, 118, 121–2, 123, 125, 244, 257
  voluntary groups/charities and 60
  youth services 130, *131*, 132–3, 257, 258
Local Government Association 155, 257
Local Welfare Assistance Schemes 57
London 121, 166, 198
  benefit cap 42–3
  climate change and 193, 196
  food 250–1, 255–6
  housing 46, 142, 229
  Mayoral Office 154, 250
  transport 137, 252–3
London School of Economics 43
  Centre for Analysis of Social Exclusion 220
low income households
  benefits cuts and 36
  costs of low-carbon energy transition and 203
  deprivation 23–4
  food and financial insecurity 29
  housing 140
  inflation and 102, 104
  minimum wage worker 95
  poverty 11–12
  relative income and 19–20
  tax credits 106
  transport 135
  UC uplift 58
  water bills 198

M

Mahmood, Shabana 169
Manchester/Greater Manchester 137, 186, 252–3, 254, 273
  Live Well initiative 281
May, Theresa 109, 143–4, 165, 169
McFadden, Pat 86
mental health 80, 82
  conditionality and sanctions' impact on 66–7, 69, 85
  poverty and 12, 30, 47, 53
  suicide 69, 74, 75, 187
Met Office 190, 192, 193

Index

Middlesbrough 256
migrants *see* immigration/migrants
minorities and ethnic communities 43, 101, 165, 167, 168
Moore-Bick, Sir Martin 154
Murphy, Richard 288

N

National Audit Office 144, 209
National Health Service (NHS) 9, 126, 219, 223
 COVID-19 pandemic 239
 Lord Darzi's report on 238–9
 outsourcing/private sector and 240–1
 rebuilding the NHS 238–42
 underinvestment and spending cuts 239
National Housing Federation (NHF) 158, 160
 The Better Social Housing Review 157
National Infrastructure Committee 195
National Institute of Economic and Social Research 98–9
National Insurance (NI) 263
 abolition of 289
 insurance unemployment benefit 266–7
 NI contributions 107, 263, 264, 269, 286, 289
 NI 'credit' 264
 self-employment 289
National Residential Landlords Association 153
National Resources Wales 197
National Wealth Fund 210
Netherlands 265, 266
New Economics Foundation (NEF) 173, 210, 222–3, 272, 284–5
non-profit providers 242
 childcare 245, 246, 247
 housing 156, 238
 social care 124, 125, 244

Northern Ireland 149, 164, 188, 252, 299n25
Nuffield Foundation 43

O

Octopus Energy 225
Office of National Statistics (ONS) 102, 289–90
OFGEM (Office of Gas and Electricity Markets) 224
OFWAT (Water Services Regulation Authority) 197, 198
Oldham Council: Oldham Community Power 205, 254
Organisation for Economic Co-operation and Development (OECD) 63, 82, 228, 237, 285
Osborne, George 38, 39, 83, 94–5, 106, 107

P

pensioners 16, 23, 252
 higher-income pensioners 273, 274, 276, 289
 low-income pensioners 41, 213, 274
 pension credit 3, 274, 276
 pension incomes 273–4
 pension tax-free withdrawal 288–9
 poverty 16–17, *18*
 private pensions 273, 274–5
 tax relief for pension contributions 288
 winter fuel allowance for 3, 6–7, 227
 see also state pension
Phillipson, Bridget 245, 248
poverty 1, 9–10
 asylum seekers 179, 183, 184–8
 benefits cuts and 7, 8, 19, 36, 39, 44, 48
 climate change and 191
 debt and 52, 53, 54
 definition 13, 215

disabled people 5, 76–7, 94
families with children 23, 61, 93, 94, 175, 176, 277
food poverty 26, 215–16, 232, 254, 255
fuel poverty 207, 208, 209, 210, 225, 227
housing and 139, 140, **212**
mental health and 12, 30, 47, 53
migrants 5, 165, 167, 171, 174–6
out of work poverty 89, 266
part-time work and 94, 98, 108
pensioners 16–17, *18*
poverty trap 113, 250, 279
single-parent families 69, 94
see also child poverty; impoverishment; in-work poverty
poverty, measures of 13–14, 33, 219
absolute income measure 14
absolute poverty 13, 14, 15, 16, *17*, 32–3
deprivation 13, 22–6
household incomes 13, 14–15
material deprivation index 23–6, *25*, 219–21
Minimum Income Standard (MIS) 20–2, 217–18, 219
official poverty measures 14–19
poverty *before/after* housing costs 15
relative income measure 14, 19–22, *21*, 217
relative poverty 10, 13, 15–16, *15*, 18, 19, 20–1, 61, 69, 76, 89, 92–3, 116, 221, 222
Preston (Lancashire) 253–4
PricewaterhouseCoopers (PwC) 251–2
private/for-profit providers
buses 133, 136–7
care services 124–9, 242, 243, 244
childcare 111–12, 242, 244–5, 246–7
energy sector 224–5

NHS and 240–1
private renting 49, 50, 103, 139–40, 143, 150, 152, 211, 213, 227, 229–30
public services and 10, 240, 241, 246, 286
water privatisation 196–200, 224
public debt 3–4, 284–5, 286
public services
affordability 220, 222
anti-poverty strategies and 220, 222–7, 236, 237–8, 241, 250, 252, 254, 258, 284, 286
children's services 127–32, *128*, *131*, 235–6
collective/public ownership of 200, 224, 226
collective services 22, 217, 222–3, 246
fair pricing 222, 224, 226
free provision of 22, 217, 218, 222–4, 237
free provision for some 217, 218
outsourcing to private sector 10, 240, 241, 246, 286
paid for 217, 218, 222–4
quality 222, 223
redistributive impact of 236–8
service deprivation indicators 221
Universal Basic Services (UBS) guarantee 236, 237–8
youth services 130, *131*, 132–3, 236
see also care services; childcare; education; energy sector; healthcare; internet services; transport
Public Services International 270–1

R

race/racism 154–5, 169
racist/anti-immigration riots 163–5, 184, 188
Rama, Edi 182
Rayner, Angela 104, 105, 158
Reed, Howard 268–70

Index

Reeves, Rachel 3, 4, 8, 48, 53, 82, 88, 96, 115, 233, 286, 288, 289, 291
  see also Chancellor (of Exchequer)
Reform UK 201
Refugee and Asylum Participatory Action Research (RAPAR) 186
Research England 59
Residential Landlords Association 167
Resolution Foundation 76, 84, 194, 257–8, 267
Retail Price Index (RPI) 37–8, 39–41, *40*
Robinson, Tommy (Stephen Yaxley-Lennon) 183
'Rossi' Index 37–8
Russia's invasion of Ukraine 58, 101, 179, 203, 224

S

Savills 155, 160
savings 29, 216
  discouraging savings 262, 263, 265
  pensions and 274, 275
  UC and 101, 107, 262
Scope 70–1
Scotland
  anti-poverty strategies 260–1
  Carer's Allowance 116
  childcare 110, 246
  disabled people 77–8
  free school meals 250
  homelessness 146
  housing 141, 210
  local councils 118, 256–7
  Social Security Experience Panels 78
  social security system 77
  transport 133, 137
  UC 77
Scottish National Party (SNP) 2–3
Shelter 143, 153, 158, 160, 228–9
single-parent families 30, 47, 107, 263
  conditionality regimes 64, 68–9, 109–10
  poverty 69, 94
Social Fund 57
social housing 49, 50, 141–2, 143, 156, 160, 227, 238
  decline of 10, 140–3, 154
  energy efficiency 210–11, **212**
  housebuilding 142, 158–60, 161–2, 228–9
  pensioners 275, 276
  poor conditions 154–6, 157
  poverty **212**
  shortage and need for more 49, 139, 157–62, 228
  see also housing
Social Market Foundation 200
social security 4, 45, 48, 77
  minimalist view of 264–5
social security benefits *see* benefits
South East Water 198
South Korea 213, 267
Starmer, Keir 2, 5, 82, 83, 233, 234
state pension
  anti-poverty strategies and 264, 273–6
  housing and 275–6
  raise of state pension age 275, 276
  savings and 274, 275
  triple lock 40, 41, 273, 276
  uprating 39–40, 41
  women 274, 275
StepChange 52, 54
stigma 54, 64, 89, 154, 165, 250, 268
  food banks and 27, 256
Streeting, Wes 80
subsidies
  childcare 112, 242, 246
  energy sector 202, 204, 211, 212, 213
  homeownership 160, 161
  transport 133–4, *134*, 136, 137
Sunak, Rishi 58–9, 103, 164, 181
Sweden 205, 266

T

taxation 4, 6
  'bedroom tax' 48–50
  capital gains tax 231, 290

council tax 118, 120, 170, 231, 257–8, 290
foreign investments tax 290
higher-income households and 237
income taxes, increase of 276, 286–9
inheritance tax 290
marginal tax rates 270, 278, 287
online sales tax 291
property tax 231, 290–1
stamp duty 212, 231, 290
tax allowances 271–2, 287
tax cuts for high earners 102
tax reliefs 288
tax revenue 262, 285, 286, 288, 290
tax wedge 287
wealth, taxes on 289–92
Wealth Tax Commission 291
on working people 284, 286–7
tax credits 16, 37, 19, 69
impact of 105–9
tax rates 107, 108, *108*
see also Child Tax Credit; Working Tax Credit
Telegraph (newspaper) 166
Thames Water 196, 198, 199–200
Thatcher, Margaret 16, 136, 138, 140, 197
Timms, Stephen 86
Trade Union Congress (TUC) 226, 260
trade unions 97, 105
training 44, 67, 130, 132, 174, 227, 242, 277
transport 23, 185, 201, 218, 270, 285
Bus Back Better 134–5
costs of 11, 12, 22, 44, 70, 135, 136, 236
COVID-19 pandemic 133, 137, 252
expanding free/discounted public transport 252–3
franchising system 137–8, 252–3

impact on people's lives 135–6, 138, 236
local bus services, decline of 133–7
price caps 252
privatisation and deregulation 133, 136–7
promise of better bus service 137–8
subsidies 133–4, *134*, 136, 137
Transport for the North 236
Treasury 141, 272, 285, 286
Trump, Donald 192, 271
Truss, Liz 102–3
Trussell Trust 26, 51
two-child benefit limit 2–3, 6, 8, 9, 43, 44–5, 260

U

unemployment/out of work 89, 100, 115
COVID-19 pandemic 55, 100, 101
out of work poverty 89, 266
unemployment/out of work benefits 38, 63, 64, 108, 264, 280, 281–2
as insufficient/low 41–2, 63, 108
insurance unemployment benefit 266–7
Jobseeker's Allowance (JSA) 4, 41, 63, 170, 267
Work Support Allowance 41
UK Energy Research Centre 202, 207
UNICEF 233
UNISON 132, 243
Universal Basic Income (UBI) 268–72
Universal Credit (UC) 2, 7–8, 50–5
anti-poverty strategies 260, 261, 263, 269
cap for deductions 53–4
Child Tax Credit component of 50, 107, 277
conditionality regimes 55, 64–5, 67, 68
COVID-19 pandemic 55–6, 85
debt and 52, 54

Index

disabled people 75–7, 84, 85, 86
effective tax rates 107–8, **108**
free school meals 249–50
housing component of 48, 50, 51, 107, 261
as incentive to move into work 108
increasing the value of 260
as insufficient/low 52, 60–1
migrants and 175, 261
sanctions 65
Scotland 77
shortcomings 51–5, 262, 269
two-child benefit limit 43, 260
UC uplift 56, 58, 85
Working Tax Credit component of 50, 56, 95, 107, 108, **108**
University College London (UCL)
Institute for Global Prosperity 253
Social Research Unit 111–12
University of Edinburgh 236
University of Glasgow 66
University of Leeds 135–6
University of Malaga (Spain) 278
University of Oxford: Migration Observatory 171, 173, 181, 184
University of Southampton 175
University of Warwick 126, 167
University of Worcester 254
University of York 11, 43
United States (US) 241, 287

V

voluntary groups and charities 32, 59–60, 176, 256

W

wages
earnings inequality 96–8, 106
earnings insecurity 97
immigration's impact on 172, 173
in-work poverty and 104
Low Pay Commission 96
means-tested minimum income schemes 265
minimum wage, impact of 94–6
minimum wage as compensation for lower benefits 95–6
National Minimum Wage/ National Living Wage 94–6, 100, 112, 114
part-time work 108
'social wage' 238
stagnation in 19, 98, *99*, 104, 265
wage progression 109
see also income; in-work poverty
Wales
bus services 133
care leavers 273
childcare 110
extreme weather 189
free school meals 250, 251
homelessness 146
housing 141, 149, 150
local councils 118, 256–7
water privatisation 197
Warsi, Sayeeda (Baroness) 165
water
bills 57, 198–9
companies 197–200
supply 196, 223
wealth 143, 210, 257, 268, 272, 286, 288, 289–92
welfare system 1
as broken safety net 35, 36–7, 117–18, 256
shadow welfare system 256, 271
welfare dependency 42, 60, 62, 69
welfare spending 4–5, 38, 45, 292n25
welfare spending cuts 4–5, 9, 45, 82
welfare state, introduction of 263
see also benefits; social security
We Own It 200
Women's Budget Group (WBG) 51, 110, 248, 278–9
Worcester 254

377

working-age benefits 36, 38–9, 69–70, 81–2, *81*, 264
   erosion of value/cuts of 37–9, 41, 61, 94
   uprating 37, 39
Working Tax Credit 64, 69, 106–7, **108**
   moving unemployed into paid work as aim of 63, 105, 107
   taper rate 106–7, 262–3
   as UC component 50, 56, 95, 107, 108, **108**
   work allowance 106, 262
   see also tax credits
Wright, Peter 153

Y

Yield Investing 157
young people
   Better Futures Fund 258
   care leavers 268, 272–3
   COVID-19 pandemic and 56, 101
   education 132, 135
   health-related issues 12, 80
   homelessness 144
   transport 135, 252
   UC 84
   youth services 130, *131*, 132–3, 236, 257, 258

www.ingramcontent.com/pod-product-compliance
Lightning Source LLC
Chambersburg PA
CBHW020350080526
44584CB00014B/957